The experience of music

The experience of music

BENNETT REIMER *Case Western Reserve University*

EDWARD G. EVANS, JR. *Eastman School of Music of the University of Rochester*

PRENTICE-HALL, INC., *Englewood Cliffs, New Jersey*

To our mothers

PRINTED IN THE UNITED STATES OF AMERICA.

Library of Congress Cataloging in Publication data

Reimer, Bennett.
The experience of music.

Includes bibliographies.
1. Music—Analysis, appreciation. I. Evans, Edward G., 1916–   joint author. II. Title.
MT6.R33E9   780'.15   77-37428
ISBN 0-13-294553-3

○● *This book has been principally composed in Galaxy, a film version of a contemporary typeface designed by Adrian Frutiger, with headings and other supplemental material in various styles of Garamond, a typeface adapted from a sixteenth-century model.*
  The editing, design, and art direction are by David R. Esner; the production was handled by Norma T. Karlin; and the layout and line illustrations were executed by Winifred M. Schneider. The photographs introducing the parts are of (Part 1) the New York Philharmonic Orchestra in Philharmonic Hall, Lincoln Center (Sandor Acs), (Part 2) organ pipes (Sarge Marsh photograph, Cincinnati), (Part 3) excerpts from manuscripts by G. F. Handel, W. A. Mozart, and J. Brahms (New York Public Library), and (Part 4) a Nepalese musician (Peace Corps photograph by Paul Conklin). The photographs in Chapter 7 are by Barry Allan Perlus.

10 9 8 7 6 5 4 3 2 1

PRENTICE-HALL INTERNATIONAL, INC., *London*
PRENTICE-HALL OF AUSTRALIA, PTY. LTD., *Sydney*
PRENTICE-HALL OF CANADA, LTD., *Toronto*
PRENTICE-HALL OF INDIA PRIVATE LTD., *New Delhi*
PRENTICE-HALL OF JAPAN, INC., *Tokyo*

Preface

THERE ARE MANY SPECIAL WAYS THAT PEOPLE DEAL WITH MUSIC: THE COMPOSER creates it, the performer and conductor re-create it (and sometimes create it), the musicologist studies its historical-social-philosophical dimensions, the music theorist examines its internal structure, the music educator is concerned with problems of teaching and learning it, the music critic makes judgments about pieces and performances, the music therapist influences physical and psychological behavior with it, the acoustician handles problems of sound and its production, the record manufacturer is involved with performances and markets, the movie maker and dancer use it to enhance their creations, the department-store manager employs it as a background for selling, the religious leader depends on it to enrich ritual, and so on and on.

Most persons deal with music only by listening to it, and the special uses of music also stem from listening. All encounters with music must rest on a foundation of listening, for music is made of sound, and sound must be heard to be experienced.

The ability to listen can be improved. This textbook is a member of a learning system designed to improve your perception of what goes on in music so that your response can be more sophisticated, more secure, more profound, more enjoyable. The system is further embodied in the following materials: *Developing the Experience of Music: Listening Charts*, a fourteen-record set (*Library for Developing the Experience of Music*) to accompany the charts, and a seven-record set (*Listening for the Experience of Music*) of basic listening examples. All will serve to heighten your experience of music. The introduction to Part 1 of this book gives details about its organization and explains how the Listenings are keyed to the fourteen- and seven-record sets. The Preface to *Developing the Experience of Music: Listening Charts* explains how the charts work and how they can increase your musical perception.

The selections studied in *The Experience of Music* range over a wide spectrum: old and new compositions, jazz, rock, opera, and chamber, choral, orchestral, band, electronic, and nonwestern musics. The goal is not to persuade you to prefer any particular type of music over any other but to acquaint you with many kinds of music and provide you with better skills for enjoying any music you choose to enjoy.

The authors express their gratitude to Bruno Nettl, of the University of Illinois, for his willingness to write the entire chapter on music of other cultures. By bringing his authoritative scholarship to this difficult subject matter, Dr. Nettl has added a dimension of vital import to students enrolled in today's colleges and universities.

In the preparation of the manuscript numerous graduate students at the Eastman School of Music lent assistance in various ways; special thanks are due to two doctoral condidates, Leon Foster and Barbara Thomson, and to staff members of Sibley Music Library, especially Dr. Klaus Speer, Gerald Gibson, and Charles Lindahl.

To Robert Goodling, of Corning, New York, the authors are deeply indebted, for he is almost solely responsible for assembling and forming both indexes to the book, a task that involved judgment and knowledge.

Contents

Contents   *ix*

Contents   *xiii*

Contents   *xiv*

Part 1 ∘ *Musical experience*

Music is by people for people. Part 1 explores the three major ways people deal with music: composing, performing, and listening. Our concern here is to give a broad overview of the nature of musical experience. First, the study will focus on the composer—his role in the total musical process, the qualities he needs to be successful, the ways he goes about creating. Then we shall turn to the performer and the conductor: Just what are their functions? How do they operate as creative artists? What qualities must they have in order to fulfill their roles? Finally, our attention will be turned toward the listener—his responsibilities and opportunities, how he can improve his musical experience.

After this general treatment of how people experience music, we shall be ready to explore the specifics of musical expressiveness: Part 2 deals with the major expressive qualities of rhythm, melody, harmony and counterpoint,

tone color, and form, and in Part 3 the specifics are put into historical perspective and then applied to representative compositions of each major style in Western music. Part 4 presents a brief survey of the music of other cultures.

Each major point raised in this book is immediately applied to a listening experience. The examples in the LISTENINGS *have been drawn primarily from pieces recorded on the fourteen-record set available for the text (Library for Developing the Experience of Music). A small open circle accompanying a composition indicates that at least a part of this piece is included in these fourteen Concentration Chart and Perception Chart records. A small solid circle indicates that the complete piece or movement is also on a seven-record student set (Listening for the Experience of Music). The pieces listed without a symbol are supplements to the*

recorded selections and are available on standard recordings.

The LISTENINGS *in Part 1 call attention to general qualities of musical expression and organization. Those in Parts 2 and 3 will be more specific in focusing your perception on particular musical events and relations among events. Part 4 contains examples of musical creativity in nonwestern cultures. It is not necessary to listen to every composition in every list. But you should not just read the text and neglect the listening examples. Music cannot be experienced by merely reading about it; listening is not in any sense an extra, or secondary, activity. It is the payoff of your musical study and should therefore receive a major portion of the time that you intend to devote to this course.*

All your study should be understood as a means to a larger end—a heightened ability to experience the joy and meaning of music.

Chapter 1 ○ Aesthetic creation: the composer

MUCH OF THE WORLD IN WHICH HUMAN BEINGS LIVE CAN BE EXPERIENCED aesthetically—that is, for its own self-contained expressiveness. Practically all nature has aesthetic qualities that can be experienced for beauty rather than for practical, scientific, religious, political, or other meanings. Man-made things that are manufactured to serve nonartistic purposes (such as machines) can be regarded for their aesthetic qualities if we see them as expressive arrangements of shapes, colors, lines, textures, or forces. A great many things that serve nonaesthetic purposes are made to include aesthetic qualities so that their usefulness will be enhanced by the pleasure of their appearance: cars, clothing, furniture, refrigerators, dishes, typewriters, and numerous other items.

A work of art is a man-made thing that is to be regarded *primarily* for its aesthetic qualities. The work may serve many nonaesthetic functions as well. It may earn money for the person who created it; it may be part of a social ceremony; it may provide pleasant social contacts for the persons engaged in its production; it may cover a crack in a wall. But the essential thing about a work of art is that its aesthetic qualities outweigh other considerations. When art is regarded as art, rather than as a means to nonartistic ends, it is regarded for the value of its inner, expressive qualities.

Much music is intended to serve primarily nonmusical functions and contains little musical interest. Background music piped into a department store, for example, would be quickly eliminated if customers found it so interesting that they began to pay too much attention to it and forgot what they came in to buy. An army band supplying music for drilling would be less than helpful if the maneuvers were ruined because the soldiers became so involved with the music that they forgot their marching routines. Since our concern in this book is with the artistic value of music, music that has little such value will seldom be of interest to us.

Some music serves nonmusical functions but has in addition a high level of musical value. Wolfgang Amadeus Mozart's Requiem, for example, is a utilitarian piece of music in that it can serve a specific religious function. But in addition to, and including, its religious content it is a work of art; that is, its aesthetic qualities are a principal part of its nature. The music of *Histoire du Soldat* (*The Soldier's Tale*), by Igor Stravinsky, was conceived as an accompaniment to a ballet. But it is so artistically valuable by itself that it deserves to be (and usually is) listened to for its purely musical interest. The Blood, Sweat and Tears's "God Bless the Child" has a strong comment to make about the value structure of modern society. Yet this comment is integrated into music of intrinsic worth, which offers aesthetic qualities expressive in and of themselves.

Finally, much music is *entirely* musical, having no other purpose than to be experienced for its aesthetic qualities. Such music is basic to what we are interested in: the full experience of the artistic power of music.

The topic for this chapter is how a composer uses sounds to make them musical, that is, aesthetically expressive. An understanding of the way a composer works and what he is trying to do will be helpful in increasing your ability to share the value of the things he creates.

As do all other creative artists, the composer uses a certain material to capture the way life feels to him. The basic material of the composer is sound. His primary purpose as an artist is the manipulation of sound to create a sense of significance, interest, meaning, and pleasure: in a word, *expressiveness*. The drive to create expressive sounds is strong in a composer. He has a need to come to grips with the sense of life, immersing himself in this sense, shaping it, refining it, and sharing it with others through the pieces he creates.

The need to create could not be satisfied, however, without certain qualities that allow the composer to carry his creative drive to fulfillment. Three qualities are very strong in successful composers: craftsmanship, sensitivity, and imagination. Although they are interdependent, it is possible to focus our attention on them in turn, to explore the function of each as it contributes to the total phenomenon of the creative artist.

Craftsmanship

Musical craftsmanship is a highly developed ability to organize sounds skillfully. The composer must be so familiar with the complex ways that sound can be handled that he scarcely has to think about them as he works. He must be so steeped in the characteristics and possibilities of musical instruments and voices that he can put them to exactly the use he wishes. He must be able to notate—to put down on paper—the exact sounds his mind conceives so that those sounds can be re-created accurately by the performer. All these skills are demanding to a high degree, and composers usually spend a large part of their lives developing, perfecting, and widening their musical craftsmanship (LISTENING 1.1).

Sensitivity

LISTENING 1.1

LUDWIG VAN BEETHOVEN ○● Sonata for Piano in c,* op. 13.†
Even when a composition is for a single instrument, such as the
piano, musical complexities require a high degree of craftsmanship.
You need not be able to read music or perform it to be able to
sense from listening how skillful the composer must be to handle
all the complexities of musical sound. Each note has its separate
pitch (high to low), its duration (long to short), its volume (loud
to soft), its articulation (type of attack), its particular function in
both the immediate sound and the developing structure. All must
be fully controlled by the mind and the feelings of the composer.
For instance, note that in Example 1.1 the outlined measure 6
contains ninety-two notes, each important in the brief time it takes
to play that measure.

JOHANN SEBASTIAN BACH ○ Fugue for Organ in g, S. 578. This
time the single instrument is the organ, but the complexities are
similar. Note how the need for craftsmanship increases as the
music becomes more and more involved (Example 1.2). Later we
shall take a close look at the inner workings of this piece.

I. STRAVINSKY ○ The Soldier's Tale, I. Other aspects of
craftsmanship are called into play when more than one instrument
is involved. This piece calls for ten instruments, including a
collection of percussion instruments. To control the expressive
possibilities of each instrument and their various combinations, as
well as the rhythmic, melodic, harmonic, and structural
components of the developing sounds, requires musical skill of
great depth. As your eye scans the score (Example 1.3), whether or
not you can read music, and as your ear follows the sounds, try to
sense the expertness necessary to handle the complex tonal events
created by the composer. (See Chapter 13 for a more complete
discussion of this work.)

THOMAS MORLEY "Now Is the Month of Maying," from The
First Booke of Balletts to fiue voyces (1595). The voices intertwine in
complex ways, weaving a web of sounds. The composer has the

(continued on page 8)

In addition to craftsmanship, the successful composer must have a high
level of personal and musical sensitivity. On the personal side, he must
be a human being whose reactions to the world are keen, perceptive,
and deeply felt. Feeling is what the composer is dealing with, through
sounds that move as feelings do. A composer must constantly increase
his sensitivity to the way his experience of life feels.

Based on a romanticized view, a popular idea exists that, in order to
develop his understanding of life, the artist must throw himself into all
the exotic, passionate, unconventional experiences he can, tasting the
"forbidden fruits" so that he can learn the hidden secrets of the human
soul. The artist is therefore expected to be a bit bizarre, more or less

(continued on page 11)

*The problem of identifying thousands of musical compositions, many of which
are similar in form or other characteristics, is gradually being systematized by
scholars. A few of the identifications and abbreviations used are explained in this
footnote and the following one.

It is customary—as in this book—to indicate compositions in a major key (see
Chapters 5 and 6 for these terms) by using a capital letter as in, for example,
Quartet for Strings in D, and those in a minor key by a small letter as in, for
example, Concerto for Piano and Orchestra in d.

† The abbreviation "op.," or "Op.," stands for opus and literally means "work."
Opus numbers are a rough chronological guide to a composer's output. Sometimes one opus number may contain more than one complete composition, for
example, Quartet for Strings in B♭, op. 18, no. 6.

Some other means of identification to be found in this and other books are the
following: "BWV" (Bach-Werke-Verzeichnis) is the symbol for a comprehensive
catalogue of J. S. Bach's music compiled by numerous scholars, most recently
by Wolfgang Schmieder. The number following BWV (or "S." as in this book)
precisely identifies a specific work by Bach. "D." identifies a specific work by
Franz Peter Schubert as found in the catalogue by Otto Deutsch, but opus numbers are often used. Fanna ("F.") numbers identify music by Antonio Vivaldi; other
scholars' and opus numbers are frequently used. Hoboken ("H.") numbers identify
works by Franz Joseph Haydn although the string quartets are most commonly
referred to by opus number and the symphonies by numbers and keys only (for
example, Symphony 102 in B♭). Georg Kinsky's thematic catalogue identifies
music by Beethoven, especially those works which do not have an opus number.
Köchel numbers have long identified works by W. A. Mozart, but this numbering
has been revised by Alfred Einstein and others. The Library of Congress has
adopted the Einstein numbering. Longo numbers identify the keyboard music of
Domenico Scarlatti, but the numeration by Ralph Kirkpatrick is replacing the Longo
system. Franklin Zimmerman has catalogued the works of Henry Purcell.

Example 1.1 • L. van Beethoven: Sonata for Piano in c, op. 13, I (excerpt).
(By permission of J. W. Edwards.)

Example 1.2 • J. S. Bach: Fugue for Organ in g, S. 578 (excerpt). (By
permission of Breitkopf & Härtel, Wiesbaden.)

HISTOIRE DU SOLDAT
GESCHICHTE VOM SOLDATEN / THE SOLDIER'S TALE
1ère PARTIE / 1. TEIL / PART I

MARCHE DU SOLDAT / MARSCH DES SOLDATEN / THE SOLDIER'S MARCH
Airs de marche / Marschmelodien / Marching-Tunes

Igor Strawinsky
(*1882)

Example 1.3 • I. Stravinsky: Histoire du Soldat (The Soldier's Tale), *I
(excerpt).* (By permission of J. & W. Chester Ltd. and Edwin F. Kalmus,
Publisher.)

problem here of absorbing the words into a totally unified musical effect. Part of his success in doing so (an important part, but certainly not the whole story) is the technical ability at his command to wed the words to the music.

WILLIAM SCHUMAN ○● *Symphony 3* (1941), II. With a full orchestra the demands for craftsmanship are great. The composer must have in mind the particular qualities of each sound and how each sound affects every other. All must be coordinated in a master plan: the musical score, the technicalities of which are, by themselves, formidable. And all this technical skill is simply a means to a larger end—the creation of a musically compelling experience. Example 1.4 is an excerpt from the score (the start of movement II), which should allow your eye to help your ear appreciate the staggering problems of technique that must be solved in order to create a successful piece of complex music.

Example 1.4 • W. Schuman: Symphony 3 (1941), II. (For technical reasons this excerpt is preceded by the last measure of the first movement.) (By permission of G. Schirmer, Inc.)

(*continued on page 10*)

different from the common run of men, an "original." During the nineteenth century this was a particularly attractive idea, and it persists today among many laymen and some artists.

Some persons are disappointed to find, when they meet an outstanding artist, that he may well give a very ordinary impression. In manners, dress, life style, many of the world's important composers are remarkably unremarkable. This is not to say that unconventionality is never found among composers nor that someone who is a nonconformist cannot be a good composer. It is simply to call attention to the fact that inward sensitivity need not be, and often is not, shown in any noticeable outward way.

But whatever the outward appearance, the inner, hidden perceptions of the way life feels are always highly developed in the composer capable of creating sensitive works. A major way that his inner sensitivity deepens is through *musical creation itself*, for in exploring the expressive possibilities of sound (which is what composing largely consists in), the composer is at one and the same time exploring feeling. We cannot just sit around making ourselves feel sensitively, deeply, or freshly when we are not involved with something that arouses our feeling. Sounds are the something the composer uses to arouse his sense of feeling, to develop it, to examine its subtleties, to discover new and deeper and more satisfying shadings of expression. As he does this, he keeps a record (a score) of the sounds that he has created. If a particular creative effort has gone well—that is, if it has come to grips with feeling in a strong way and if his record is sufficiently accurate so that someone else can reproduce the sounds—an expressive piece of music has been born. (In some cases no record is needed, as in jazz. We shall discuss this mode of musical creation farther on.)

As the composer explores feeling through exploring the expressive qualities of sound he is faced with constant decisions: What to do next? How should a melody move? How should a rhythmic pattern be expanded? Is some heaviness of sound needed here, some lightness there? Can an idea be continued or is a contrast needed? Of course, he is seldom conscious of such questions, his decisions being made at least partly below the level of consciousness. But the decisions must be made, and sensitivity—personal and musical—is the constant guide.

Contrary to what people often believe, the composer is not entirely free to make any decision he cares to make. As soon as his music begins

LISTENING 1.2

CLAUDE (ACHILLE) DEBUSSY   ○● *Prélude à l'après-midi d'un faune* (*The Afternoon of a Faun*). Many elements of sensitivity to sound are apparent here. In particular, notice the exquisite blending and

(*continued on page 12*)

contrasting and balancing of instrumental tone colors. To achieve this subtlety, Debussy chose *timbres* (the characteristic "colors" of different tone producers) with great care and insight, guided by his awareness of the special effect of each and of several combined. Also note the sensitive handling of silences, which punctuate the movement of the music, giving it an unusually interesting flavor. When music is as transparent or "wide open" as this, with every note standing out so clearly, the composer's sensitivity is particularly on display.

L. VAN BEETHOVEN ○ Sonata for Piano in c, op. 13, II (*Pathétique*). The 8-measure theme that opens the movement is in itself a striking illustration of sensitivity to the subtleties of pitch relationships. The shape of the melody as it rises and falls, the creation of very slight tensions and resolutions as the theme unfolds, the accompaniment, which enhances the sense of movement—all show a deep musical sensitivity in operation. The theme is then used with slight changes (a higher register, a bit more motion in the accompaniment) and is set off by another theme of different musical character. As the movement proceeds, the expressiveness of the music becomes more intense and the total effect builds in power. Using very simple yet subtle materials, Beethoven's sensitivity guides the development of a short movement in which each note seems to add its necessary contribution to the whole.

STAN GETZ AND JOÃO GILBERTO "The Girl from Ipanema," from *Getz/Gilberto*. Subtle tensions are built by stretching the rhythm a bit here and there in the melody against the steady beat in the accompaniment. The resulting clashes create a shifting, complex, skillful tangle of rhythmic interplays. The voice is sensitively handled, with slight changes in color, a bit of stress on dissonances here and there, and an intrusion of a "straight" sound (without vibrato), the veiled voice quality blending with the guitar accompaniment. As other musicians take the stage we are shown other sensibilities at work.

OTHER LISTENINGS

F. P. SCHUBERT ○● "Der Wanderer," op. 4, no. 1. Sensitive setting of text. (See Chapter 12 for a more complete discussion of this work.)

SAMUEL BARBER ○● *Adagio* for Strings, op. 11. Sensitive development of a musical line. (See Chapter 13 for a more complete discussion of this work.)

W. A. MOZART ○ *Eine kleine Nachtmusik* in G, K. 525, I. Sensitive balancing of structure.

to take shape, it makes its own demands. Once a melody has started, for example, it suggests by its own nature how it might effectively continue. As a musical idea becomes clear, it indicates how it might be used. As a musical structure unfolds, its own intrinsic, developing form suggests the growth and end of its career. A composer (Roger Sessions) explains:

> The process of execution is first of all that of listening inwardly to the music as it shapes itself; of allowing the music to grow; of following both inspiration and conception wherever they may lead. A phrase, a motif, a rhythm, even a chord, may contain within itself, in the composer's imagination, the energy which produces movement. It will lead the composer on, through the force of its own momentum or tension, to other phrases, other motifs, other chords.*

So the composer finds himself in a two-way relationship with his music: On the one hand, he is the one doing the creating; on the other, the music constantly provides feedback as to what would be effective. This interplay of forces is a basic element in aesthetic creation. The factor that keeps the interplay alive and makes it fruitful is the composer's sensitive balancing of the demands on both sides of the relationship. If the situation becomes unbalanced toward either side, the result is likely to be musical disaster. If the composer forces the music, the result is usually emptiness and sterility. If the music is just followed, the result is blandness and impersonality. Out of an intimate involvement between composer and sound, guided by the composer's sensitivity, can come music that is compelling, "right," intense, human.

Of course, all good music shows sensitivity, as it shows craftsmanship. And sensitivity is a subtle quality, of which some measure in the *listener* is required if he is to notice the sensitivity in the music. LISTENING 1.2 calls attention to what seems to be a high level of sensitivity in some representative pieces.

---

*Roger Sessions, "The Composer and His Message," in August Centeno (ed.), *The Intent of the Artist*, Princeton University Press, Princeton, N.J., 1941, p. 128. ⓒ Princeton University Press, 1969. Reprinted by permission of Princeton University Press.

Imagination

The third necessary quality for successful musical creation, imagination, is as subtle as sensitivity but still identifiable. Imagination in composing is the ability to create a musical event with originality and freshness. Without musical inventiveness—a fertility of ideas in the realm of sound—a composer's work would be dull, uninteresting, or ineffective. Each piece a composer creates has to have some tonal imagination, or it would not get beyond the first note or first idea. The most effective composers are those whose imagination, combined with their craftsmanship and sensitivity, leads them through musical experiences that result in pieces of high interest and a sense of adventure (LISTENING 1.3).

Perhaps the worst thing one can say of a composer is that he lacks imagination. For no matter how skillful his work and how sensitive he may be personally or musically, little of interest can happen unless those qualities are used in imaginative ways. The *style* of his composition may not be very different from that of other music of his time, but the piece had better be different in some way if it is not to be regarded as imitative, as lacking in individuality, as a cliché.

Creative processes

Given a sufficient amount of musical craftsmanship, sensitivity, and imagination, the composer is equipped for his job. But what, exactly, does he do when composing? How does he get started? And what does he do after he gets started?

Every composer is an individual, and every creative act is, in a sense, unique. But although it may be difficult to pinpoint the various behaviors involved in musical creation, it is not impossible to do so. As with the *qualities* necessary for composing discussed above, the more striking creative *processes* can be identified. This can be done without implying that a mere few categories can explain the complex act called "composing." Our aim must be quite modest, yet of practical value in increasing your sensitivity to the nature of music. Taken this way, a look at some processes of composing can add another level to your understanding of what music does. The most important of these processes may be described as spontaneity, building, pattern using, and exploring.

LISTENING 1.3

ARNOLD SCHOENBERG ○● *Pierrot lunaire,* op. 21, I. Few pieces show the quality of musical imagination as strikingly as Schoenberg's setting of twenty-one poems by Albert Giraud, having to do with the weird adventures of the poet Pierrot. The first movement calls for flute, violin, violoncello, piano, and voice, the voice being used in a half-speaking, half-singing manner called *Sprechstimme.* We shall return later to this movement and others to explore specific aspects of their expressiveness. For now, your attention is called to the imaginative way that Schoenberg combines sounds to produce a striking musical adventure. With a minimum of materials he creates an endlessly interesting, highly

(continued on page 14)

organized succession of sounds, which transform the word meanings of the poem into a musical experience. (This poem is a description of the poet's drinking with his eyes the lovely wine pouring from the moon.) (See Chapter 13 for a more complete discussion of this work.)

BÉLA BARTÓK   *Music for String Instruments, Percussion, and Celesta*, III. In this movement we are presented with unusual, imaginative sound qualities. At one point, over a string *tremolo* (the same note quickly played over and over), some violins play a *glissando* (slide) up and down while others play a slow, small-step melody in the high register. The piano punctuates with downbeat chords. This is just one imaginative moment in a highly original movement. To think up such sounds, to create musical events that have newness and freshness and excitement, requires a continually renewable musical imagination, which Bartók seemed to have in abundance.

W. A. MOZART   ○ Twelve Variations for Piano on "Ah, vous dirai-je, Maman" in C, K. 265 (300*e*). The quality of musical imagination exists in many ways in addition to that of unusual sounds and sound combinations. The ability to take a musical idea and use it in a variety of interesting ways is a basic requirement for composing. Mozart's use of a nursery tune as the theme upon which he builds variations is, in a sense, a bold display of imagination. "Give me the simplest possible material with which to work," he seems to say, "and I'll show you what real imagination can do." The twelve variations (after the theme is presented) bear out Mozart's implied claim. We sense that his fertile musical mind could have gone on producing variations forever, each as imaginative as the one before.

OTHER LISTENINGS

L. VAN BEETHOVEN   ○● Sonata for Violin and Piano in A, op. 47, II (*Kreutzer*). Imaginative variations on a simple theme.

ILLINOIS JACQUET   ○ "How High the Moon," from *The King*. Imaginative transformations of a tune idea. (See Chapter 13 for a further discussion of this work.)

DONALD ERB   ○● *Reconnaissance* (1967), I. Imaginative use of tone colors. (See Chapter 13 for a further discussion of this work.)

SPONTANEITY

Most composers start the process of musical creation with some sort of musical idea. The idea may be a bit of melody, an interesting rhythm, a sequence of chords, some intriguing tone colors, or a provocative formal plan. It might be a melody the composer had thought up previously but had never taken the time to do anything with. A piece of music he hears may suggest some new ideas; a poem he wishes to set to music may arouse ideas as he toys with its rhythms and word sounds.

No one is certain just how musical ideas spring into a composer's mind. In other times a Muse, one of the goddesses of art, was credited with giving artists their ideas; today it is more acceptable to talk of the source as a combination of the conscious and the unconscious. Whatever the explanation, the spontaneous flow of ideas, usually called "inspiration," is a necessity to every composer.

But the popular notion that a composer must wait for inspiration to seize him and that he can compose only then is far from accurate. Composers consciously *cultivate* inspiration by working regularly: by sitting down to compose, starting to work with sounds, and watching for a new, fresh insight to arise. The working composer expects—in fact, counts on—the appearance of flashes of musical insight as he works. This spontaneity is part of every composer's stock in trade.

Some composers, however, depend more on the spontaneous element in composition than do others. For example, the jazz musician must have a great deal of spontaneity. Jazz requires that composition be carried out on the spot, at the very moment of performance. There is no time for an idea to occur and for its implications to be mulled over in the mind or for an attempt to be made to write it out on paper, look at it, consider it, tinker with it, try to use it here and there. That is a perfectly proper and common way to compose, but "it isn't jazz"! The immediate, spontaneous, and uninterrupted expression of musical ideas (called "improvisation") is a basic condition of jazz, giving this style of music its immediate, "right-now" character (LISTENING 1.4).

All composers of the spontaneous type share with the jazz musician the ability to give the impression that their musical ideas gush out quickly. But no matter how impulsive the music might seem in jazz or

LISTENING 1.4

JOHN COLTRANE   "Summertime," from *My Favorite Things*. The typical jazz improvisation begins with a statement of a tune to serve as the organizing structure for the piece (in modern jazz the tune is seldom played straight but is altered and embellished even on its first presentation). Then the performers—more properly, performer-composers—play with the tune, spontaneously re-creating it in a variety of ways. John Coltrane followed this time-honored jazz formula but left the original tune far behind in his improvisations. We sense a keen originality of musical ideas coming so fast as to be almost breathtaking.

The fine line between controlled musicianship and uncontrolled bursts of meaningless sounds is the line between musical and nonmusical expression. Some persons say that Coltrane occasionally crossed that line, committing the sin of becoming unmusical, which is the chief weakness of "bad jazz." Others say that he flirted with the line but always had sufficient musical sense not to cross over into uncontrolled emotionalism. Perhaps part of the excitement of his playing is this musical brinkmanship.

THE MILES DAVIS SEXTET   "Fran-Dance," from *Miles and Monk at Newport*. Again, we hear the classic statement of the theme followed by variations (improvisations). The style is much cooler than the heat of Coltrane, but Davis's performance illustrates clearly the combination of spontaneity and control that makes jazz what it is. The fresh embellishments turn the tune into a vital musical statement.

OTHER LISTENING

THAD JONES, MEL LEWIS, AND THE JAZZ ORCHESTRA   ○● "Don't Ever Leave Me." Individual and collective spontaneity. (See Chapter 13 for a further discussion of this work.)

LISTENING 1.5

F. P. SCHUBERT   *Die schöne Müllerin* (*The Pretty Miller Girl*), op. 25, no. 7: ○ "Ungeduld" ("Impatience"). Spontaneity is particularly evident in art songs of the nineteenth century. Highly romantic in both poetry and music, they often seem to be impassioned outbursts of feeling. But their composers control the emotionality in order to transform them into convincing music.

Die schöne Müllerin is a series of related songs. We shall explore

(continued on page 16)

any other style, convincing music never crosses from art to sheer expression of emotion. When someone expresses his emotions, he gives vent to the way he feels at that very moment. He cries, laughs, jumps for joy, slaps his forehead, wrings his hands, shakes with fear, trembles with excitement. All these are expressions of emotion. None requires shaping to the ends of a coherent, unified, and compelling artistic event.

Good composers, as any other artists, do not express emotion. Instead, as we have stated, they explore and discover feeling, forming sounds according to the patterns disclosed while creating. This is true of jazz, and it is true of any other music. No matter how spontaneous a composition may be, it is musical as long as it shapes sound artistically (LISTENING 1.5).

Sometimes we sense that sound is no longer musical but has become a symbol for a particular emotion. A bad jazz trumpeter will "scream" on his horn, not adding to the music but simply crying in public. We may sympathize with the expression of his emotion or be embarrassed by such a display, depending on our personalities, but the expression is not a musical one. This does *not* mean that music is less powerful than screaming is; it means that music (and all art) can explore the wide realm of feeling, whereas expressing emotion uses a particular physical action as a symptom of an immediately present sensation.

BUILDING

Although all composers depend to a greater or lesser extent on spontaneity, they must also be able to take an idea, manipulate it in different ways, use it in various contexts, and try it out in different settings. Many pieces of music take a long time to create (Brahms labored for some ten years on his first symphony). As a composer works along on a piece, he must add to it carefully until the whole structure of sounds takes on a finished quality. To some extent the composer must be a builder. The structure he builds is a structure of tonal relationships, and it must be a well-built structure or it will sound weak and sloppy. Musical ideas, like all ideas, should be organized with skill and care so that each idea is related with others in a coherent way, the whole piece holding together in a musically unified manner. Even the jazz musician and the most spontaneous art-song composer must be at least partly builders, giving their music a sense of shape and form.

several of the songs at various times. Notice for now the highly spontaneous character of the music, especially on the words "dein ist mein Herz/Dein ist mein Herz" ("my heart is yours").

HOWARD HANSON   Symphony 2, op. 30, II (*Romantic*). The principal theme (the main melody idea) is heard immediately in the woodwinds as the strings weave decorations around it. The free-flowing melodic line has a strong feeling of spontaneity, of uninhibited outpouring. As the statement of the theme draws to a close, the character of the music becomes more restrained and complex. The immediacy of expression of such music characterizes it as being "romantic," and since Hanson is a contemporary composer, his music is often called "neoromantic." We shall take a closer look at modern romanticism in Chapter 13.

OTHER LISTENINGS

FRÉDÉRIC FRANÇOIS CHOPIN   o Étude for Piano in E, op. 10, no. 3. Songlike, spontaneous flow of ideas.

GEORGE FRIDERIC HANDEL   *Messiah:* o● "Hallelujah" chorus. Though the music is highly structured, the effect is that of an outburst of feeling.

LISTENING 1.6

L. VAN BEETHOVEN   o● Symphony 5 in c, op. 67, I. Using a brief musical idea (*motive*) of three short repeated notes followed by a longer note, Beethoven builds a complex movement. Try to follow the many musical transformations of the opening motive. It is used as a building block, allows for musical imagination to operate, and at the same time provides an element to unify the movement.

LISTENING 1.7

J. S. BACH   o Fugue for Organ in g, S. 578 ("Little").

W. SCHUMAN   o● Symphony 3 (1941), II: Fugue. Fugue is a musical pattern or procedure that has challenged the creative powers of composers for at least three hundred years. In this procedure an idea (subject) is stated alone at first and is then repeated in turn by different instruments (or voices) while those which have already stated the subject go on to other material. The music becomes progressively more complicated in its web of interrelated strands.

Some composers, however, tend to be primarily musical builders. They usually work slowly and carefully, changing things around frequently, adding ideas here and there, taking out ideas when they seem not to work well, constantly reshaping and reforming and rethinking. All composers do this to some extent, but some do it at every point in their work. Composers of the builder type usually produce large, involved pieces that are complicated structures of musical ideas. Each such composition is likely to contain a world of expressive possibilities, which the listener can explore again and again, finding new insights each time. Many of the monuments of music literature—great and powerful creations containing complex and deep insights—are results of the craftsmanship, sensitivity, and imagination of musical builders (as in LISTENING 1.6).

PATTERN USING

All composers are partly spontaneous and partly builders. Also, composers work with some well-established means of musical creation known to, and shared by, the composers working at any one time in history. As all other artists, composers are intensely interested in the important artistic ideas of their time and are influenced by them.

In any one period in the history of music, certain ideas or patterns mold the work of most of the composers of that period. Some patterns are so useful that they persist over long periods even though the general style of music may have changed. The basic pattern *ABA*, for example, in which some musical material (*A*) is presented, some contrasting music (*B*) is introduced, and the first material is then repeated, has guided the creative output of countless composers over hundreds of years through works ranging from the simplest to the most complex. Indeed, so productive of musical ideas is this pattern that composers throughout history have turned to it, altered it, expanded it, added to it, and sometimes used it in its purest state, joyfully displaying its musical beauty. We shall later explore the principal patterns in music in detail (Chapter 8) because each one serves as a key to a great deal of material.

Some composers depend more on well-established patterns than do others. Such composers are concerned not so much with doing things *differently* from their colleagues as with doing them *better*. The music of such composers is predictable in pattern but may be quite unpre-

Chapter 8 contains an explanation of fugue.

The examples given here (also see the score excerpts, Examples 1.2 and 1.4) are by the baroque master of fugue and by a contemporary composer, spanning some two hundred fifty years of musical history. Note how the pattern remains basically unchanged even though the musical style has changed dramatically.

J. S. BACH ○● Passacaglia and Fugue for Organ in c, S. 582: Passacaglia. W. SCHUMAN Symphony 3 (1941), I: Passacaglia. The same two composers provide another opportunity to illustrate the staying power of some musical patterns. The passacaglia is a variation form in which a single idea is played (usually alone and in the bass register) and is then almost exactly repeated over and over throughout the composition, each time accompanied by different music (see the score excerpt, Example 2.1). The problem for the composer is to create many interesting settings for the same idea, the whole piece giving a sense of progression and unity. Again we find Bach and Schuman using the identical pattern but in the very different styles of their own times.

OTHER LISTENINGS

W. A. MOZART *Eine kleine Nachtmusik* in G, K. 525, III; ○ Symphony 41 in C, K. 551, III. L. VAN BEETHOVEN Symphony 5 in c, op. 67, III. Three examples of *ABA* pattern. Chapter 8 will explain how this pattern works.

LISTENING 1.8

CARLO GESUALDO "O vos omnes," from *Sacrae Cantione*. A nobleman of Venosa, an Italian city, Gesualdo (*ca.* 1560–1613) lived at a time of change in musical style, from the late renaissance to the early baroque. His later music (this piece was published in 1603) exhibits a level of chromaticism (use of pitches not contained in the basic scale of a piece) and dissonance (use of pitches that clash with one another) so remarkable that some scholars claim that only now, with contemporary music under our belts, can we understand its sophistication. The exploratory nature of Gesualdo's work opened up new expressive horizons for music.

All ye that pass by behold and see: if there be any sorrow like unto my sorrow.	*O vos omnes, qui transitis per viam attendite et videte: si est dolor similis sicut dolor meus.*

(continued on page 18)

dictable in the actual content of the pattern. This tension between established forms and fresh ideas has provided the impulse for numerous works of art (LISTENING 1.7).

EXPLORING

Whereas spontaneity, building, and pattern using account for three basic processes of creation, a fourth—exploring—adds to each of the other three and is important in and of itself. We have suggested that the act of composition is largely an act of discovery, of searching out expressive sound events and embodying them in a thing called a "composition." This searching out, whether heavily flavored by spontaneity or building or pattern using or all three in combination, is essential to all creative work. Without the quality of exploration—novelty, adventure, the element of risk—spontaneity would be stillborn, building would be mechanical, and pattern using would be academic.

So even if a composer is working on his one hundred fourth symphony (Haydn) or his thirty-second piano sonata (Beethoven), his craftsmanship, sensitivity, and imagination must be touched with exploration if his work is not to be stale or dull. No matter how conservative his style or careful his work, some degree of investigating new territory must be present if his work is to come off. All successful composers, therefore, are at least *partly* explorers.

Some composers, however, are *primarily* explorers; in the history of music certain composers have made dramatic breaks with the established practices of their times, striking out in new directions (LISTENING 1.8). Such breaks tend to occur when the music in a particular style has reached full growth, its potentialities having been fulfilled as thoroughly as seems possible for that style. At such points new ideas are needed, and composers appear who are able to open new paths to musical creation.

That such composers have been regarded with suspicion is not astonishing. Explorers rock the boat of habit and familiarity, and this is unpleasant for many. But once the new practices have taken hold, they become quite acceptable to everyone and later tend to seem tame and even old-fashioned. Compositions that had once been shocking seem, to modern ears, to be quite inoffensive. In their time they opened new musical possibilities for exploration.

L. VAN BEETHOVEN ○● Symphony 3 in E♭, op. 55, I. After the classic era had reached its height, Beethoven (1770–1827) revealed a new world of musical potential with his bold departures from general practice and brought the romantic period to birth. In his early works, including the first and (to a lesser extent) second symphonies, Beethoven's style was basically classic even though highly original in flavor. The third symphony added another dimension to music. In length, complexity, and immediacy of expression, it can be called "revolutionary"—a giant step away from the existing musical style. We shall study various aspects of this work in several places, but at this point its nature as a dramatic musical exploration need only be sensed.

Example 1.5

Example 1.6

Example 1.7

A. SCHOENBERG   Quartet for Strings 4, op. 37, I. Schoenberg's twelve-tone system of composition uses a series of pitches that becomes the basis for all that follows it in the same movement. The series must contain all twelve pitches of the chromatic scale, but no pitch may reappear until all twelve have been sounded (a pitch may be repeated when first sounded as long as no other pitch comes in between). The radical nature of this procedure will become clear after we have discussed tonality and lack of tonality in Chapters 5 and 6; but for now the following sketch will suffice as an introduction.

The twelve tones of the chromatic scale (traditionally, one starts the scale on middle c) are shown in Example 1.5, and the first movement of this piece arranges the twelve tones as in the series of Example 1.6. With the addition of the rhythm, the series sounds like Example 1.7.

So highly organized is Schoenberg's music that all that follows stems from the original series used in various ways. However, the ease or difficulty with which the organization of the music can actually be *heard* is quite another matter.

ANTON VON WEBERN   ○● Five Pieces for Orchestra, op. 10. See the discussion in Chapter 13.

EDGARD VARÈSE   *Ionisation*. Born in 1885, Varèse was one of the major twentieth-century musical revolutionaries, having composed music of remarkable originality during every stage of his long career until his death in 1965. *Ionisation* was first performed in 1931; so it can hardly be called brand new. Yet it gives a strong impression of newness and, because of its inventiveness, will perhaps continue to seem new for many years to come.

The work calls for thirteen performers, who play thirty-seven different percussion instruments, including three that sound actual pitches: chimes, celesta, and piano. These last are used very little so that the piece depends primarily on rhythm and tone color for its impact. With these two elements Varèse demonstrated novel expressive possibilities—possibilities still being explored by many composers. As a seminal work, therefore, *Ionisation* is an important contribution to the music of our day. But its value is not just historical; to experience it continues to provide pleasure for those who can open themselves to its power.

VLADIMIR USSACHEVSKY   *Piece for Tape Recorder*. One of the first electronic devices to be used for musical composition was the common tape recorder. Given a composer with sufficient technical know-how and an urge for musical exploration, the tape recorder can generate a great many musical ideas. With the ability to alter musical sounds and everyday noises in an endless variety of ways, this machine opens up a new world of tonal possibilities to the composer. Still other electronic devices, far more sophisticated than the tape recorder, have multiplied the available sound materials dramatically. There seem to be so many new sound possibilities that we can assume that composers will be exploring the realm of electronically produced music for many years.

Ussachevsky's *Piece. . .* is especially interesting in that the sense of musical progression, of sounds moving purposefully in an expressive, goal-oriented, coherent fashion, is quite evident. Much electronic music is musical in that sense; it is made of interrelated sounds used for their expressive power, as music has been for its entire history. All such music has the same purpose and the same materials—the capturing of conditions of feeling in conditions of sound—and so it can be called "traditional music." Further on we shall discuss music that departs from this tradition. Although in one way *Piece for Tape Recorder* is traditional music, in the way it goes about being musical it represents a new departure within the frame of music as an art.

OTHER LISTENING

LUCIANO BERIO   o *Omaggio a Joyce.* See the discussion in Chapter 13.

Summary

The twentieth century has been a time of adventure in the arts (including music) as well as in science and technology. The rate of change in music has been more rapid than it has at any other time in history, producing a large number of works of the exploratory type.

Of the many new musical ideas generated in our century, three have been particularly fruitful. The first of these is the system of composition developed by Schoenberg (1874–1951) and called variously ''twelve-tone music,'' or ''dodecaphonic music,'' or ''serial music,'' or ''atonal music,'' or ''expressionistic music,'' or, in Schoenberg's own words, ''[a] method of composing with twelve tones which are related only with one another.'' Schoenberg's new ways of organizing music have proved to be so interesting and powerful that they have guided the compositions of a group of composers closely associated with him and a constantly increasing number of later ones adapting the ideas to novel uses.

The second important twentieth-century departure from tradition has been the expanded conception of what is proper for musical instruments and the voice to do. Using traditional instruments in all sorts of untraditional ways, exploiting the potential of percussion instruments, inventing new instruments to add new sound possibilities, imaginatively combining new and old instruments and the voice—all have led to a growing musical literature of fresh, challenging content.

Finally, the use of many electronic devices as sound producers and sound manipulators has been a great departure from tradition and has opened up a seemingly endless realm of exploratory potentialities.

Each of these contemporary movements (and their various combinations) will be examined in appropriate places throughout this text so that, by the time we meet them in historical perspective in Chapter 13, you should find them quite familiar and no longer puzzling. The examples in LISTENING 1.9 are the first formal introduction to them.

With qualities of craftsmanship, sensitivity, and imagination and with creative processes including spontaneity, building, pattern using, and exploring, the composer does his work, embodying in sound his sense of the nature of feeling. In most cases his embodiment (his composition) is not available for sharing until it has been transformed from idea to actuality by the act of re-creation. We turn now to the next essential contribution to music experience, that of the performer and conductor.

Chapter 2 ∘ Aesthetic re-creation: the performer and the conductor

THE SEVEN MAJOR ARTS ARE USUALLY CONSIDERED TO BE LITERATURE, DRAMA, music, dance, painting, sculpture, and architecture. Many feel that the film, or the cinema, should be added as an eighth art. Each has its own identity even though some elements (such as words, actions, sounds, colors, shapes) are used by more than one of them. Each contains subcategories: literature includes poetry and the novel; dance, ballet and modern; painting, drawing and printmaking. Each one of these individual arts has what seems to be an endless potential for doing what art in general does: exploring human feeling and capturing a sense of feeling in a formed thing. Because of the great capacity to explore feeling in a variety of ways and the ability to examine human feeling deeply, each has acquired the description ''major.''

In literature, painting, and sculpture the work of art exists in final form as soon as the artist has finished creating. When the last word has been added, the poem is completed and can be immediately read or heard and enjoyed (even if it has to be published in a book for many people to be able to read or hear it). When the painter applies the last brush stroke, the painting is immediately ready to be looked at and experienced. When the last bit of material has been shaped, the sculpture is in final form.

One of the major arts, architecture, presents an interesting problem: The architect has accomplished his creative and aesthetic task when he has conceived the shape of a building and has fixed his conception in a set of plans (blueprints) for its construction. But the work of art—the building—does not yet exist, for workmen, often so highly skilled as to be called ''craftsmen,'' must still carry out the instructions given by the blueprints (often the architect guides the construction process). Only when they are finished is the work of art finished. The workmen, however, have simply followed directions, and their craft consists in following complex directions exactly and skillfully. They are artisans in that they are adept in the *application* part of a complex task, such as erecting a cathedral; but because the aesthetic decisions are made by someone else, the builders are not usually considered to have engaged in aesthetic creation.

In drama, music, dance, and film someone—a playwright, a composer, a choreographer, a screenwriter—conceives a work of art that does not completely exist at the moment he has finished creating (but there are a few exceptions, such as jazz). As with the architect's brainchild, someone else must complete the process in order for the "formed thing" to come into existence. But in the arts of drama, music, dance, and film the persons involved in actualizing the original creation are themselves considered to be aesthetic creators. Why is this so? The answer lies in the matter of aesthetic decision making. In drama, music, dance and film many decisions of a *creative* nature must be made in order to transform the original conception into a completed creation. Often there must be a complex chain of creative decisions, each link contributing to the effect of the finished work. In a play, for example, the director, the actors, the stage designer, the costume designer, and the lighting specialist all add their own creativity to the creativity of the playwright. The total of their contributions is the production that an audience experiences, which is intended to be so unified that the separate contributions merge into a single whole larger than the sum of its individual parts.

How do the persons involved in the actualizing process make aesthetically creative decisions in their work? That is, how do they function as artists rather than as artisans? Each of the four arts that we have been speaking of, which are called "performing arts" because of the creative role played by various performers, goes about its work in its own ways. This chapter will focus on the kind of aesthetic re-creation that takes place in the art of music. Performance is crucial to the musical process, and an understanding of the performer's and the conductor's contributions can deepen your musical enjoyment.

Most often (we shall mention some exceptions later) music is brought to the point of actual sound by a person who did not create the original musical ideas. Sometimes the composer knows exactly who will perform his work, as is the situation where he is commissioned to compose a piece for a particular performer or where he agrees that, when a piece is finished, a particular performer will play it. In such instances the composer knows the musical capabilities of the person who is going to bring his concepts to life and can take them into account as he composes. He may even be able to work with that person to help guide the process of actualization. Yet in most cases the composer does not know who might perform his pieces; and he will usually not have the opportunity to work with a performer, giving advice as to how he thinks a piece should go. He is in the uncomfortable position of having to depend on another's notion of how his piece should sound, and although he can control some of the things that will take place in a performance, he cannot control everything. A great deal must be left to the performer. Is it any wonder that composers tend to be a bit nervous about the fate of their music when much of that fate is out of their hands?

What would a composer hope for as the attributes of a person who is going to perform his music? What does it take to be a good performer? We have suggested that, among the many characteristics making up a total human personality, three are especially necessary if a person is to be a successful composer: craftsmanship, sensitivity, and imagination. The same characteristics are basic to being a successful performer. Of course, the *content* of these attributes is different for the performer than it is for the composer because performing differs from composing.

A look at these attributes as they operate in performers will help make clear how and why a performer is a creative artist, but as with our discussion of the composer, we must recognize that human characteristics do not exist in watertight compartments. Nevertheless, we can focus our attention on first one and then another to clarify processes that in the whole would be difficult—if not impossible—to deal with.

The performer's craftsmanship

Among performers there is a saying that ''art begins where technique ends.'' Every musical instrument, including the voice, presents a great many problems of a purely technical sort: fingers must be moved accurately, breath must be controlled in special ways, inner and outer muscles must be made to respond immediately and with great precision, hearing must be extraordinarily keen, eye and body must be in perfect partnership. Anyone who has ever tried to play or sing has some notion of the technical difficulties presented by musical sound-producing devices; but very few people ever achieve the technical mastery required of a performing artist. It is doubtful that many, no matter how much they struggled with their early music lessons, have a clear understanding of what mastery means in performance, for a change in kind rather than mere degree, seems to take place when mastery is reached. It is not just a matter of *more* skill but a *transformation* of skill into a natural function of the body such as breathing, walking, reaching, or chewing. When the performer has made his instrument a part of himself, he is free to be an artist.

In order to get to that point, the would-be performer must submit himself to the long apprenticeship required and then must be willing to keep his technique sharpened by constant effort. It takes a special sort of person to do this: one who has the physical, mental, and musical potential for mastery and who is willing to achieve it and maintain it.

In every period of the history of music the best performers have been expected to have sufficient craftsmanship to cope with whatever performance problems existed in contemporary music. And they have also been expected to be able to deal with the difficult music of all earlier times. Naturally, as the body of music increases, it becomes harder and harder to handle the special technical demands of the most complex music from every musical period. Many performers come remarkably close to doing this. But some performers will concentrate on the music of one era or perhaps a few eras as their own, special, literature. Such performers base their reputation on being, for example, especially excellent in the piano music of the romantics or the vocal music of the renaissance or baroque organ music, whereas other performers will attempt challenging music from many periods and become known for their ability to master a wide variety of performance problems.

Today new ideas about music have created challenges different from any in history: For instance, although the piano techniques of previous times presented a variety of problems, all were basically alike. Now, in some modern pieces, the pianist is expected to pluck the strings, to crash his arms on the keyboard, to tap on the lid, to improvise music at specified moments, or to handle rhythms and melodies given only in bare outline. Traditional technique will be of little help in these pieces.

Many performers simply refuse to have anything to do with the radical changes in technique required by some modern music; others have become expert in such music. All performers, teachers of performance, and students of performance face real difficulties because of new demands on craftsmanship. Does one try to add radically new techniques to those one has spent a lifetime perfecting? Should the young performer in training be introduced to such problems immediately, or should his training first be traditional? Is it necessary to learn the traditions of craftsmanship at all, or can one jump immediately to the new, excluding the old? Must the well-rounded performer of the future be able to do everything, or will specialization have to become more and more narrow? No one can give final answers to such questions although, as might

(continued on page 27)

LISTENING 2.1

The following selections for a single performer or for a featured performer with accompaniment illustrate some obvious problems of craftsmanship. The score excerpts show the notational directions that the performer must translate into sound. The ability to read complex music is in itself an important aspect of craftsmanship. Note the radical changes in musical notation from traditional to contemporary.

J. S. BACH ○● Passacaglia and Fugue for Organ in c, S. 582: Passacaglia. See the excerpt in Example 2.1

L. VAN BEETHOVEN ○● Sonata for Violin and Piano in A, op. 47, II (*Kreutzer*). See Example 2.2 for an excerpt.

KARLHEINZ STOCKHAUSEN *Zyklus* (1950). For a single percussion player, this composition is excerpted in Example 2.3.

PASSACAGLIA.

Example 2.1 • *J. S. Bach: Passacaglia and Fugue for Organ in c, S. 582* (*excerpt*). (By permission of Breitkopf & Härtel, Wiesbaden.)

Example 2.2 • L. van Beethoven: Sonata for Violin and Piano in A, op. 47, II (*excerpt*). (By permission of J. W. Edwards.)

Part 1 • Musical experience

ZYKLUS for one percussionist

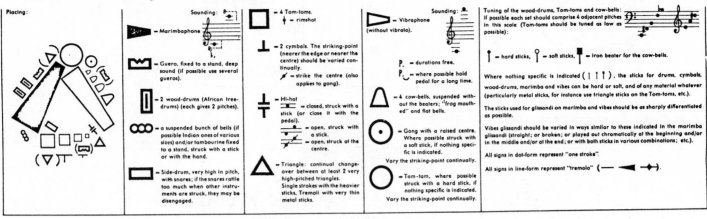

Placing:

Durations and intervals of entry (time-interval between attacks) are drawn to scale; equal distances correspond to equal amounts of time.

One interpretation can begin with any page, and must then run through all pages in the given order without interruption and finish with the first stroke of the page you started with.

For resonating instruments: ● and ◄ are damped sounds. ◠ and ◄◠ undamped (laissez vibrer); ⌒ at the beginning of a group, applies to all the tones in the group. ∿∿∿ laissez vibrer until the end of the wavy line.

◖ and ●●●● always as fast as possible. ◖●◗ observe the proportions of the intervals of entry. ⌐ ⌐ ⌐ closed system: follow up with a tone or group immediately on reaching the final barline (with resonating instruments, the sound may be damped at the final barline, instead of the above procedure). ╱ = accelerando, ╲ = ritardando: intervals of entry in these are free, and so is the total duration.

Intensities are given by the different thicknesses of the points and lines: they vary between ·— and ●▬. The intensities of the guero strokes are not differentiated in the score; they are free, but should be chosen with reference to the instruments with which the strokes are combined (see below, last sentence).

Structure types: 1. Composed straight through as usual; all dots and/or groups are fixed by the time-scale.

2. Where several bracketed staves ⊟ occur, one is to be chosen for one performance.

3. Groups and/or dots in triangles ⊠ ⊠ are interchangeable (as regards their succession), but they must begin at the indicated points ∧ ∨ in the measured time-lapse.

4. Groups and/or dots in rectangles ⬜ are interchangeable (as regards their succession) and can be folded into the measured time-lapse at any point within the length of the rectangle: both successively and simultaneously (wherever possible).

5. Groups and/or dots in 2 rectangles drawn one above the other ⊟ are just as in single rectangles. But a group or dot from one rectangle should be followed by a group or dot from the other ↕ (alternate). In some rectangles and pairs of rectangles, only connections and changes indicated by arrows may be played.

6. Groups and/or dots in bracketed rectangles ⊂⊃ drawn simultaneously above and below the continuous measured stave: the procedure is the same as for single rectangles, but in one performance only the contents of one of the rectangles are to ⊂⊃ be played.

7. Groups and/or dots in rectangles which are occasionally widened ⌐⌐ : the procedure is the same as for simple rectangles, but the reservoir of elements is increased during the time of the widening.

8. Dots without stave-lines for the 4 Tom-toms: the distribution of the points is determined statistically by their density (speed) and thickness (intensity); the pitches are free; intervals of entry are – taking account of density – relatively free.

In structure types 1, 3, 4, 5, 7, 8, all elements are to be played. In none of the structure types may an element be repeated. In the variable structure types 3–8 the player should leave as much silence as possible. In structure types 3–8 the dots and groups that are variable as regards their placing in time, should be folded into the fixed time-lapse in such a way that variable and fixed attacks occur simultaneously as often as possible, so that complex sound-mixtures result, consisting of the sounds of 2 or more instruments. The **variable** sound-elements can be played within the attack (– process), and in the course of, and during the decay or release (– process) of the **fixed** sound-elements and vice versa. In particular the guero strokes should be combined with the attack of a different instrument.

(continued on page 26)

Example 2.3 • *K. Stockhausen:* Zyklus *(1950; excerpt).* © 1961, Universal Edition, Vienna. Used by permission. Theodore Presser Company sole representative U.S.A., Canada, and Mexico.)

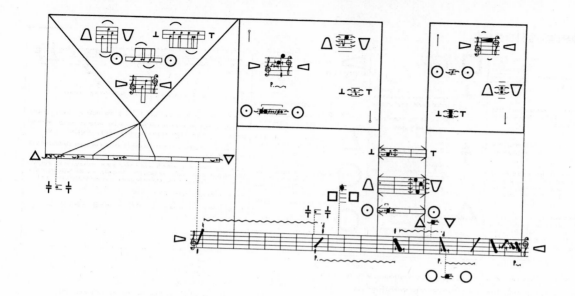

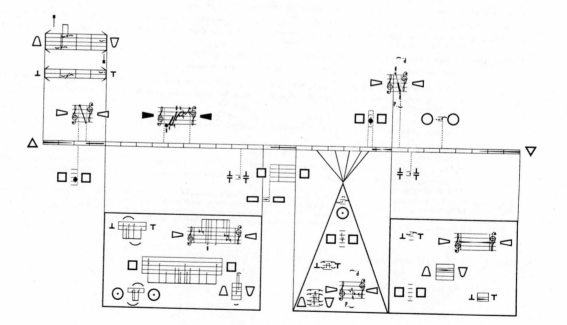

be expected, very strong opinions are held by those involved. It will be most interesting to observe the controversies and trends of performance craftsmanship in the years ahead.

Now listen to LISTENING 2.1.

The performer's sensitivity

Craftsmanship is necessary if a person is to be an artist-performer, but it is not sufficient. Technical mastery is a means, not an end. The end is aesthetic re-creation; for this end to be attained, craftsmanship must be transformed into artistry by the performer's sensitivity and imagination. Some performers seem to be strong in technique but weak in the ability to use it to produce music that is expressive, gripping, and compelling. We think of such performers as admirable for their virtuosity but as lacking in the qualities for making technique artistic. On the other hand, some performers, by the way they shape the unfolding musical events, give hints that they have deep musical insights but are prevented from fully expressing them by weaknesses in technique that cause many blunders. The great performers are those who are highly developed in craftsmanship and sensitivity and imagination.

The performer's sensitivity is the ability to translate the composer's musical insights into sounds that clearly display those insights. The performer must be so sensitive to the nuances of sound suggested by a composer's instructions that he can exhibit all the subtleties in their proper perspective. He must grasp the sense implied in a melody: its unfolding, its movement up and down, its creation of hesitation here and forward motion there, its use as a unifying force in an entire piece. He must be perfectly attuned to rhythm: its underlying movement, its stresses and strains as it proceeds, its function in emphasizing an event here and submerging it there. Harmony must be sensitively handled to produce a convincing effect, with precise balancing of tones, highlighting backgrounds or throwing them into shadow, and blending accompaniment and melody. Tone color must be just right, with exact amounts of shading here and there and of altering color to point up or play down this or that event, to add its own expressive quality to the whole. Balancing of musical texture—melody with melody, melody with harmony—must clarify the expressive intent of a piece. The form of a composition—its structure as a unified sound event—must be shown by the way the performer contrasts and balances and repeats and varies

LISTENING 2.2

The score excerpts in Examples 2.4 to 2.6 show how composers try to guide the performer's decisions by suggesting how the music should be treated. In every case the performer must decide how to follow the directions. As you listen, pick out some of the marked directions and focus your attention on how they are performed. Foreign words and musical signs are defined with the scores.

F. F. CHOPIN ○ Étude for Piano in E, op. 10, no. 3. (Example 2.4.)

C. DEBUSSY "Des Pas sur la neige" ("Footsteps in the Snow"). (Example 2.5.)

FRANZ LISZT ○ Concerto for Piano and Orchestra 1 in E♭, I. (Example 2.6.)

The performer's imagination

events as the music goes on. And since each of the musical elements—melody, rhythm, harmony, tone color, form—is dependent on all the others, the performer must be sensitive not only to the impact of each but also to the total aesthetic impact emerging from their unification.

Perhaps this discussion gives some notion of how necessary it is that the performer be the sort of person who is sensitive to sound in all its dimensions. Any weakness in sensitivity to a composer's ideas will desensitize those ideas when they are being executed. How does the performer bring music to life in sensitive ways? By making sensitive decisions. At every moment in the act of re-creation, he must make musical decisions: The composer has indicated "louder" in the score. But how much louder? Just a little? A great deal? Somewhere in between? What the performer decides will make the music sound one way or another; so the decision must be a good one. A moment after, the written music says *legato* (smooth). But how smooth? And when a similar *legato* melody occurs later, should it sound just like this one or a bit different? Now the music says "fast but not too fast." Too fast as compared with what? Too fast for whom? Then comes the instruction "with feeling." What feeling? How much feeling? What does one do to the music to make it sound "with feeling"? And so on and on.

When there are many instructions in the music, the performer must decide *how* to follow each one. When there are no instructions in the music except the notes themselves (as is often the case), the performer must decide *what* treatment to apply to the notes, for merely playing them is never enough to create an expressive musical event. There is no escape. Every sound the performer makes will reflect his sensitivity to musical "rightness" at that particular moment (LISTENING 2.2).

A performer makes conscious and unconscious musical decisions. Usually decisions are more conscious when a piece is first being learned, and then they become less conscious—more internalized—as practice proceeds. By the time a composition is ready for public performance, a professional will have made it so much a part of himself that few, if any, conscious decisions remain. But no matter how conscious or unconscious the decisions, there is no way, in the traditional composer-performer roles, for a performer to avoid creatively deciding what he

(continued on page 32)

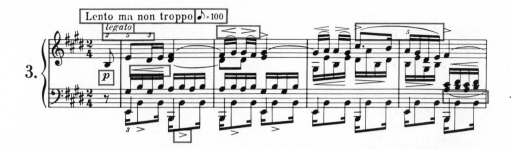

Lento ma non troppo	Slow but not too slow
(♪ = 100)	100 eighth notes per minute
legato	smooth
1, 2, . . . , 5	suggestions for fingering the notes
p [piano]	soft
< or cresc. [crescendo]	getting gradually louder
> [decrescendo or diminuendo]	getting gradually softer
⌢ and ⌣	slurs (play these notes smoothly together)
stretto	hurried
ten. [tenuto]	the note held its full value
ritenuto	[the speed] held back

Example 2.4 • F. Chopin: *Étude for Piano in E, op, 10, no. 3 (excerpt)*. (By permission of G. Henle Verlag, Munich.)

Example 2.5 ° *C. Debussy: "Footsteps in the Snow" (excerpt).*

Triste et lente	Sad and slow
♩ = 44	44 quarter notes per minute
pp [*pianissimo*]	very soft
< > [*crescendo* and *decrescendo* or *diminuendo*]	getting gradually louder and then softer
expressif et douleureux	expressive and full of pain
⌐	hold this note its full value
Ce rythme doit avoir la valeur sonore d'un fond de paysage triste et glacé	This rhythm must be the sound equivalent of a dull and frozen landscape background
più pp	more soft
p [*piano*]	soft
'	end of a phrase
⌒ and ⌣	slurs (play these notes smoothly together)
3 [*triplet*]	3 notes to a beat
m.d. [*main droite*]	right hand
♪ [*staccato*]	short note, detached
Cédez – –	Get slower
Retenu	[The movement] held back
//	halt the movement

Allegro maestoso. Tempo giusto.	Fast [but with] majesty. Proper speed.
ff [*fortissimo*]	very loud
Ped.	pedal on
∧	accent
♫♫ [*staccato*]	short note, detached
< [*crescendo*]	getting gradually louder
sf [*sforzando*]	sudden stress
Cadenza	a brilliant solo part (see the discussion in this chapter)
grandioso	with grandeur
8 · · · · ·	play an octave (8 notes) higher
sempre ff e marcatissimo	always very loud and very marked
ten. [*tenuto*]	the note held its full value
un poco riten. [*ritenuto*]	
e molto rinforz. [*rinforzando*]	[the speed] held back a little with much emphasis
a capriccio	at will, in a free style
strepitoso	noisy and impetuous
un poco marc. [*marcato*]	a little emphasized
tr ⌇⌇	trill (rapid alternation between the written tone and the one above it)

Example 2.6 • F. Liszt: Concerto for Piano and Orchestra 1 in E♭, I (excerpt of piano part only). (By permission of Breitkopf & Härtel, Wiesbaden.)

thinks the music should sound like. By necessity, a performer must *imagine* the musical ideas that have been incorporated into a piece and indicated by the conventions of musical notation. In doing so, he automatically brings his own personality into the picture.

That a performer's job calls for him to use his own imagination and therefore to add his personality to a composer's leads to the performer's unquestioned status as a creative artist and all sorts of problems of keeping the composer's imagination and the performer's imagination in balance. Should the performer try to eliminate his own conception of the music, submerging himself in the composer's imagination? Or, since this is impossible to do entirely, should the performer boldly assert his own imagination, insisting on an equal share of the creative responsibility?

These are old questions, and they will no doubt continue to be asked as long as composing and performing are separate roles. Every performing art contains such built-in dilemmas. But although they cause many theoretical and practical difficulties, they are also the source of some of the greatest pleasures to be had from art. Performing arts require multiple creation as part of their essential nature; so whatever the problems, the opportunities for excitement, complexity, freshness, variety, and individuality are very great in music, dance, drama, and film.

Some composers find it hard, if not impossible, to tolerate the notion that someone else's imagination might supplement their own: "Just follow my orders," they say. And some performers are willing to try, even to the extreme of adding little if anything to what is given in the musical score.

Other composers are quite agreeable to entrusting their music to the imagination of performers, and some performers are happy to take advantage of this license by ignoring whatever they please of the composer's instructions and making the music very much their own creation. At this extreme performances can be public displays, lacking depth and musical conviction.

Between the two extremes is an area that permits reasonable differences in balancing composer's and performer's creative imaginations. Most musicians operate within this area, constantly seeking that balance which will make a piece of music deeply expressive because of the combined insights of composer and performer, as LISTENING 2.3 will show.

LISTENING 2.3

Each of the following pieces has been recorded by several outstanding performers. Compare performances, concentrating on the differences in interpretation, which will range from the very subtle to the very obvious. Every difference comes about because each performer uses his own, personal sensitivity and imagination. Each begins from identical instructions (the musical score) but adds his own identity through thoughtful decisions on how the instructions should be carried out. Every difference in interpretation, no matter how slight, will make the music sound different to the sensitive listener.

F. F. CHOPIN   o Étude for Piano in E, op. 10, no. 3. Score excerpt in Example 2.4.

F. LISZT   o Concerto for Piano and Orchestra 1 in E♭. Score excerpt in Example 2.6.

L. VAN BEETHOVEN   o● Sonata for Violin and Piano in A, op. 47 (*Kreutzer*). Score excerpt in Example 2.2.

PIOTR ILYICH TCHAIKOVSKY   o Concerto for Piano and Orchestra in b♭, op. 23.

W. A. MOZART   o Twelve Variations for Piano on "Ah, vous dirai-je, Maman" in C, K. 265 (300e).

Group craftsmanship, sensitivity, and imagination

LISTENING 2.4

Compare performances of the following pieces, in which the number of players ranges from two to several. Which performances seem to achieve the most unified, expressive, and convincing effect?

GIOVANNI GABRIELI   "Canzon septimi toni."

W. A. MOZART   Quintet for Piano and Winds in E♭, K. 452.

L. VAN BEETHOVEN   ○● Quartet for Strings in B♭, op. 130.

JOHANNES BRAHMS   Quintet for Clarinet and Strings in b, op. 115.

JACQUES IBERT   "Trois Pièces brèves" ("Three Short Pieces"). (For woodwind quintet.)

MAURICE RAVEL   Quartet for Strings in F.

The performer as composer

Our discussion so far has centered on the individual performer and the qualities that make him a creative artist. The same qualities—craftsmanship, sensitivity, and imagination—are present when several performers create together, but a whole new dimension is added to each quality. At this point our interest is in the performer when he is a member of a small group (small ensemble) such as a string quartet, a woodwind quintet, or a brass quintet. (Chapter 7 will explain some of the details of such ensembles.)

In a string quartet, for example, each of the four players must have, in addition to his own technical mastery of his instrument, the ability to hear, understand, evaluate, and adjust to the sounds being produced by the other three players and his sounds as related to theirs. This process must be instantaneous. It requires a kind of skill, a stretching of the ears and mind, that can take, and often has taken, years of experience to develop.

The sensitivity of each player in the quartet must be to his own part of the music, to the parts of all the others, to the very subtle relationships among all the parts, and to the total effect of all four parts, which is always larger than the sum of the four. The complexity of this multiple sensitivity is so great that words can only hint at it.

In addition, each player has his own idea of how the music should sound. A crucial job for the quartet in their rehearsals is to merge the separate ideas into a unified one, in which each player adds to the whole and the whole gives the effect of a single interpretation.

Simultaneous creation, then, is a staggeringly complex process. It is also highly rewarding, both for the listener who can share its sense of adventure and for the performer, whose musical qualities are challenged in a large variety of special ways by the demands of "ensemble" (LISTENING 2.4).

In some kinds of music the performer is expected to use his craftsmanship, sensitivity, and imagination to create new musical ideas as a composer does. The most obvious example is the jazz musician. Our discussion of jazz in Chapter 1 focused on the spontaneous character of jazz composition, the immediate creation of musical ideas, that is, improvisation. We can deepen our understanding of jazz if we approach it through our discussion of the qualities to be expected of a successful performer.

In jazz, in addition to performance craftsmanship, the musician must have composing skill as well—the ability to create fresh, unified, and convincing music while he is performing. His sensitivity consists in being keenly aware of the creative possibilities suggested by the tune he is working with and, at the same time, being so highly responsive to the musical ideas of the other performers in the ensemble that his own sensitivity contributes to theirs. His imagination must be vivid and quick, grasping musical ideas instantly and sensing their implications at the moment the ideas occur. This all adds up to very large demands, which, when skillfully fulfilled, can produce music of great excitement and expressive power (LISTENING 2.5).

At various times in the history of music, performers have been expected to act at least partly as composers. The expectations range from jazz, in which the music is almost entirely composed by the performer, to styles that ask the performer to supply only decorative details to a composed piece. In the sixteenth century, singers were often expected to improvise on some parts of the composed music. In the baroque period (ca. 1600–ca. 1750), much music left details of harmonization and decoration (the addition of various ornaments to the music) to the performer. Some baroque performers, including Bach and Handel, who are now well known as composers rather than as performers, were famous in their own day for their ability to improvise music to the extent that jazz performers do now. In the romantic period (most of the nineteenth century), famous improvisers included Liszt, César Franck, and Anton Bruckner.

In our own time, improvisation enjoys renewed interest. Some compositions have performers make random sounds at various points as the music proceeds. Others give a few directions about the general nature of the piece but leave most of the details to performers. And some attempts have been made to leave *everything* to the performers, with no guides except chance and chance alone. We shall look more closely at these and other developments later in this chapter and in Chapters 8 and 13. At the moment we need only note that performers in various ways continue to be asked to act as composers, as they have for centuries (LISTENING 2.6).

LISTENING 2.5

Listen again to some of the jazz pieces introduced in Chapter 1 (listed here with a few additions), this time keeping in mind the requirements of craftsmanship, sensitivity, and imagination as other dimensions along with spontaneity. Surely no one can accuse jazz performance of being a simple matter!

J. COLTRANE   "Summertime," from *My Favorite Things.*

THE MILES DAVIS SEXTET   "Fran-Dance," from *Miles and Monk at Newport.*

LOUIS ARMSTRONG   "When the Saints Go Marching In," from *Louis Armstrong at the Crescendo.*

ORNETTE COLEMAN   ○ "Sadness," from *Town Hall, 1962.*

LESTER YOUNG   "Lester's Blues No. 2," from *Jazz Immortal Series, Vol. 2: Lester Young.*

T. JONES, M. LEWIS, AND THE JAZZ ORCHESTRA   ○● "Don't Ever Leave Me," from *The Jazz Orchestra.*

ELLA FITZGERALD   "How High the Moon," from *The Best of Ella Fitzgerald.*

The Art of Ornamentation and Embellishment in the Renaissance and Baroque, Bach Guild 70697, 70698. These interesting records contain selections in which a plain version is followed by an ornamented and embellished version. You can hear immediately how the performer's skill in improvisation was an important element in the effect of the music.

W. A. MOZART   Concerto for Piano and Orchestra in c, K. 491, I. L. VAN BEETHOVEN   Concerto for Piano and Orchestra in c, op. 37, I. P. I. TCHAIKOVSKY   o Concerto for Piano and Orchestra in b♭, op. 23, I. In classic and romantic concertos (large compositions for a solo instrument with orchestral accompaniment) the composer gave the performer a chance to show his virtuosity of technique and skill of improvisation in a section (usually toward the end of the first movement) called "cadenza," where the orchestra comes to a halt and the soloist displays his brilliance of craftsmanship, sensitivity, and imagination by creating a breathtaking improvisation.

As might be expected, many performers ignored the musical context, creating cadenzas totally out of style with the concerto. Owing to this abuse and other musical considerations, Beethoven composed the cadenza for his fifth (and last) piano concerto (in E♭, op. 73, *Emperor* Concerto) as an integral part of the music, and most composers after him followed his lead. Beethoven and Mozart also composed cadenzas for their other concertos (not all Mozart's concertos were so provided for by the composer) so that a cadenza one hears today may have been composed by the original composer, by a famous performer of the past, or by a contemporary performer.

KRZYSZTOF PENDERECKI   o *Passion According to St. Luke* (1965). At several places in this piece the players and singers find some general directions about what to do but must fill in the actual sounds on their own. This produces moments when chance plays a large part in what occurs. Thus the composer consciously gives up a large measure of control to the performers, introducing an element of uncertainty and unpredictability. (See the discussion of this piece in Chapter 13.)

JOHN CAGE   *Cartridge Music* (1960). This piece gets its title from the fact that many of the sounds are made by phonograph cartridges into which toothpicks, matches, feathers, bits of wire, and the like have been inserted. The cartridges are hooked up to amplifiers. The performers scrape or bounce the cartridges in various ways, thus producing sounds. Microphones are also used to pick up sounds from a variety of objects such as chairs and wastebaskets, which the performers tap or rub. Each performer is given some general idea of what to do but must make most of the decisions himself. The recording superimposes four different performances by two performers, further compounding the amount of sheer chance involved.

The composer as performer

LISTENING 2.7

SERGEY VASSILIEVICH RAKHMANINOV   Concertos for Piano and
Orchestra in f♯, c, d, g, opp. 1, 18, 30, 40. Recordings of each of
Rakhmaninov's concertos are available with the composer and with
other pianists performing. Compare the composer's performance
with others. Is Rakhmaninov's necessarily the "best" performance,
that is, the performance with the highest level of craftsmanship,
sensitivity and imagination?
  In the following pieces, compare the composer's performance with
other available ones:
SERGEY PROKOFIEV   Concerto for Piano and Orchestra in C,
op. 26.
  B. BARTÓK   *For Children* Suite for Piano, op. 14.
  DIMITRY SHOSTAKOVICH   Concerto for Piano and Orchestra, op.
102; Quintet for Piano and Strings, op. 57.

LISTENING 2.8

Collective composing by performers is illustrated by most popular
group albums. The following groups have produced some
particularly successful examples: The Beatles; Simon and Garfunkel;
The Who; Blood, Sweat and Tears; The Rolling Stones; The
Doors.

LISTENING 2.9

V. USSACHEVSKY   *Piece for Tape Recorder.* (Discussion in Chapter
1.)
  LEJAREN HILLER   *Computer Cantata*, Prolog and Epilog to
Strophe III. Computers are being used more and more to help
composers generate and manipulate musical ideas. Computers can

Often composers perform their own compositions, taking the role of
interpreter of their own creations. When this happens, there is no guar-
antee that a performance will be the best possible interpretation. We
can certainly assume that the performance reflects a composer's ideas
as closely as he can express them at the particular moment. But he
may very well perform the piece a bit differently the next time! The
composer must do what every performer does—make countless creative
decisions about the music—and his decisions are not likely to be the
only ones that can be made (consult LISTENING 2.7). As Roger Sessions*
explains, a performance

*is the result of a collaboration between the composer and a
particular performer on a particular occasion. This is true also when
the composer himself performs; the occasion is just as specific and
the problems are similar. The composer is as unlikely as anyone else
to play his work twice in the same way, and the more able the
performance—the more eloquent and convincing, that is—the truer
this is likely to be. The composer, too, must be faithful to the
composition; he must in fact, and presumably will, learn to be. But
he, too, will present one aspect of the work, and only one of various
possible aspects.*

Much popular music is composed by performing groups in a process
of "collective creation." Each member of the group adds his own ideas
about how to treat the rhythm, melody, harmony, tone color, and form.
What emerges is not an improvisation, on the one hand, nor an interpretation of someone else's ideas, on the other. It is most like what jazz
musicians call a "head arrangement," in which the decisions about what
to do throughout the piece are made together "off the top of the head"
and then immediately carried out (LISTENING 2.8). In later performances
of the same piece the original decisions are usually the ones followed.
  Several new technological developments have given composers the
opportunity to produce sounds by machine and to manipulate them in

*The Musical Experience of Composer, Performer, Listener, Princeton Paperback,
Princeton, N.J., 1971, p. 85. © Princeton University Press, 1950. Reprinted
by permission of Princeton University Press.

also be used to give off electronic sounds, these sounds being organized into musical compositions in the same way that sounds given off by a piano or violin or trumpet or tape recorder can be organized into music. Hiller's piece uses the computer to organize ideas, which are then performed by voices and traditional instruments, and to produce sounds directly, as in the Prolog (introduction) and Epilog (concluding section) to Strophe (section) III. In the record-jacket notes on this and similar pieces Hiller says, "Much nonsense has been written about computers 'thinking' and 'creating.' After all, a computer is really nothing more than a complex array of hardware. It can be tremendously useful hardware, however. . . . These pieces are truly experimental because they are concerned with revealing process as well as being final product. They are embodiments of objective research results. They are laboratory notebooks."

MILTON BABBITT ○ *Composition for Synthesizer*. The synthesizer used by Babbitt was built by RCA. Its full name is the RCA Electronic Sound Synthesizer, and it does exactly what its name implies—produces sounds by electronic means. These sounds are then organized into music by the composer, using whatever compositional techniques he chooses.

A major problem for the composer who uses such a machine is to keep his music within the bounds of what human ears are capable of hearing. For example, the Synthesizer can produce the twelve tones of the traditional scale so quickly that only a few of them can be heard; or it can repeat the same tone so rapidly that it sounds to the ear like one long tone; or it can produce pitches too high or too low for human ears to distinguish. Given such possibilities, the composer must be constantly aware of whether the sounds he is working with can be heard in the way he intends. It is easy to understand why composers using such sophisticated machines are fascinated with the outer limits of aural perception, and it should be no surprise that much of their music stretches the abilities of the listener. But much is also quite easy to share if one is not put off by the newness of the sounds, allowing himself to become absorbed in the sound events and the way they unfold.

THE UNITED STATES OF AMERICA "The American Metaphysical Circus," ○ "The Garden of Earthly Delights," from *Music of Our Times*. THE BEATLES "A Day in the Life," from *Sgt. Pepper's Lonely Hearts Club Band*. These are further examples of a combination of sounds produced by performers and by electronic devices, this time in pop style. The versatility of such combinations may well lead to their use in ways impossible to foresee.

a variety of expressive ways. This process does away with the traditional role of the performer, the composer and the machine being all that are needed to make music. This appeals to many composers who, for artistic and economic reasons, are pleased to bypass dependence on performers. But machine-produced sound also opens up a whole new world of expressive possibilities to the composer, and it is this rather than doing away with the need for performers which is the major attraction of the new technology. Some composers have imitated traditional musical sounds with machines, but most are not at all interested in reproducing by machine what live performers can do, for they want to explore new musical possibilities, either for entire pieces or in combination with live performers. The future will undoubtedly bring a wealth of music with no performer in the traditional sense, as well as music with various combinations of machine-produced and performer-produced sounds (LISTENING 2.9).

As the number of musicians performing together increases and the music they are re-creating becomes more complex, a point is reached where it becomes impossible for aesthetic decisions to be made collectively. A leader is needed: someone who can mold the individuals into a unified group. A conductor enters the picture.

The conductor's simplest task is to keep a steady beat so that all the musicians know exactly where they are as the music moves along. This was accomplished at various times in history by foot stamping, finger snapping, clapping, beating on the floor with a cane, or tapping on a music stand with a stick, or baton. Such methods of keeping a group together left something to be desired, and by the seventeenth century protests began to be made against the incessant din accompanying group music making. For a while the problem was solved by the head nodding of the harpsichordist, who also played chords in a steady beat, much like the rhythm section (drums, string bass, and piano) of a modern jazz group. Also, the first-violin player took to waving his bow at crucial times to keep everyone going at the same speed. Early in the nineteenth century some conductors tried out a new idea: *waving* a baton as a means of directing the group, a practice that met a good deal of opposition. But by the middle of the nineteenth century the specialist conductor had become so well established, so dominant in his role, and so attractive as a part of music making that concerts were often personal displays by virtuoso conductors, each of whom had a worshipful following of admirers. Some of this personality-cult atmosphere survives to this day; but the evolution of conducting responsibilities and the artistic complexities of music of the last hundred years have made conducting a necessary and demanding part of the art of music.

What does it take to be a successful conductor? It will come as no surprise to learn that the attributes of successful conducting are the same as those necessary for successful composing and performing: craftsmanship, sensitivity, and imagination. Much of what has been said about those three qualities in relation to the composer and performer is relevant for any musical role, but some important differences from role to role exist. An increased sensitivity to these differences can increase your enjoyment of the richness of music.

The conductor's craftsmanship

As leader of performers, a conductor must communicate musical ideas to them so that they do exactly what he wants them to do in exactly the way he has in mind. Each performer has his part, and a conductor must make clear to each performer how that part will best contribute to the whole. The means of communication between conductor and performer are the following: (1) the notes a composer has put on paper, giving conductor and player a common frame of reference from which to work; (2) words, as the conductor during rehearsals describes, explains, or instructs how he wants the music to sound; and (3) the conductor's body, which he uses to express his sense of how the music should unfold. Each of these means of communication requires its own kind of craftsmanship.

1. When a composer devises a piece for a group of performers, he translates his musical ideas into notation. Each performer has his own part, and all the parts are indicated on a master plan of the music—the score. In Chapter 1 we illustrated the complexities for the composer of creating a score for a group of performers (pages 5, 7–10). The conductor's task is to comprehend the score in all its details so that he can help every performer do his part properly. Each performer has only his own part of the score in front of him and is responsible for only that part; in itself this is an extremely complex responsibility, as our discussion of the performer has demonstrated. But the conductor has before him the full score, containing *all* the parts, and he must have the mental and musical capacity to hear in his mind how all the

LISTENING 2.10

Refer to the score excerpts by Stravinsky in Example 1.3 and by Schuman in Example 1.4. Each line of the score contains the part for the instrument named at the left-hand side of the line. The conductor's eyes and ears must read and hear the notes from top to bottom of the score at every moment.

In the score excerpt in Example 2.7, the beginning of Act II of the opera *La Bohème* by Giacomo Puccini, the instruments and voices to be used in the act are listed in a traditionally determined order from top to bottom. The music begins with the trumpets (Italian, *trombe*) playing a fanfare. They are soon joined by other instruments and voices until by rehearsal number 2 practically all are performing. The conductor must see and hear each pitch, each rhythm, each dynamic marking (loud or soft), each articulation (dots for short notes, curved lines for smooth notes, and so forth), each expression mark (*Allegro focoso*, "rapidly and fiery"; *marcatissimo*, "with the most marked emphasis"; *gridando*, "shouting style"). Everything that occurs must be fully under the conductor's control at each split second of its occurrence. As you listen, try to imagine the skill required in merely this first aspect of the conductor's total craftsmanship.

LISTENING 2.11

W. A. MOZART o Symphony 36 in C, K. 425 (*Linz*) (Bruno Walter rehearsing the Columbia Symphony Orchestra on Columbia record DSL-224). In this interesting recording three record sides are devoted to Walter's actual rehearsal of this symphony. You will hear him explaining, describing, cajoling, advising, and singing, as he works with the musicians to mold the music as he wants it to sound. The musicians are top-notch professionals who have probably performed this composition many times. However, Walter wants it to sound the way *he* thinks it should sound, and this requires that he be a skillful teacher. The fourth record side is the uninterrupted performance, which is the result of the rehearsals.

separate parts should sound when performed together. His eyes must take in almost countless separate bits of instructions; his ears must tell him exactly what each instruction sounds like and whether the performers are making the sounds as they should; and he must be able to identify immediately any detail that is not just right and know exactly what to say or do to correct it. Imagine this process with a full orchestra of over one hundred players! You will begin to get the sense of the craftsmanship required just to comprehend each part of the score and the total of all the parts together (LISTENING 2.10).

2. Having himself learned all the details in a score, in rehearsals a conductor must help his group learn to perform the music effectively. In an amateur group he must be a skilled teacher at a level that may include telling the performers how to finger certain notes on their instruments, how this or that rhythm goes, how to sing from this note to that note. With a professional group, of course, a conductor can devote himself to instructions about slight shadings of expression, delicate balances of sound, or small details of rhythmic precision, dealing with the music at a high level of artistry. But at every level of performance a conductor has problems of teaching, and he must be skilled in the technical, psychological, emotional, and musical aspects of being an effective teacher-director (LISTENING 2.11).

3. The other means by which a conductor communicates his ideas to his performers, aside from using his voice during rehearsals, is his body. Traditional ways of using the hands and arms have developed over the years so that a common sign language exists, which musicians learn as part of their training. A conductor must be thoroughly at home with these complex signs, able to make them clearly, adapt them to a wide variety of musical situations, and use them to the best possible advantage at every moment in the music.

In addition to the usual beat patterns, loud and soft indications, and cuing directions (indicating the precise moment for a performer to begin), a conductor's head, eyes, mouth, shoulders, and trunk will all add to the language by which he controls the musical events as they occur. The slightest toss of his head will bring a response from seasoned performers. A raised eyebrow, a bit of a smile, a hunching of shoulders, a slight movement from the waist—all are immediately meaningful and will cause the music to sound one way rather than another. The interplay

(continued on page 42)

Example 2.7 • G. Puccini: La Bohème, Act II: beginning. (Used by permission of the publisher, Bellwin-Mills Publishing Corp.)

LISTENING 2.12

K. PENDERECKI *Fluorescences* (1961). (The score, with instructions, is excerpted in Example 2.8.)

The conductor's sensitivity and imagination

between conductor and performers in a highly professional group may be as subtle and sensitive as any human interaction, the many so precisely attuned to one another that all think and feel and act as if they were one person. The interaction guide is the body of the conductor.

As music becomes more complex, especially in rhythm, the technique of conducting must be expanded to handle new demands. Much contemporary music is so rhythmically changeable, with many difficulties in getting things to sound together in the right place at the right time, that the performers could not possibly figure things out without the guidance of a conductor (see LISTENING 2.12). Yet a conductor is faced with the problem of clearly communicating incredibly complex ideas with limitations imposed by nature on what the human body can do. Four arms rather than two would help a great deal in some music, and in fact there are pieces that *do* call for a second conductor, who beats time for some of the performers while others follow the regular conductor. (An example is the second movement of Elliott Carter's piano concerto.) Nevertheless, in most cases a conductor must do the best he can by himself, adapting his old technique in new ways to meet new demands and inventing new techniques when the old no longer help.

Most of what we stated about the sensitivity and imagination of the performer also applies to the conductor. The major differences are the scope of the musical material and the technique of producing sound. As we have said, a conductor has to make aesthetic decisions affecting all aspects of multiperformer music; although he does not himself make musical sounds, he is responsible for unifying the sensitivity and imagination of each performer with his own and with his conception of the composer's desires.

So he is responsible for bringing about a successful merger of three different levels of sensitivity and imagination. First is the level of the composer, which is the foundation for the process of aesthetic creation in music, for the composer's ideas must be presented as faithfully and as vividly as possible; the sensitivity and imagination of the composer must come through if a performance is to be valid. Second is the level of the performers as individuals and as a group; the sensitivity and imagination of each must be preserved and at the same time amal-

(continued on page 46)

Example 2.8 • K. Penderecki: Fluorescences (1961; excerpt). (Copyright © 1972 by Moeck Verlag. Sole and exclusive agent for the United States of America and Canada, Deshon Music, Inc. Used by permission.)

ORCHESTRA

4 Flauti (anche 4 Fl picc.) - Fl.
4 Oboi - Ob.
4 Clarinetti in sib - Cl.
4 Fagotti - Fg.

6 Corni in fa - Cr.
4 Trombe in sib - Tr.
3 Tromboni - Tn.
2 Tuba - Tb.

Batteria I
Piatto soprano - Pto S.
Lastra (Donnermaschine) - Lar.
Triangolo - Trgl.
4 Blocchi di legno (Tempelblocks) - Bl.d.Lgn.
Bongos - Bgs.
Fischietto - Fio.

Batteria II
Piatto alto - Pto A.
Gong - Gng.
Vibrafono - Vbf.
Un pezzo di vetro - Vtr.
Bongos - Bgs.
Fischietto - Fio.

Batteria III
Gong javanese - Gng jav.
Guiro - Gro.
Campane - Cmp.
Flexaton - Flexaton.
3 Tom-Tom (SAT) - Tom-t.
Fischietto - Fio.

Batteria I'
Tam-Tam - Tmt.
Claves - Claves.
Raganella - Rgl.
2 Campanacci - Cmp.
Tom-Tom (B) - Tom.
2 Tamburi (militare) e.c., a.c. - Tmb.
Fischietto - Fio.

Batteria II'
Triangolo - Trgl.
Tam-Tam - Tmt.
Claves - Claves.
Un pezzo di ferro - Fro.
4 Timpani - Tmp.
Fischietto - Fio.

Batteria IV
Campanella elettrico - Cmp. eltr.
Un pezzo di legno - Lgn.
Sega (Singende Säge) - Sega.
Macchina da scrivere - Macchina da scrivere.
Surna (Altsrumlator) - Surna.
Fischietto - Fio.

24 Violini - Vn.
8 Viole - Vl.

8 Violoncelli - Vc.
6 Violinbassi - Vb.

Pianoforte - Pfte.

Alle Instrumente sind in C notiert. Piccolo-Flöten klingen eine Oktave höher, Kontrabässe eine Oktave tiefer als notiert. Die durch Sägen, Feilen und Pfeifen zu erzeugenden Geräusche können auch auf Tonband aufgenommen und dann eingeblendet werden. All instruments are written in C. The piccolo flutes sound an octave higher, the double basses sound an octave lower than notated.

The noises to be produced by saws, files and whistles may be tape-recorded and reproduced during the performance. Tous les instruments vont écrits en do. Les flûtes piccolo sonnent une octave plus haut, les contrebasses une octave plus bas que notées. Les bruits à produire par des scies, limes et sifflets peuvent être enregistrés et reproduits pendant l'exécution.

ABKÜRZUNGEN UND SYMBOLE · Abbreviations and symbols · Signes d'abréviation et symboles

a) allgemein · general · général

+ = Erhöhung um ¼ Ton · raised by ¼ tone · hausse la note d'un quart de ton
+ = Erhöhung um ¾ Ton · raised by ¾ tone · hausse la note de trois quart de ton
◄ = höchster Ton des Instruments (unbestimmte Tonhöhe) · highest note of the instrument (no definite pitch) · le son le plus haut de l'instrument (hauteur non déterminée)
► = tiefster Ton · deepest · lowest note · likewise · le son le plus bas · de même
= molto vibrato
= sehr langsames Vibrato mit ¼ Ton Frequenzdifferenz · very slow vibrato with ¼ tone frequency difference · vibrato très lent à interval d'un quart de ton
✕ = sehr schneller, nicht rhythmisiertes Tremolo · very rapid non-rhythmical tremolo · tremolo très rapide, mais sans rythme précis
= Tonrepetition so schnell wie möglich · repeat tone as rapidly as possible · son répété le plus vite possible
= unbestimmte Tongruppierung so schnell wie möglich wiederholen · repeat the notated tone grouping as rapidly as possible · répéter le groupement de sons notés le plus vite possible
= sägen · to saw · scier
= reiben · to rub · frotter

b) Blasinstrumente · wind instruments · instruments à vent
+ = nur auf Mundstück blasen · to be played on reed or mouthpiece only · jouer seulement de l'anche ou de l'embouchure
+ = nur die Klappen anschlagen · strike the keys only · seulement toucher les clés
✕ = frullato

c) Schlaginstrumente · percussion instruments · instruments de percussion
= mit Triangelschlägel · with triangle rod · avec baute de triangle
= mit Trommelschlägel · with drumstick · avec baguettes de caisse claire
= mit Paukenschlägel (für Vbf mit weichem Kopf) · with a kettledrum stick (with a soft head in case of Vbf) · avec mailloche de timbales (pour Vbf avec la tête douce)
= mit Holzhammer · with a mallet · avec du maillet
= mit Jazzbesen · with jazz brushes · avec balais
= Schlag auf die Mitte eines auf die Schlagfläche gelegten Schlägels mit einem anderen · Strike one drumstick after having laid it on the striking surface of the instrument · Frapper le milieu d'une baguette posée sur la peau avec une autre baguette
= Schlagfläche und Rand des Instruments mit demselben Schlägel gleichzeitig anschlagen · Strike the striking surface and the edge of the instrument with the same drumstick simultaneously · Frapper en même temps la peau et le cercle avec la même baguette
= Schlag auf den Rand des Instruments · Strike the edge of the instrument · Frapper sur le rebord de l'instrument

d) Streichinstrumente · stringed instruments · instruments à cordes
s.t. = sul tasto
s.p. = sul ponticello
c.l. = col legno
l. batt. = legno battuto
ord. = ordinario
nv = mehrere unregelmäßige Bogenwechsel nacheinander · several irregular bow strokes up and down in succession · successivement plusieurs coups d'archet irréguliers
✛ = zwischen Steg und Saitenhalter spielen (eine Saite) · play between bridge and tailpiece (one string) · jouer entre le chevalet et le cordier (une seule corde)
⋕ = dasselbe (zwei Saiten) · likewise (two strings) · de même (deux cordes)
⊥ = dasselbe (arpeggio über vier Saiten) · likewise (arpeggio on four strings) · de même (arpeggio à quatre cordes)
= mit dem Bogen über den Saitenhalter streichen (rechtwinklig zu dessen Längsachse) · to be played on the tailpiece · jouer sur le cordier
E = Bogenstrich über das Holz des Steges rechter Kante · strike the strings with the open hand or with the bored of the finger-tip · frapper les cordes avec la paume ou les doigts
E = mit der flachen Hand oder mit dem Fingerspitze auf die Decke klopfen · tap the soundboard with the bored or the finger-tip · frapper sur la table d'harmonie avec le talon ou le bout du doigt
E = mit dem Bogen auf das Pult klopfen · tap the desk with the bow · frapper sur le pupitre avec l'archet

Notengrafik: Julian Zaryski

(continued on page 44)

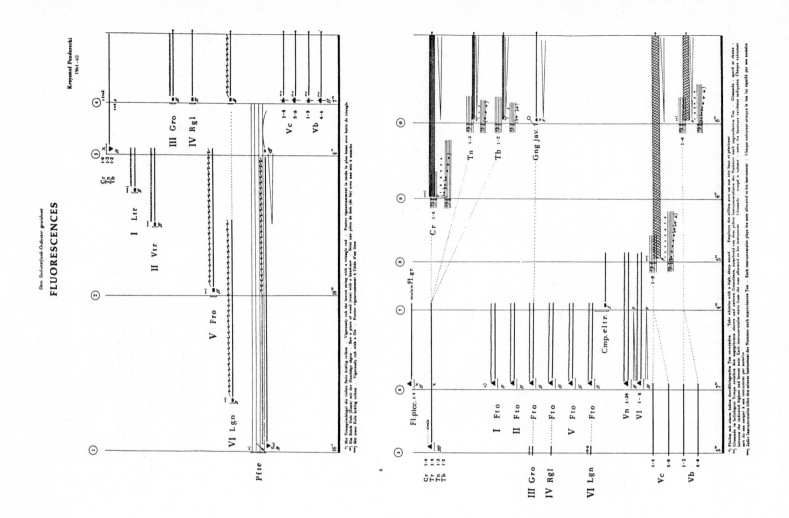

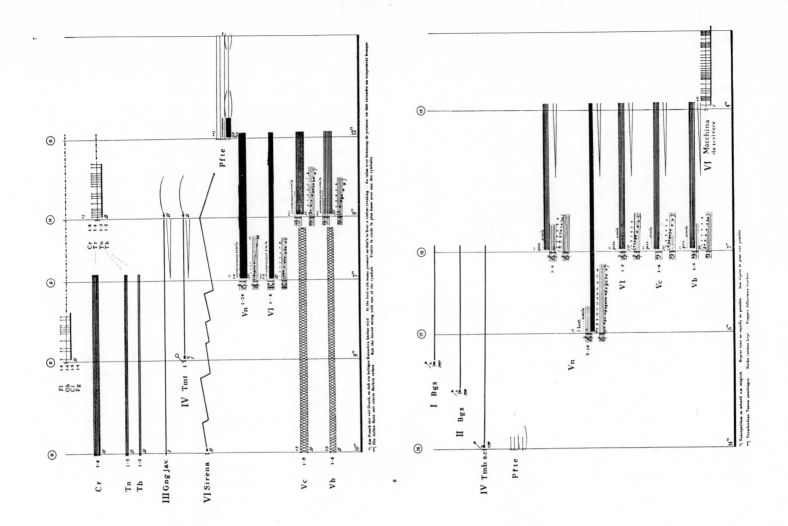

The following works have been recorded by several conductors. Compare performances, trying to sense the different effect of different sensitivities and imaginations. The works preceded by an asterisk have been recorded with the composer as conductor. As in composers as performers, compare the composer who interprets his own creation with other conductors who interpret his music.

J. S. BACH   ○ Suite for Orchestra in b, S. 1067.

F. J. HAYDN   ○● Symphony 101 in D.

W. A. MOZART   ○● *Don Giovanni*, K. 527.

L. VAN BEETHOVEN   ○● Symphony 5 in c, op. 67.

RICHARD WAGNER   ○● *Tristan und Isolde*, Act IV: "Liebestod."

I. STRAVINSKY   *○ *Le Sacre du printemps* (*The Rite of Spring*).

AARON COPLAND   *Billy the Kid.* (Suite.)

S. PROKOFIEV   *Romeo and Juliet*, op. 64. (Excerpts.)

DARIUS MILHAUD   *La Création du monde (The Creation of the World).

The performer and conductor (*summary*)

gamated into a larger whole. Finally, a conductor's own sensitivity and imagination are added to the process. The conductor must make many creative decisions based on his sensitivity to the composer's intentions, his imagination of how to realize those intentions in a compelling way, his sensitivity to the musical contributions of his performers, his imagination of how to take best advantage of his performers in the service of an expressive performance, and, finally, his ability to create a musical event that includes all three levels of aesthetic creation while transcending each of them.

There is probably no more complex aesthetic situation than this in all of art. For the listener the excitement, the challenges, the problems, and the rewards are very great in these interlocked creativities. With an excellent conductor, excellent performers, and an excellent composition (the word "excellent" in all three cases meaning, again, a high level of craftsmanship, sensitivity, and imagination), the opportunities for aesthetic enjoyment are offered to the listener in abundance (LISTENING 2.13).

In Chapter 1 we suggested that the composer does not express emotion, as many people seem to think. Instead, he explores the realm of feeling, shaping sounds to reflect his discoveries of how feelings go.

The same can be said of performer and conductor: they also do not express their emotions through performance. Their own personalities are certainly involved in what they do; but their musical job is to capture the sense of feeling in the music they are performing and to display that sense by the sounds they make or cause to be made. What might sometimes appear to be self-expression in a performance is instead the complete absorption of the performer or the conductor in the expressive conditions of the sounds. If the performer or the conductor begins to express *himself* and not music, he has abandoned art for emotionality.

The musical process that begins with the composer and is carried further by the performer and the conductor ends with the listener. The composer listens as he composes, the performer listens as he performs, the conductor listens as he conducts; but it is not necessary to do any of those things in order to share music. So it is now time to discuss how the listener can share the expressive sounds created by composers, performers, and conductors.

Chapter 3 ○ Aesthetic experience: the listener

THE EXPERIENCE OF A WORK OF ART IS ONE OF THE MOST PERSONAL AND most complex of human responses. Discussions about such experience can only hint at its richness, for as with other powerful occurrences in life, there is no substitute for *having* the experience. But it is possible for a discussion about the nature of aesthetic experience to have a helpful effect on its quality.

Many persons carry a heavy load of misconceptions about aesthetic encounters. This makes them act in unhelpful ways when confronted with a work of art and blocks their interaction with it. Clear thinking about aesthetic experience can get rid of some of the rubble that may block the experience and allow the interchange between a human being and a work of art to be as free and as direct as it should be.

What is an aesthetic encounter like? One answer to this question is that aesthetic experience is primarily an intellectual thing. It is a matter of the mind, and any pleasure comes from using the mind in the peculiar way appropriate to the contemplation of works of art. Perceiving the formal relationships in a work produces its own kind of pleasure, and that particular kind of pleasure is what art is supposed to provide. There is an element of truth in this notion. The aesthetic interrelations, whether of colors, movements, verbal images, sounds, or spaces, open up new and powerful ways of perception. We can recognize that this is one of the essentials that are involved in experiencing art. Yet something is missing.

A second answer, which contradicts the first, says that the inner mechanisms of art are not important by themselves; they only help to call attention to something in the nonart world outside the work of art. Thus a good work of art aids in responding to the everyday world more keenly. According to this view, the aesthetic experience is not different from other experiences; it is just another way to undergo things that can also be undergone nonaesthetically. There is something reasonable about this view also. The experience of art seems to share elements of other kinds of experience. At the same time, there are qualities in aesthetic transactions that appear unique, and to deny this is to rob art of its peculiar contributions to human understanding.

A third answer recognizes the truth in both other views but adds a distinctive dimension to each. This third view regards the created interrelations in art as expressive of the underlying qualities of human feeling. To share the sense of feeling captured in works of art, one must perceive and react to properties of sounds, colors, or shapes. A combination of *perceiving* the inner qualities of art and *reacting* to the expressiveness of those qualities is what we call "aesthetic experience."

Suppose, for a moment, that three people are looking out of the windows of a jet airplane as it is preparing to land at a large airport. The first person is a geologist going to lecture at a local university; the second is a design engineer for the company that built this particular jet; and the third, a college student returning home for vacation.

The geologist observes that the river to the north of the airport makes a curious bend as it gets close to the city. Just at the bend is a cliff formation and some low hills. "That's strange," he thinks; "I had no idea that this river was diverted that way. I don't remember reading anything about the effects of that kind of land formation on water flow in this area of the country. I wish some of my graduate students were here to see this: maybe one of them could do a dissertation on it."

The geologist's observation is predominantly scientific, and his reaction is appropriate to his perception. His experience might be called "intellectual" or "scientific" or "knowledge oriented."

The engineer is looking out the next window. "We shouldn't be this low so soon," he says to himself. "I wonder if the pilot is having trouble with those new altitude controls we installed last month. If pilots don't use them correctly, they're going to burn a lot more fuel and the profit margin for this plane is going to drop. I'd better have a talk with our flight-training director tomorrow."

The perception in this experience is primarily practical, and the reaction is of the same sort. We might call the engineer's experience "technical" or "practical" or "action oriented."

The college student is also at the window. He perceives the rough texture of the buildings, the grays and blacks and patches of bright color, the glint of the sun on the river, the contour of the hills in the background, the clouds close overhead, the movement of the jet as it swoops closer to the ground. "How lovely!" he thinks. And in wordless contemplation he becomes absorbed in the qualities of sight, sound, and movement presented to his senses.

The perception here is of aesthetic qualities, and the student's reaction is one of sensing the loveliness or significance or import of those qualities. The experience is aesthetic: It leads to no particular practical action and offers no particular knowledge of a scientific kind. It is complete in itself, moving in itself, fulfilling in itself. The experience adds nothing in the way of quantity, materially or practically, but it adds a dimension of quality. It seems to deepen the sense of what experience can be, to open the human being to awareness and involvement not usually present in ordinary experiences. The student may feel changed by such an experience—more alive, more sensitive, more in touch with a level of feeling below the surface. In this sense the experience is humanizing: It expands those qualities peculiar to the human condition: self-awareness, inwardness, subjectivity, and significance.

The three types of experience were presented as if each were pure, untouched by the other types or by various other kinds of human experience. Experiences can be of one or another type, but they often have bits and pieces of several types mixed in. The three in the jet could be one person, experiencing the landing differently from moment to moment. Human experience is too complicated to be separated as neatly as in our example. Nevertheless, it is possible to point to differing features of experience, and our job is to call attention to those features which are primarily aesthetic so that we can concentrate on them and help you develop your ability to experience music aesthetically.

Suppose that our three subjects are now sitting in a concert hall listening to a performance of Beethoven's ninth symphony. The first person has become a musicologist. "This movement shouldn't go so fast," he comments to himself. "The original notation shows it as slower. This conductor is not doing it the way it should be done."

Next to him sits a high-school orchestra director: "I'd give anything if my orchestra could play this. But even if it could, the school chorus couldn't handle it. Maybe I could do some of the easier parts and leave out the harder ones."

The college student is absorbed in the qualities of sound that are expressive in and of themselves: the melody, the harmony, the rhythm, the tone color, and the form—and in the meanings of the words as they have been transformed into parts of the musical events. He is perceiving the aesthetic aspect of the music rather than the scholarly or practical or other aspect, and his reaction is caused by what he is aesthetically perceiving. It is this particular kind of experience that music (and all art) is designed to give in the first place. The other experiences of art are not wrong. They are, however, beside the point for sharing that which art exists to share. They may be useful in one way or another, but they do not allow the power of art to be experienced in its own, unique way. Our concern is to help you experience the aesthetic power of music directly and immediately.

Several kinds of response to music are productive of a deeper sharing of its aesthetic power, and several kinds are not. We have already mentioned some musically unproductive ways to respond: reactions to the scientific or practical aspects of the experience, or to others, such as the religious, political or social. No one would argue that music should not be used for such purposes; they are perfectly legitimate uses of music for nonmusical ends, and music has served such ends through-out history and no doubt will continue to do so in the future. But none of them leads to more sensitivity to the *musical* use of music.

There are still other responses to music that do not deepen the experience of its artistic power. One such response is to hear music but not to listen to it, for it is possible for sounds to reach the ear without penetrating the mind. In modern society we are surrounded by music that is intended not to be listened to but to provide a pleasant setting for other activities. Restaurants, shops, elevators, lounges, airplanes—all endeavor to soothe, calm, and relax the nerves with a quiet background of sound. Such sound, in order to serve its purpose, must never intrude much on your consciousness. You are not supposed to become absorbed in the music; if you did, it would produce unwanted consequences: you might be too busy listening to spend your money, get off the elevator, or eat your food. So the music is kept soft and simple, not very interesting, and certainly not challenging to the mind or feelings.

The kind of response we want to help you develop is exactly opposite. In order to share the impact of music, you must be willing to throw yourself into the experience with all your powers of concentration and all your capacity for feeling. The music we are concerned with *demands* your involvement; it was not created to soothe you or to calm you or to tickle your ears without intruding into your brain but was created to absorb you, to challenge you, to excite your mind and your feelings, to add *more* awareness rather than less. It cannot do these things without your help. So when you listen to music *musically*, you must put aside letter writing, knitting, chatting, reading a magazine, or doing homework. We do not say that you should never use music that way; but when you are involved with learning about music, you must be willing to let music come first. The rewards can be very great.

Another kind of ''nonlistening'' response is to daydream to the music, the sounds fading into the background as the events of life, things scheduled to do, people, places, and problems file past. The music recedes again, not really listened to but just providing an excuse for reverie. Everyone listens this way some of the time. But such listening will not let you participate in the excitement and challenge and impact of the music itself. If you are to receive what music can give, you must be willing to put aside your daydreams and focus on the sounds and what they are doing. So much happens in good music (music that has qualities of skillful construction and deep expressiveness) that you will find it impossible to share if your mind is wandering around. Daydreaming to music is a hard habit to break. But unless it is broken, you will not benefit fully from the art of music. As you get more experienced in concentrating on music, you will become more skilled in turning off daydreams and turning on musical experience.

A closely related way to hear music without really listening is to make up fantasies while the music is going on: ''I imagined a jungle, steaming hot, with sunlight filtering through the leaves''; or ''I thought of clouds drifting along and changing shapes and getting darker and lighter''; or ''it was a haunted house with ghosts and witches and creaking staircases.'' Many persons use music as a way to let their imagination go, devising all sorts of scenes, stories, or dreamlike images. This can be a pleasant diversion, but it has little to do with musical experience. Of course, some music does tell a story or suggest a scene or a mood (and is then called ''program music''), which can become part of the musical experience. However, for many the music is not the important thing at all, the fantasy making pushing it into the background; the power of the music gets lost or diluted.

Finally, another way to miss the music is to focus only on the technical matters surrounding the business of music making. ''How young this quartet is! I wonder how they got famous so fast.'' ''That soprano is built like a battleship.'' ''The drummer looks like he's in his own little world.'' ''Did you hear the violins come in at the wrong place? That would never happen in a professional orchestra.'' ''This pianist has changed his style since I heard him last.'' ''What a glorious sound the chorus has in the Brahms! But it's a little heavy for the Mozart.'' ''Listen to the bass on this recording—it's distorted.'' So much of interest surrounds music and music making that it is easy to concentrate on such externals and not go beyond them to the music itself. Some of them *can* help the musical experience because they bring to prominence this or that event in the music or some bit of technical material related to the music. When we learn about music, it is necessary and useful to cover many of these matters. Some approaches to studying music stress them: the personal lives of musicians, techniques of performance, the historical background of music, the way certain pieces were received when first performed. Our approach, however, is direct; we want to help you perceive musical sounds and react to them. We shall include *some* background and technical information because it can influence the quality of your interaction with music. But this information is always a means, never an end.

There are three major ways to experience music musically. Each touches on the others, but we shall discuss them in turn so that we can clarify their particular qualities.

The first level of musical response, called the "sensuous" level, is to the surface impact of sound itself. There is something about hearing sounds that has powerful effects on the human body and mind. Many explanations have been advanced for this phenomenon, but whatever its causes, stimulation of the sense of hearing does result in strong responses in human beings.

The sounds of music serve none of the warning-signal or message-carrying functions that man depends on for survival. Musical sounds give us no signals to get out of the way of danger; they give us no practical information about the immediate environment; they do not carry specific messages that we can translate into statements, commands, ideas, warnings, propositions, or questions—all the things that spoken language does. Music is interesting, absorbing, exciting, and satisfying partly for the sake of the sounds themselves.

Music takes advantage of the power of sound to affect people through rhythmic devices, such as the pounding of a beat; melodic devices, such as the swooping upward and downward of a series of pitches; harmonic devices, such as layering pitches into thick and thin clusters of sound; and tone-color devices, such as loudness, softness, sudden accents, and the different tone qualities of musical instruments. These and other ways that music utilizes the impact of sound will be explored in detail in Part 2. Your increasing sensitivity to sound itself can increase the enjoyment you get from music.

LISTENING 3.1

The following pieces contain a large amount of sensuous impact. Some use rhythm as a primary way to involve the listener's body, whereas others depend on melody and harmony. All use big, heavy, and colorful sounds, which wash over the listener, making him feel as if he were immersed in an almost physical sound environment. In each piece the sensuous qualities are complex, calling for concentrated involvement on the part of the listener if he is to share the subtleties as well as the more obvious aspects of the music.

J. S. BACH   ○ Cantata 80, *Ein feste Burg ist unser Gott*, I.

G. F. HANDEL   *Messiah:* ○● "Hallelujah" chorus.

W. A. MOZART   *Don Giovanni*, K. 527: ○● Finale.

L. VAN BEETHOVEN   ○● Symphony 5 in c, op. 67, I.

P. I. TCHAIKOVSKY   ○● Symphony 5 in e, op. 64, II. Listen to the entire movement, for the sensuous quality builds as the movement proceeds.

G. PUCCINI   *La Bohème*, Act I: end, including ○ "Che gelida manina" and   ○● "Mi chiamano Mimi." Act II: beginning.

R. WAGNER   *Tristan und Isolde*, Acts I and IV: Prelude and ○● "Liebestod." Long, slow building up of sensuosity.

M. RAVEL   *Daphnis et Chloé*. (Suite.)

W. SCHUMAN   Symphony 3 (1941), IV.

WITOLD LUTOSŁAWSKI   *Trois Poèmes d'Henri Michaux (Three Poems by Henri Michaux)*, II.

T. JONES, M. LEWIS, AND THE JAZZ ORCHESTRA   ○● "Don't Ever Leave Me."

TEO MACERO   "Sounds of May," from *Outstanding Jazz Compositions of the 20th Century*.

BLOOD, SWEAT AND TEARS   ○● "God Bless the Child."

Some kinds of sensuous response to music are almost entirely an involvement of the body with little, if any, involvement of the mind. The pounding, throbbing, gut-shaking roar of some all-out hard-rock pieces is a body experience first and foremost. Loudness is intended to blot out thinking so that the physical feeling of the sound itself can be experienced directly. To call such pieces "unsophisticated" or "simple-minded," as many critics of rock do, is to miss the point entirely. Such pieces are not sophisticated or complex in their musical organization, but they are not *supposed* to be. They are directed toward a particular kind of sound involvement—a sensuous one—and produce such involvement very effectively. Other rock pieces, of course, go far beyond the strictly sensuous level and contain music of sophistication and complexity.

Some persons (notably those over age 30) find the temperature of much rock a little high for their thinning blood. There is plenty of "body music" available for them; it is just a bit less strenuous, as befits those of ancient years. The tickling bubbles of Lawrence Welk, the soothing syrup of Mantovani, the comforting stroking of the skin by Melachrino, the Jackie Gleason orchestra, the 101 Strings—all cater to the sheerly sensuous response to music. As in some rock, there is a bare minimum of musical interest, the emphasis being on the skin rather than on the brain. An entire industry exists to supply such experience at varying levels of excitement.

There is nothing wrong with the sheerly sensuous response to music, whether hot or lukewarm. There is also nothing to be taught and learned about this response. It is just a case of doing what comes naturally. Our only advice about this kind of response to music is "enjoy."

All music, no matter how sophisticated and brainy and calculated, depends to some extent on the sensuous quality of sound. Some composers lean more heavily on the sensuous than do others, but all use the impact of sound as an essential part of the expressiveness of their music (LISTENING 3.1). In most important music the sensuous response is one part of a more inclusive experience.

The next level of response to music, the "perceptual," includes the sensuous, as all musical experiences must. But now, in addition to responding to the sound impact, the careful listener responds to *how the sounds are related to each other*. He hears the rise and fall of a melody as it unfolds, the points of hesitation and forward motion, the repetition of bits of it, and the way it is changed as the piece continues. He hears the rhythm as it moves in various ways, becoming stronger then weaker or simpler then more complex, and as it adds to the unity of a composition by the way it is repeated and varied. He hears the harmony in its progress through moments of stress and moments of release, in its density, and in its relation to the melody it supports. The tone color of various instruments and voices is responded to not only for its sheer sound but also for the flavor it contributes to melody, harmony, and rhythm. The texture of the music—the way melody and harmony are organized—is perceived as part of the expressiveness of the events: at one moment a melody with chords underneath, at another two different melodies contrasted, or at still another several melodies mixed with harmony in complex interweavings. The form of the music— its structure as it proceeds from instant to instant and its overall orga- nization—is responded to as a unifying force holding the events together and as a generating force for the new and unexpected. And since none of the musical elements—melody, rhythm, harmony, tone color, texture, form—can exist separately from the others, the listener at this level responds to each element as it affects all the others, the parts adding up to a larger whole called ''a piece of music.''

If this description impresses you with how complex musical experience can be, you are beginning to get an idea of the richness of this art. Actually, this short description only hints at the possibilities for involving the mind in musical experience; all of Part 2 and most of Part 3 are devoted to a fuller explanation of how music is organized. And no matter how much is said about musical organization, there will always be much that cannot be said, for the possibilities of sounds to be structured far exceed the ability of words to describe what the sounds are doing. Nevertheless, some of the major ways music uses shaped sounds can be made clear through study.

Why should one perceive what is going on in music? We must reply, ''Because what cannot be perceived cannot be felt.'' Even the body experience of some hard rock is a kind of perception, the feeling it arouses depending on an awareness of the beat, the loudness, the tone color, the density, and the repetitions. These qualities are quite obvious and need little mind power to share them. Much music thought of as great or important or serious *also* has qualities that can be shared with a minimum of perception. But the richer the music, the more there is

LISTENING 3.2

The pieces in LISTENING 3.1 have a high degree of sensuous content but also contain a great deal of musical expressiveness in addition to, and including, their sensuous aspects. We shall come back many times to those and other pieces, each time focusing on a different aspect of their content.

For now, listen to several of them again, concentrating as hard as you can on what the sounds are doing. Do not expect to be clear about everything that is going on, but try to notice the many sound events each piece presents. After going through Part 2, we shall return to some of these compositions in Part 3, to listen to them as a whole again.

LISTENING 3.3

Choose a few of the pieces listed on page 53 with which you feel somewhat familiar. Attempt to add the dimension of expectation as you listen. You will find that it takes a kind of concentration—a total involvement—that you may not have thought possible with music. No one proposes that every moment of listening must be at this level; but it is there, and you can enjoy it if you are willing to try.

(both in quantity and quality) to perceive and to feel (LISTENING 3.2). If you are to do more than skim the surface of music, you must perceive more than the surface in order that you can *feel* more than the surface.

We must mention one more level of musical response, the "imaginal," which includes the sensuous and the perceptual but throws a new light on each. In this kind of response the listener does not only perceive the musical events as they unfold and react to their expressiveness. He also *anticipates* events before they happen. He feels the melody moving in a certain direction and predicts a change of direction. He feels a place of rest (a cadence) coming and waits for it to happen. He hears a bit of rhythm altered and begins to expect a return to its original use. He senses the harmony as it develops and foresees that it will create more and more tension as it goes. He hears a melody embellished by a different melody and looks ahead to how the two will be used later on. He feels the arrival of the end of a section and anticipates that new material will soon be introduced. He knows the music is coming to an end and waits for the sound to taper off until the piece is over. His imagination, in all these examples, is actively creating along with the music. He anticipates tendencies; he is absorbed in deviations from patterns; he is surprised by improbable events, is delighted by the fulfillment of an expectation, is challenged by delays in the unfolding ideas, is puzzled by an unusual situation, wonders how it will be resolved, watches and waits and follows and jumps ahead, totally absorbed in the world of structured sound that is presented to his mind and feelings.

At this level of response it is truly possible to say that the listener becomes one with the music. He emerges from such an experience exhausted and wrung out but also rejuvenated, excited, and exalted. A new and deeper level of experience has enriched his life. People who cherish music have shared some of this excitement; they know how special such experience is and how fulfilling it can be. It is little wonder that they seek it out at every opportunity. The imaginal response to music is not, however, reserved for the talented: Everyone can become absorbed to some degree in the world created by a piece of music. It takes some practice, a committment to permit the absorption, and sufficient familiarity with musical processes and particular compositions that one is not completely lost about what is going on (LISTENING 3.3).

None of this is mystical or magical; it is simply a matter of studying music willingly and well.

In Chapters 1 and 2 we suggested that the dominant qualities needed for successful composing, performing, and conducting are craftsmanship, sensitivity, and imagination. These are precisely the qualities needed for successful listening.

For the listener craftsmanship is the ability to perceive music keenly. Most of this book is devoted to helping you improve your craftsmanship as a listener.

Sensitivity for the listener is the willingness to feel music and the kind of feeling shared. You are responsible for this aspect of musical experience: No one can make you feel, and the nature of your feelings are determined by all you are as a human being. We shall continually emphasize those aspects of music which can cause feeling, and we shall constantly remind you that the reason you should *hear* what is going on in music is so that you can *feel* what is going on. As with just about everything else in life, practice at responding sensitively to music will make you better at it. We can supply the musical conditions that can involve your feelings. You must supply the involvement out of your own being.

Imagination in musical experience is the active participation in the creative process. The amount of imagination you use is partly a matter of listening ability and partly a matter of how much effort you are willing to put into musical experience. This kind of listening is not for the lazy. As in the case of sensitivity, we can help with the listening-ability part. The amount of mental and emotional energy you invest will be determined by you.

We can summarize our discussion of aesthetic experience in music by listing the traits that make a person a good listener, the listener that composers and performers look forward to finding among their audience:

1. A good listener knows what to listen for in music. He concentrates on what the sounds are doing, how they relate to one another, and how they create a series of events moving through points of tension, relaxation, stress, release, expectation, and fulfillment.

2. A good listener is able to concentrate on the music. He puts non-musical matters out of his mind for a while, giving the music his un-

divided attention. He knows that he is not supposed to go off to dreamland but that he is to be prepared to attend to the sounds and what they are doing.

3. A good listener feels as the music makes him feel. His investment in listening includes his feelings as well as his mind. He opens himself to the experience wholeheartedly, entering into the relation with music as a concerned partner.

4. A good listener adds something of himself to the experience, taking responsibility for an active encounter with the music. He is willing to give in order to get, the giving being an approach to listening that is creative as well as receptive.

5. A good listener will try to hear more in a piece of music each time he listens to it. He will not be content with the obvious but will try to get deeper into the music and absorb more of its significance at every opportunity.

6. A good listener is open to new musical adventures. Recognizing that every significant listening experience is an exploration in the realm of feeling, he seeks out challenging experiences as well· as comfortable ones. He is unafraid of fresh encounters with musical feeling, regarding them as opportunities rather than threats.

7. A good listener is less concerned with liking music than experiencing music. He does not bank on simple pleasure—liking—as the only payoff of listening. Instead, he tries to hear more and feel more from every piece of music, valuing those experiences which challenge his hearing and expand his feelings.

8. A good listener does not prejudge music. He tries to put aside attitudes that might prejudice the experience, allowing the music to speak for itself openly and honestly. Judgments about a piece can be made after the piece has been given a chance to be heard and felt, although a good listener has no need always to judge music: He is often willing to share music freely and not worry about whether the music is good or bad. When he makes judgments, he makes them thoughtfully and makes them on the basis of several experiences in listening to the piece.

9. Finally, a good listener is willing to make some effort in improving his ability to share music. He cherishes musical experience enough and so understands the nature of music that he knows that everyone can get better at listening if he tries. He may not intend to devote his life

to music; nevertheless, he recognizes the contribution it can make to his life and therefore does what he can to take advantage of opportunities to learn.

Our study of the composer, the performer, the conductor, and the listener has covered the most important persons involved in the process of music. Now we must turn to the actual material these persons use, the conditions of sound that make sound musical.

Part 2 ∘ *Musical expressiveness*

Some important characteristics of each of the three major roles in musical experience were examined in Part 1: aesthetic creation, aesthetic re-creation, and aesthetic sharing (aesthetic experience). Having been introduced to the general nature of these three roles, we are now ready to direct attention to the actual musical content of composing, performing, and listening. In Part 2 our study will focus on the elements that organize music in expressive ways: rhythm, melody, harmony, counterpoint, tone color, and form. We shall explore the most important means by which each element contributes to musical expressiveness.

To make the expressive conditions of music more perceptible, we must give them names so that they can be pointed to, discussed, compared, and identified in various contexts. The words in this book that name the expressive qualities of music are—as much as it is possible to make them—descriptive instead of interpretive. For example, two words that will be used to name a particular quality of sound will be "long" and "short." They describe the duration of individual notes. Because it is such a fundamental means of organizing movement, the length, or duration, of notes should be something you can perceive and react to. But the reaction you have to the particular durations in a particular piece must be entirely a matter between you and the music. The words "long" and "short" objectively describe important qualities of sound and help to call your attention to them; they in no way impose a subjective reaction on you, as would be the case if we named them, for example, "sober" and "frivolous." With the latter

words, your reaction is not entirely free: another's interpretation is being imposed upon you. You ought to be free of any reactions except those caused by the music itself. We have tried to use words that avoid interpretive meanings, words that also are useful tool concepts about sound and its workings and are commonly employed in the field of music.

Another important aspect of our using words as an aid to musical perception is the arrangement of such words on continua. Whenever possible, words like "long" and "short" will be presented as follows: long . . . short. The arrangement indicates a fundamental characteristic of music and a fundamental limitation of any language applied to music. This characteristic is that music exhibits an infinite number of subtle differences within each means and has the ability to shift constantly among these differences. For example, between extremely long notes and extremely short notes is an infinite number of possible note lengths; and the progress of the music might well include subtle or dramatic combinations of, and motion between, notes of various lengths. Words are limited in that it is quite impossible to name the countless points, combinations, and shifts between the extremes of any continuum. Music is as powerful as it is largely because of its fluid nature, whereas language is static and blunt. So we must not expect words to do the same things that music does. What we can expect from words is that they point out the existence of expressive means such as long . . . short, recognizing that we can usually identify that means with a word only when the music approaches

either end of the continuum. Still, that will be a big help. As your musical perception becomes more refined, you should be able to hear many of the subtleties in each category and many of the interrelations among categories. The more of such musical content you hear, the more you will be able to share the significance and pleasure of music. This is because the content of music to be studied in Part 2 constitutes the heart of music as an art: the expressive conditions of sound.

One further comment must be made at this point: The art of music is probably the best possible example of the principle that the whole is larger than the sum of its parts. Music does not consist of separate sounds, separate elements, separate means. In a work of art every part is meaningful because it contributes to a total impact. So to fragment music, as we are going to do to some extent, is to run the risk of distorting it. It would be a great pity if you were to get the impression that the parts of music are important in and of themselves. They are not. Just as cells plus organs do not equal a human personality, the elements of music do not simply add up to the art of music.

Yet the study of any complex phenomenon, whether a physical thing, an idea, a social institution, or a work of art, requires the examination of its parts, with the recognition that the parts must be understood in relation to the whole. So we have tried to ensure that the separate means you are studying will be heard as integral portions of actual musical experience. You should find that your increasing ability to hear them within their contexts will add much to your musical pleasure.

Chapter 4 ∘ The expressiveness of rhythm

THE ORGANIZATION OF MOVEMENT IN MUSIC IS CALLED "RHYTHM." (THIS definition also applies to the other arts, for each one has its characteristic way of creating a sense of movement.) Because of the striking ability of sounds to create an illusion of movement, rhythm is a particularly gripping musical element, and the more sensitive you become to the endless expressive possibilities of musical movement—of rhythm—the more you can share its sense of significance.

The movement of music is organized in three basic ways: speed, called "tempo"; "beat," or division into units; "quality," the kind of movement exhibited. In the margin is an outline of what we shall study about musical rhythm.

Tempo

SLOW . . . FAST

The speed of music might seem like such an obvious matter that it hardly needs to be mentioned. Yet it is so basic a factor in musical affect and can be so subtle in the hands of a sensitive musician that your awareness of it should be sharpened. Few decisions of composers or performers are as crucial as those having to do with tempo: A piece played a shade too fast or slow can be a piece robbed of its character, whereas subtle changes in tempo, under the control of a sensitive artist, can bring a piece to new, fresh life.

Since around 1600, composers have indicated the tempo they have in mind for a particular piece or section of a piece by one of several traditional words, of which the most common, with their meanings as usually interpreted, are:

RHYTHM (ORGANIZATION OF MOVEMENT)

TEMPO

Slow . . . fast.
Ritardando . . . accelerando.

BEAT

Grouping (meter): duple, triple, compound: regular meter . . . irregular meter.
Strong beat . . . weak beat.

QUALITY

Duration: long . . . short; articulation: *legato . . . staccato.*
Accents: strong . . . weak; regular . . . irregular.
Rubato: none . . . much.
Patterns: simple . . . complex.
Motion: static . . . active.

Largo	broad and slow
Lento	slow
Adagio	slow (literally, "at ease")
Andante	moderately slow (literally, "walking")
Moderato	moderate
Allegro or *allegretto*	fast (literally, "cheerful")
Presto	very fast
Prestissimo	as fast as possible

As was discussed in Chapter 2, such words give performers and conductors only a rough indication of tempo, there being a good deal of leeway

LISTENING 4.1

Below are examples of pieces in each of the traditional tempo categories. Compare different performances of the same piece to experience the difference in feeling produced by a different tempo. Note the wide variation in tempo from one composition to another in the same category. Surely the practice of music cannot be accused of being overly logical!

LARGO

L. VAN BEETHOVEN   ○ Concerto for Violin and Orchestra in D, op. 61, II; ○● Sonata for Piano in c, op. 13, Introduction.

A. VIVALDI   ○ Concerto for Violin and Orchestra in E, op. 8, no. 1, II (*La primavera* [*Spring*]).

HECTOR BERLIOZ   *Symphonie fantastique*, op. 14, I.

A. SCHOENBERG   Quartet for Strings 4, op. 37, III.

LENTO

F. LISZT   Sonata for Piano in b: beginning and ending.

I. STRAVINSKY   ○ *Le Sacre du printemps:* beginning.

ADAGIO

W. A. MOZART   ○ Symphony 36 in C, K. 425, I (Introduction); ○ Requiem in d, K. 626, I.

L. VAN BEETHOVEN   ○ Symphony 3 in E♭, op. 55, II; ○ Sonata for Piano in c, op. 13, II.

S. BARBER   ○● *Adagio* for Strings, op. 11.

J. COLTRANE   "Every Time We Say Goodbye," from *My Favorite Things.*

ANDANTE

J. S. BACH   ○● Italian Concerto for Harpsichord Solo in F, S. 971, II.

F. J. HAYDN   ○● Symphony 101 in D, II

P. I. TCHAIKOVSKY   Symphony 5 in e, op. 64, I, ○● II, ○ IV.

B. BARTÓK   ○● *Music for String Instruments, Percussion, and Celesta*, I.

"Walking in Space," from *Hair.*

MODERATO

W. A. MOZART   Twelve Variations for Piano on "Ah, vous dirai-je, Maman" in C, K. 265 (300*e*): theme and first variation.

F. P. SCHUBERT   *Die schöne Müllerin*, op. 25, no. 9: "Des Müllers Blumen" ("Miller Flowers").

C. DEBUSSY   ○● *The Afternoon of a Faun:* beginning.

A. SCHOENBERG   Quartet for Strings 4, op. 37, II.

ALLEGRO

A. VIVALDI   ○ Concerto for Violin and Orchestra in E, op. 8, no. 1, I.

W. A. MOZART   ○● Symphony 40 in g, K. 550, I; ○ Symphony 41 in C, K. 551, IV.

H. HANSON   ○ Symphony 2, op. 30, III.

A. SCHOENBERG   Quartet for Strings 4, op. 37, I.

S. GETZ AND J. GILBERTO   "So Danco Samba," from *Getz/Gilberto.*

THE BEATLES   "When I'm Sixty-four," from *Sgt. Pepper's Lonely Hearts Club Band.*

PRESTO

W. A. MOZART   ○ Symphony 36 in C, K. 425, IV.

J. S. BACH   Italian Concerto for Harpsichord Solo in F, S. 971, III.

O. COLEMAN   "Congeniality," from *The Shape of Jazz to Come.*

---

in what might be considered "slow" or "moderate" or "very fast." Many composers are quite willing to accept the looseness of the words and to encourage the re-creator to use his own judgment in this matter. Other composers will not tolerate having such important decisions made by anyone but themselves, and they use elaborate instructions to keep the performer from changing what was originally conceived as the proper tempo. The composer's best weapon for this purpose is the *metronome*, which, set to the number indicated by the composer, will tick off exactly the tempo he has in mind and give the performer little room to maneuver. In actual practice, metronome markings are as often changed or ignored by performers as the less exact word indications. Also, much music is so complex in tempo changes, both sudden and gradual, that metronome markings would be futile. So both in traditional music, where tempo indications give rough guidelines (hear LISTENING 4.1), and in contemporary music, where many of the guidelines have become less useful or even irrelevant (see the later discussion under Motion), tempo is a complex, vital matter in the creation of musical expressiveness.

LISTENING 4.2

RITARDANDO

H. BERLIOZ   *Symphonie fantastique*, op. 14, I: ending.
ALBAN BERG   *Lyric Suite* for Strings, II.
A. COPLAND   ○● *El Salón México:* beginning.
Many jazz pieces end with an obvious *ritardando*.

ACCELERANDO

H. BERLIOZ   *Symphonie fantastique*, op. 14, II: *animato più vivo stringendo* section.
W. SCHUMAN   Symphony 3 (1941), IV: measures 260 to 311.

Beat

RITARDANDO . . . ACCELERANDO

Some compositions depend for part of their expressiveness on a constant, unchanging tempo: Marches, many dances, and much jazz begin with a particular tempo and maintain it unchanged. But a great deal of music, although generally at the speed that characterizes it, depends also on moments of increased or decreased speed. A gradual increase of speed is called *accelerando*; a gradual decrease, *ritardando*.

The amount of *accelerando* and *ritardando* can vary all the way from a sudden slowing down at the end of a piece to a long, sustained, dramatic buildup of speed over the course of an entire composition. These alterations of tempo, whether slight and subtle or obvious and startling, add a whole new dimension to the expressiveness of rhythm (as in LISTENING 4.2) and give flexibility immensely useful to the composer.

A pervasive part of human experience is pulse, or beat—the recurrence of strokes of emphasis to mark off movement into units. The speed of beats determines tempo, but the expressive possibilities of beat include other important matters in addition to the most obvious one of how fast the beat goes.

Beat is so closely tied to the condition of life and is so natural a quality of movement that the expressiveness of music depends heavily on it.

GROUPING (METER)

The simplest way to use beat is to have it occur in a steady repetition, with slight and regular emphasis so that one feels a division of movement into groups, or measures. The practice of grouping beats into recurrent units is so widespread in music that many persons assume that it is always present or *should* be. So powerful are the effects of steadily repeated beat groupings that people, no matter how musically sophisticated, seldom, if ever, seem to tire of it. The weakening or elimination of a regular beat has probably caused as much difficulty in responding to some contemporary music as any other single characteristic.

The most common beat groupings are in duple or triple. *Duple* meters (duple groupings) are organized on the basis of two or four beats, with

DUPLE METER

J. S. BACH   ○ Fugue for Organ in g, S. 578.

W. A. MOZART   ○● Symphony 40 in g, K. 550, I, IV.

L. VAN BEETHOVEN   ○ Symphony 5 in c, op. 67, ●I,
IV; ○ Symphony 3 in E♭, op. 55, II.

J. BRAHMS   ○● Symphony 2 in D, op. 73, II.

H. HANSON   ○ Symphony 2, op. 30, III.

W. SCHUMAN   ○● Symphony 3 (1941), III.

A. SCHOENBERG   ○ *Pierrot lunaire*, op. 21, VI.

L. ARMSTRONG   "Tin Roof Blues," from *Ambassador Satch*.

DAVE BRUBECK   "Bossa Nova U.S.A.," from *Dave Brubeck's
Greatest Hits*.

TRIPLE METER

J. S. BACH   ○● Italian Concerto for Harpsichord Solo in F,
S. 971, II.

A. VIVALDI   ○ Concerto for Violin and Orchestra in E, op. 8, no.
1, II.

W. A. MOZART   ○ Symphony 36 in C, K. 425 III;
○● Symphony 40 in g, K. 550, III.

L. VAN BEETHOVEN   ○● Symphony 3 in E♭, op. 55, I; Symphony
5 in c, op. 67, II, III.

P. I. TCHAIKOVSKY   ○● Symphony 5 in e, op. 64, III.

J. BRAHMS   ○ Symphony 2 in D, op. 73, III.

A. SCHOENBERG   *Pierrot lunaire*, op. 21, VIII.

ROBERT RUSSELL BENNETT   *Suite of Old American Dances*, IV.

D. BRUBECK   "It's a Raggy Waltz," from *Dave Brubeck's
Greatest Hits*. This piece remains in triple meter but shifts beats to
give the impression of duple *within* triple.

COMPOUND METER

A. VIVALDI   Concerto for Violin and Orchestra in E, op. 8, no.
1, III.

W. A. MOZART   ○ Requiem in d, K. 626, VII; ○● Symphony 40
in g, K. 550, II.

L. VAN BEETHOVEN   Concerto for Violin and Orchestra in D, op.
61, III; Sonata for Violin and Piano in A, op. 47, III.

F. P. SCHUBERT   *Die schöne Müllerin*, op. 25, nos. 3, ○ 5, 10, 14:
"Halt!" ("Stop!"), "Am Feierabend" ("Evening Rest"),
"Tränenregen" ("Falling Tears"), "Der Jäger" ("The Hunter").

emphasis on the first and third beats: *one*-two *one*-two or *one*-two-*three*-
four. *Triple* meters are based on divisions of three: *one*-two-three *one*-
two-three. A combination of duple and triple meters (*compound* meter)
exists when the beat is grouped into two (or more) groups of three,
such as *one*-two-three-*four*-five-six, so that both a duple feeling and a
triple feeling exist at the same time. Duple, triple, and compound meters
account for the vast majority of regular-beat music (which in turn is
the majority of all music). LISTENING 4.3 selects just a few examples.

REGULAR METER · · · IRREGULAR METER   As we have implied, regular-
beat organization, such as in the music in LISTENING 4.3, is typical of
music until the late nineteenth century, when composers began to
increase experiments with new groupings of beats and with sudden
shifting of meters for expressive effects. One of the simple ways to
achieve some irregularity of meter is to alternate measures of duple and
triple meter, *one*-two *one*-two-three (or *one*-two-*three*-four-five), or the
reverse, *one*-two-three *one*-two (or *one*-two-three-*four*-five). If this pattern continues for some time, however, the effect is regular—a regularly
recurring five-beat, as in LISTENING 4.4.

Another common way to add irregularity to a basically regular beat
is to shift strong beats from the expected places in the measure to
unexpected and irregular places. This is an old and widely used device
to create an off-balance rhythmic flow. The beat remains evenly divided
on paper, giving the impression that it has not been abandoned, while
it is being altered. A sequence might be *one*-*two*-three-four *one*-two-
three-four *one*-two-three-*four* *one*-two-*three*-four (LISTENING 4.5).

Finally, irregularity of measured beat is achieved by changing the actual
meter as the music moves along, by putting one meter over another,
or by doing both at the same time. Some contemporary music has
become so irregular in meter, with such enormous complexity of beat
organization, that professional performers and conductors find themselves having to learn to think in new ways about how to produce music.
From the early metrical complexities of Stravinsky (once considered
terribly difficult to perform but now standard technique), through the
tortuous beat organizations of Schoenberg and his followers, to the
mathematically controlled but unperceivable constructions of the avant-
garde, irregularity of meter has become progressively more important
as a means for producing musical effects (LISTENING 4.6). The old masters
would have been astonished at how far meter has been pushed—as

LISTENING 4.4

P. I. TCHAIKOVSKY   Symphony 6 in b, op. 74, II. This movement is organized in five beats to the measure, with the five beats a regular recurrence of *one-two-three-four-five* (2 + 3).

D. BRUBECK   "Take Five," "Blue Rondo à la Turk," from *Time Out.* "Take Five" is in five beats to the measure, organized as *one-two-three-four-five* (3 + 2). "Blue Rondo à la Turk" is based on the pattern *one-two-one-two-one-two-one-two-three* (2 + 2 + 2 + 3), with interruptions of *one-two-three-one-two-three-one-two-three* (3 + 3 + 3), exhibiting a curious regularity within an irregular context. The meter shifts to 3 + 3 + 3 2 + 2 and then goes into a regular duple meter for the saxophone and piano solos, giving the common duple meter a fresh feeling when heard in an irregular context.

LISTENING 4.5

A. COPLAND   o● *El Salón México:* ending.
J. BRAHMS   Symphony 2 in D, op. 73, IV.
L. VAN BEETHOVEN   o● Symphony 3 in E♭, op. 55, I.
W. SCHUMAN   Symphony 3 (1941), IV.

Quality

LISTENING 4.6

I. STRAVINSKY   *The Soldier's Tale:* o "The Soldier's March," "Music to Scene I," o● "The Royal March"; *Le Sacre du printemps:* o "Dance of the Adolescents," "Sacrificial Dance."
A. SCHOENBERG   Quartet 4 for Strings, op. 37, II: ending.
B. BARTÓK   o● *Music for String Instruments, Percussion, and Celesta,* I.
PIERRE BOULEZ   *Le Marteau sans maître:* any part.
O. COLEMAN   *Free Jazz.*

astonished, no doubt, as the contemporary listener still expecting to feel the beat when he goes to a concert of modern music.

STRONG BEAT . . . WEAK BEAT

The discussion of beat so far has concentrated on "strong" beat organizations, those which are easily perceptible in regular groupings and present but more complex in irregular groupings. Naturally, the strength of the beat, its heaviness or obviousness or clarity, is more apparent when it is regular, but it can be strong even though irregular, as in Stravinsky. Some musical motion, however, is so fluid and flexible that little or no sense of beat is given. In some pieces the beat recurs over and over but with so little emphasis that one barely feels it. In other pieces there are constant changes in speed from point to point, and the points, or beats, are so weak that they do not seem to be there at all. The movement floats rather than marching along. Such music, usually composed before 1600 and after 1900, depends for part of its effectiveness on the weakness or absence of a felt beat; a rootless, subtle sense of motion is given by the sound events (LISTENING 4.7). In much contemporary music beat has been entirely abandoned, making the words "pulse" or "meter" (as the word "tempo") irrelevant. Many listeners regret the absence of a strong beat; but composers often argue that their freedom from the "tyranny of the bar line" has opened up whole new worlds of rhythmic expressiveness for exploration.

The third basic way, after tempo and beat, that musical movement is organized is through the quality of the movement, the inner content of the rhythmic flow. This, of course, is the aspect of rhythm least capable of being verbalized: The possibilities of creating an illusion of movement with sounds are so great that language can only stumble along behind, pointing out important landmarks along the way. In addition, rhythmical considerations overlap those of melody, harmony, and to some extent tone color and form. The power of music to blend many elements together is one of its fundamental characteristics, one that language can only partially explain. So the treatment of rhythmic quality, as of many other musical elements, must be regarded simply as an entry point to better perception.

LISTENING 4.7

GREGORIAN CHANT   ○ "Veni creator spiritus"; ○● "Alleluia vidimus stellam."

E. VARÈSE   *Ionisation.*

M. BABBITT   ○ *Composition for Synthesizer.*

L. BERIO   ○ *Omaggio a Joyce.*

O. COLEMAN   ○ "Sadness," from *Town Hall, 1962.*

LISTENING 4.8

LEGATO

L. VAN BEETHOVEN   ○ Symphony 3 in E♭, op, 55, II.

J. BRAHMS   ○● Symphony 2 in D, op. 73, II.

B. BARTÓK   ○● *Music for String Instruments, Percussion, and Celesta,* I.

S. BARBER   ○● *Adagio* for Strings, op. 11.

W. SCHUMAN   ○● Symphony 3 (1941), III.

STACCATO

L. VAN BEETHOVEN   ○● Symphony 3 in E♭, op. 55, III.

J. S. BACH   ○ Suite for Orchestra in b, S. 1067, II.

H. BERLIOZ   ○● *Symphonie fantastique,* op. 14, V: "Ronde du Sabbat."

I. STRAVINSKY   ○ *Le Sacre du printemps:* "Dance of the Adolescents."

LEGATO AND *STACCATO* COMBINED

W. A. MOZART   *Eine kleine Nachtmusik* in G, K. 525, II.

F. J. HAYDN   ○● Symphony 101 in D, II.

L. VAN BEETHOVEN   ○ Symphony 5 in c, op. 67, IV.

S. GETZ AND J. GILBERTO   "Corcovado," from *Getz/Gilberto.* After the *legato* introduction, a *legato* melody is set against a basically *staccato* accompaniment.

DURATION: LONG . . . SHORT; ARTICULATION: *LEGATO* . . . *STACCATO*

Long and short durations of sound determine the inner rhythmic movement of music. The combination of long and short sounds into patterns, the relations among patterns, and the alterations, variations, and developments of patterns provide the composer with rhythmic possibilities approaching infinity. Even with traditional instruments and the human voice and traditional abilities of performance, rhythmic diversity seems to be endless. With increased technical abilities in performance during recent years, the advent of newly invented instruments, the widened use of percussion instruments and new devices in conjunction with traditional instruments, and the invention of electronic sound-producing and sound-manipulating instruments, the possibilities for the creation of movement patterns and relations among them are staggering.

Every presentation of sounds includes, in addition to their length, or duration, the quality of movement from one sound to another (articulation). At one end of the continuum is smooth, uninterrupted gliding from sound to sound so that there is continuous, unbroken motion. This quality of articulation is called *legato*. At the opposite pole is the short, detached, interrupted succession of sounds called *staccato*. Here the sounds are separated by spaces (rests), and the effect is quite different from *legato*. Of course, a great many points exist between extreme *legato* and extreme *staccato* as well as all sorts of combinations of the two and constant shiftings from one to the other (LISTENING 4.8). Articulation adds another expressive layer over the rhythmic base of duration.

ACCENTS: STRONG . . . WEAK; REGULAR . . . IRREGULAR

As musical movement proceeds, dramatic highlights are often added in the form of sudden stresses called "accents." Beat is also a matter of emphasis, but accent means a level of emphasis beyond that of the normal beat for a particular piece. In a piece with a weak beat, therefore, a slight accent will be heard as a greater stress than its surroundings have; thus it is similar to a very heavy accent in a strong-beat context.

A sensation of accent can be produced by holding certain notes longer than others or by moving to a higher pitch. The most common type

LISTENING 4.9

ACCENTS

W. A. MOZART   ○ Symphony 41 in C, K. 551, II.

L. VAN BEETHOVEN   ○ Symphony 5 in c, op. 67, IV: end of movement.

B. BARTÓK   *Music for String Instruments, Percussion, and Celesta*, IV.

W. SCHUMAN   ○● Symphony 3 (1941), II.

I. STRAVINSKY   ○● *The Soldier's Tale:* "Royal March"; ○● *Symphony of Psalms*, I.

SYNCOPATION

L. VAN BEETHOVEN   Symphony 5 in c, op. 67, III: end of movement and transition to ○ IV.

R. R. BENNETT   ○ *Suite of Old American Dances*, V: "Rag."

B. BARTÓK   ○● *Music for String Instruments, Percussion, and Celesta*, II.

I. STRAVINSKY   *The Soldier's Tale:* ○ "The Soldier's March," "Triumphal March of the Devil."

A. COPLAND   ○● *El Salón México.*

D. BRUBECK   "Bossa Nova U.S.A.," from *Dave Brubeck's Greatest Hits.*

S. GETZ AND J. GILBERTO   "The Girl from Ipanema," from *Getz/Gilberto.*

I. JACQUET   ○ "How High the Moon," from *The King.*

of accent is that which depends on sudden loudness, with or without the reinforcement of length and pitch. That a wide range of soft to loud can produce accent, that there are complex possibilities of interrelation between accents and the beat of a particular composition, and that the reinforcing effects of note length and pitch placement exist make of accent a most fruitful device.

Also to be taken into account is the regularity or irregularity of accent in the ongoing motion of the music. At one extreme accents occur so regularly that they merge with the beat. In this situation strong beat and regular accent are essentially the same qualities. From that starting point a wide range of differences can exist between the underlying beat and the sounding of accents; accents may regularly coincide with some beats, or they may not coincide in any predictable way with the beat. The further removed the accents are from regularity, the more uncertain and unexpected are their expressive results.

The intimate relationship between accent and beat gives rise to a particular rhythmic effect so widely used that it has its own name: "syncopation." This changes the normal beat pattern by accenting weak beats; thus unexpected beats are stressed, and usually stressed ones are not. The resulting irregularity produces a disjointed movement that is most effective. The syncopated pattern is sounded at the same time that the normal beat goes on so that the two overlap clearly. Jazz constantly does this: the regular beat is kept by rhythm instruments while many syncopated patterns are played by melody instruments. Sometimes the entire rhythmic content of the music becomes syncopated and produces a dramatic loss of beat sense and therefore a great deal of musical uncertainty. Of course, this device must be used sparingly since, if it goes on too long, it will be perceived as regular and lose its impact. Syncopation of all sorts, in the hands of sophisticated composers, adds another dimension to the many subtleties of rhythmic accent. (Now hear LISTENING 4.9.)

RUBATO: NONE . . . MUCH

The movement of music with a definite beat organization is often perfectly steady, each beat recurring with machinelike precision. But much music calls for a loosening up of the beat by slight hesitation or slight pushing ahead, called "*rubato*." This is not so evident as to

LISTENING 4.10

Whenever possible, listen to several performances to compare *rubato.*

L. VAN BEETHOVEN ○ Sonata for Piano in c, op. 13, II.

F. F. CHOPIN ○ Étude for Piano in E, op. 10, no. 3; "Polonaise-Fantaisie" for Piano, op. 61.

P. I. TCHAIKOVSKY ○● Symphony 5 in e, op. 64, II.

J. BRAHMS ○● Symphony 2 in D, op. 73, II.

C. DEBUSSY ○● *The Afternoon of a Faun.*

F. P. SCHUBERT ○ *Die schöne Müllerin,* op. 25, nos. 18, 19: "Trockne Blumen" ("Wither'd Flowers"), "Der Müller und der Bach" ("The Miller and the Brook").

be called *ritardando* or *accelerando* but is a subtle deviation from the beat, creating tensions by stretching it here and there.

Some *rubato* occurs in the melody only, the beat of the accompaniment remaining steady. As in the similar type of syncopation, this style produces an expressive tension between the steady and unsteady rhythms—a tension that can be used in subtle ways by both composers and performers. At other times, all parts of the music deviate from the steady beat, creating uncertainty, which resolves when steadiness returns.

Much music would sound square if played without *rubato.* Other music would sound ridiculous *with rubato.* This rhythmic means is so delicate that musical notation cannot express it in any precise way. A composer will usually resort to writing the word *rubato* under particular sections or indicating that an entire movement or piece is to be performed "with expression," or "sweetly," or even "with heart." Such is the gap between actual sound events and any known means to indicate them precisely that such suggestive terms continue to be relied upon for subtle effects. Naturally this leaves a great deal to the judgment of the performer. It is interesting to listen to several different performances (LISTENING 4.10) of a piece that calls for *rubato* and notice the differences in each performer's interpretation. The artist-performer is the one who can add the right touch of *rubato* that brings a piece to expressive life.

PATTERNS: SIMPLE . . . COMPLEX

In much music rhythm patterns as building blocks for the creation of a unified whole are as important as any other elements. Such patterns can be purely rhythmic, (for example, in percussion music) but usually are an integral part of melodic or harmonic patterns. For example, the melody fragment (motive) on which the first movement of Beethoven's Symphony 5 is based has the following rhythm: $\frac{2}{4}$ ♪♪♪ | ♩. Obviously, this is presented by particular pitches so that its melodic aspect and its rhythmic aspect (as well as its tone-color aspect) cannot be separated. For the moment, however, we shall focus on the rhythmic dimension of patterns so that you can become more conscious of their role in musical expressiveness.

Until recent years, practically all music used rhythm patterns. Simple patterns, repeated over and over (often with different pitches), ensure

LISTENING 4.11

Here are examples of complex pieces that use relatively simple rhythm patterns as foundations:

J. S. BACH ○ Suite for Orchestra in b, S. 1067, II. The basic pattern is (musical notation)

W. A. MOZART ○● Symphony 40 in g, K. 550, I. The basic pattern is (musical notation)

W. A. MOZART ○ Symphony 41 in C, K. 551, III. The basic pattern is (musical notation)

L. VAN BEETHOVEN ○● Symphony 5 in c, op. 67, I. The basic pattern is (musical notation)

LISTENING 4.12

These examples illustrate complex rhythm patterns that are still quite recognizable to the ear:

B. BARTÓK *Music for String Instruments, Percussion, and Celesta,* IV. The basic pattern is (musical notation)

H. HANSON Symphony 2, op. 30, II. The basic pattern is (musical notation)

W. SCHUMAN Symphony 3 (1941), IV. The basic pattern is (musical notation)

As complexities increase and rhythms are piled atop rhythms, the ability to perceive patterns becomes so stretched that it no longer can operate because of either the complexity or the nonuse of patterns as musical organizers.

A. SCHOENBERG ○ *Pierrot lunaire,* op. 21, XIV.
A. BERG *Lyric Suite* for Strings, III.
P. BOULEZ *Le Marteau sans maître.*
YANNIS XENAKIS ○● *Pithoprakta.*

that the music will be experienced as sensible—as holding together, logical, related, and unified. Popular music, patriotic music, folk music, or ceremonial music all depend for part of their easy accessibility on simple rhythm patterns often repeated:

"The Star-Spangled Banner" is based on (musical notation)

"My Country 'Tis of Thee" is based on (musical notation)

"America the Beautiful" is based on (musical notation)

"Auld Lang Syne" is based on (musical notation)

"Home on the Range" is based on (musical notation)

The simplicity of such patterns and their constant repetition make the music easy to grasp, as it must be to serve its social functions.

Composers of concert music also have depended on rhythm patterns for building a sense of form into their music, but their use of patterns becomes more complex as the music leaves the level of the obvious and moves toward deeper levels of expressiveness. Some music is shaped by simple patterns but develops, alters, and builds on the patterns in complex ways, as LISTENING 4.11 shows.

Although simple rhythm patterns can generate complex music, more involved patterns interest and challenge both composer and listener. At every point in history, music has contained rhythm patterns both simple and complex for the style context of the time; but with the passage of centuries, the span between simple and complex has lengthened as more and more rhythmic challenge has been added. This challenge includes both complexity of patterns and their intricate overlapping. In a great deal of recent music, rhythmic patterns continue to be used and recognizable, but they have become stretched in length, in intricacy, in irregularity, or in the use of one over another (LISTENING 4.12).

MOTION: STATIC . . . ACTIVE

The rhythmic means described above account for major aspects of the organization of musical movement. The result of them all, including subtleties beyond the capacity of words to describe, is a sense of motion.

LISTENING 4.13

The following pieces use traditional rhythmic means for producing a sense of motion:

RELATIVELY STATIC MOTION

F. J. HAYDN   o● Symphony 101 in D, II.

A. VIVALDI   o Concerto for Violin and Orchestra in E, op. 8, no. 1, II.

I. STRAVINSKY   o● *Symphony of Psalms,* I, III.

L. VAN BEETHOVEN   Sonata for Piano in c, op, 13, o● Introduction, o II.

THE MODERN JAZZ QUARTET   "Yesterdays," from *The Modern Jazz Quartet.*

RELATIVELY ACTIVE MOTION

J. S. BACH   o Cantata 80, *Ein feste Burg ist unser Gott,* I.

W. A. MOZART   o Requiem in d, K. 626, I: Kyrie Eleison.

I. STRAVINSKY   o *Le Sacre du printemps:* "Dance of the Adolescents."

B. BARTÓK   *Music for String Instruments, Percussion, and Celesta,* IV.

W. SCHUMAN   Symphony 3 (1941), IV.

O. COLEMAN   "Congeniality," from *The Shape of Jazz to Come.*

Here is some contemporary music producing motion with nontraditional means:

E. VARÈSE   *Poème électronique.*

M. BABBITT   o *Composition for Synthesizer.*

V. USSACHEVSKY   *Piece for Tape Recorder.*

OTTO LUENING AND V. USSACHEVSKY   *King Lear.* (Suite.)

HALIM EL-DABH   *Leiyla and the Poet.*

This motion sense is musical rhythm in its widest yet most accurate definition, for although many separate means in music can be isolated and described, their existence in musical experience adds up to something more than any of their combinations. That something more is a sensation of movement as powerful, as affecting, as subtle, and as rich as any available to human experience.

The overall impression of motion (also called "pace") in a particular piece can range from very static to very active. At the static end, there is a sense of stillness, of hovering, of cessation, of quiescence. These nouns very roughly describe the general flavor of static motion; but the actual feeling of relative lack of motion, as of all feelingful musical experiences, cannot be described in words. At the opposite end of the continuum, music gives a sense of extreme activity, of great animation, rushing, or speed, of tumbling motion. Of course, infinite shadings exist between static and active pace as well as constant changes from one to the other and overlappings of the two.

The amount of motion in a piece is usually determined by tempo, by length of notes, by arrangement of beat and accent, and by repetition of patterns. Yet it would be too easy to assume, for example, that fast tempo always produces active motion or that long notes always make motion static. A relative lack of rhythmic motion may be felt as static because it is set against a fast-beat background; a slow tempo may provide a background against which a quick series of notes can produce an impression of pressing action.

Further, much contemporary music cannot be described with traditional rhythm terms; nevertheless, it may give strong effects of static to active motion. The word "tempo" loses its meaning when applied to most electronic music, where "fast" and "slow" are quite inappropriate descriptions of the rhythmic movement. Such music certainly gives a sense of motion, which is often the music's main expressive content; but one will search in vain for tempo, for beat groupings, for *rubato*, or for rhythm patterns. In fact, it is just this ability to produce motion sense without dependence on traditional rhythmic means which fascinates many composers of electronic music and which challenges the listener. Cut loose from customary restraints, a different world of motion experience has come into view, to be explored for its expressive riches. As with all explorations, an element of risk exists, with inevitable disappointments, false moves, and wasted efforts; but the possible gains in depth of musical insight are so great as to lead many people to want very much to share in the adventure. If one can give oneself up to the motion content of some contemporary music, free from expectations of traditional devices, one can expect some interesting and absorbing musical experiences. This is not in any way to rule out similar experiences with traditional rhythmic organization, for a basic component of anything that can be called music is its sense of motion (LISTENING 4.13). Another dimension has been added to that component, however, which no doubt will provide a fertile field for exploration in the years ahead.

Summary

As we have seen, musical rhythm is a complex element, capable of producing a wide range of expressive sound characteristics. Even if music consisted only of rhythm, a great deal of artistic material would be generated that could be experienced as compelling and significant. But music contains much more than rhythm, and rhythm seldom exists separated from other musical elements. We shall now look at a second major element of music: melody.

Chapter 5 ∘ *The expressiveness of melody*

MELODY (ORGANIZATION OF SERIES OF TONES)

INTERVALS

Small steps . . . large leaps.

MELODIES

Mode: major, minor, modal, other.
Length: short . . . long.
Cadences: strong . . . weak.
Direction: upward . . . downward.
Shape: smooth . . . jagged.
Register: high . . . low.
Pitch range: narrow . . . wide.
Structure: simple . . . complex.
Usage: motivic, thematic, complete.

Example 5.1 • The chromatic scale.

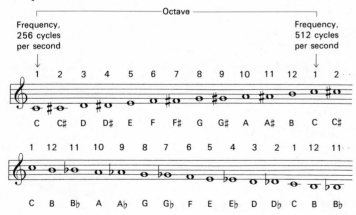

AS WE HAVE SHOWN IN CHAPTER 4, ALL MUSIC MOVES FROM ONE POINT in time to another, the organization of the movement being rhythm. A sense of movement is produced by sounds that take up a certain amount of time (they have duration) and have other qualities explained in Chapter 4. Movement, in and of itself, is a fundamental characteristic of musical expressiveness.

Most music is made of sounds that, in addition to duration, have pitch—a sensation of highness or lowness produced by heard vibrations. The number of vibrations per unit of time is called "frequency," and the higher the frequency, the higher the pitch. Musical instruments and the human voice produce tones from high to low by generating vibrations at different frequencies.

The organization of series of tones, each of which has duration and pitch, is *melody*. Melody always has to do with the horizontal dimension of tones—movement from one tone to another in a single file, or series, or line. When tones are sounded together, one on top of another, the term applied to them is "harmony." That dimension of music will be explored in Chapter 6.

Many regard melody as the most important expressive element of music. Of course, no single element is the most important, but surely melody provides music with a powerful means by which to explore the realm of feeling: The rise and fall of a melodic line seems to correspond to the rise and fall of feeling itself; the movement of a melody from its beginning to its conclusion gives a sense of how feelings move from a start to an end. Points of tension and relaxation, movement to a climax, direction and contour and structure—all seem to offer profound insights into the comparable qualities of feeling.

It is not surprising, therefore, that many persons listen to music by listening only to melodies, especially when it stresses melody over other expressive elements. There is no competition among the several elements of music, of course; each contributes to the whole of which it is a part. Our concern will be to share the expressiveness of each element and of all together.

There is more to melody than meets the casual ear. It is one thing to hear the obvious things about melody, the overall shape of its line and its general mood; it is quite another to hear the many subtleties of melody. For some music is melodically simple, requiring little of the listener's mind or feelings, but much music has melody that is not

Intervals

LISTENING 5.1

In the following examples concentrate on the way the melodic line moves by small steps, large leaps, or both.

These melodies are characterized by small steps (chromatic intervals):

ANONYMOUS ○● Early organum, "Rex coeli, Domine."

JOANNES OKEGHEM ○● *Missa prolationum:* Sanctus.

W. A. MOZART ○ Symphony 41 in C, K. 551, III.

H. BERLIOZ ○● *Symphonie fantastique,* op. 14, V.

C. DEBUSSY ○● *The Afternoon of a Faun.*

I. STRAVINSKY *Symphony of Psalms,* II. Note the small-step melody (beginning in measure 6) against the large-leap melody of the beginning; this creates a small-step line against a large-leap line.

Here are some melodies characterized by large leaps:

J. S. BACH ○ Fugue for Organ in g, S. 578 ("Little"). The beginning melody (subject) contains many large leaps and then smooths out to small-step intervals. When the subject enters again (measure 6), the countersubject played against it is a mixture of small steps and larger leaps. As the fugue unfolds, there are many changes between small steps, large leaps, and combinations of the two.

(continued on page 74)

obvious and demands keen ears if the expressiveness is to be shared. Just as rhythm may include complexities far below the surface, melody also can challenge our hearing with complex expressive events. An outline of our exploration in melody is in the margin on page 72.

SMALL STEPS . . . LARGE LEAPS

Every melody is made of a series of pitches. The distance between two pitches is an *interval*. In most music of the Western world, intervals are arranged in a particular way, in which the smallest distance between pitches is a *half step*. A half step is the distance heard between two adjacent notes on the piano keyboard (usually from a white key to a black or a black to a white but in a few cases from a white to a white). Because the half step is the smallest interval in the traditional Western system of music, standard musical instruments are built to sound half steps, one after another from low to high, although some instruments can slide in between the half steps (string instruments, trombone), as can the voice. Nevertheless, the half-step interval remains the foundation for organizing the pitch aspect of music.

When notes are arranged in order from low to high or high to low, the series of pitches is called a "scale." If such a series includes every half step between an octave, the name of that particular scale is the "chromatic scale." Example 5.1 shows how the chromatic scale looks in musical notation.

An important phenomenon in Western music is the identity of the octave. Each pitch has a particular frequency of vibration: C is 275 cycles per second, A is 440, and so on. When the frequency is halved or doubled, we perceive the pitch to be "the same" even though lower or higher. The note A, for example, is heard as very low A to very high A when we hear frequencies of 55, 110, 220, 440, 880, and 1,760; each A is separated by an *octave*—eight steps of a scale (not counting intermediate half steps). Every pitch exists as the same in octave intervals, each higher octave having twice the frequency as the one below it. This kind of identity gives a large measure of stability to pitch in Western music. You will notice that there is a total of twelve pitches in the chromatic scale (the pitches are named and symbolized differently according to whether they are going up or coming down, but that is just a matter of convenience for the musician). No matter what pitch

W. A. MOZART   ○● Requiem in d, K. 626: Tuba Mirum.

W. SCHUMAN   ○● Symphony 3 (1941), II: Fugue.

A. VON WEBERN   ○ Three Songs, op. 18, nos. 1, 3.

P. BOULEZ   *Le Marteau sans maître*, I.

MARIAN BROWN   "27 Cooper Square," from *Marian Brown Quartet.*

And these melodies have both steps and leaps:

W. A. MOZART   ○● Symphony 40 in g, K. 550, I; ○ Requiem in d, K. 626, I: Kyrie Eleison.

L. VAN BEETHOVEN   Symphony 3 in E♭, op. 55, ○ II, IV.

F. P. SCHUBERT   *Die schöne Müllerin*, op. 25, nos. ○ 7, 17: "Ungeduld" ("Impatience"), "Die böse Farbe" ("The Hateful Color").

P. I. TCHAIKOVSKY   ○● Symphony 5 in e, op. 64, II.

H. HANSON   Symphony 2, op. 30, II.

M. DAVIS   "Rogue," from *Birth of the Cool.*

LISTENING 5.2

The following are examples of music using quarter-tone intervals:

ALOIS HÁBA   Fantasy for Violin Solo, op. 9a.

CHARLES EDWARD IVES   Symphony 4 (1910–1916).

ERNEST BLOCH   Quintet for Piano and Strings.

New Music in Quarter-Tones, Odyssey 32-16-0162. This recording contains Ives's *Three Quarter-tone Pieces for Two Pianos* and music by T. Macero, Calvin Hampton, and Donald Lybbert.

HARRY PARTCH   *Windsong* and other pieces; *The Bewitched; Oedipus.* Partch's music uses scales of more than twelve pitches, played on various instruments he invented and built himself.

In jazz, pitches are constantly being bent slightly below or above the norm. This pitch looseness is one of the important factors in jazz expressiveness, giving it its peculiarly vital quality. The most frequently altered pitches are the third, fifth, and seventh notes of the major scale (see Example 5.2 below), each being flatted a half step against nonflatted harmony to create the characteristic jazz dissonances. However, all pitches in jazz melody are fair game for subtle deviations.

E. FITZGERALD   "How High the Moon," from *The Best of Ella Fitzgerald.*

CHARLIE BYRD   "Ella Me Dexou," from *Byrd at the Gate.*

S. GETZ AND J. GILBERTO   "The Girl from Ipanema," "Desafinado," from *Getz/Gilberto.*

you start on, there will be twelve half steps, and then you will be back at the "same" pitch again and must start counting over from 1. So all the notes on a piano keyboard (or any instrument) are actually just twelve pitches repeated over and over from low to high.

Some melodies move mostly by half steps, the distance between pitches being generally toward the small-step side of the continuum (*conjunct* motion). Other melodies are characterized by large leaps, the pitches jumping from one to another one far away (*disjunct* motion). In between is an area in which the intervals are neither small steps nor large leaps—the middle of the continuum. Of course, many, if not most, melodies move by small steps, small leaps, and large leaps mixed together in an endless variety of ways.

The expressiveness of a melody is determined to a great extent by its use of steps and leaps. The feeling of a small-step line is quite different from that of a large-leap line. The shaping of a melodic line by its movement through small, medium, and large intervals is a fundamental way that music shapes a sense of the movement of feeling (LISTENING 5.1).

Most Western music continues to use the traditional half-step interval as the smallest distance between pitches. Smaller intervals were used in ancient Greece and occasionally in the Middle Ages and renaissance, but until the middle of the nineteenth century there was little interest in changing the twelve-note scale. Then a few composers began to experiment with new ways to organize pitches, and in this century interest has continued to grow. The use of quarter tones (which divide each half-step interval in half) was an obvious and early attempt to break away from the restrictions of a twelve-note scale. Other scales made of more than twelve notes were devised by various composers to exploit new pitch possibilities. These departures required that traditional instruments, such as the piano, be retuned to sound the new intervals or that new instruments be invented, built to whatever scale the composer wanted. Both these approaches have been taken.

With the advent of the tape recorder and more sophisticated electronic means of manipulating pitches, composers now have available an endless spectrum of pitch gradation. As mentioned earlier (page 37), one of the problems facing composers who use electronic pitch generators is that the machines can easily produce pitch differences so small that no one can actually hear them. So the composer must constantly check

L. ARMSTRONG   "Rockin Chair," from *At the Crescendo;* "When It's Sleepytime Down South," from *Louis Armstrong's Greatest Hits.*
CHARLEY PARKER   "Funky Blues," from *The Essential Charley Parker.*
COLEMAN HAWKINS   "Body and Soul," from *The Essential Coleman Hawkins.*
O. COLEMAN ○● "Sadness," from *Town Hall, 1962.*
BLOOD, SWEAT AND TEARS ○● "God Bless the Child."
Much electronically generated music has abandoned the traditional chromatic scale. Examples are numerous; consult the Music Index for listening suggestions.

Melodies

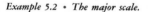

Example 5.2 • The major scale.

Example 5.3 • Minor scales: (a) harmonic; (b) natural; (c) melodic (different going up from coming down).

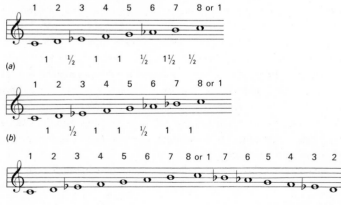

his music to be sure that it falls within the boundaries of what the human ear can perceive; yet the boundaries of perception are constantly being pushed back by people eager to explore the farthest reaches of what can be heard.

Contemporary music includes a wealth of pitch possibilities beyond those of the traditional twelve half steps (LISTENING 5.2). The use of these possibilities ranges from purely electronic music (with few or no remnants from traditional practices) to basically traditional music with slight touches of microtones (intervals smaller than a half step). The challenges for the listener are great when faced with possibilities far wider than what tradition has accustomed him to; but the opportunities to share new musical experiences are equally great.

MODE: MAJOR, MINOR, MODAL, OTHER

Until the seventeenth century music in the Western world was based on several different arrangements of intervals into scales called "modes." Each had its own series of half steps and whole steps, and each therefore had its peculiar flavor.

Then two scales, the major and the minor, began to be used more than any others, to the extent that music from the seventeenth century to this day has been almost entirely composed in just these two scales; and they have been basic for so long that many cannot conceive of music that is neither major nor minor. Any pitch arrangements other than major or minor, such as the old modes or microtone scales or a few other scales to be mentioned below, are usually considered exotic or experimental. Since the past three centuries include most of the music people living today are likely to hear, it is understandable that our ears have become accustomed to these scales, with other arrangements of pitch regarded as foreign to our experience. One of the exciting things about music today is its wholesale assault on the old major-minor system.

The major scale has the arrangement of half steps and whole steps shown in Example 5.2; and the three versions of the minor scale, each with its slightly different sequence of half and whole steps, are presented in Example 5.3.

Finally, two other scales, the whole-tone and the pentatonic have occasionally been used in traditional music (Example 5.4).

(a)

(b)

Example 5.4 • (a) Whole-tone scale (no half steps). (b) Pentatonic (five-toned) scale (no half steps).

LISTENING 5.3

All the following examples are tonal music, based on scales in which each pitch serves its particular organizing function. Try to sense the difference in flavor between major, minor, and the other scales.

Here is some music in major keys. Switches to minor are not uncommon; try to be aware of such changes when they take place.

A. VIVALDI ○ Concerto for Violin and Orchestra in E, op. 8, no. 1, I.

G. F. HANDEL ○● *Messiah:* "For unto us a child is born," "Hallelujah" chorus.

F. J. HAYDN ○● Symphony 101 in D, II. Note the sudden change from major in the first section to minor in the middle section and a return to the original major in the concluding section.

L. VAN BEETHOVEN ○● Symphony 3 in E♭, op. 55, III; ○ Sonata for Piano in c, op. 13, II.

F. F. CHOPIN ○ Étude for Piano in E, op. 10, no. 3.

THE BEATLES "All You Need Is Love," from *Magical Mystery Tour.*

THE WHO "Welcome," from *Tommy.*

SIMON AND GARFUNKEL "Mrs. Robinson," from *Bookends.*

In the following music in minor keys, be on the lookout for temporary switches to major:

A. VIVALDI ○ Concerto for Violin and Orchestra in E, op. 8, no. 1, II.

When the title of a piece includes its key (the scale around which the piece is organized), we are being given the information that the music is based on, for example, the major scale beginning on the note D (Symphony 2 in D); or the title might be Sonata for Piano in b, which tells us that the piece is based on a minor scale beginning on the note B. (In this book, as explained in the first footnote in Chapter 1, a minor key is designated by a small letter—Sonata in b—and a major key by a capital letter—Symphony in D.) Of course, an entire piece is not likely to remain in the same key from beginning to end (see the section on modulation in Chapter 6), but the title informs us which scale is the most important one in the piece.

The important thing in all this is not the details of half steps, whole steps, keys, or scales. Underlying the technicalities is an important idea about how music is organized: the idea of tonality.

Until this century music depended on a system, the tonal system, in which each pitch in a scale performed a particular function. In tonal music the principal pitch in a scale is always the first, the tonic. This is the pitch to which all the others gravitate, giving a sense of center, or home base, so that movement can be felt as away from the center or back to the center. The tonic supplies a security base that allows tonal music to offer a sense of exploration and tension when it wanders from home and a sense of return and relaxation when it moves back. Therefore every pitch in a scale serves a unique function in relation to the tonic. The listener need not know the functional technicalities, for they are so much a part of our lives, like the language we learn as babies, that they can be regarded as a given, as one of the basic ways our minds operate. Tonal music makes sense to us because we have internalized the system. Particular pieces of tonal music may be more or less understandable, as particular books in English are more or less understandable, depending on their complexity and the experience of the reader. But the basis for understanding is present, in tonal music or in a book in English; neither requires that a new language be learned.

The major and minor scales are the foundations of the language of tonal music. The old modes and the few other scales occasionally used are like dialects—a bit different but still quite understandable. With all tonal music (LISTENING 5.3) the listener can feel, at the very least, that it is speaking his language.

Tonality continues to be a powerful organizing force in music, and many

J. S. BACH   ○ Suite for Orchestra in b, S. 1067; ○ Fugue for Organ in g, S. 578; ○● Cantata 80, *Ein feste Burg ist unser Gott,* IV.

W. A. MOZART   ○● Symphony 40 in g, K. 550, I, II, IV. In the third movement, the first section is in minor, the second is in major, and the conclusion is a repeat of the first minor section.

L. VAN BEETHOVEN   ○ Symphony 3 in E♭, op. 55, II. This movement, one of the most famous funeral marches in music, has many complex shiftings from minor to major. The dominant tonality is minor, with a dramatic change to major in the middle section.

F. P. SCHUBERT   ○ *Die schöne Müllerin,* op. 25, no. 19: "Der Müller und der Bach." Beginning in minor, this song changes to major, returns to minor, and ends in major.

SIMON AND GARFUNKEL   "America," "Old Friends," from *Bookends.*

PETER, PAUL AND MARY   "Brother, Can You Spare a Dime?" from *See What Tomorrow Brings.*

THE BEATLES   "The Fool on the Hill," from *Magical Mystery Tour.*

The following pieces use the medieval church modes, which preceded the domination of major and minor:

L. VAN BEETHOVEN   Quartet for Strings in a, op. 132, III. In the Lydian mode.

F. F. CHOPIN   Mazurka for Piano in c, op. 24, no. 2. Uses the Lydian mode.

MODEST PETROVICH MUSSORGSKY   *Boris Godunov:* Prelude. The opening is in the Dorian mode.

C. DEBUSSY   "La Cathédrale engloutie" ("The Sunken Cathedral"); Quartet for Strings in g, op. 10, I; "Ondine" ("Undine").

RALPH VAUGHAN WILLIAMS   *Fantasia on a Theme by Tallis; Fantasia on "Greensleeves."*

SIMON AND GARFUNKEL   "Scarborough Fair," "Canticle," from *Parsley, Sage, Rosemary and Thyme.*

"Aquarius," from *Hair.*

M. RAVEL   "Alborada del gracioso"; *Le Tombeau de Couperin.*

Here is music using the pentatonic scale:

"Auld Lang Syne" and "Comin' through the Rye" are typical pentatonic folk melodies.

C. DEBUSSY   "La Fille aux cheveux de lin" ("The Girl with the Flaxen Hair"); "Le Vent dans la plaine" ("The Wind in the Plain"); "Les Collines d'Anacapri" ("The Hills of Anacapri").

(continued on page 78)

persons argue that it always will be; but several kinds of contemporary music have abandoned tonality. The first system of composition based on nontonal, or "atonal," pitch relationships was that created by Schoenberg in the early years of this century (you will recall that we discussed Schoenberg's system in Chapter 1, as an example of a major exploratory venture). Schoenberg realized that tonality was becoming so stretched by composers such as Wagner and Debussy, with the old pitch functions becoming less and less binding on composers' choices, that it would be logical to recognize that music need not depend on traditional pitch expectations.

With this recognition, a whole new world of possibilities presented itself. So limitless were the new choices that some kind of system was required to bring order into the chaos of possibilities. Schoenberg's response to the need for a new order was the twelve-tone system of composition, in which the traditional twelve pitches of the chromatic scale were used in such a way as to avoid any hint of their old interrelations. To be certain that no sense of tonality crept in, rules and regulations were set up to help a composer create a structured piece without the crutch of the traditional pitch relations. But because the old, tonal organization was not present, twelve-tone music sounded (and may still sound) unorganized to ears accustomed to tonality. This was indeed a new language—not just a dialect of the old language. So it was not surprising that many, listening according to one musical language, did not know what to make of sounds organized according to another.

Schoenberg's system of composition was taken up by several other composers, most notably Alban Berg and Anton von Webern, each of whom adapted the new atonal language to his own purposes. The use of a series of pitches related only to one another (rather than having traditional functions within a scale) became a powerful generating force in musical composition. Serial music has developed in various ways, with several composers' applying the idea of a series of pitches to other aspects of music, such as rhythm, dynamics, or tone color. Most of this new music remains atonal in that, no matter how highly organized it is, the old major-minor language is no longer spoken.

Atonality of one sort or another (LISTENING 5.4) is thus a principal force in contemporary music, whether of the serial variety, the electronic variety, the aleatoric (chance, or random) variety, or various combinations and offshoots of these. It is no longer possible to state that music

EDVARD HAGERUP GRIEG   Suite for Orchestra I from *Peer Gynt*, op. 46: "Morning," beginning.

R. VAUGHAN WILLIAMS   *The Lark Ascending:* final violin-solo cadenza; Symphony 2, I; Symphony 3, IV.

ERIK SATIE   *Parade.*

And here is music using the whole-tone scale:

C. DEBUSSY   "Voiles" ("Veils"); *Pelléas et Mélisande*, Act III; ○● *The Afternoon of a Faun;* "Reflets dans l'eau" ("Reflections on the Water").

F. LISZT   *A Faust Symphony:* beginning.

NIKOLAY ANDREYEVICH RIMSKY-KORSAKOV   Suite for Orchestra from *Le Coq d'or,* II: beginning.

M. RAVEL   *Gaspard de la Nuit,* I, II.

CHARLES MARTIN LOEFFLER   *A Pagan Poem,* op. 14.

LISTENING 5.4

There follows a selection of atonal music stemming from Schoenberg's serial system:

A. SCHOENBERG   Quartet for Strings 4, op. 37; Concerto for Violin and Orchestra, op. 36; Quintet for Winds, op. 26; Variations for Orchestra, op. 31; *Moses und Aron.* Earlier works by Schoenberg that were still tonal are the following: *Verklärte Nacht,* op. 4; *Pelléas and Mélisande,* op. 5; *Gurrelieder.* His early atonal works, before the full working out of serial techniques, include: *Erwartung,* op. 17; Five Pieces for Orchestra, op. 16; ○● *Pierrot lunaire,* op. 21. Later works, in which tonal implications return, include: Suite for Strings in G; *Kol Nidrei,* op. 39; Theme and Variations for Band, op. 43*a.*

A. BERG   *Lyric Suite* for Strings; Chamber Concerto for Piano, Violin, and Thirteen Winds; *Wozzeck; Lulu;* Concerto for Violin and Orchestra.

A. VON WEBERN   ○● Five Pieces for Orchestra, op. 10; Six Bagatelles for String Quartet, op. 9; ○ Three Songs, op. 18; Symphony, op. 21; Variations for Piano, op. 27; Two Cantatas, opp. 29, 31.

ERNST KŘENEK   *Eleven Transparencies; Pentagram for Winds; Sechs Vermessene.*

LUIGI DALLAPICCOLA   *Canti di prigionia: Variazioni per orchestra.*

GEORGE PERLE   Quintet for Strings, op. 35; Rhapsody for Orchestra.

must be based on major and minor scales. At the same time, however, a great deal of music, concert as well as popular, stays as tonal as any music of the past three hundred fifty years. So the ability to understand several musical languages is necessary if the contemporary listener is to share all that music is capable of giving.

LENGTH: SHORT . . . LONG; CADENCES: STRONG . . . WEAK

Every melody, no matter how its intervals are arranged, has certain qualities that contribute to its expressiveness. One of these qualities is length: Some melodies are very short, just a few notes in a coherent pattern; other melodies are very long, moving in broad, leisurely arcs covering a wide span from beginning to end. As with every other musical quality, the center of the continuum contains melodies that are neither very short nor very long.

As a melody moves from start to finish, it usually passes through several points of lessened tension where the sense of movement comes to a partial or complete rest. Such resting places are called "cadences." Just as many sentences have places that require a comma, signifying a brief pause, many melodies are broken into parts called "phrases," each phrase ending with a brief easing of tension, or a cadence. And as a sentence comes to an end with a period, a melody ends with a strong cadence, which gives a sense of finality.

Some melodies are composed solely of short phrases, each of which is separated from the others by a fairly strong cadence. The impression of such melodies is that of old-style primary readers: "See Spot run." "Spot runs." "Run, Spot, run." Short phrase construction like this need not be musically simple; some of the most profound music ever written has used small melody fragments with frequent cadences, just as some profound literature uses short sentences or short poetic phrases (Ernest Hemingway or e. e. cummings). The very brevity of the ideas can be a powerful factor in their expressiveness.

Other melodies spin out in time with few cadences to break up the movement or with weak cadences that only hint at a lessening of tension. Such melodic lines are like the long rambling sentences of novels by James Joyce or William Faulkner. They move along by gathering speed and gradually winding down, with no real pause until the long-awaited final note. Many contemporary melodies are so lacking in resting

M. BABBITT   Composition for Viola and Piano; *All Set;*
Partitions.

I. STRAVINSKY   *Threni.*

Here is some other atonal music (in many of these pieces the
word "melody," in the traditional sense of a coherent series of
tones, is no longer applicable):

K. STOCKHAUSEN   *Gruppen; Kontakte; Kontra-Punkte; Zeitmasse;
Zyklus* (1950).

M. BABBITT   o *Composition for Synthesizer; Ensembles for
Synthesizer.*

O. LUENING AND V. USSACHEVSKY   *Poem in Cycles and Bells;* Suite
from *King Lear.*

E. VARÈSE   *Ionisation; Poème électronique.*

P. BOULEZ   *Le Marteau sans maître; Soleil des eaux.*

J. CAGE   *Fontana Mix; Atlas Eclipticalis; Cartridge Music* (1960);
Indeterminacy; Variations II, III, o IV.

MORTON SUBOTNICK   *Silver Apples; Wild Bull.*

LISTENING 5.5

In the following examples try to anticipate the movement of the
melodies *to* points of rest and *away from* points of rest. Note the
differences among melodies that come to cadences frequently and
predictably and those which tantalize by just hinting at cadences
or withholding them for long periods of time. Let yourself be
caught up in the phrase patterns as they unfold and intertwine.

SHORT PHRASES AND STRONG CADENCES

W. A. MOZART   o *Eine kleine Nachtmusik* in G, K. 525,
I; o Symphony 36 in C, K. 425, I, II, III, IV; o● Symphony 40
in g, K. 550, II, III, IV.

J. S. BACH   o Suite for Orchestra in b, S. 1067, II.

L. VAN BEETHOVEN   Symphony 3 in E♭, op. 55, o II, o● III, IV
(the last movement is a complex treatment of a short-phrase,
strong-cadence melodic idea); o● Symphony 5 in c, op. 67, I.

J. BRAHMS   o Symphony 2 in D, op. 73, III.

JOAN BAEZ   "East Virginia," "Wildwood Flower," from *Joan
Baez, Vol. I.*

BLOOD, SWEAT AND TEARS   "Smiling Phases," from *Blood, Sweat
and Tears.*

(continued on page 80)

places that they give a rootless, breathless impression, and in combination with a lack of pulse, these melodies can present strong feelings
of constant tension and motion, with no letup until the music is over.

Of course, many melodies are neither very short nor very long and use
both weak and strong cadences, and much music shifts constantly
between long and short melodies or sets one off against the other
(LISTENING 5.5). Phrases and cadences provide melody with syntax—a
sequence of patterns perceptible as parts of a larger whole. As organizers
of musical movement, they allow sounds to structure feeling.

DIRECTION: UPWARD . . . DOWNWARD

One of the most powerful illusions created by changes of pitch is a
sense of upwardness or downwardness. Of course, pitches do not
actually move up or down; they simply have more vibrations or fewer.
Yet our language testifies to the illusion of direction: A pitch with many
vibrations is called "high," and a pitch with few vibrations is called
"low." Whatever the physiological, psychological, or social reasons for
this sensation, it is an important means by which a melodic line seems
shaped, organized, and expressive.

Melodies are carefully laid out to move in upward and downward lines.
Sometimes the direction is primarily upward—in a single sweep or in
several overlapping upward sweeps—the overall illusion being a movement from low to high. Other melodies start high and move primarily
downward, either directly or gradually. Most melodies move *both* upward
and downward, creating direction tendencies that can be extremely
expressive as the listener follows the unfolding of the melodic line. The
movement upward to a peak and the tapering downward to a point of
rest, the swooping over and over in a single direction, the sudden
changes of course, the delays and diversions in expected directions,
all make for a fascinating dimension of expressive possibilities, as exem-
plified in LISTENING 5.6.

SHAPE: SMOOTH . . . JAGGED

As melodies unfold through upward and downward movement, we get
a sense of their overall shape, or contour. Some melodies flow effortlessly from one note to another in graceful curves, forming even, un-

LONG PHRASES AND WEAK CADENCES

J. S. BACH   ○ Suite for Orchestra in b, S. 1067, I.

B. BARTÓK   ○● *Music for String Instruments, Percussion, and Celesta,* I, II.

J. BRAHMS   ○● Symphony 2 in D, op. 73, II.

R. WAGNER   *Tristan und Isolde,* Acts I, IV: Prelude, ○● "Liebestod."

S. BARBER   ○● *Adagio* for Strings, op. 11.

W. SCHUMAN   ○● Symphony 3 (1941), III: Chorale.

SIMON AND GARFUNKEL   "Like a Bridge over Troubled Water," from *Bridge over Troubled Water.*

J. BAEZ   "The House of the Rising Sun," "All My Trials," from *Joan Baez, Vol. I.*

The following pieces depend very little or not at all on structured phrases with cadences. Note, however, that, although traditional phrases and cadences may be missing, the music has points of relaxed tension that mark off the motion into perceptible segments.

A. SCHOENBERG   Quartet for Strings 4, op. 37; ○● *Pierrot lunaire,* op. 21.

A. BERG   *Lyric Suite* for Strings, II, III.

K. STOCKHAUSEN   *Gesang der Jünglinge.*

ILHAN MIMAROGLU   *Agony.*

Y. XENAKIS   ○● *Pithoprakta.*

LISTENING 5.6

The following melodies have clear directional tendencies that you can easily follow by concentrating on this particular aspect of their expressiveness:

J. S. BACH   ○● Italian Concerto for Harpsichord Solo in F, S. 971, II. This movement begins with an accompaniment figure, continuing throughout. The figure is a constant, short, upward and downward line. Against it the melody spins out in complex and subtle shiftings of direction. So we have a straightforward bottom part over which an elaborate line meanders in endless decoration.

W. A. MOZART   ○ Requiem in d, K. 626, VII: Lacrimosa.

L. VAN BEETHOVEN   Symphony 7 in A, op. 92, II. This movement is based on a melody line that is nearly as straight

(lacking in upwardness and downwardness) as a melody is likely to be. Yet the subtleties of direction and the wider fluctuations occurring later give an unusual flavor to a movement rich in many aspects of expressiveness.

H. BERLIOZ   ○● *Symphonie fantastique,* op. 14, V.

H. HANSON   Symphony 2, op. 30, I.

S. BARBER   ○● *Adagio* for Strings, op. 11.

Upwardness and downwardness are essential components of much electronic music. Even though the moving line is not tonal, the music derives much of its expressiveness from the illusion of direction, often dramatically used.

M. BABBITT   ○ *Composition for Synthesizer.*

E. VARESE   *Poème électronique.*

V. USSACHEVSKY   *Piece for Tape Recorder.*

H. EL-DABH   *Leiyla and the Poet.*

MARIO DAVIDOVSKY   *Electronic Study No. 1.*

LISTENING 5.7

GENERALLY SMOOTH SHAPE

W. A. MOZART   *Eine kleine Nachtmusik* in G, K. 525, III.

P. I. TCHAIKOVSKY   Symphony 5 in e, op. 64, I, ○● III.

H. BERLIOZ   *Symphonie fantastique,* op. 14, II.

J. BRAHMS   ○● *Ein deutsches Requiem,* op. 45: "How lovely is thy dwelling place."

H. HANSON   Symphony 2, op. 30, I.

S. BARBER   ○● *Adagio* for Strings, op. 11.

GENERALLY JAGGED SHAPE

J. S. BACH   Suite for Orchestra in b, S. 1067, I.

L. VAN BEETHOVEN   ○● Symphony 3 in E♭, op. 55, III.

S. PROKOFIEV   Symphony 5, op. 100, II.

B. BARTÓK   *Concerto for Orchestra,* I.

I. STRAVINSKY   *Ragtime for 11 Instruments;* ○● *Histoire du soldat.*

A. BERG   Concerto for Violin and Orchestra, I, II.

O. COLEMAN   "Peace," from *The Shape of Jazz to Come.*

broken contours; there is little tension between the notes, one leading to another easily and inevitably. In other melodies the movement from one note to another is uncertain, with large leaps in unpredictable directions and awkwardness, or tension, between the notes; the shape of such melodies is jagged, sudden changes in direction and awkward leaps creating a rugged, rough contour.

Naturally, the shape of melodies will affect how they feel to us. Subtle changes from smooth to jagged shape, dramatic shifts of shape, or surprising combinations of shapes superimposed one over another all contribute an important dimension to the power of music (LISTENING 5.7).

REGISTER: HIGH . . . LOW

A basic characteristic of the human mind is the ability to recognize a thing even though several aspects of it are changed from instance to instance. We say to a clerk, "I want the same dishes but in yellow and brown instead of green and white." Or, "Do you have the same lampshade in a larger size?" That we can recognize the essential nature of a thing even when it is manifested differently allows us to organize our world in manageable ways.

In music there is constant use of sound patterns that retain an identity throughout many changes. A common example of this is the placement of a melody in several different levels of highness or lowness (*registers*) as a piece proceeds. The melody is "the same" in our perception even though it is sometimes in a high register, sometimes in a low register, or anywhere in between. Yet each register adds its own expressive flavor to the melody; it is the same yet different. It is no wonder that composers make constant use of register changes to display a melodic idea in a variety of guises. As we follow the appearance of a melody in different registers (as in LISTENING 5.8), we get a strong impression of unity within variety.

PITCH RANGE: NARROW . . . WIDE

As a composer creates a melody, he chooses from all available pitches those which capture the right melodic idea for his expressive purposes. Sometimes a melody will use just a narrow range of pitches from low to high: the lowest and the highest notes may be separated by only

LISTENING 5.8

The following examples contain melodic ideas that reappear in various registers. Note the different expressive effect of the same idea in various pitch placements.

J. S. BACH   o● Fugue for Organ in g, S. 578 ("Little").

W. A. MOZART   o Symphony 41 in C, K. 551, I, II, III, IV; o● Symphony 40 in g, K. 550, I, II.

L. VAN BEETHOVEN   o● Quartet for Strings in B♭, op. 130, IV: *Alla danza tedesca.*

J. BRAHMS   o● Symphony 2 in D, op. 73, II.

H. BERLIOZ   o● *Symphonie fantastique*, op. 14, V.

A. SCHOENBERG   *Verklärte Nacht*, op. 4.

W. LUTOSŁAWSKI   *Postlude for Orchestra.*

LISTENING 5.9

These pieces have fairly obvious pitch-range organizations. Try to perceive the spread of pitch as a factor in the impact of the music.

NARROW-RANGE IDEAS

W. A. MOZART   Twelve Variations for Piano on "Ah, vous dirai-je, Maman" in C, K. 265 (300*e*): Theme.

A. VIVALDI   Concerto for Violin and Orchestra in E, op. 8, no. 1, o I, III.

GIOVANNI PIERLUIGI DA PALESTRINA   o *Missa Papae Marcelli*, I.

(continued on page 82)

P. I. TCHAIKOVSKY   Symphony 5 in e, op. 64, I.

B. BARTÓK   ○● *Music for String Instruments, Percussion, and Celesta*, I

H. HANSON   Symphony 2, op. 30, II.

WIDE-RANGE IDEAS

J. S. BACH   ○● Passacaglia and Fugue for Organ in c, S. 582: Passacaglia.

L. VAN BEETHOVEN   Symphony 5 in c, op. 67, III.

J. BRAHMS   ○● Symphony 2 in D, op. 73, II.

RICHARD STRAUSS   *Don Juan*, op. 20.

A. SCHOENBERG   ○● *Pierrot lunaire*, op. 21: most movements.

M. BABBITT   ○ *Composition for Synthesizer.*

O. LUENING   *Gargoyles.*

O. COLEMAN   "Focus on Sanity," "Congeniality," from *The Shape of Jazz to Come.*

LISTENING 5.10

These melodies are generally toward the simpler end of the spectrum as compared with other music of the past four hundred or so years. Of course, within each style period (Part 3) melodies can be judged as simple or complex in relation to other melodies of that period. The comparisons here are much more broad in that our purpose is to illustrate the notion of simple and complex structure without regard for style constraints, whereas Part 3 will raise some issues of judging musical complexity within particular styles.

A. VIVALDI   Concerto for Violin and Orchestra in E, op. 8, no. 1, ○ I.

J. S. BACH   ○ Suite for Orchestra in b, S. 1067, II.

W. A. MOZART   ○ Symphony 36 in C, K. 425, III.

L. VAN BEETHOVEN   Concerto for Violin and Orchestra in D, op. 61, III. The simple opening theme returns again and again, with more complex material in between the reappearances.

J. BRAHMS   *Variations on a Theme by Haydn* in B♭, op. 56a. The straightforward chorale melody is subjected to eight variations and a finale, each much more complex than the original simple melody.

These melodies are at the complex end of the spectrum:

J. S. BACH   ○ Fugue for Organ in g, S. 578;   ○● Italian Concerto for Harpsichord Solo in F, S. 971, II; ○ Cantata 80, *Ein*

five or six degrees of the scale. Within this restricted range the melody line unfolds, never straying very far from the small section of the scale it uses. Other melodies encompass a wide range of pitch: if you found the lowest note in a melody and the highest, the distance between them might stretch over a wide band of pitches. The effect of such a melody will be quite different from that of a narrow-range melody.

Music constantly makes use of pitch range to create a varied and interesting line. Whereas some pieces stay within a narrow range and some create a wide range, many, if not most, pieces shift from one to the other in constant line alteration (LISTENING 5.9). If a narrow-range piece were represented like this:

and a wide-range piece like this:

most pieces would combine the two like this:

In a great deal of contemporary music the pitch range has been extended dramatically—sometimes to the limits of highness and lowness the human ear can perceive. As in all music, the range of pitches is nevertheless a basic means of organizing sounds into expressive events.

STRUCTURE: SIMPLE . . . COMPLEX

A combination of all the previously discussed melodic dimensions forms the overall structure of any particular melody. The intervals it uses, its scale organization, the length of its ideas, the number and strength of cadences, its direction and shape, and its register changes and pitch range add up to a particular melody with its own particular structure. If many or all dimensions of a melody are simple in nature—predictable intervals, clear scale organization, regular cadences—it will make a simple impression. This is not to say that it will therefore be superficial; its simplicity may be an important factor in giving a powerful sense of *feste Burg ist unser Gott,* I. Compare the melodic complexity of this movement with the simplicity of the chorale melody of VIII.

P. I. TCHAIKOVSKY   ○● Symphony 5 in e, op. 64, II;
○ Concerto for Piano and Orchestra in b♭, op. 23, I.

G. PUCCINI   *La Bohème,* Act I: ○ "Che gelida manina,"
○● "Mi chiamano Mimi."

I. STRAVINSKY   ○● *Symphony of Psalms,* I, III.

A. SCHOENBERG   ○● *Pierrot lunaire,* op. 21.

LEONARD BERNSTEIN   Symphony 3 (*Kaddish*). This entire work uses highly complex melodic ideas, both atonal and tonal, as part of the dramatic setting for speaker, choruses, and orchestra.

LISTENING 5.11

These pieces depend heavily on motives:

L. VAN BEETHOVEN   Symphony 5 in c, op. 67, I.

W. A. MOZART   ○ Symphony 41 in C, K. 551, IV. This movement utilizes five distinct motives, which reappear in complex ways.

F. LISZT   Sonata for Piano in b.

PAUL HINDEMITH   Sonata for Piano 3 (1936), II.

The following pieces use themes as basic components of their structure:

J. S. BACH   ○● Passacaglia and Fugue for Organ in c, S. 582. The passacaglia theme is stated in the bass and is then repeated over and over throughout.

W. A. MOZART   ○● Symphony 40 in g, K. 550, I (the three-note figure ♫ ♩ may be considered a motive; the idea of which it is a part is a theme), IV (here also the distinction between motive and theme is blurred, the opening theme being made of two motives that recur throughout the movement).

L. VAN BEETHOVEN   ○● Symphony 3 in E♭, op. 55, I; ○ Sonata for Piano in c, op. 13, III; ○ Symphony 5 in c, op. 67, IV; ○● Quartet for Strings in B♭, op. 130, IV.

P. I. TCHAIKOVSKY   ○ Symphony 5 in e, op. 64, IV.

H. BERLIOZ   *Symphonie fantastique,* op. 14. This symphony uses a theme idea (first stated after the slow introduction of movement I) in each of the five movements. The theme is varied in expressiveness to give a sense of the different occurrences in the life of the hero of this musical tale.

C. FRANCK   Symphony in d. This work also uses several theme

(continued on page 84)

feeling. If a melody is so simple that it causes little interest, contains little uncertainty, or follows predictable formulas, it is likely to have little impact on the listener; but in the hands of a skillful composer the simplest of materials can be made to give profound musical insights.

At the other end of the continuum are melodies of complex structure, involving unpredictable intervals and hazy scale organizations, long, nonsymmetrical phrases with few or unusual cadences, many direction changes, complex shapes, and wide swings in register and pitch range. The dangers here are obscurity and intellectualism; the opportunities are for a high level of involvement, challenging insights, and long-lasting interest (LISTENING 5.10).

USAGE: MOTIVIC, THEMATIC, COMPLETE

Every melodic means discussed in this chapter contributes to the structuring, or forming, of sounds into coherent pieces of music. The same is true of every rhythmic means studied in Chapter 4, and it will be true of all the aspects of harmony, counterpoint, and tone color discussed in the next two chapters. Music is *formed* by the countless, intertwined sound dimensions that we are exploring in this part of our book.

Some aspects of rhythm, melody, harmony, counterpoint, and tone color are concerned with form in the direct sense of the structural outline of a piece: Rhythmic patterns, for example, contribute directly to the structure of music, for they are building blocks for shaping an ordered sequence of sound events. In melodies too there are common usages that are "formal," means for forming a piece into some particular structure. These are basically *motives, themes* or *subjects,* and complete, self-contained entities. The distinctions among these three usages are sufficiently clear that the listener can easily grasp them, thus adding to his ability to perceive musical coherence.

A motive is the smallest building block of the several available to the composer. It is a short, easily recognizable figure that is repeated over and over in various ways throughout a composition both as a unifying and as a generating element. As with most aspects of melody, it is difficult, if not impossible, to separate the pitch dimension from the rhythm dimension of a motive (see Chapter 4, page 68). So we can regard a motive as an inseparable combination of melody and rhythm, ideas, sometimes short enough to be considered motives, which reappear from movement to movement.

Fugues, all of which begin with a subject that is repeated several times and variously manipulated as the music unfolds, include:

J. S. BACH   o Fugue for Organ in g, S. 578; Passacaglia and Fugue for Organ in c, S. 582; Toccata and Fugue for Organ in d, S. 565.

W. A. MOZART   o Requiem in d, K. 626, I: Kyrie Eleison.

B. BARTÓK   o● *Music for String Instruments, Percussion, and Celesta,* I.

W. SCHUMAN   o● Symphony 3 (1941), II.

The theme-and-variations form employs a theme, stated by itself at the beginning, as the basis for what follows, each reappearance being varied in some way (see Chapter 8):

W. A. MOZART   o Twelve Variations for Piano on "Ah, vous dirai-je, Maman" in C, K. 265 (300*e*).

L. VAN BEETHOVEN   o● Sonata for Violin and Piano in A, op. 47, II; o Concerto for Violin and Orchestra in D, op. 61, II.

BENJAMIN BRITTEN   *The Young Person's Guide to the Orchestra,* op. 34.

Pieces in which more complete melodic ideas exist:

A. VIVALDI   o Concerto for Violin and Orchestra in E, op. 8, no. 1, II.

J. S. BACH   o● Italian Concerto for Harpsichord Solo in F, S. 971, II.

L. VAN BEETHOVEN   o Sonata for Piano in c, op. 13, II.

F. F. CHOPIN   o Étude for Piano in E, op. 10, no. 3; ● Impromptu for Piano in c♯, op. 66, no. 4.

F. P. SCHUBERT   o● "Der Wanderer," op. 4, no. 1.

P. I. TCHAIKOVSKY   o● Symphony 5 in e, op. 64, II, III.

Practically all popular songs present a complete melodic idea as the major content.

Conclusion

the two yielding a small musical idea to be used and reused as the music proceeds. The opening notes of the first movement of Beethoven's Symphony 5 in c make perhaps the most famous musical motive, and it is certainly one of the clearest examples of how a tiny idea can generate a whole movement of varied, profound, and coherent insights.

A theme is longer and better developed than a motive is. It is a melodic idea that serves as a point of departure for a piece, recurring several times but not so constantly as does a motive. If a motive can be regarded as a single brick in a house, a theme can be regarded as a preformed section of wall; the theme is not so compact as the motive, but it too is only a component part and not the whole. The words "theme" and "subject" can be regarded as synonyms. Traditionally, the main theme of a fugue (see Chapter 8) is a "subject," as is also often the case for the sonata form. However, we need not concern ourselves with the subtleties of terminology here because it will suffice if we recognize the two structural levels of melodic usage: the smaller one of the motive and the larger one of the theme or subject.

Finally, many pieces use melody ideas that are more complete in themselves than are either motives or themes. Such melodies might be thought of as preformed rooms of a house. Each is a complete entity. A composition might repeat the melody several times (as a three-bedroom house) and might have more than one melody (a kitchen, a living room, a den), but each melody of this sort gives a sense of wholeness beyond that of a typical theme.

Naturally, there are some subtle gradations between theme and complete melody (as there are between motive and theme), where distinctions are difficult or impossible to make. Nevertheless, our purposes will be well served if we settle for the idea of three rough levels of melodic usage: motivic, thematic, and complete. These will help you perceive the structure of complex musical works (LISTENING 5.11).

The richness of melody as a generator of musical expressiveness is such that a study of it could go on forever. In combination with rhythm, itself endlessly interesting, melody has available a wealth of material out of which to shape artistic events. Several other dimensions of sound have yet to be explored, however, and next we turn our attention to two other major components of music: harmony and counterpoint.

Chapter 6 ∘ *The expressiveness of harmony and counterpoint*

OUR DISCUSSION OF RHYTHM AND MELODY HAS CALLED ATTENTION TO TWO fundamental elements of music: its movement through time and with pitch. For centuries rhythm and a single melody line (and the tone color of the instruments and voices used) were the only materials, the total content, of music. That kind of music is said to have "monophonic texture" (Greek, *monos*, "single," *phōnē*, "sound"). Further comments about monophonic music and listening examples are on pages 94–95.

In the Middle Ages a second line of pitch was added to the first, giving a musical organization, or "texture," in which two melodies were heard at the same time. As the centuries passed, the practice of using two or more melodies together increased in popularity and complexity. Music in which more than one melody exists simultaneously is said to have "polyphonic" (Greek, *polys*, "many"), or "contrapuntal," texture (sometimes such music is described as in "counterpoint").

During the sixteenth and seventeenth centuries attention began to be paid to the effect of several pitches sounding together, and by the early 1700s this vertical, or up-and-down, aspect of music was thoroughly recognized as a basic element through which music could be expressive. Various theories, or guidelines, on how to organize tones sounding together began to evolve; and to this day a major part of writing about music and of the study of music is concerned with the organization of tones sounding together, or "harmony."

When music has a melody with harmony, its texture is said to be "homophonic" (Greek, *homos*, "same"), and it can be diagrammed as in Example 6.1. Listening to homophonic music requires attention to both its horizontal (melodic) and vertical (harmonic) aspects. Of course, many listeners concentrate on the melody and let the harmony take care of itself, thus unfortunately allowing a lot of interesting material to slip by unnoticed. As our study will demonstrate, however, the harmonic

Example 6.1

Melody

Harmony

Harmony (homophony)

HARMONY AND COUNTERPOINT

HARMONY (HOMOPHONY; ORGANIZATION OF TONES SOUNDING TOGETHER)

Structure: simple . . . complex.
Quality: consonant . . . dissonant.
Tonality: tonal . . . atonal.
Density: thick . . . thin; block chords . . . harmonic patterns.
Cadences: strong . . . weak.
Modulation: few . . . many; gradual . . . abrupt;
usual . . . unusual.
Shape: smooth . . . jagged.
Harmonic-rhythm: infrequent change . . . frequent change.
Prominence: accompaniment . . . main content.

MONOPHONY (SINGLE MELODY)

COUNTERPOINT (POLYPHONY; ORGANIZATION OF MELODIES SOUNDING TOGETHER)

Imitative . . . nonimitative.
Colors: blending . . . contrasting.
Density: thick . . . thin.

MIXED TEXTURE

Homophonic . . . polyphonic.

dimension of music is so rich in expressiveness that it deserves special attention. After our exploration of harmony, we shall discuss counterpoint, or polyphony. An outline to guide our study is in the margin.

STRUCTURE: SIMPLE . . . COMPLEX

In Chapter 5 (on melody) a definition of an interval was given: the distance between two pitches. Our interest there was in pitches sounded one after another, producing a *melodic interval*. When two pitches are sounded *together*, the interval produced is a *harmonic interval*. When three or more pitches are sounded together, the result is a *chord*. Our concern now is chords and how they are used in music.

If we number the pitches in a scale 1 through 8, the simplest chords for that scale would be made of pitches 1–3–5, 2–4–6, 3–5–7, 4–6–8, 5–7–9(2), 6–8–10(3), 7–9(2)–11(4), and so on. Example 6.2 shows how they look in musical notation. Each chord has a number (traditionally a Roman numeral) so that it can be identified as being the I chord (built on the first note of the scale), or the V chord (built on the fifth note of the scale), or whatever. When a composer is using chords to accompany a melody, he chooses those which enhance the sound of the melody, chords that add just the right touch of richness, of movement, of highlight, to dress up the melody and make it sound as expressive as possible. The chords also have their *own* expressiveness and are interesting because they create a sense of movement, expectation, and tendency, which carries the listener along as the chords move from one to another. Just as each single melodic pitch has its own part to add to the total melody, each chord adds its own flavor to the ongoing chord movement of the music.

The harmonies available to the composer are not limited to the seven chords built on the seven pitches of the major scale. Each half step of the chromatic scale can yield a chord, giving a total of twelve from which to choose. Each of the twelve can be arranged in different orders of the three pitches. The C chord, for example, can be arranged in the ways in Example 6.3, the three pitches being positioned differently—(*a*) is named ''root position'' because C, the chord name, or root, is on the bottom; the other arrangements, (*b*) and (*c*), are called ''inversions'' of the C chord.

Each arrangement of pitches has its own sound, subtly different from

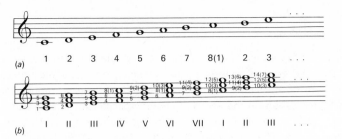

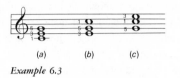

Example 6.2 • (a) Pitches in a scale; (b) pitches in chords.

Example 6.3

Example 6.4

that of the others. With all the possible positions of all twelve chords, the composer's choice widens. Further, each chord and inversion can be spaced with the notes close together, as in Examples 6.2 and 6.3, or the notes can be spread out with wide gaps between them, thus adding still another set of possibilities for variety (Example 6.4).

Another thing that multiplies chord choice is the practice of altering one or more pitches of the basic chord. A basic C chord, C–E–G, can be altered in the following traditional ways: lowering the E a half step; lowering both the E and the G a half step; or raising the G a half step. The original C–E–G is called a "major" chord; C–Eb–G is a "minor" chord; C–Eb–Gb is a "diminished" chord; and C–E–G♯ is an "augmented" chord. Each of these chords has its own, particular flavor, which the composer can "mix and match" as he sees fit. Also, each of the altered chords can be arranged in various inversions and spacings. So the possibilities for chord choice become numerous indeed.

We have still not run out of ways to build chords. Another important practice in harmony is the addition of pitches to the basic three. The simplest way to do this is to *double* one of the three pitches, such as C–E–G–C. But it is possible to add *new* notes to the basic three, such as C–E–G–B and C–E–G–Bb, and in fact several new notes can be added to the basic three: C–E–G–Bb–D. Each time a new pitch is added, the sound becomes more complex; and each additional pitch adds new possibilities of inversions and spacings.

If we total all the possible combinations of chords built in the traditional way—that is, out of superimposed thirds—we find that the number of choices becomes very large. Yet during this century even more possibilities have been added: chords built on nontraditional intervals such as C–F–Bb–Eb; chords piling up note upon note until everything blurs together; the sounding of two different and clashing chords together; clusters of sound in which the pitches are used only because of the sheer color or effect they produce. Students of music spend years exploring the intricacies of traditional harmony; and now there are the new challenges of nontraditional harmony. Harmony offers many challenges for the listener also. People not studying music professionally do not need to learn all the details and complexities of harmony. Our purpose here is mainly to give you some sense of what is involved in this element of music and some hints on how to enjoy more of its expressiveness.

LISTENING 6.1

The following pieces (all tonal music) include average dissonance and much dissonance for the period under which they are listed. Try to get the flavor of the dissonance possibilities in each style.

MEDIEVAL AND RENAISSANCE

ANONYMOUS ○ "Ave, Virgo–Ave Gloriosa Mater–Domino." Thirteenth-century motet.

GUILLAUME DUFAY ○● "Ce jour de l'an."

CLAUDE LE JEUNE ○● "La bel'Aronde."

BAROQUE

CLAUDIO MONTEVERDI ○● *Orfeo:* "Tu se' morta."

J. S. BACH ○ Suite for Orchestra in b, S. 1067; ○● Italian Concerto for Harpsichord Solo in F, S. 971; ○● Cantata 80, *Ein feste Burg ist unser Gott;* Mass in b, S. 232.

G. F. HANDEL ○● *Messiah;* "Royal Fireworks" Music.

GEORG PHILIPP TELEMANN ○ Quartet for Recorder, Oboe, Violin, and Continuo in G.

A. VIVALDI ○ Concerto for Violin and Orchestra in E, op. 8, no. 1.

CLASSIC

F. J. HAYDN ○● Symphony 101 in D; *Die Schöpfung (The Creation);* Quartet for Strings in d, op. 76, no. 2.

W. A. MOZART ○ *Eine kleine Nachtmusik* in G, K. 525; Symphonies ○ 36 in C, K. 425, ○● 40 in g, K. 550, ○ 41 in C, K. 551; ○● Requiem in d, K. 626; ○● *Don Giovanni,* K. 527, Act II: Scene 5 (final scene). The ending of *Don Giovanni* has such a high level of dissonance that one can only marvel that the same composer could have created both the serenade *Eine kleine Nachtmusik* and this scene. The serenade uses dissonance so sparingly that each little touch of it adds a delightful bit of spice to a basically consonant context; the last scene of the opera lays it on so thickly that the sheer power and sensuousness of the dissonant sounds can be overwhelming.

L. VAN BEETHOVEN ○● Symphonies 3 in E♭, op. 55, 5 in c, op. 67; ○● Sonata for Violin and Piano in A, op. 47; ○● Quartet for Strings in B♭, op. 130.

NINETEENTH CENTURY

F. P. SCHUBERT ○ *Die schöne Müllerin;* Symphony 8 in b (*Unfinished*).

QUALITY: CONSONANT . . . DISSONANT

The words "consonant" and "dissonant" indicate the relative amount of "clash," or tension, between pitches sounding together. If the pitches in a chord do not clash with each other and produce no rubbing or grating impression on the ear, that chord is consonant. Most persons would agree that C–E–G–C is a consonant chord. If we add a note between C and E and between G and C, to get C–D–E–G–B–C, we get a combination of pitches with a good deal of tension between them: the C and D and E clash with each other as do the B and C. Most would agree that the resultant sound is dissonant.

With a few exceptions (to be discussed next) music of the past four hundred or so years has depended on consonance and dissonance to give a sense of tension and relaxation. Tonal music (review pages 76–78) would be an impossibility without the force, drive, and interest created by movement between tension and relaxation, and the power of music to affect us—to make us feel—is largely based on this motion. An important way to produce such motion is to use dissonance to create tension and consonance to relieve the tension.

How much dissonance is needed to create a feeling of tension in the listener? A broad generality would be that music has become more and more dissonant over the centuries. What was at one time considered a shocking dissonance became less and less shocking as people got used to it; when it no longer produced the desired tension, composers had to think up new ways to add interest, drama, and forward motion to their music. So a bit more dissonance was used, and then, as that became commonplace, still more.

Contemporary tonal music contains a good deal of dissonance, partly because of the influence of atonality (see below) and partly because modern ears have become accustomed to a high level of dissonance. But *every* period in the history of music has used dissonance to create feeling. If one has some general idea of what the music of a certain period sounds like, he can find some pieces very dissonant for that particular time; so our responses to dissonance and consonance should be relative. Some of the music of Gesualdo (*ca.* 1560–1613), for example, is shockingly dissonant as compared with other music of his day. Much of the music of Mozart (1756–1791) uses dissonance very

H. BERLIOZ　○● *Symphonie fantastique,* op. 14; Requiem, op. 5.

J. BRAHMS　○● Symphony 2 in D, op. 73; ○● *Ein deutsches Requiem,* op. 45; Variations on a Theme by Haydn in B♭, op. 56a.

P. I. TCHAIKOVSKY　○● Symphony 5 in e, op. 64; ○ Concerto for Piano and Orchestra in b♭, op. 23.

R. WAGNER　*Tristan und Isolde:* Prelude and ○● "Liebestod"; "Siegfried Idyll."

TWENTIETH CENTURY

C. DEBUSSY　○● *The Afternoon of a Faun;* "Footsteps in the Snow."

A. SCHOENBERG　*Verklärte Nacht,* op. 4.

I. STRAVINSKY　○ *The Rite of Spring;* ○● *Symphony of Psalms.*

B. BARTÓK　○● *Music for String Instruments, Percussion, and Celesta; Concerto for Orchestra.*

W. SCHUMAN　○● Symphony 3 (1941).

R. VAUGHAN WILLIAMS　Symphony 5.

L. ARMSTRONG　*Satchmo's Collectors' Items.*

O. COLEMAN　○● *Town Hall, 1962; Free Jazz.*

C. PARKER　*The Essential Charley Parker.*

J. COLTRANE　*My Favorite Things.*

THE WHO　*Tommy.*

sparingly, as did most of the music of his contemporaries. But in some of Mozart's music there is so much dissonance, *for his time,* that the effect is a shocking one for the listener who knows what to expect from classic music. As one gets more sensitive to the dissonance-consonance possibilities within musical styles, one can enjoy the great differences that exist in them (LISTENING 6.1).

TONALITY: TONAL . . . ATONAL

Tonal music depends on harmony as well as melody to help create a sense of movement away from a tonal center and back. Just as each pitch in a scale has its particular function in relation to the others, so each chord has its function in the total scheme of chord relations. We can hear a progression of chords move logically and expressively from one to another because each leads us to expect the next. Our expectations are based on the tonal language, whether or not we happen to know the formal melodic or harmonic rules of that language. Harmony and melody together determine whether a piece is considered to be tonal or atonal.

When Arnold Schoenberg devised his twelve-tone system of composition, creating atonal music as an extension of the earlier breakdown of tonality in Wagner, Debussy, and others, a kind of sound emerged that is dissonant all the time. The melody line gives no sense of returning to a home base where one can relax for a moment. The harmonies are not made of traditional chords that move from consonance to dissonance as an important part of their flow. The pitches sounding together at any single moment do not blend in easy consonance but instead are in a constant state of tension (according to traditional norms). So if you listen to a tonal piece, say, the Haydn Quartet for Strings in d in LISTENING 6.1 and compare it for amount of dissonance with an atonal piece, say, Schoenberg's Quartet for Strings 4, you would have to say that the Schoenberg is infinitely more dissonant than the Haydn.

But that is a bit like comparing apples and houses. Atonal music, as *all* music, gives a sense of movement—of expectations, of tendencies, of tensions and relaxations. But it does not use traditional consonance and dissonance to do so. If we ignore the requirement that consonance and dissonance, as traditionally used, must be present in music, we can be free to share the expressiveness of that music which has aban-

LISTENING 6.2

Choose some of the works in LISTENING 5.4. This time concentrate on the total effect of the music as it creates a sense of structured movement.

The pieces performed by traditional instruments (listed before Other Atonal Music) contain many sounds that are not, strictly speaking, "harmony." Our discussion of counterpoint will clarify this. For now just get a feeling for the total sound in atonal contexts. The pieces under Other Atonal Music often have nothing that can properly be called melody or harmony. You must allow the unfolding sounds to carry you along, unconcerned about hearing a melody line with chords. There are still moments of more and less tension, but the concepts melody and harmony have no real bearing.

LISTENING 6.3

The following pieces contain some clear examples of thin chordal harmony:

F. J. HAYDN   ○● Symphony 101 in D, II.

L. VAN BEETHOVEN   ○ Concerto for Violin and Orchestra in D, op. 61, II: variation 3.

F. P. SCHUBERT   ○ *Die schöne Müllerin,* op. 25, no. 19: "The Miller and the Brook." This song begins with thin chordal harmony (28 measures) and then uses a broken-chord pattern throughout.

C. DEBUSSY   "Claire de lune": beginning.

G. PUCCINI   ○● *La Bohème,* Act I: "Mi chiamano Mimi."

The following contain thick chordal harmony:

L. VAN BEETHOVEN   ○● Sonata for Piano in c, op. 13, I: beginning (*Grave*)

F. P. SCHUBERT   ○ *Die schöne Müllerin,* op. 25, no. 5: "At Leisure." This song begins with 4 measures of thick chords. The harmony then changes to a broken-chord pattern and back to thick chords again. After a slower, more elaborate interlude, thick chords return ("und der Meister sagt zu allen") and then the faster broken-chord pattern. Two thick chords end the song.

P. I. TCHAIKOVSKY   Symphony 5 in e, op. 64, ○● II: beginning, IV: ending (*Presto*); ○ Concerto for Piano and Orchestra in b♭, op. 23, I: beginning and ending.

A. SCHOENBERG   ○ *Pierrot lunaire,* op. 21, XIV: "Die Kreuze."

doned it. Such music creates sound conditions to be heard and felt; it can be experienced musically if met on its own terms (LISTENING 6.2).

DENSITY: THICK . . . THIN; BLOCK CHORDS . . . HARMONIC PATTERNS

Let us now return to music that has harmony in the traditional sense: that is, a vertical dimension in which the pitches sounding together have been chosen for their expressive effects on each other and on the melodic aspect of the music.

One of the important ways harmony is used is to give an illusion of density, or weight, or thickness. Of course, sounds do not actually have density; they have no weight and they occupy no space. Yet they can *feel* as if they do. When tones are piled up one on top of another in close spacing with many low pitches included (especially if played or sung loudly), they produce a distinct impression of thickness. And if tones are spaced out widely with just a few pitches used and placement toward the high end of the pitch spectrum (especially if played or sung softly and delicately), they give an impression of lightness, thinness, or spaciousness. Density presents the composer with another opportunity to create a sense of dynamic movement. From the most thick and heavy sounds to the most thin and light, a rich spectrum of possibilities for variety exists.

The density of harmony depends on another important factor in addition to the number of pitches in a chord and how they are spaced. Often a chord is broken up into a pattern in which the pitches are not sounded together but are sounded one after another; for example, the simple chord C–E–G can be broken up into several patterns in which the three pitches are repeated over and over, as in Example 6.5. The effect is still harmony even though, strictly speaking, no chord is sounded. Instead of a chord we have a broken-chord pattern, which makes a quite different effect from that of the same pitches sounded together.

Example 6.5

Clear examples of broken-chord patterns are:

W. A. MOZART   *Eine kleine Nachtmusik* in G, K. 525, III:
Trio; ○ Symphony 41 in C, K. 550, III: beginning; Twelve
Variations for Piano on "Ah, vous dirai-je, Maman," in C, K. 265
(300*e*), Variations II, IV, X.

L. VAN BEETHOVEN   ○ Sonata for Piano in c, op. 13, II:
beginning (16 measures).

F. F. CHOPIN   ○ Étude for Piano in E, op. 10, no. 3: beginning.

F. P. SCHUBERT   *Die schöne Müllerin*, op. 25, nos. 1–3, 11, 15:
"Wandering," "Whither," "Stop!," "Mine!," "Jealousy and Pride."

Relatively thicker and thinner harmonic material is conveniently
illustrated in Mozart's variations on "Ah, vous dirai-je, Maman":

Variation (Theme	Texture thin)	Variation	Texture
1	thin	7	thick
2	thick	8	thin
3	thin	9	thin
4	thick	10	thick
5	thin	11	thin
6	thick	12	thick

Contemporary nontraditional music often uses density as a basic
part of its expressiveness and formal structure, even though
nothing that can be traditionally thought of as harmony is present.
Listen for the different thicknesses and thinnesses, or weights, in
the following:

M. BABBITT   ○ *Composition for Synthesizer.*

K. STOCKHAUSEN   *Gesang der Jünglinge; Kontakte.*

O. LUENING   *Concerted Piece for Electronic Sounds and Orchestra.*

E. VARÈSE   *Poème électronique.*

LISTENING 6.4

Listen again to some of the selections listed under the topic of
cadence in melody (LISTENING 5.5). This time concentrate on the
harmonic material accompanying the melody as it strengthens the
sense of cadence in the music. Compare the effect of traditionally
built cadences with the pauses in the recent music. Although none
of the old cadence formulas is found in the latter music, points of
relaxation continue to be major factors in musical structure.

It is extremely important to realize that not all harmony consists of
chordal harmony—chords played in separate blocks of sound, chord after
chord after chord. Composers constantly break up harmonies into all
sorts of simple and complex patterns, in which the notes of chords are
strung out in a great variety of ways. All this material is *harmony* because
it is used as a background against which a melody stands out more
expressively than it could if it were alone. However, the harmonic patterns play an important part in the music and sometimes are highlighted
for their own sake; so harmony is not a matter of mere background.
Much music would make no sense without harmonic material, whether
chordal or in various patterns. The ways to create harmonic material
are endless, each slight variation of density giving a slight variation of
feeling (LISTENING 6.3).

CADENCES: STRONG . . . WEAK

In Chapter 5 we discussed the idea of cadences in melody. What was
said there applies as well to harmony. The movement of music to places
of relaxation or rest (to cadences) depends on harmony in addition to
melody. Both operate together to bring motion to a halt, whether permanently, as at the end of a composition, or temporarily, as during its
course.

Harmony can be allied with rhythm to give a sense of a strong ending.
This is done with a progression of chords leading to an expected I (tonic)
chord and then reaching that home-base chord in a forthright way. Most
endings of tonal pieces have this kind of strong cadence, which creates
an unmistakable feeling of finality.

Other harmonic progressions give a more temporary sense of rest; they
may end on some other chord than the I chord, or the I chord may
be prepared for in a subtle way that allows the music to proceed easily
after it is reached. Some cadences have been used so often that they
have settled down to a formula: Most music students can easily write
out a "perfect," a "plagal," a "half," or a "deceptive" cadence. It
is not necessary for you to know the technical details of these musical
formulas (any good music dictionary or theory text will give more details
if you want them), for our interest is in the expressiveness of cadence—
the way it helps music to have an organized, sensible structure (LISTENING
6.4).

There are obvious modulations in the following short pieces. A helpful way to follow the modulations is to hum the key tone to yourself as the music goes along, wait until a change is made, and then hum the new key tone until *it* changes. With some practice you can begin to tell when a modulation is coming and what the new key tone might be.

w. a. mozart   *Eine kleine Nachtmusic* in G, K. 525, III. The opening minuet is in G, the trio part is in D, and then the minuet is repeated. Symphony 35 in D, K. 385, III. Following common practice in the classic period, this *Menuetto* and Trio is in the key scheme D (tonic) for the *Menuetto* and A (dominant) for the Trio; the *Menuetto* then returns in D.

f. j. haydn   Symphony 94 in G, II (*Surprise*). This famous movement contains a surprise loud chord that was supposed to have awakened a sleepy audience. It also contains constant modulations from the opening G (tonic) to C and back to G. There is a sudden change to c and then a return to the alternating G and C to end in C.

f. p. schubert   *Die schöne Müllerin*, op. 25, no. 11: "Mein!" ("Mine!"). A series of modulations proceeds as follows:

Words	Key
Beginning	D
"Durch den Hain" (measure 22)	A
"Die geliebte Müllerin" (measure 30)	D
"Mein Frühling" (measure 40)	B♭
"Bachlein, lass dein" (measure 64)	D
"Durch den Hain" (measure 77)	A
"Die geliebte Müllerin" (measure 85)	D

o *Die schöne Müllerin*, op. 25, no. 18: "Trockne Blumen" ("Wither'd Flowers"). This song begins in G, modulates to E ("Und wenn sie wandelt am Hugel vorbei"), and switches to e for the closing 4 measures (piano alone).

More complex modulations, but still detectable with practice, can be heard in the following:

w. a. mozart   Symphonies o● 40 in g, K. 550,   41 in C, K. 551, especially III.

l. van beethoven   o Sonata for Piano in c, op. 13, I.

r. r. bennett   o *Suite of Old American Dances*, V: "Rag."

r. vaughan williams   o *Folksong Suite*.

MODULATION: FEW . . . MANY; GRADUAL . . . ABRUPT; USUAL . . . UNUSUAL

In the discussion of scales in Chapter 5 it was mentioned that tonal music depends on the existence of a home-base note (the tonic), which is the first note of any particular scale. The key of a piece of music is the same as the name of that note and the kind of scale built on it: if the music is based on the scale beginning on the note C, the key is C (major or minor depending on where the half steps come); music built on the major scale beginning on E♭ is in the key of E♭ (major); if a piece is built on the minor scale beginning on F, the key is f (minor). As long as the music (melody plus harmony) is based on a particular scale, it will give a sense of rest, or cadence, when it returns to the first note, or key note, or tonic, of that scale. We feel the movement coming back home as it returns to the key note, and we feel it going away from home as the music strays from the key note. This is a basic way for music to create feelings of relaxation and tension.

Harmony is an important element in the sensation of key. Chords add enormously to the strength and clarity with which a key can be felt, so that composers use harmony with great care to establish a feeling for a particular key and to stray from the key chord.

If a piece remained in the same key from beginning to end, that is, if the same scale were the basis for the entire piece, the amount of tension possible in that piece would be limited; the musical territory available for exploration would be confined to the single scale in which the piece began. To widen the territory and make room for greater possibilities of uncertainty, composers often begin a piece in one key and then switch to another key as the music is going along. Such a change from one key to another is called a "modulation." A modulation can affect the listener very strongly: His ears have become accustomed to a particular key; all of a sudden he finds himself in a *different* key. Then, when he is just getting accustomed to the new key, he may find himself back at the first one again. The possibilities for tension and uncertainty are obviously rich.

Some music modulates frequently from key to key. This constantly throws the listener off balance. Other music remains in a single key for long periods of time and results in stability and security. Some modula-

LISTENING 6.6

GENERALLY SMOOTH HARMONIC MOVEMENT

J. S. BACH   ○ Cantata 80, *Ein feste Burg ist unser Gott,* VIII: chorale.

F. F. CHOPIN   ○ Étude for Piano in E, op. 10, no. 3.

P. I. TCHAIKOVSKY   ○● Symphony 5 in e, op. 64, II: beginning.

C. DEBUSSY   "The Girl with the Flaxen Hair."

W. SCHUMAN   ○● Symphony 3 (1941), III: Chorale.

GEORGE SHEARING   "Yesterdays," from *The Capitol History of Jazz, Vol. 4.*

GENERALLY JAGGED HARMONIC MOVEMENT

W. A. MOZART   ○ Requiem in d, K. 626, X: Sanctus (beginning).

C. DEBUSSY   "The Hills of Anacapri," "What the West Wind Saw," "The Interrupted Serènade," "The Dance of Puck," "Minstrels."

B. BARTÓK   ○● *Music for String Instruments, Percussion, and Celesta,* II.

A. SCHOENBERG   ○ *Pierrot lunaire,* op. 21, XIV.

LISTENING 6.7

L. VAN BEETHOVEN   Sonata for Piano in c, op. 13, ○● I. The fast sections have a high degree of harmonic action, whereas the slower sections have less frequent changes. ○ II. Here the harmonic rhythm is quite slow, partly because of the slow tempo but also because of the moderate rate of change from harmony to harmony, seldom faster than beat to beat.

W. A. MOZART   Requiem in d, K. 626, II: Dies Irae. The harmonic rhythm is generally fast, but some measures use the same harmonic pattern throughout.

F. F. CHOPIN   ○ Étude for Piano in E, op. 10, no. 3. The smooth harmonic shape is carried by a generally static harmonic rhythm. Polonaise for Piano in A, op. 40, no. 1. The active rhythmic content of this polonaise is matched by a generally high degree of harmonic change.

(continued on page 94)

tions are gradual: A composer will move slowly and carefully from one key to another so that the listener hardly realizes that a switch has been made. Other modulations are very abrupt: One minute the music is in a certain key, and the next it has boldly switched to another. Naturally these differences will *feel* different to the listener who is able to perceive them.

A modulation can be from one key to another closely related to it. This is the usual kind of modulation, in which the amount of imbalance is moderate. But some modulations take the music to a key far removed from the original. The imbalance is much greater, creating more tension and thereby resulting in a much stronger need for resolution. (Try LISTENING 6.5.)

Tonal music uses modulation constantly. A piece that is longer than a simple song is almost sure to modulate during its course. In the late nineteenth century some compositions modulated so often that it became impossible to tell when they were in any particular key. In them no home base at all can be definitely identified so that constant uncertainty is felt. The later music of Richard Wagner and many pieces of Claude Debussy are of this sort. It was a short step beyond their music to abandon tonality (and, therefore, modulation) entirely, as Schoenberg and his followers did. Contemporary tonal music continues to use modulation, but nontonal music contains no modulation in any traditional sense of the word.

SHAPE: SMOOTH . . . JAGGED

A melody can move in a smooth, unbroken line, each note following another with little or no awkwardness. Harmonic material can also move in a smooth, gradual contour. In many chord progressions or harmonic passages the movement shape seems effortless and even; the listener is carried along by the flowing quality of the harmony. (Rhythm plays an important part in creating this sense of flow.) But just as a melody can be jagged, harmony can also contain a great many awkward jumps, sudden changes of direction, or rough contours as chords and single pitches leap with great tension from one to another. (Again, the rhythmic setting of the harmony will contribute greatly to its shape.) The musical landscape will be quite different according to the harmonic arrangement; so it will feel different to the perceptive listener (LISTENING 6.6).

R. WAGNER   *Das Rheingold:* Prelude. The opening measures are harmonically static on an E♭ chord for over a hundred measures.

C. DEBUSSY   "Footsteps in the Snow." Although the tempo is moderate, the harmonic action is quite intense, with frequent changes from harmony to harmony.

O. COLEMAN   "Dedication to Poets and Writers," from *Town Hall, 1962.* The jagged shape and active harmonic rhythm create a driving, restless feeling in this composition for strings by a famous jazz saxophonist.

LISTENING 6.8

These pieces rely on harmonic material for much of their expressiveness:

W. A. MOZART   Requiem in d, K. 626, II: Dies Irae; VI: Confutatis; ○ VII: Lacrimosa; ○ X: Sanctus (*Adagio,* beginning).

L. VAN BEETHOVEN   ○● Symphony 3 in E♭, op. 55, III; Symphony 5 in c, op. 67, III, ○ IV.

H. BERLIOZ   ○● *Symphonie fantastique,* op. 14, V.

P. I. TCHAIKOVSKY   Symphony 5 in e, op. 64, ○● II: beginning; ○ IV.

W. SCHUMAN   Symphony 3 (1941), IV: Toccata.

A. SCHOENBERG   ○● *Pierrot lunaire,* op. 21, most pieces.

THE MODERN JAZZ QUARTET   *Third Stream Music.* Much of the effect of this kind of cool jazz depends on rich harmonic material as well as on the melodic inventiveness that is the most important content of much jazz.

Monophony

HARMONIC RHYTHM: INFREQUENT CHANGE . . . FREQUENT CHANGE

In some music a particular chord is used with little change for several measures; then another chord is used for a while. The rate of harmonic change, or "harmonic rhythm," is slow. Such music has a minimum of harmonic action; it seems static. (Again, the overall rhythm of the music is involved in the rhythm of its harmony.) When there are constant and quick changes from harmony to harmony (fast harmonic rhythm), a very active impression is given, with resulting excitement and drive. Of course, much music is neither always static nor always active in harmonic rhythm. As all other musical means, this one often creates many subtle and obvious differences by subtle and obvious movement between the two extremes (LISTENING 6.7).

PROMINENCE: ACCOMPANIMENT . . . MAIN CONTENT

In homophonic texture the melody is often prominent, and the harmony is accompaniment. But as we have seen, harmony is much more than just a pleasant background against which the melody stands out; in and of itself, it is a complex and expressive dimension of music. In fact, in many pieces harmonic material plays such an important part that it sometimes becomes the main musical content; melody is not heard at all for a time while harmony takes the limelight. The listener must not think that, because melody is missing, the music is just marking time at that point. The shifting of interest from melody to harmony should be followed and enjoyed by the perceptive listener (LISTENING 6.8).

Music consisting in a single melody without any implied additional parts or implied accompaniment is rarely heard today. Ever since the birth of polyphony in the Middle Ages, the music of western Europe has quickly developed into more complex textures, a complexity that seems more appreciated by audiences than does the purity of an unadorned solo melody.

The vast bulk of monophonic music exists in various types of chant. Except for a brief excursion into secular monophonic music of the late

Middle Ages and a few isolated examples in later music (LISTENING 6.9), composers have not been attracted to the writing of pieces that are entirely monophonic. They have not hesitated, however, to include brief monophonic passages (one to a dozen or so measures) in works of homophonic and polyphonic textures.

Counterpoint (polyphony)

LISTENING 6.9

This list includes early monophonic works and a few more modern examples that use this texture entirely or in part:

GREGORIAN CHANT o "Veni creator spiritus," o● "Alleluia vidimus stellam."

GIRAUT DE BORNEIL o "Reis glorios."

There are examples of chant up to the year 1000 in *L'Anthologie Sonore*, in Archive Production Research Period I, in the first and second volumes of *The History of Music in Sound*, in *History of European Music*, in *Masterpieces of Music before 1750*, in *A Treasury of Early Music*, and in *Music of the Middle Ages*. The record collections also contain monophonic pieces other than chant. See the end of Chapter 9 (Other Important Music) for further information about them.

J. S. BACH Partita for Violin Solo in d, S. 1004, I, IV.

R. WAGNER *Tristan und Isolde*, Act I: opening of Scene 1, tenor solo; Act III: opening of Scene 1, English-horn solo.

C. DEBUSSY "Syrinx" for Flute Solo.

R. VAUGHAN WILLIAMS Mass in g, I: Kyrie.

LISTENING 6.10

In these pieces concentrate on the ideas that enter time and time again. Try to feel how the imitation gives a sense of unity to the music while creating an ongoing, ever-changing sequence of events.

J. OKEGHEM o● *Missa prolationum:* Sanctus (see Chapter 9).

JOSQUIN DES PRÉS o● "Ave Maria."

G. P. DA PALESTRINA o● *Missa brevis:* Agnus Dei II.

(continued on page 96)

When music consists of two or more melodies stated at the same time, it is polyphonic, or contrapuntal, or in counterpoint. Homophonic music, melody with harmony, requires that we hear the relationship of the melody to its harmony. Polyphonic music requires that we hear the relations among the separate melodies. The essence of polyphonic music is that each horizontal line has its own identity and yet relates and balances with the others. The enjoyment and challenge of counterpoint is to hear and feel the separateness and togetherness all at once.

Example 6.6 is a diagram of polyphonic music, in this case with four different melody lines. The number of lines will, of course, depend on the number of melodies in a particular piece, and the length of the lines will depend on how the melodies enter and drop out. The minimum for counterpoint is two melodies that overlap at least sometimes.

Example 6.6

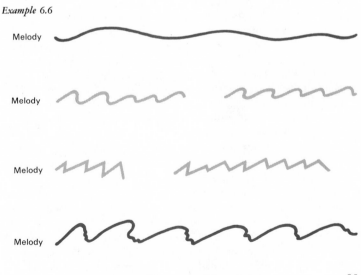

Melody

Melody

Melody

Melody

LUCA MARENZIO ○ "S'io parto, i' moro."

T. MORLEY   The vocal madrigals are a treasure of contrapuntal devices. A good collection is sung by The Deller Consort, *Madrigals of Thomas Morley,* Vanguard record BGS-5002. The following ones depend heavily on imitation, although nonimitative parts (see the text farther on) are often present to some degree: "In dew of roses," "Miraculous love's wounding," "Hark, alleluia cheerily," "Arise, get up, my dear," "I go before, my darling," "Say, gentle nymphs," "Good morrow, fair ladies," "Hard by a crystal fountain," "Whither away so fast," "When, lo, by break of morning."

J. S. BACH   ○ Cantata 80, *Ein feste Burg ist unser Gott,* I; ○ Fugue for Organ in g, S. 578.

G. F. HANDEL   ○● *Messiah:* "For unto us a child is born."

W. A. MOZART   ○ Requiem in d, K. 626, I: Requiem, *Allegro* (Kyrie); V: Recordare; X: Sanctus, *Allegro.*

I. STRAVINSKY   *Symphony of Psalms,* II.

W. SCHUMAN   ○● Symphony 3 (1941), II: Fugue.

LISTENING 6.11

G. F. HANDEL   *Messiah:* "Thou art gone up on high," "Thou shalt break them," ○● "Hallelujah." This last, a famous chorus, contains both imitative and nonimitative counterpoint.

P. I. TCHAIKOVSKY   ○● Symphony 5 in e, op. 64, II. The main melody (played by the French horn) is embellished with imitative decorations. When the strings play the melody afterward, the embellishments are nonimitative.

A. SCHOENBERG   Quartet for Strings 4, op. 37, III, IV. Much twelve-tone, or serial, music is polyphonic in texture, with much use of nonimitative counterpoint.

W. SCHUMAN   ○● Symphony 3 (1941), III: Chorale, beginning. Dixieland jazz depends on nonimitative counterpoint for much of its unique flavor. The tune is embellished by several players together and in turn. It then becomes the basis for the last, all-out chorus, in which the separate improvisations are woven together in one grand, nonimitative melodic tapestry. Typical Dixie performances can be found in *The Capitol History of Jazz, Vol. I,* and most recordings by L. Armstrong, The Dukes of Dixieland, Pete Fountain, Sidney Bechet, Jimmy McPartland, Jelly Roll Morton, Kid Ory, and Al Hirt.

IMITATIVE . . . NONIMITATIVE

A simple kind of counterpoint consists in a single melody line that is repeated in overlapping imitations, of which a round is an obvious example. A melody, say, "Row, Row, Row Your Boat," begins and is then repeated, or imitated, by other voices in an overlapped texture (Example 6.7). A round is purely imitative counterpoint, each voice identical yet balancing off with a different part of the melody.

Imitative counterpoint can be much more complex than this, however. The imitation need not be exact: Sometimes only a part of a melody is imitated, and sometimes there are two or more melodies busily imitating various parts of each other. One particular procedure for creating a complex imitative texture, the *fugue,* became very popular during the seventeenth century and has been used by composers ever since. We shall take a look at this procedure in Chapter 8. Our concern now (LISTENING 6.10) is to call attention to how a contrapuntal texture can be built by imitating what has happened before.

Imitation helps the listener hear how overlapped melodies are related. The challenges become greater when the overlapped melodies are quite

Example 6.7 • A round: (a) melody alone; (b) in counterpoint.

Row, row . . . gently down. . . . Merrily, merrily, . . . , life is but. . . .

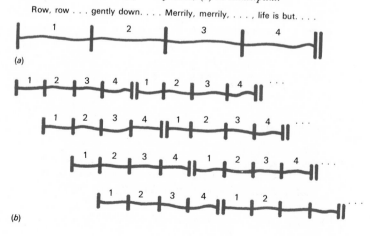

LISTENING 6.12

Blending colors in the following pieces give a homogenized sound to the counterpoint:

G. P. DA PALESTRINA   *Missa Papae Marcelli:* Benedictus.

G. GABRIELI   *Canzon septimi toni.*

A. BERG   *Lyric Suite, Andante amoroso.*

B. BARTÓK   ○● *Music for String Instruments, Percussion, and Celesta,* I: beginning.

The contrasting colors in the following produce a rich, varied effect:

W. A. MOZART   ○ Requiem in d, K. 626, I: Kyrie (voices, strings, and winds).

J. S. BACH   ○ Cantata 80, *Ein feste Burg ist unser Gott,* I. Voices, strings, and high brass.

L. VAN BEETHOVEN   ○ Symphony 3 in E♭, op. 55, II: fugue section (measures 114–150); strings, woodwinds, brass, and percussion.

G. PUCCINI   *La Bohème,* Act III: beginning with "Addio, dolce sveglia alla mattina," sung by Mimi and Rodolfo (rich contrasts among the voices and orchestral instruments).

Dixieland always uses contrasting colors, such as clarinet, trumpet, and trombone.

LISTENING 6.13

GENERALLY THIN POLYPHONY

FRANCESCO LANDINI   ○ "Chi più le vuol sapere."

W. A. MOZART   ○ Requiem in d, K. 626, I. This starts thin and soon builds to a thick sound.

I. STRAVINSKY   *Symphony of Psalms,* II: beginning; ○ *The Rite of Spring:* beginning.

GENERALLY THICK POLYPHONY

J. S. BACH   ○ Cantata 80, *Ein feste Burg ist unser Gott,* I.

G. GABRIELI   *Canzon septimi toni.*

G. F. HANDEL   ○● *Messiah:* "Hallelujah" chorus.

W. SCHUMAN   Symphony 3 (1941), ○ I, ○● II. The Passacaglia keeps adding voices until the thinness has been transformed into extreme thickness. The first and second variations are thick, the

(continued on page 98)

different from one another, or "nonimitative." Of course, the melodies musically fit each other as they unfold, but at the same time they are distinct. The manners in which they blend, clash, merge, separate, go in the same direction or different directions all add to the interest of the musical texture as it develops (LISTENING 6.11). A very simple kind of nonimitative counterpoint occurs when two different but complementary songs are sung together, such as "Ten Little Indians" with "Skip to My Lou," "When the Saints Go Marching In" with "Goodnight, Ladies," or "Humoresque" with "Old Folks at Home." At the other extreme is some contemporary atonal music, which overlaps melody fragments in a variety of complex ways.

COLORS: BLENDING . . . CONTRASTING

In much polyphonic music the several strands of melody are produced by the same or similar types of voices or instruments. For example, four violins might be used for a four-part polyphonic piece or four soprano voices. Or perhaps the melodies will be produced by the same family of instruments, such as two violins, a viola, and a cello or two sopranos and two altos. In these cases the melodies will blend together in sound because the quality of each sound is much like the others. It is as if a weaver used four strands of yarn of the same color or of closely matched shadings of the same color. The strands will blend together in a unified, merged fabric.

If, however, the same four melodies played by four violins were played by a flute, a trumpet, a violin, and a guitar, the contrasting tone colors will produce quite another effect. This is like the weaver's using alternating strands of blue, orange, green, and white yarn. The weave may be the same, but the result is very different. Composers carefully pick and choose blending and contrasting colors to give the unfolding texture just the desired amount of sameness and difference (LISTENING 6.12).

DENSITY: THICK . . . THIN

Some polyphonic music is made of just a few strands of melody sounded by only a few instruments or voices. This gives a thin, transparent sound like an open-weave fabric for some curtains or clothing. You can see through the fabric or "hear through" the music.

third is thinner, getting thicker, and the fourth is thick, leading to the Fugue, which is generally quite thick with a few dramatic shifts to thin.

Mixed texture

LISTENING 6.14

Shifts from homophonic sections to polyphonic sections can be heard in the following:

G. F. HANDEL   ○● *Messiah:* "Hallelujah" chorus.

L. VAN BEETHOVEN   ○ Symphony 3 in E♭, op. 55, II.

J. BRAHMS   ○● Symphony 2 in D, op. 73, II.

W. SCHUMAN   ○● Symphony 3 (1941), III: Chorale.

I. STRAVINSKY   ○● *Symphony of Psalms,* III.

G. SHEARING   "Yesterdays," from *The Capitol History of Jazz, Vol. 4.*

Two or more melodies with harmonic accompaniment are found in the following:

G. DE MACHAUT   Benedictus (*The History of Music in Sound,* vol. III).

P. I. TCHAIKOVSKY   ○● Symphony 5 in e, op. 64, II.

I. STRAVINSKY   ○ *The Rite of Spring:* "Ritual Performance of the Ancestors."

Practically all Dixieland has several melody lines plus piano and bass playing a harmonic accompaniment.

At the other extreme is the piling up of many melodies sounded by many instruments or voices. Here the effect is like a heavy rug or tapestry, with a dense, weighty feeling. Thin and thick densities give composers means for creating varied expressive values as useful in polyphonic texture as in homophonic texture (LISTENING 6.13).

HOMOPHONIC . . . POLYPHONIC

It is important to realize that a great deal of music is neither all homophonic nor all polyphonic. The most obvious kind of mixture of the two can be found in a piece that has separate homophonic sections and polyphonic sections. The music simply shifts from one texture to another as it goes along. This is extremely common, and the listener must be prepared to shift gears as the texture shifts so that the proper kind of concentration can take place (LISTENING 6.14).

Another kind of mixed texture is one in which harmony and counterpoint exist at the same time. This happens when there are two or more melodies going along in counterpoint while harmonies are being sounded. A simple example would be two different songs sung together, say, "When the Saints Go Marching In" and "Goodnight, Ladies," while a piano plays chords as accompaniment, as diagramed in Example 6.8.

Another way counterpoint and harmony can exist at the same time is for several melodies to be so constructed that each note forms a chord with the notes sounding together in the other melodies. This is

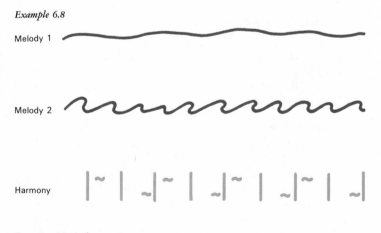

Example 6.8

Melody 1

Melody 2

Harmony

LISTENING 6.15

These compositions exhibit hymnlike (chorale) texture:

J. S. BACH   ○ Cantata 80, *Ein feste Burg ist unser Gott,* VIII. Also other last movements of German cantatas.

W. A. MOZART   Requiem in d, K. 626, VIII (voices), IX: first section (voices).

L. VAN BEETHOVEN   ○ Concerto for Violin and Orchestra in D, op. 61, II: beginning. The solo violin decorates the hymn texture in the orchestra.

W. SCHUMAN   ○● Symphony 3 (1941), III: Chorale, several sections.

LISTENING 6.16

Here are examples of traditional music with complex blendings of textures:

I. STRAVINSKY   *Petrushka;* ○ *The Rite of Spring; The Firebird.*

GUSTAV MAHLER   Symphony 2 in c.

C. DEBUSSY   *La Mer.*

D. SHOSTAKOVICH   Symphony 5, op. 47.

L. BERNSTEIN   Symphony 3.

A. COPLAND   Symphony 3.

B. BARTÓK   *Concerto for Orchestra.*

Nontraditional musical textures:

K. PENDERECKI   ○● *Passion According to St. Luke; Three Poems of Henri Michaux.*

K. STOCKHAUSEN   *Zeitmasse; Zyklus; Kontakte; Mikrophonie I.*

L. BERIO   *Visage;* ○ *Omaggio a Joyce.*

I. MIMAROGLU   *Agony.*

OLIVIER MESSIAEN   *Chronochromie.*

Y. XENAKIS   ○● *Pithoprakta.*

D. ERB   ○● *Reconnaissance.*

the way most hymns (or chorales) are constructed. Each of the four parts can be thought of as a separate melody, but at every moment chords are heard as the result of the four melodies together. A diagram might look like Example 6.9, where each dot is a note of the melody.

This particular blend of counterpoint and harmony was developed to a high degree in the music of J. S. Bach (1685–1750) and other composers of his time. It has been used only occasionally since then, perhaps because just about any music of this texture tends to sound like a hymn (LISTENING 6.15).

Our exploration of harmony and counterpoint has concentrated on music that can be easily recognized as one or the other or a particular blend of the two. We must now acknowledge that much music cannot be classified so neatly, for some music is so complex in texture, mixing bits and pieces of harmony and counterpoint in a jumble of overlapping and shifting organizations, that a simple description becomes impossible. Such music is certainly of a mixed texture, sometimes including monophonic texture to widen the possibilities further, but there is no simple way to separate the homophonic from the polyphonic components.

Finally, much contemporary music is made of sounds that cannot be identified as melody or harmony, so that the words "homophonic" or

Example 6.9

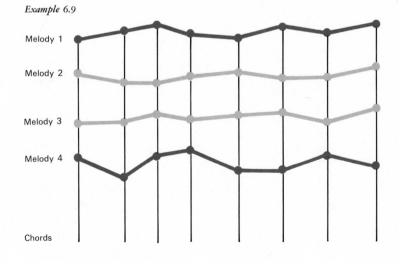

"polyphonic" or "counterpoint" do not apply in their traditional meanings. Such music is not without texture, but we have no common terms to describe it. Harmony, counterpoint, monophonic, homophonic, polyphonic—all are useful tool words with which to grasp traditional musical practices; but they may no longer serve in the new world of recent musical departures. We must listen to new music with as much concentration and involvement as we do to the older, or more traditional, but we must be ready to experience sound organizations so different that the comfortable labels of the past cannot easily be applied (LISTENING 6.16).

Harmony and counterpoint concluded

Rhythm, melody, harmony, counterpoint: each is an endless source of musical material, and each depends on, and enhances, the others. None could exist, however, without sound itself. Underneath each element and all of them together is this single factor, on which all music depends. It is time now to look at the expressiveness of tone color, of sound itself.

Chapter 7 ° The expressiveness of tone color

Quality (*kind of sound*)

TONE COLOR (SOUNDS OF MUSIC)

QUALITY (KIND OF SOUND)

MEDIUM

The voice (and groups of voices). The instruments (and groups of instruments). Other sounds of music.

DYNAMICS (AMOUNT OF SOUND)

Soft . . . loud; *crescendo, decrescendo;* accents.

IN CHAPTER 3 WE DISCUSSED THE SENSUOUS RESPONSE TO MUSIC AND THE peculiar power of sound to move people. Some music contains little else but sound for the sake of sound; other music uses the expressiveness of sound as one way among others (rhythm, melody, harmony, counterpoint, form) to create an interesting sequence of events. Our investigation of rhythm, melody, harmony, and counterpoint has shown how each contributes to a total thing, a piece of music. We now turn to sound, the medium of music: its quality and usage, its amount. In music, as in all art, the medium is an essential part of the message. The marginal outline, as in previous chapters, will guide our study of musical tone color.

The term "tone color" is inaccurate, of course, since tones have no visual properties. Borrowed from the art of painting, color in music refers to the distinctive quality of different sounds. The ability to distinguish among different sounds is so common as to be accepted unthinkingly: For example, everyone with normal ears and brain can immediately tell the difference between a telephone's ringing and a car engine's starting, for if telephones and cars are part of his life, he has learned to associate the correct sound with each. But even the most common sounds can be highly complex, requiring special training if their subtleties are to be grasped. The telephone technician can detect the slight difference in the quality of a ring that immediately indicates a problem in the equipment. The trained automobile mechanic is so sensitive to the sound of a starting motor that the least bit of variation will be perceived clearly. Such refinements escape most of us because our level of sensitivity to these sounds is not high.

Imagine, then, the sensitivity to sound required by a successful composer. Sound is the stuff with which he works—sound infinitely various, subtle, transient, and intangible. From the vast universe of possible sounds he must select those which give the right expressive values to his ideas, as the slightest change in the sound he chooses will immediately change the effect of his music. Just as a painter adds a dab of yellow to brown, a drop of orange to red, or a bit of white and blue to get the precise shade that is right, a composer adds and mixes and contrasts and blends sounds to achieve the tone color that will make his music vital and alive.

LISTENING 7.1

In the following pieces compare the effect of the same music in the various different tone-color settings:

J. S. BACH   Toccata and Fugue in d, S. 565. Versions for organ and for orchestra. Cantata 147, *Herz und Mund:* "Jesu, Joy of Man's Desiring." Versions for chorus and orchestra, guitar, organ, piano, solo voice, and Moog Synthesizer.

The Moog Synthesizer, an elaborate set of electronic sound-producing equipment, has been used to reproduce some baroque music. Compare the machine-produced tone colors in *Switched-on Bach* (Columbia record MS-7194) and *The Well-tempered Synthesizer* (Columbia record MS-7286) with performances on traditional instruments. Some Moog-produced rock can be heard on *Switched-on Rock* (Columbia record CS-9921).

Many piano pieces by F. F. CHOPIN have been arranged for orchestra. It is instructive to compare the piano original with its orchestral version and to compare several orchestral versions of the same piece.

C. DEBUSSY   *The Afternoon of a Faun.* Versions for ○● orchestra, piano, and two pianos. "Claire de lune." Versions for orchestra, guitar, piano, organ, harp, and concert band.

M. RAVEL   "Pavane pour une infante défunte." Versions for orchestra, guitar, flute ensemble, piano, and clarinet choir.

Before the baroque era (*ca.* 1600–*ca.* 1750) composers seldom thought in terms of specific tone-color choices for their music. They more commonly wrote a piece for, say, four parts, leaving to convenience the instruments or voices to perform the parts. As time went on, however, more and more attention began to be paid to the specifics of each tone color so that choices became more conscious and careful. From the end of the baroque to the present the choice of tone color has been a major responsibility of a composer although some interesting attempts are being made by modern composers to leave tone-color choices to others, as was the practice long ago. More comments about this matter will be made in Part 3 when we explore the particulars of tone color in each historical period.

A performer too must be extremely sensitive to the expressiveness of sound. As he imagines the effect of the music he is performing, he controls all the subtleties of its sound in order to have every bit serve the expressiveness of the music. He may be playing a violin, which means that the tone color he can produce is a particular one. But within that color is an enormous range of possibilities over which he exerts complete control: a slight edge to the sound here, a bit of heaviness there, a touch of brightness at this point and that—all add up to a performance with its own special quality. A first-rate performer is master of every slight nuance of sound his instrument is capable of making.

The conductor shares the sensitivity to sound required for successful musicianship. The orchestra conductor, for example, has before him a vast array of possible sounds: The composer has stipulated which sounds are to be made when, so that the broad outlines of tone color have been drawn; the performers make the actual sounds, adding their own imaginations to that of the composer. The conductor must now mold all the parts into a unified whole. He senses that more sound is needed from the cellos here, a bit more from the oboe there, a less cutting sound from the brass in this spot, a warmer sound from the violins in another. He shapes and molds and blends until the mix is just right—the music has the quality of sound that seems satisfying.

The listener also has some responsibilities. Just as sensitivity to rhythm, melody, harmony, and counterpoint can be developed, so can sensitivity to the subtleties of tone color. It is not enough to settle for the obvious, for beyond that level are possibilities of perception and reaction that can add a world of pleasure to every person's musical experience.

Before we explore each of the major tone producers (each medium), we can get an overall sense of the importance of tone color by attending to some compositions that have been performed in different mediums (LISTENING 7.1). In these cases the musical events remain essentially the same, but the medium changes, as if a painting were kept exactly the same except for the colors—one version in blues and yellows or another in browns and oranges. The expressiveness of each musical tone color is unique, just as is a particular color used in a painting. Concentrating on the medium itself will help you focus attention on the coloristic element of music in the remainder of this chapter.

THE VOICE

As a natural sound producer, the human voice is the most widely used, and no doubt the oldest, medium of music. It is a rare person who has never made music with his voice. Paradoxically, the closeness of the voice to natural human functions can limit it as a musical instrument. Sheer emotional self-expression often depends on the use of the voice; but self-expression is not *musical* expression. The difficulty in using such an integral part of the body as a means of producing music is to balance the self-expression aspect with the musical aspect. No vocal training is needed to express emotion with the voice, as does a baby when he cries. To transform voice sounds into musical expressiveness, however, requires the transformation of a natural function into an instrument of music. This is done to some extent by anyone who sings a song; but to raise the level of singing to the point where the voice becomes a musical instrument of sophistication, subtlety, and tonal beauty requires long and serious study. The perfect outcome, seldom achieved, is a powerfully expressive blending of the human and the musical, each reinforcing and refining the other.

Voices fall naturally into high, medium, and low ranges for both women and men. From high to low the major voice ranges for women are traditionally named "soprano," "mezzosoprano," and "contralto" (or "alto"); and for men, "tenor," "baritone," and "bass." Some male singers have a range between baritone and bass and so are called "bass-baritones." A very high male voice, comparable to contralto, is called "countertenor."

In addition to being classified by range, singers (especially in opera)

Medium

LISTENING 7.2

Most of the great singers of our time have recorded collections of pieces in their repertory. Because we are concentrating on tone color as such, we shall find it helpful to listen to examples by voice types, comparing one type with another and comparing different singers of the same type. A convenient way to do this is to use the Schwann *Artist Issue,* a catalogue of recordings published each year. Under the category "Vocalists" is a list of recordings by various singers, each labeled by voice type. Listen to available recordings by several sopranos, mezzosopranos, and so on, noting the similarities and differences in their tonal qualities.

LISTENING 7.3

The distinction between jazz and popular music is often artificial. It continues to be used, however, even though it produces some inevitable overlaps. The monthly Schwann record catalogue, for example, has separate sections for jazz and current pop. Choose some singers in each category, concentrating on their use of the voice in a blend of the musical and the personal.

LISTENING 7.4

The following are only a few examples from the vast literature of major vocal types. Solos, arias, duets, trios, and quartets are found in most of the larger works.

SONG CYCLES

L. VAN BEETHOVEN   *An die ferne Geliebte,* op. 98.

F. P. SCHUBERT   o *Die schöne Müllerin,* op. 25; *Die Winterreise,* op. 89.

ROBERT SCHUMANN   *Frauenliebe und -leben,* op. 42; *Dichterliebe,* op. 48.

G. MAHLER   *Kindertotenlieder.*

A. SCHOENBERG   o● *Pierrot lunaire,* op. 21.

R. VAUGHAN WILLIAMS   *On Wenlock Edge.*

NED ROREM   *Poems of Love and the Rain.*

MADRIGALS

C. GESUALDO   Madrigals.

HEINRICH SCHUTZ   Italian madrigals.

WILLIAM BYRD   Madrigals.

ORLANDO DI LASSO   Madrigals.

JOHN DOWLAND   Songs and madrigals.

C. MONTEVERDI   Madrigals.

N. ROREM   *Four Madrigals.*

CANTATAS AND SIMILAR WORKS

J. S. BACH   Cantatas 4, o● 80, 106, 212.

G. P. TELEMANN   Cantatas.

I. STRAVINSKY   Cantata.

ARTHUR HONEGGER   *Christmas Cantata.*

are classified by the particular character, or quality, of their voice. The dramatic soprano is a specialist in heavy, powerful roles that require a full tone quality. The coloratura soprano has great flexibility and agility in the very high range. The lyric soprano has a light, smooth quality, with concentration on the beauty of tone itself. The lyric tenor is comparable to the lyric soprano, with light, lovely vocal quality (Irish tenors are usually lyric tenors). The tenor robusto has power to spare and specializes in using it. The dramatic tenor, or *Heldentenor* (heroic tenor), has a big voice of heavy quality despite its high range. The basso cantante specializes in lyrical, smooth use of the voice. The basso profundo has the deepest voice of all, with great power and weight. These voice classifications (LISTENING 7.2) may be summarized as follows:

Female:
  Soprano (lyric, coloratura, dramatic)
  Mezzosoprano
  Contralto (alto)
Male:
  Countertenor
  Tenor (lyric, robusto, dramatic)
  Baritone
  Bass-baritone
  Bass (cantante, profundo)

THE VOICE IN JAZZ AND POP   For concert music a voice must be so highly cultivated that it can be distinguished as a particular type and even subtype. This is not the case in jazz or popular music, where a free-wheeling, unstructured approach to singing exists. Here the only distinction needed is that between male voice and female voice, and even this is not an especially meaningful classification. What matters most about the voice in jazz and pop is not its type or beauty of tone or particular specialized use but the personal character it adds to the expressiveness of the music. Concert vocalists must also have their individual qualities, of course, but in jazz and pop the voice personality is of primary importance. There is simply no point in comparing anyone else with Louis Armstrong, for example, or Ella Fitzgerald or Joan Baez or Johnny Cash.

It is paradoxical, then, that in jazz the voice is used almost entirely

MASSES

JACOB OBRECHT   Mass (*Sub tuum praesidium*).

J. DES PRÉS   *Missa pange lingua.*

G. P. DA PALESTRINA   o *Missa Papae Marcelli; Missa sine nomine.*

J. S. BACH   Mass in b, S. 232.

F. J. HAYDN   Mass in C (*Paukenmesse*); Mass in d (*Nelson*).

W. A. MOZART   Mass in C, K. 317 (*Coronation*); o● Requiem in d, K. 626.

L. VAN BEETHOVEN   Mass in C, op. 86; *Missa Solemnis* in D, op. 123.

H. BERLIOZ   Requiem, op. 5.

J. BRAHMS   o● *A German Requiem*, op. 45.

GABRIEL URBAIN FAURÉ   Requiem Mass, op. 48.

B. BRITTEN   *War Requiem*, op. 66.

I. STRAVINSKY   *Mass.*

ORATORIOS

GIACOMO CARISSIMI   *Balthazar; Jephte.*

J. S. BACH   *Christmas Oratorio*, S. 248; *Easter Oratorio*, S. 249.

G. F. HANDEL   *Israel in Egypt; Judas Maccabaeus;* o● *Messiah; Samson; Solomon.*

F. J. HAYDN   *The Creation; The Seasons.*

H. BERLIOZ   *L'Enfance du Christ*, op. 25.

FELIX MENDELSSOHN   *Elijah*, op. 70; *St. Paul*, op. 36.

D. BRUBECK   *Light in the Wilderness.*

A. HONEGGER   *King David.*

I. STRAVINSKY   *Oedipus Rex.*

WILLIAM TURNER WALTON   *Belshazzar's Feast.*

Miscellaneous choral works with light accompaniment or no accompaniment (a cappella) are:

JOHN DUNSTABLE   Sacred and secular music for four voices.

J. DES PRÉS   Motets.

O. DI LASSO   Motets; "Echo Song."

J. S. BACH   Six motets.

H. PURCELL   *Te Deum.*

J. BRAHMS   Motets, opp. 29, 74, 110; "Liebeslieder" waltzes, opp. 52, 65; *Marienlieder*, op. 22.

B. BRITTEN   *Ceremony of Carols.*

LUKAS FOSS   *Behold I Build a House.*

C. IVES   *Psalms* 14, 25, 54, 135.

A. SCHOENBERG   *Six Pieces for Men's Chorus*, op. 35.

A few important operas from each historical period are:

(*continued on page 106*)

as another instrument rather than retaining its function as a means of communicating emotion. At the same time that the singer's personality pervades his music, his voice becomes an instrument serving the musical ideas. It is this tension between the personal and the musical, resolved by the skillful jazz singer whose personality and musicianship become merged, that gives jazz singing its peculiarly powerful character. The personality of Armstrong, for example, shines through every note he sings. Yet his voice is in actuality another dimension of his trumpet playing, and his trumpet playing is another dimension of his voice. In good jazz, singing becomes "instrumental," and instrument playing becomes "vocal". This is true in concert music as well but is perhaps more clearly displayed in jazz.

In pop the voice usually retains even more of the singer's personality than it does in jazz, and the concern with personal expression can easily overbalance the concern with musical expression. When a pop singer succeeds in transforming his voice into an instrument of musical expressiveness, the result can be music of lasting value (LISTENING 7.3).

GROUPS OF VOICES   The use of voices to make music together is probably as old as human society, for both psychologically and musically there are great benefits in group singing. The shared experience can be extremely fulfilling while the musical results can be deeply significant. From two people casually humming a tune to the thunder of a massed chorus singing a masterwork, groups of voices exist in every possible combination and at every possible musical level.

The most common groupings are the duet (two voices), trio (three), and quartet (four). The vocal quartet in concert music usually consists of soprano, alto, tenor, and bass although any combination can be found if one looks hard enough. The words "choir" and "chorus" refer to a larger group of singers, the distinction being that a choir sings church music and a chorus sings secular music. (Sometimes the word "chorale" is meant to be a synonym for either a choir or a chorus; properly, however, a chorale is a hymn tune.) The adjective "choral" pertains to either choir or chorus. The term "a cappella" means without accompaniment and refers to choral music for voice only (LISTENING 7.4).

Some kinds of music written for voices are shown in the following list:

Song (German, *Lied;* French, *chanson*): a short piece for a single (solo) voice, usually with instrumental accompaniment.

BAROQUE

PIETRO FRANCESCO CAVALLI *L'Ormindo.*

PIETRO ANTONIO CESTI *Orontea.*

G. F. HANDEL *Julius Caesar; Alcina.*

C. MONTEVERDI ○● *Orfeo; The Coronation of Poppaea.*

H. PURCELL *Dido and Aeneas.*

JEAN-BAPTISTE LULLY *Alceste.*

CLASSIC

CHRISTOPH WILLIBALD GLUCK *Orfeo; Alceste.*

W. A. MOZART *Così fan tutte,* K. 588; ○● *Don Giovanni,* K. 527; *Die Zauberflöte (The Magic Flute),* K. 620; *Le Nozze di Figaro (The Marriage of Figaro),* K. 492.

L. VAN BEETHOVEN *Fidelio,* op. 72.

ROMANTIC

GEORGES BIZET *Carmen.*

GAETANO DONIZETTI *Lucia di Lammermoor.*

JULES EMILE FRÉDÉRIC MASSENET *Manon.*

G. PUCCINI ○● *La Bohème; Madame Butterfly; Tosca.*

GIOACCHINO ANTONIO ROSSINI *Barber of Seville.*

GIUSEPPE VERDI *Aida; Otello; Rigoletto; La Traviata; Il Trovatore.*

R. WAGNER *The Flying Dutchman; Lohengrin; Tannhäuser; The Ring of the Nibelungs (includes The Rhine Gold; The Valkyrie; Siegfried; Twilight of the Gods);* ○● *Tristan und Isolde; The Mastersingers of Nuremberg; Parsifal.*

TWENTIETH CENTURY

S. BARBER *Vanessa.*

A. BERG *Lulu; Wozzeck.*

B. BRITTEN *Peter Grimes; The Turn of the Screw.*

GIAN CARLO MENOTTI *The Medium; Amahl and the Night Visitors.*

FRANCIS POULENC *Dialogue of the Carmelites.*

A. SCHOENBERG *Moses und Aron.*

I. STRAVINSKY *Mavra; The Rake's Progress.*

Some large choral-instrumental works of a varied nature are:

G. P. DA PALESTRINA *Magnificat.*

H. SCHÜTZ *Seven Last Words.*

J. S. BACH *St. Matthew Passion,* S. 244; *St. John Passion,* S. 245; *Magnificat in D,* S. 243.

L. VAN BEETHOVEN *Symphony 9 in d,* op. 125.

B. BRITTEN *Festival Te Deum; Rejoice in the Lamb.*

Aria: a long, elaborate song ("air"), used especially in operas.

Song cycle: a group of related songs.

Madrigal: a short poem set to music for a small group of voices. Most madrigals were written from about 1250 to 1750.

Cantata: music for the voice with instrumental accompaniment, in several movements varying among solos, duets, choruses, and the like. The text can be sacred or secular. Many cantatas were composed from about 1600 to 1750.

Mass: the music sung for the important service of the Catholic Church.

Oratorio: a large dramatic work for voices and instruments in varied movements ranging from solos to full choruses. The text of most oratorios is religious or contemplative in character. An oratorio is usually performed in concert version, without the costumes, scenery, or dramatic action found in opera.

Opera: a drama in which vocal and instrumental music play a major part. Operas use all the trappings of theater (costumes, stage sets, lighting) and many of the musical forms, ranging from purely instrumental pieces (*overture*) through vocal solos, duets, trios, quartets, and choruses. Sometimes the story line is spoken, and sometimes it is sung in a kind of speech singing (*recitative*). Offshoots and variants of opera include musical comedies, operettas, comic operas, and light operas, each using elements of opera to suit particular purposes.

THE INSTRUMENTS

Musical instruments are devices for making sounds. It would be impossible even to estimate how many such devices have been used to make music over the years. From the simplest of natural materials, such as a hollow log, to an ingenious mechanism, such as a grand piano, men have searched constantly for ways to add to the repertory of sounds that could be put to musical uses. As in the history of other kinds of devices, musical instruments have developed from the primitive to the sophisticated; many older types continue to exist along with new inventions although many others have been dropped along the way. A kind of natural selection has taken place, in which instruments of particular usefulness have continued to survive and to be improved upon while others have faded out of sight after a longer or shorter period of life. Your awareness of the rich realm of instrumental tone color should

Figure 7.1 • Double bass, violin, viola, and cello.

help you share more of the enjoyment to be found in it. Instruments are not just means; they are also ends, in the sense that each tone color has its own, unique expressive values; each *feels* to us in its distinctive way. A melody played by a particular instrument has one feeling; but when the same melody is repeated by a different instrument, the feel of that melody is quite different. This is no small matter. It is one of the fundamental ways music presents sound conditions that can cause feeling. To hear a melody as the same without perceiving the difference made by its different tone color is to miss a basic component of music's expressiveness.

In this part of the book we shall discuss the major families of traditional instruments, those presently used which have a rather long history. Then we shall take a brief look at new musical instruments invented during our own century. The four families of traditional instruments are (1) strings, (2) woodwinds, (3) brasses, and (4) percussion. To this we add (5) keyboard instruments.

1. STRINGS   String instruments are built on a simple principle: When a string is stretched and then made to vibrate, a tone will be produced. Attach some strings to an amplifying device, such as a wooden box, and you have a primitive violin. With refinements in the shape of the amplifying body, the materials used, the arrangement by which the fingers can control the length of the strings to produce different pitches, and the mechanism for making the strings vibrate, the modern violin emerges. The simplicity of the principle remains while the refinements create a tone-producing mechanism of enormous versatility.

Chief members of this family (Figure 7.1) are the violin, viola, violoncello (cello), and bass viol (bass, double bass, string bass, contrabass, bass fiddle). Each is essentially the same instrument except for the length of the strings and the correspondingly larger size of the body (technical differences among them need not concern us here). Each produces vibrations either by a plucking of the strings (*pizzicato*) or by the drawing of a bow across them, the friction between the hair of the bow and the string setting the string into continuous motion and therefore sustaining a tone for as long as the bow is drawn.

The lowest pitch of the string bass through the cello and the viola to the highest pitch of the violin represents an enormous range in essentially the same tone color. This in itself makes the violin family an extremely useful medium, of which the importance to music is en-

LISTENING 7.5

The musical literature for violin, viola, and cello is enormous. (The string bass does not lend itself well to solo performance; its solo literature is quite limited.) Following is a representative list of important solo works for each string instrument. When a solo instrument is accompanied by a piano or other keyboard instrument, the piece is commonly a sonata; when the accompaniment is an orchestra, the piece is a concerto.

Note that, for all the instruments to be discussed in this chapter, artist-performers have recorded collections of pieces for which the record information can be found under the name of the instrument in the latest Schwann *Artist Issue* catalogue. Compare performances of the same piece by several different artists, and observe the different musical results produced by each artist's characteristic tone quality and interpretation.

VIOLIN

J. S. BACH   Three sonatas and three partitas for unaccompanied violin; two concertos for violin and orchestra; six sonatas for violin and harpsichord.

ARCANGELO CORELLI   Twelve sonatas for violin and continuo.

A. VIVALDI   Numerous concertos for violin and orchestra, including o *Le quattro stagione* (*The Four Seasons*); Sonata for Violin and Continuo in A, op. 2, no. 2.

F. J. HAYDN   Eight sonatas for violin and keyboard; Concerto for Violin and Orchestra in B♭.

W. A. MOZART   Sonatas for Violin and Piano in C, e, K. 296, 304; seven concertos for violin and orchestra.

L. VAN BEETHOVEN   o Concerto for Violin and Orchestra in D, op. 61; ten o● sonatas for violin and piano.

F. P. SCHUBERT   Sonata for Violin and Piano in A, op. 162.

P. I. TCHAIKOVSKY   Concerto for Violin and Orchestra in D, op. 35.

B. BARTÓK   Sonata for Violin Solo; Concerto for Violin and Orchestra; two sonatas for violin and piano.

M. RAVEL   Sonata for Violin and Piano.

A. SCHOENBERG   Concerto for Violin and Orchestra, op. 36.

A. BERG   Concerto for Violin and Orchestra.

A. COPLAND   Sonata for Violin and Piano.

S. PROKOFIEV   Two concertos for violin and orchestra.

VIOLA

G. F. HANDEL   Three concertos for viola and orchestra.

hanced by the great variety of expressive effects available through special bowing and fingering techniques, the wide range of loudness and softness the strings can produce, their extreme agility in producing fast notes and their capacity to sustain very long notes, and—not least—their characteristic tonal quality, which can be among the most attractive sounds available to the human ear, as LISTENING 7.5 demonstrates.

Strings in groups   Although a variety of small groups of string instruments (trios, quintets, and so on) exists, the most important is the string quartet, which is made up of two violins, a viola, and a cello. Many regard this grouping as the most important small instrumental ensemble (chamber group); certainly the music composed for it constitutes one of the most significant parts of musical literature. From the late eighteenth century, when Mozart and Haydn composed many pieces for this combination, to the present day, major composers have created some of their most profound music for string quartet. Its consistency of tone color from instrument to instrument, its wide range from the low cello to the high violin, the broad range of expressive devices these instruments can handle, their extreme technical agility, and the loveliness of their characteristic sound quality have combined to make the string quartet the most popular of chamber groups. Some persons will seldom bother to listen to any other group, and all can find in the string-quartet literature an abundant source of musical enjoyment (LISTENING 7.6).

More than any other family of instruments, the violin family is capable of producing excellent musical results in a massed group. Many musical instruments have been used in large numbers, but none has become so basic to instrumental music as the large string ensemble. The symphony orchestra is normally a large string group supplemented by winds and percussion; and much music exists for string orchestra, which is basically the string section of a normal orchestra used alone. A typical string orchestra will contain some thirty to thirty-five violins (divided into two parts called first and second violins), about a dozen violas and as many cellos, and eight to ten string basses. This number produces a sound that is not just louder or bigger than a group containing only one of each instrument but is unique in richness of color. The sound of a large string ensemble is generally accepted to be among the most attractive in the realm of music (LISTENING 7.6).

Other string instruments   A great many miscellaneous instruments use vibrating strings as the basis for sound production. The most impor-

G. P. TELEMANN   Concerto for Viola and Orchestra in G.

A. VIVALDI   Concerto for Viola d'Amore and Orchestra in d, F. II, no. 2.

CARL PHILIPP STAMITZ   Two concertos for viola and orchestra.

IVAN EVASTAFIEVICH KHANDOSHKIN   Concerto for Viola and Orchestra.

W. A. MOZART   *Sinfonia concertante* for Violin, Viola, and Orchestra in E♭, K. 364.

J. BRAHMS   Two songs for alto, viola, and piano; Sonatas for Clarinet (Viola) and Piano in f, E♭, op. 120, nos. 1, 2.

NICCOLO PAGANINI   *Terzetto concertante* for Viola, Guitar, and Cello in D, op. 68.

B. BARTOK   Concerto for Viola and Orchestra.

D. MILHAUD   Concerto for Viola and Orchestra.

P. HINDEMITH   Two sonatas for viola and piano; Sonata for Viola Solo, op. 25, no. 1.

CELLO

A. VIVALDI   Concerto for Cello and Orchestra in G, F. III, no. 12.

J. S. BACH   Six unaccompanied-cello suites.

F. J. HAYDN   Concerto for Cello and Orchestra in C.

LUIGI BOCCHERINI   Concerto for Cello and Orchestra in B♭.

L. VAN BEETHOVEN   Sonata for Cello and Piano in g, op. 5, no. 2.

J. BRAHMS   Sonata for Cello and Piano in e, op. 38.

EDWARD WILLIAM ELGAR   Concerto for Cello and Orchestra in e, op. 85.

MAX BRUCH   *Kol Nidrei* for Cello and Orchestra, op. 47.

C. DEBUSSY   Sonata for Cello and Piano.

E. BLOCH   *Schelomo* for Cello and Orchestra.

E. CARTER   Sonata for Cello and Piano.

RICHARD ORTON   *Cycle, for 2 or 4 Players.*

STRING BASS

KARL DITTERS VON DITTERSDORF   Concerto in E for Double Bass and Orchestra.

JAN KŘTITEL VAŇHAL   Concerto in E for Double Bass and Orchestra.

SERGE KOUSSEVITZKY   Concerto for Double Bass and Orchestra.

ALEC WILDER   Sonata for String Bass and Piano.

D. ERB   *VII Miscellaneous* for Flute and Double Bass.

G. PERLE   *Monody II* for Double Bass Solo.

LISTENING 7.6

Following is a representative selection of important string-quartet music:

F. J. HAYDN   Quartet in D, op. 64, no. 5 (*Lark*); Quartet in d, op. 76, no. 2 (*Quinten*).

W. A. MOZART   Quartet in B♭, K. 458 (*Hunting*); Quartet in C, K. 465 (*Dissonant*); Quartet in F, K. 590.

L. VAN BEETHOVEN   Many performances of Beethoven's quartets exist. Sample some from the low, middle, and high opus numbers, which represent earlier and later works.

F. P. SCHUBERT   Quartet in c (*Quartettsatz*); Quartet in d (*Death and the Maiden*).

J. BRAHMS   Complete Quartets 1–3, op. 51, nos. 1, 2, op. 67.

C. DEBUSSY   Quartet in g, op. 10.

M. RAVEL   Quartet in F.

B. BARTÓK   Complete Quartets 1–6.

P. HINDEMITH   Quartet 4, op. 22.

A. SCHOENBERG   Complete Quartets 1–4, opp. 7, 10, 30, 37.

A. BERG   Quartet, op. 3; *Lyric Suite.*

A. VON WEBERN   *Five Movements,* op. 5.

D. SHOSTAKOVICH   Quartet 10, op. 118.

E. CARTER   Quartet (1951).

IRVING FINE   Quartet (1952).

Here is some music for string orchestra (large string ensemble):

A. CORELLI   *Concerto grosso* in g, op. 6, no. 8.

W. A. MOZART   ○ *Eine kleine Nachtmusik* in G, K. 525.

F. MENDELSSOHN   Eleven "Symphonies."

P. I. TCHAIKOVSKY   Serenade in C, op. 48.

ALEXANDER PORFIREVICH BORODIN   Nocturne.

B. BARTÓK   *Divertimento.*

B. BRITTEN   *Simple Symphony,* op. 4; *Variations on a Theme by Frank Bridge,* op. 10.

E. W. ELGAR   Introduction and *Allegro,* op. 47.

P. HINDEMITH   *Five Pieces.*

I. STRAVINSKY   Concerto in D.

A. SCHOENBERG   Suite in G.

S. BARBER   ○● *Adagio,* op. 11.

L. BERIO   *Fortunate Islands.*

LISTENING 7.7

Representative guitar, lute, mandolin, and harp music, old and new, may be heard in the recordings of performers listed in the Schwann *Artist Issue* catalogue under the heading "Instrumental Soloists." Jazz and popular guitarists are easily accessible on records.

Some orchestral pieces featuring the harp are:

REINHOLD MORITZOVICH GLIÈRE   Concerto for Harp and Orchestra in E♭, op. 74.

P. I. TCHAIKOVSKY   *Nutcracker* Suite, op. 71*a*.

M. RAVEL   *Introduction et Allegro; Ma Mère l'oye.*

C. DEBUSSY   *Danse sacrée et danse profane.*

H. HANSON   Serenade for Flute, Strings, Harp, and Orchestra (1945).

R. VAUGHAN WILLIAMS   Fantasia on "Greensleeves."

Figure 7.2 • Harp.

tant of these are the guitar and its relatives and the harp (LISTENING 7.7). (Instruments with keyboard mechanisms to set strings in motion will be considered separately.)

Although the acoustical principles underlying the violin family apply to the guitar family, the strings of the latter are always plucked, never bowed. When the stretched string is plucked by the finger or a pick, the resulting pitch is amplified by the wooden body or, in the electric guitar, by electronic means. The same principles apply to the banjo and ukelele. The differences among all these instruments depend on different body shapes and sizes, proportion of body to length of strings, number of strings, and material used to make the body. All have bodies with flat backs, a distinguishing characteristic of the guitar family. A similar group, the lute family, has rounded backs. Lute music (mostly from the sixteenth and seventeenth centuries) and lutes are still played by specialists, as is music for mandolin, a member of the lute family.

A good deal of composed concert music exists for guitar (and much more arranged for guitar) as does an enormous folk-music literature. Jazz has depended heavily on the guitar for both its background and its soloistic capabilities. And, of course, contemporary popular music would be unthinkable without a wide variety of guitars, usually electronically amplified.

The harp (Figure 7.2) also uses plucked strings and a body for amplification, but here the strings are perpendicular to the body rather than parallel, as in the instruments discussed so far. Modern harps have pedals attached to the base of the body that are capable of automatically changing the lengths of the strings and therefore the pitches, whereas all the other string instruments must tune each string separately. Much solo and ensemble literature for harp exists, and it is an important contributor to the special tone colors of the symphony orchestra.

2. WOODWINDS   All wind instruments use the human breath to set a column of air into motion. The woodwinds and the brasses are the two major categories, between which the differences, surprisingly, are due less to the use of wood or brass than to more fundamental principles of sound production.

Although all the older families of woodwinds were at one time made of wood, several are now almost always made of metal. A relative newcomer to this category, the saxophone, has always been made of metal. Besides producing sound by setting a column of air to vibrating

LISTENING 7.8

Some representative music for flute is:

A. VIVALDI ○● Concerto for Two Flutes and Orchestra in C, F. VI, no. 2.

CARL PHILIPP EMANUEL BACH Sonatas for flute and continuo.

J. S. BACH Seven sonatas for flute and harpsichord; Sonata for Flute Solo in a, S. 1013.

G. F. HANDEL Sonatas for flute (recorder) and continuo.

W. A. MOZART Quartets for Flute and Strings in D, G, C, A, K. 285, 285*a*, 285*b* (Anh. 171), 298; Concertos for Flute and Orchestra in C, D, K. 313 (285*c*), 314 (285*d*); Concerto for Flute, Harp, and Orchestra, K. 299 (297*c*).

J. IBERT Concerto for Flute and Orchestra.

CHARLES TOMLINSON GRIFFES *Poem* for Flute and Orchestra.

C. DEBUSSY *Syrinx* for Flute Solo.

P. HINDEMITH Sonata for Flute and Piano.

D. ERB *VII Miscellaneous for Flute and Double Bass.*

Compositions in which the piccolo can be heard include:

A. VIVALDI Concertos for Piccolo and Orchestra in C, D, a, F. VI, nos. 4, 5, 9.

P. I. TCHAIKOVSKY Symphony 4 in f, op. 36, III; *The Nutcracker* Suite, op. 71*a*: "Chinese Dance."

GABRIEL PIERNÉ *Cydalise:* "Entrance of the Little Fauns."

C. DEBUSSY *Ibéria*, I.

M. RAVEL *Mother Goose* Suite; *Daphnis et Chloé* Suite 2.

ZOLTÁN KODÁLY *Háry János* Suite, II, IV.

D. SHOSTAKOVICH Symphony 7, op. 60, I.

S. PROKOFIEV *Lieutenant Kije* Suite, op. 60.

A. SCHOENBERG *Pierrot lunaire*, op. 21: "The Dandy."

GUNTER SCHULLER *Seven Studies on Themes of Paul Klee:* "The Twittering Machine."

The alto flute is heard in:

R. VAUGHAN WILLIAMS *Job, a Masque for Dancing*, Scene IX.

I. STRAVINSKY ○ *Le Sacre du printemps*, Introduction (middle).

The recorder is heard in the following:

ALESSANDRO SCARLATTI Sonata for Recorder and Strings in F.

G. P. TELEMANN Sonatas for Recorder and Continuo; Concerto for Recorder and Strings in C.

J. S. BACH "Brandenburg" Concerto for Two Recorders, Violin, and Strings in G, S. 1049.

A. VIVALDI Concertos for Recorder and Orchestra.

JEAN BAPTISTE LOEILLET Sonatas for Recorder and Harpsichord.

G. F. HANDEL Concertos for Recorder and Strings in F, G.

(as do the brasses), the woodwinds are loosely united into a family by their method of causing pitch changes through opening and closing holes in the tube enclosing the air column: If all the holes are closed, the full length of the air column will vibrate, producing the instrument's lowest pitch; the longer the instrument, the lower will be its lowest pitch. This accounts for the difference in length among the woodwinds, from the shortest and therefore highest (the piccolo) to the longest and lowest (the contrabassoon). Thus along the length of each woodwind instrument are holes drilled through its body. When the bottom hole is opened, it has the effect of shortening the air column to that point and therefore raising the pitch, and as more holes are opened, the pitch continues to rise. Antique woodwinds depended on the number of fingers available for the number of holes they could have and were consequently limited in the number of pitches they could produce; modern instruments have elaborate mechanisms that extend the pitch range and allow for dexterity in changing pitches.

In basic sound the subgroups in the woodwind family differ much more from one another than do the strings. The major subgroups, each with its own family, are those of flutes, clarinets, oboes, bassoons, and saxophones.

Flutes Ancestors of the modern flute existed far back in human history, probably because it is easy to produce sound by blowing across the top of a tube. In modern instruments the top end of the tube is closed, and close to the end is a hole in the body across which the player blows, setting the air in the column into motion. As in all woodwinds, the fingers control mechanisms that open and close holes to produce changes of pitch. These changes can be performed extremely quickly and with great agility on the flute; the mechanisms enable it to play complex passages in addition to those with long, flowing notes.

Three flutes are in common use today: the smallest, the piccolo (Figure 7.3), produces the highest sounds of any wind instrument; next larger is the flute itself (Figure 7.3), the most widely used of the three; the alto flute (sometimes called "bass flute") is larger than the flute, producing deeper tones subtly different from the flute.

Most flutes are now made of metal although various other materials—wood or ivory—have been used in the past, and modern flutists argue about the relative merits of different metals—silver, gold, alloys. Some flutists insist on using wooden instruments still; most prefer one of the

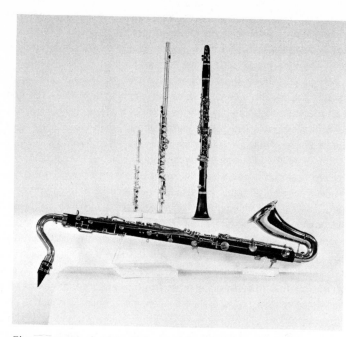

Figure 7.3 • Piccolo, flute, clarinet, and bass clarinet.

LISTENING 7.9

Some works for clarinet include:

W. A. MOZART   Concerto for Clarinet and Orchestra in A, K. 622; Quintet for Clarinet and Strings in A, K. 581.

J. BRAHMS   Sonatas for Clarinet and Piano in f, E♭, op. 120, nos. 1, 2; Quintet for Clarinet and Strings in b, op. 115.

CARL MARIA VON WEBER   Concertino for Clarinet and Orchestra in E♭, op. 26; Concertos for Clarinet and Orchestra in f, E♭, opp. 73, 74.

F. POULENC   Sonata for Clarinet and Bassoon; Sonata for Clarinet and Piano.

B. BARTÓK   *Contrasts* for Clarinet, Violin, and Piano.

CARL AUGUST NIELSEN   Concerto for Clarinet and Orchestra, op. 57.

C. DEBUSSY   *Première Rapsodie* for Clarinet and Piano (Orchestra).

available metals. The piccolo continues to be more commonly made of wood.

Cousin to the flute is the recorder. It is blown into from the end, having a whistle-type mouthpiece. Its tone is softer than that of the modern side-blown (transverse) flutes. Recorders were extremely popular until around 1750, after which they gradually faded out of use. No significant technical growth took place so that recorders made today are copies of seventeenth- or eighteenth-century instruments and are used primarily to play early music. The most common sizes today are soprano, alto, tenor, and bass.

The flute family can be heard in LISTENING 7.8.

Clarinets   A performer produces sound on the clarinet by blowing through a mouthpiece to which is attached a *single reed*, a flat piece of cane shaved to a very thin edge. The vibrating reed sets the air in the column to vibrating, and as in all woodwinds, the fingers control the mechanism by which holes are opened and closed to change pitches. Clarinets are usually made of wood, but metal and plastic compositions are often utilized today, especially for less expensive instruments.

From around the seventeenth century to the present there have been many versions of clarinetlike instruments, most of which have disappeared. At present clarinets in common use (Figure 7.3) include: small clarinet in E♭ (sopranino); clarinet in B♭ (soprano), by far the most common, and a slightly larger version pitched in A; alto clarinet in E♭, which has an upward-pointing bell (the bottom end of the instrument); bass clarinet in B♭, a larger version of the alto; and, finally, contrabass clarinet, the deepest sounding of this family (LISTENING 7.9). The entire family is often used in the concert band, where it is the dominant group of instruments.

Oboes   The very characteristic oboe sound is produced by a *double reed*, two small, thin slivers of cane tied to a metal tube that fits into the body of the instrument. The two pieces of cane leave a tiny opening at the end through which air is forced to set the canes and the air column into vibration. The delicacy of this double reed requires constant attention by the performing artist, who usually must also be an expert reed maker and adjuster. The body of professional-grade oboes is wood, to which is attached an elaborate metal key system (Figure 7.4). Some student instruments are plastic.

A. COPLAND   *Concerto* for Clarinet and Orchestra.

I. STRAVINSKY   *Three Pieces* for Clarinet Solo.

M. DAVIDOVSKY   *Synchronisms 2* for Clarinet, Violin, and Cello.

The bass clarinet is heard in the following:

R. WAGNER   *Tristan und Isolde*, Act II: "King Mark's Song."

P. I. TCHAIKOVSKY   *The Nutcracker* Suite, op. 71*a*: "Dance of the Sugar-plum Fairy."

R. STRAUSS   *Don Quixote*, op. 35, Variation III.

I. STRAVINSKY   *Petrushka*: "The Moor Dances."

MORTON GOULD   *American Salute.*

W. SCHUMAN   Symphony 3 (1941), IV: beginning.

Here are a few works for E♭ clarinet:

H. BERLIOZ   ○● *Symphonie fantastique*, op. 14, V.

R. STRAUSS   *Till Eulenspiegels lustige Streiche*, op. 28: scaffold scene; *Ein Heldenleben*, op. 40: critics' section.

M. RAVEL   *Daphnis et Chloé* Suite 2.

LISTENING 7.10

Oboe literature includes:

J. S. BACH   "Brandenburg" Concertos for Winds and Strings in F, F, S. 1046, 1047; Concerto for Violin and Oboe in c, S. 1060.

A. VIVALDI   Concertos for Oboe and Orchestra.

F. J. HAYDN   Concerto for Oboe and Orchestra in C.

W. A. MOZART   Concerto for Oboe and Orchestra in D, K. 314 (285*d*); Quartet for Oboe and Strings in F, K. 370 (368*b*).

B. BRITTEN   *Fantasy Quartet* for Oboe and Strings, op. 2.

P. HINDEMITH   Sonata for Oboe and Piano.

WALTER PISTON   Suite for Oboe and Piano.

F. POULENC   Sonata for Oboe and Piano.

Solos for English horn are heard in these pieces:

C. FRANCK   Symphony in d, II.

G. DONIZETTI   Concerto for English Horn and Orchestra in G.

JEAN SIBELIUS   *The Swan of Tuonela*, op. 22, no. 3.

A. COPLAND   *Quiet City.*

G. A. ROSSINI   *William Tell* Overture.

ANTONÍN DVOŘÁK   Symphony 5 in e, op. 95, II.

H. BERLIOZ   *Roman Carnival* Overture; *Symphonie fantastique*, op. 14, III.

The oboe is essentially a solo instrument (LISTENING 7.10). Sometimes two or three are played together, but the tone color does not lend itself to large groupings as does that of the clarinet or strings (or, to some extent, the flutes).

A larger version is the English horn (Figure 7.4), which also has a double reed (larger than that of the oboe) and a similar body. Its reed is attached to the body by means of a short curved metal pipe; its bell is pear-shaped rather than flared like the oboe or clarinet bell. The English horn is a solo instrument; even the largest orchestra or band will seldom employ more than one (LISTENING 7.10).

Bassoons   Like the oboe, the bassoon uses a double reed as the means of producing vibrations. The reed is much larger, however, suitable for the larger, longer body of the instrument. The body of the bassoon is bent back on itself, the player's breath going from the reed through a thin curved metal pipe attached to the instrument, down the wooden body, around a U curve, and upward to the end of the pipe, the entire journey being some $8\frac{1}{2}$ feet. Naturally this length results in a low sound; on the other hand the *top* register of the bassoon is way up into the range of the oboe. (See Figure 7.4.)

The contrabassoon, or double bassoon, outbasses its smaller brother in that it has a body slightly over 16 feet long, doubled back on itself four times (the end pointing downward). It provides a bedrock low range for the woodwind family.

Like the oboe, the bassoon is essentially a solo instrument although two or three are often used together in duets or trios (LISTENING 7.11). Professional instruments are almost always made of wood; some plastic instruments of high quality have been made in addition to those of student grade.

Saxophones   The most recent members of the woodwind clan, the saxophones, were invented in the early 1840s by a Brussels instrument maker, Adolphe Sax. He combined a clarinetlike mouthpiece, with its single reed, a metal body flaring gradually from the mouthpiece to the upturned bell, and a key system similar to the oboe, all of which created a hybrid instrument with a distinctive tone color capable of blending well with both woodwinds and brasses and an enormously varied capacity for nuances ranging from the most strident to the most mellow. In the hands of a skillful performer this diversity of sound can be used to create particularly intriguing expressive effects. The versatility of this

LISTENING 7.11

Bassoon literature includes:

A. VIVALDI   Concertos for Bassoon and Orchestra.

FRANÇOIS COUPERIN   Concerto for Two Bassoons in G.

JOHANN CHRISTIAN BACH   Concerto for Bassoon and Orchestra in Eb.

W. A. MOZART   Concerto for Bassoon and Orchestra in Bb, K. 191 (186e).

L. VAN BEETHOVEN   Duos for Clarinet and Bassoon in C, F, Bb, op. 147, nos. 1–3.

C. P. STAMITZ   Concerto for Bassoon and Orchestra in F.

C. M. VON WEBER   *Andante* and Rondo for Bassoon and Orchestra in c, op. 35; Concerto for Bassoon and Orchestra in F, op. 75.

G. PIERNÉ   *Solo de concert* for Bassoon and Piano, op. 35.

P. HINDEMITH   Sonata for Bassoon and Piano.

HEITOR VILLA-LOBOS   *Bachianas Brasileiras* 6 for Flute and Bassoon.

The contrabassoon may be heard in:

L. VAN BEETHOVEN   o Symphony 5 in c, op. 67, IV.

J. BRAHMS   Symphony 1 in c, op. 68, I, IV; *Academic Festival Overture*, op. 80.

M. RAVEL   *Mother Goose* Suite, IV.

PAUL DUKAS   *The Sorcerer's Apprentice.*

JOSEPH DEEMS TAYLOR   *Through the Looking Glass,* Part III.

LISTENING 7.12

Works for saxophone include:

C. DEBUSSY   *Rapsodie* for Saxophone and Piano (Orchestra).

P. HINDEMITH   Sonata for Alto Horn (Saxophone) and Piano.

J. IBERT   *Concertino da camera* for Saxophone and Orchestra.

WALTER HARTLEY   Concerto for Saxophone and Band.

PAUL CRESTON   Sonata for Saxophone and Orchestra.

ALEXANDER KONSTANTINOVICH GLAZUNOV   Concerto for Saxophone, Flute, and Strings.

HAROLD FARBERMAN   Concerto for Alto Saxophone and String Orchestra.

Some orchestral works that use the saxophone in prominent solos are:

G. BIZET   *L'Arlésienne* Suite 1, Prélude.

D. MILHAUD   *La Création du Monde.*

B. BRITTEN   *Sinfonia da Requiem:* Dies Irae.

M. RAVEL   *Bolero.*

S. PROKOFIEV   *Lieutenant Kije* Suite.

M. P. MUSSORGSKY   *Pictures at an Exhibition:* "The Old Castle." Orchestration by Ravel.

R. VAUGHAN WILLIAMS   *Job, a Masque for Dancing,* Scene VI.

The saxophones are so widely used in jazz that recorded examples are easily available. Compare the tone quality and style of several performers.

LISTENING 7.13

Some important works for woodwind quintet are:

J. IBERT   *Trois Pièces brèves.*

ANTONÍN REICHA   Quintets.

FRANZ DANZI   Quintets, op. 56, nos. 1, 2, op. 67, no. 2.

D. MILHAUD   *Cheminée du Roi René.*

P. HINDEMITH   *Kleine Kammermusik,* op. 24, no. 2.

H. VILLA-LOBOS   *Quintette en forme de Choros.*

E. CARTER   *Eight Etudes and a Fantasy.*

ALVIN DERALD ETLER   Quintet.

JEAN FRANÇAIX   Quintet.

Some other works featuring woodwind combinations are the following:

W. A. MOZART   *Sinfonia concertante* for Winds and Orchestra in Eb, K. 297b (Anh. C14.01); Quintet for Winds and Piano in Eb, K. 452; various *divertimenti*; Serenades in Eb, c, K. 375, 388 (384a).

L. VAN BEETHOVEN   Sextet for Winds in Eb, op. 71; Octet for Woodwinds in Eb, op. 103; *Rondino* for Wind Octet in Eb, op. 146.

CHARLES FRANÇOIS GOUNOD   *Petite Symphonie* for Winds.

LEOŠ JANÁČEK   Sextet for Wind Instruments (1924); Sextet for Wind Instruments (*Youth*).

JOHN LESSARD   Octet for Winds.

I. STRAVINSKY   Octet for Winds.

I. FINE   Partita for Wind Quintet.

W. PISTON   Divertimento for Nine Instruments.

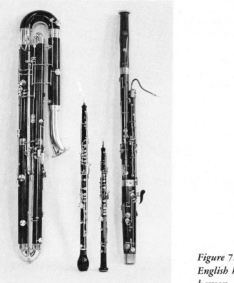

Figure 7.4 • Contrabassoon, English horn, oboe, and bassoon.

Figure 7.5 • Alto, tenor, and baritone saxophones.

instrument—its responsiveness to a variety of individual usages—has made it a natural for jazz, in which the personal element is central. In concert music the saxophone has been used only occasionally, except in the concert band, where it is a full-fledged member in good standing. Saxophones come in a variety of sizes from small to large, the smallest, the soprano, usually lacking the distinctive upturned bell at the end. The most common are the alto, tenor, and baritone (Figure 7.5), with occasional use of the soprano at the high end and the bass at the low (LISTENING 7.12).

Woodwinds in groups Woodwinds have been used together in a great variety of groupings, small and large, of which the most stable, for which a large literature exists, is the quintet (LISTENING 7.13). This chamber group is made of one each of the four traditional woodwinds—flute, oboe, clarinet, and bassoon—and one brass—the French horn.

3. BRASSES The distinguishing feature of the brass family is not the material of which its members are made, since some woodwinds are of metal and some brasses were at one time of wood, but that the lips of the players vibrate inside cups, or cone-shaped metal mouthpieces. The vibrating lips act as do the vibrating reeds of the clarinet, oboe, bassoon, and saxophone, setting the air column into motion and thus producing sound. The length and shape of the metal pipe (usually a metal alloy) from mouthpiece to bell determine the pitch range and tone quality. Pitches are changed by a combination of lip control and mechanisms to shorten and lengthen the pipe.

Over the centuries there has been a bewildering variety of brass instruments, most of which have gone the way of the dodo, as have so many of the woodwinds. What remain today are those instruments which have proved to be so musically adaptable that composers continue to depend on them for creating expressive sounds: the four major ones in current use are trumpets, trombones, horns, and tubas.

Trumpets The trumpet body is a tube that is cylindrical until near the end, where it gradually flares to a bell-shaped opening. The lowest pitch on the instrument is produced by using the entire length of the pipe and a relatively slow lip vibration. With the same length of pipe, the player can change pitches by gradually increasing the tension of his lips and therefore the rate of vibration. (This principle is clearly observed in the bugle, which depends entirely on changes in lip vibration for changes in pitch.) The trumpet combines the lip-tension principle

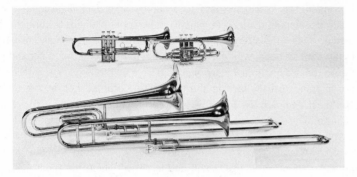

Figure 7.6 • Trumpet, cornet, bass trombone, and trombone.

LISTENING 7.14

Some representative works for trumpet are:

G. P. TELEMANN   Concertos for Trumpet and Strings in D, f.

F. J. HAYDN   Concerto for Trumpet and Orchestra in E♭.

JOHANN GEORG LEOPOLD MOZART   Concerto for Trumpet and Orchestra in D.

P. HINDEMITH   Sonata for Trumpet and Piano.

D. ERB   *Diversion for Two (Other than Sex)* for Trumpet and Percussion.

D. SHOSTAKOVICH   Concerto for Piano, Trumpet, and Strings, op. 35.

RAYMOND HANSON   Concerto for Trumpet Solo.

ALAN HOVHANESS   Sonata for Trumpet and Orchestra.

LISTENING 7.15

The trombone may be heard in the following:

W. A. MOZART   ○● Requiem in d, K. 626, III: Tuba Mirum.

PAVEL JOSEF VEJVANOVSKY   Sonata for Trumpet, Trombone, and Violin.

JOHN BAVICCHI   Three unaccompanied preludes for trombone.

ROBERT PARRIS   Concerto for Trombone and Orchestra.

L. BERIO   *Sequenza V.*

P. HINDEMITH   Sonata for Trombone and Piano.

D. ERB   *In No Strange Land.*

with a mechanism of three valves, which, when pushed down, open and close attached pipes, thus changing the length of the air column. Various combinations of pipe length and lip tension produce all the notes in the chromatic scale, enabling the instrument to fulfill a wide variety of melodic demands. The same principles apply to the cornet, which differs from the trumpet in being shorter and having more of the pipe cone-shaped. They are compared in Figure 7.6.

The cornet is seldom used outside the concert band, but the trumpet is a mainstay of the brass section of the orchestra, various brass ensembles, and of course jazz (LISTENING 7.14). Jazz trumpet playing takes advantage of a wide range of unusual and expressive effects that make the trumpet extremely versatile: growls, smears, high screams and low purrs, different colors produced by different mutes inserted into the bell—all combine to make the trumpet a rich source of expressive jazz tone colors.

Trombones   Like that of the trumpet, the trombone body is a cylinder that gradually flares toward the end to a wide bell opening. But unlike any of the other brasses, the most common trombone has no valve mechanism to change the length of the pipe. Instead there is a section of pipe doubled back on itself that slides in and out. The farther out the slide, the longer the pipe and therefore the lower the pitch. A combination of slide position and lip tension produces all the notes in the chromatic scale. Because of the time it takes to shift positions with the slide, it is very difficult to play melodic passages in which the notes change from one to another imperceptibly, although skilled trombonists get very close to being able to do this. On the other hand, the trombone can easily smear from note to note by slow motion of the slide, an effect used often, especially in jazz. Some kinds of trombone have valves to aid in pitch changes.

Trombones come in several sizes (Figure 7.6), the most popular being the ''tenor.'' The ''tenor-bass'' has a larger bore diameter, giving a quality different from the tenor. The ''bass'' is larger and longer, producing a very deep tone. The ''contrabass,'' larger still, is seldom used.

The number of characteristic expressive effects possible on the trombone is very large, making it a practical jazz instrument in addition to use in concert music. In jazz it is primarily a solo instrument, but in concert music it is often used in a group of three or four to produce a rich, blending tone color (LISTENING 7.15).

Figure 7.7 • French horn and tuba.

LISTENING 7.16

Pieces for French horn include:

G. P. TELEMANN   Concerto for Horn and Orchestra in D; Concerto for Two Horns and Strings in E.

F. J. HAYDN   Two concertos for horn and orchestra in D.

W. A. MOZART   Concertos for Horn and Orchestra in D, E♭, E♭, E♭, K. 412, (386b), 417, 447, 495.

L. VAN BEETHOVEN   Sonata for Horn and Piano in F, op. 17.

FRANCESCO ANTONIO ROSETTI   Five concertos for horn and orchestra.

R. STRAUSS   Concertos for Horn and Orchestra in E♭, op. 11, 1942.

P. HINDEMITH   Sonata for Four Horns.

A. WILDER   Sonatas for horn and piano; Suite for Horn Solo.

OTHMAR SCHOECK   Concerto for Horn and Orchestra, op. 65.

LISTENING 7.17

The tuba is heard in the following:

P. HINDEMITH   Sonata for Bass Tuba and Piano.

WILLIAM KRAFT   *Encounters II* for Unaccompanied Tuba.

A. WILDER   *Children's Suite (Effie the Elephant)*; Sonata for Tuba and Piano; Sonata for Horn, Tuba, and Piano.

W. HARTLEY   Sonatina for Tuba; Suite for Unaccompanied Tuba.

VINCENT PERSICHETTI   Serenade 12 for Tuba Solo, op. 88.

Horns   The horn (or often "French" horn) has a long and narrow conical tube wound around in several loops and ending in a widely flaring bell (Figure 7.7). The mouthpiece is funnel-shaped, not cupped as in trumpets and trombones. Three rotary valves add different loops of pipe, which, in combination with changes in lip tension, produce pitch changes. The range of the horn is very wide, and in the high register the slightest change of lip tension will produce a change of pitch. This makes it necessary for horn players to have an extremely sensitive feel as they play so that wrong notes will not creep in; nerves of steel are helpful for those who aspire to be professional hornists.

The tone quality of the horn is distinctively mellow, lending itself to groupings of several horns together and also making it an excellent partner in the woodwind quintet. Special effects are produced by mutes, or the right hand inserted into the bell, or increased wind pressure, which produces a very edgy sound.

Horns come in a variety of sizes, the most common being the horn in F (LISTENING 7.16). The "double" horn is essentially two sets of pipes connected by a valve mechanism for switching from one to the other.

Tubas   The bass instrument of the brass family comes in so many shapes and sizes that the word "tuba" has to be taken as a very general one, applying to those instruments with cup mouthpiece and large, long, tapering pipe ending in a flaring bell which produce very low pitches of the brass-instrument quality. Tubas have three to five valves that operate in the way they do in other brasses, adding sections of pipe to change pitches. (See Figure 7.7.)

In the orchestra the tubas generally used are oblong in overall shape, their bells pointing upward. These come in several sizes, from large to larger. In the concert band a tuba of circular shape with a large forward-pointing bell is common. (This shape was suggested by John Philip Sousa, after whom the sousaphone was named.) It is the instrument carried over the shoulder by players in the marching band. Other band instruments that are tubalike, but smaller, are the baritone and euphonium.

The solo literature for tuba is quite limited; it is primarily utilized as bass support in small and large ensembles. In the hands of a skillful performer, however, it is capable of real eloquence (LISTENING 7.17).

Brasses in groups   As with the woodwinds, brasses have been used in a wide variety of miscellaneous groupings: A common ensemble

LISTENING 7.18

Some representative brass-ensemble music follows:

JOHANN CHRISTOPH PETZOLD   Sonatas for five brass instruments (*Hora decima*); "Tower" music.

G. GABRIELI   *Canzoni* for brass choirs.

ANTONY HOLBORNE   *Pauans, Galliards, Almains, and other short Aeirs.*

HENRY DREYFUS BRANT   *Fourth Millenium* (*Millenium IV*).

WILLIAM BERGSMA   Suite for Brass Quartet (1945).

ALVIN BREHM   Quintet for Brass (1967).

INGOLF DAHL   Music for Five Brass Instruments (1944).

A. D. ETLER   Quintet for Brass Instruments (1964).

LISTENING 7.19

In addition to their accompaniment functions, the percussion instruments have been featured as a primary tone color in several pieces. Music for percussion ensembles of various types also exists, testifying to the powerful expressive values these instruments possess.

The following is a sample of important works in which percussion instruments play a large part:

B. BARTÓK   Sonata for Two Pianos and Percussion;   ○● *Music for String Instruments, Percussion, and Celesta.*

A. HOVHANESS   Suite for Violin, Piano, and Percussion.

D. MILHAUD   Concerto for Percussion and Small Orchestra.

D. ERB   *Diversion for Two* (*Other than Sex*) for Trumpet and Percussion.

E. VARÈSE   *Ionisation.*

There are also recordings by the Manhattan Percussion Ensemble, the American Percussion Society, and the Ithaca Percussion Ensemble.

consists of two trumpets, horn, trombone, and tuba, and larger and smaller versions of this group are also found (LISTENING 7.18).

4. PERCUSSION   This family, the most various of all, includes any device that produces a sound when it is struck, shaken, or scraped. Since almost everything will make some sort of sound when so treated, just about everything is potentially a candidate for being used as an instrument of music and *has* been employed at one time or another to serve musical purposes. However, some standard instruments have evolved that are extremely useful in a variety of musical settings. They may be grouped into (1) drums, which use a stretched membrane as a basic part of their construction, and (2) plates, bars, and tubes, which are all those soundmakers not dependent on a stretched membrane (LISTENING 7.19). Each group can in turn be divided into two types: (*a*) those which give definite, tuned pitches and (*b*) those which give an indefinite, untuned pitch.

1*a*. The important tuned drums are the kettledrums, or timpani. The membrane is stretched by means of a foot or hand mechanism—the tighter the membrane, the higher the pitch. A variety of mallets gives different percussive effects, soft to hard. When two to four timpani of different sizes are used together, a range of more than an octave becomes possible (Figure 7.8).

b. Untuned drums include the snare, which produces its characteristic sizzle when wires are stretched against the bottom membrane, and many other two-headed drums in a variety of sizes, down to the biggest football-band-type bass drum. Single-membrane untuned instruments include the bongos, which produce higher and lower untuned pitches, and the tambourine, which has a circle of metal jingles around the rim of the instrument (Figure 7.9).

2*a*. Tuned percussion instruments of the nonmembrane type include several that use metal or wooden bars arranged like a piano keyboard. Various mallets (up to four at a time) produce different percussive sounds. The major instruments of this type are the bells (glockenspiel), with metal bars, the xylophone (Figure 7.10), having wooden bars with short metal tubes hanging beneath them to help amplify the sounds, the marimba (like the xylophone, but with a deeper quality), and the vibraphone, consisting of metal bars and tubes with a rotating disk inside to give a *vibrato*. The chimes (Figure 7.10) are metal tubes tuned in

Figure 7.8 • Timpani (kettledrums).

Figure 7.10 • Chimes, gong (tam-tam), xylophone, and cymbals.

Figure 7.9 • Bass drum, bongos, and snare drum.

a scale. The tubes hang vertically on a frame and are struck on top with a hammerlike mallet, producing a church-bell effect.

b. Remaining are a miscellany of nontuned instruments to create special effects (Figure 7.10): cymbals of many sizes, the triangle, the gong (a very large metal disk to be struck with a soft mallet), claves (two resonant sticks to be struck together), maracas (rattles), whistles, whips, seed pods, scraped gourds, sandpaper blocks, sleigh bells, and so on and on. The imagination of man has been particularly fertile in putting the most unlikely sounds to musical uses.

5. KEYBOARD INSTRUMENTS   With a few exceptions (guitar, harp, or vibraphone) the instruments discussed so far produce tones one at a time as their main way of making music. It is difficult, if not impossible, for most of them to sound more than a single line of music. The keyboard instruments—piano, harpsichord, organ, and celesta—can engage all the performer's ten fingers at the same time (the organ also uses the feet), thus opening up endless possibilities for playing full-scale homophonic and polyphonic pieces. This has made the piano and the organ and, in its time, the harpsichord basic musical tools for which a great

LISTENING 7.20

Any representative list of piano literature would take several pages. The following composers have contributed unusually important pieces to this literature; you can easily sample their solo, small-ensemble, and large-orchestra works for, or featuring, the piano: MUZIO CLEMENTI, F. J. HAYDN, W. A. MOZART, L. VAN BEETHOVEN, F. P. SCHUBERT, R. SCHUMANN, F. F. CHOPIN, F. LISZT, J. BRAHMS, F. MENDELSSOHN, E. H. GRIEG, P. I. TCHAIKOVSKY, C. DEBUSSY, M. RAVEL, A. SCHOENBERG, B. BARTÓK, P. HINDEMITH.

Recent and unusual uses of the piano are found in works by J. CAGE, O. MESSIAEN, P. BOULEZ, and K. STOCKHAUSEN.

*Figure 7.11 • Harpsichord (**with two manuals, or keyboards**).*

number of important pieces have been composed over the years.

Piano   The most popular of all modern instruments (LISTENING 7.20) was invented in the early 1700s. An elaborate hammer mechanism, activated by a keyboard, strikes a set of stretched wires (which look not unlike a harp) and then falls away immediately to allow the vibrations to continue. Pedals further enrich the sound possibilities in a variety of ways. Most characteristically, a player's touch on the keyboard controls loudness and softness; this gives the piano a dimension of expressiveness lacking in earlier instruments. It also gives the instrument its name, a shortened version of the Italian *pianoforte* (soft loud).

Modern pianos have two basic shapes, horizontal (grand) and vertical (upright). Each shape comes in several sizes, but most have the same enormous range of over seven octaves, the largest practical range of any traditional instrument.

Harpsichord   From around the sixteenth to the eighteenth centuries the harpsichord was the principal keyboard instrument. It has the shape of a small grand piano, but its strings are set in motion by a mechanism that *plucks* them when a key is pushed. Many harpsichords have three or more sets (choirs) of strings, each with its mechanism to produce different tone colors, ranging from nasal to hollow, and different levels of loudness (Figure 7.11).

In our own century a revival of interest in the harpsichord has taken place; several instrument makers now produce authentic and excellent instruments. Many musicians insist that music written before the invention of the piano be performed on the instrument (often the harpsichord) for which it was conceived, while others argue that it is perfectly proper to use the piano. Those interested in appreciating the expressive qualities of such music as it was heard by those for whom it was intended will avail themselves of the many fine recordings using the harpsichord in performances that are, as far as we can tell, very close to the originals; also to be enjoyed are some twentieth-century pieces for harpsichord (LISTENING 7.21).

Organ   Perhaps the most complex—certainly the largest—of traditional instruments is the organ, which is essentially a set of pipes through which wind is forced. Its keyboard controls the mechanism (mechanical or electrical) that opens and closes valves allowing the stream of air into the pipes. The larger the organ, the more pipes of different sorts, each set having a distinctive tone color. The largest organs are com-

LISTENING 7.21

Many early ensemble works used the harpsichord as an accompaniment to play chords and decorations as the music proceeded; but a sizable solo literature exists, as well as ensemble music featuring the harpsichord.

J. S. BACH   Sixteen concertos for harpsichord solo, S. 972–987; seven concertos for harpsichord and orchestra, S. 1052–1058; Concerto for Four Harpsichords and Strings in a, S. 1065.

F. COUPERIN   Many pieces of harpsichord (*clavecin*) music.

JEAN-PHILIPPE RAMEAU   Several collections of *pièces de clavecin*.

G. F. HANDEL   o Suite for Harpsichord in E (*Harmonious Blacksmith*); Concerto for Harpsichord and Orchestra in g, op. 4, no. 1.

D. SCARLATTI   Numerous sonatas for harpsichord.

F. J. HAYDN   Four concertos for harpsichord and orchestra; Concerto for Harpsichord, Violin, and Strings in F.

Some modern works for harpsichord are:

D. ERB   Sonata for Harpsichord and Quartet.

HENRY DIXON COWELL   Prelude for Violin and Harpsichord.

A. HOVHANESS   Duet for Violin and Harpsichord.

DANIEL PINKHAM   Partita for Harpsichord Solo.

E. CARTER   Sonata for Flute, Oboe, Cello, and Harpsichord; Double Concerto for Harpsichord, Piano, and Two Chamber Orchestras.

MANUEL DE FALLA   Concerto in D for Harpsichord and Chamber Orchestra.

VIRGIL THOMSON   Sonata 4 for Harpsichord Solo.

ARTHUR BERGER   Bagatelle; Intermezzo.

LISTENING 7.22

A few of the many works for organ are:

DIDERIK BUXTEHUDE   Organ music.

LOUIS NICOLAS CLÉRAMBAULT   Organ music.

G. GABRIELI   Eleven *intonazioni d'organo*.

F. COUPERIN   *Pièces d'orgue*.

G. F. HANDEL   Sixteen concertos for organ and orchestra.

J. S. BACH   Preludes and fugues for organ, S. 531–552, S. 553–560; six concertos for organ solo, S. 592–597; much other music in collections recorded by various organists.

(continued on page 122)

prised of several keyboards, a keyboard for the feet (for bass notes), and up to a hundred sets of pipes that can be combined in various ways. With all this hardware, the organ usually must be installed in a large building, such as a church, although tiny portable organs to be held on the knee have also been built. Modern electronic equipment can approximate the sounds of the pipes, reducing the size of what would be a church organ to upright-piano measurements.

The literature for organ, as for piano, is enormous (LISTENING 7.22). Most of it is for organ solo since the instrument produces so many rich and diversified sounds that it hardly needs other instruments to add interest. It frequently accompanies choirs, and several concertos for organ and orchestra exist.

Celesta   This is a special-effect instrument that uses a keyboard to control a set of hammers that strike steel bars. It is a kind of elaborate glockenspiel, in appearance like a small upright piano (LISTENING 7.23).

GROUPS OF INSTRUMENTS   *Orchestra*   This has been the dominant large group for some two hundred fifty years. It has gone through an evolutionary process, the standard modern orchestra containing roughly the following collection of instruments:

Strings   violins (thirty to thirty-six) divided into two sections (first and second violins), violas (ten to fourteen), cellos (eight to twelve), basses (six to ten), and harps (one to three).

Woodwinds   piccolo (one), flutes (three), oboes (three), English horn (one), clarinets (three), bass clarinet (one), bassoon (three), and contrabasoon (one).

Brasses   French horns (six), trumpets (four), trombones (four), and tubas (one or two).

Percussion   timpani (four), snare and bass drums, cymbals, triangle, chimes, etc.

Other instruments as called for   piano, organ, saxophone, etc.

This combination gives the composer the full spectrum of instrumental tone colors with which to work. It is an irresistible opportunity for most composers because it is rich in possibilities for creative exploration; therefore, many of the largest and most profound compositions during the last three centuries have been for orchestra.

Many say that the heyday of the orchestra is over in that contemporary

W. A. MOZART   Seventeen sonatas for organ and orchestra; Fantasia for Organ Solo in f, K. 608.

F. J. HAYDN   Three concertos for organ and orchestra.

C. FRANCK   Three chorales for organ; *Pièce héroïque.*

J. BRAHMS   Eleven chorale preludes for organ, op. 122.

CHARLES MARIE WIDOR   Symphonies 5, 6, 9 for Organ Solo.

F. LISZT   Prelude and Fugue on B-A-C-H.

F. POULENC   Concerto for Organ, Strings, and Timpani in g.

A. SCHOENBERG   Variations on a Recitative, op. 40.

O. MESSIAEN   *Nativité du Seigneur.*

C. E. IVES   Variations on "America" for Organ Solo.

LISTENING 7.23

B. BARTOK   ○● *Music for String Instruments, Percussion, and Celesta.*

GILBERT AMY   *Inventions.*

D. PINKHAM   Concerto for Celesta and Harpsichord Soli; Concertante 1.

LISTENING 7.24

Any list of orchestral music must be only suggestive, but the following are a few important works from each style period. Notice the gradual change from the simple groupings of the early works to the complex, elaborate groupings of the later ones.

BAROQUE

J. S. BACH   ○ Four suites for orchestra, S. 1066–1069; six "Brandenburg" concertos, S. 1046–1051.

G. F. HANDEL   Twelve *concerti grossi*, op. 6; "Royal Fireworks" Music; "Water" Music.

A. VIVALDI   Numerous concertos for orchestra.

G. P. TELEMANN   *Concerto grosso* in Bb; three "productions" of *Musique de table.*

G. GABRIELI   *Sonata pian'e forte.*

GIUSEPPE TORELLI   Twelve concertos, op. 8.

TOMMASO ALBINONI   Concertos, op. 5.

H. PURCELL   *The Indian Queen:* overture.

WILLIAM BOYCE   Eight symphonies in eight parts.

music, for financial and aesthetic reasons, does not make as much use of the orchestra as was done previously. They argue that orchestras will eventually become obsolete, a few existing here and there as groups specializing in old music, much as present musical societies that specialize in medieval, renaissance, and baroque music. Others argue that the orchestra is very much alive, both as preserver of the masterworks of past centuries and as a vital source of new ideas for living composers. Certainly many major composers of this century have used the orchestra time and time again. Whether this will continue in the future as it has in the past remains to be seen. In any event, the orchestra, grandest of all music-making bodies, can be enjoyed now both for music of the past and for music of today (LISTENING 7.24).

Concert band   The second large instrumental ensemble, the concert, or symphonic, band, is found primarily in schools and colleges although there are a few full-time professional bands. Outgrowths of military bands, which have existed for centuries, concert bands became popular during the 1920s and 1930s as school groups that combined audience appeal, relatively quick results in learning to play, involvement of children in a wholesome activity, and performance of a wide variety of music, ranging from marches, through arrangements of orchestra works, to new, serious works composed specifically for band. The original literature for band has continued to grow so that much music of high quality now exists for this group (LISTENING 7.25).

A typical concert band has roughly the following instrumentation:

Woodwinds   piccolos (two), flutes (six to eight, including alto and bass as called for), oboes (four), English horn (one), Eb clarinets (one or two), Bb clarinets (twenty-two to twenty-eight), alto clarinets (two to four), bass clarinets (two to four), contrabass clarinets (one or two), alto saxophones (two), tenor saxophones (two), baritone saxophone (one), bassoons (four), and contrabassoon (one).

Brass   cornets (six to eight), trumpets (four to six), French horns (six to eight), baritones and/or euphoniums (two to four), trombones (four to six), and tubas (four to six).

Percussion   four to six players who rule over an endlessly varied domain.

Other instruments as called for   one or two string basses, piano, organ, harp, etc.

CLASSIC

C. P. STAMITZ   Symphony in E♭ (*La melodia Germania* 3).

W. A. MOZART   Symphonies ○ 36, ○● 40, ○ 41; German dances; overtures.

F. J. HAYDN   Symphonies 88, 94, ○● 101, 104; overtures; *Sinfonia concertante* in B♭, op. 84.

J. C. BACH   Six symphonies; *Sinfonia* for Double Orchestra in E.

L. VAN BEETHOVEN   ○● Nine symphonies; overtures.

C. P. E. BACH   Symphony 3 in F.

NINETEENTH CENTURY

F. P. SCHUBERT   Nine symphonies; German dances.

R. SCHUMANN   Four symphonies.

H. BERLIOZ   ○● *Symphonie fantastique*, op. 14; overtures.

F. MENDELSSOHN   Symphonies 3–5; *A Midsummer Night's Dream:* selections; overtures.

F. LISZT   *Les Préludes;* six Hungarian rhapsodies in orchestral version.

R. WAGNER   Overtures and preludes; "Siegfried Idyll."

C. FRANCK   Symphony in d.

A. BRUCKNER   Nine symphonies.

J. BRAHMS   ○● Four symphonies; *Academic Festival* Overture, op. 80; Hungarian dances; *Tragic* Overture, op. 81; Variations on a Theme by Haydn in B♭, op. 56a.

P. I. TCHAIKOVSKY   ○● Six symphonies; *1812* Overture; *The Nutcracker* Suite; *Capriccio italien.*

A. DVOŘÁK   Symphony 5 in e, op. 95 (*New World*).

G. MAHLER   Symphonies 2, 4, 9.

TWENTIETH CENTURY

C. DEBUSSY   *Images pour orchestre; La Mer; Nocturnes;* ○● *The Afternoon of a Faun.*

C. E. IVES   *Holidays;* Symphony: four symphonies; *Three Places in New England.*

M. RAVEL   *Alborado del gracioso; Bolero; Daphnis et Chloé* Suite 2; *Rapsodie espagnole; La Valse.*

A. SCHOENBERG   Five Pieces for Orchestra, op. 16; *Verklärte Nacht*, op. 4.

A. BERG   Three Orchestra Pieces, op. 6.

A. VON WEBERN   ○● Five Pieces for Orchestra, op. 10; Six Pieces for Orchestra, op. 6.

B. BARTÓK   *Concerto for Orchestra.*

I. STRAVINSKY   *Firebird* Suite; *Petrushka* Suite; ○ *Le Sacre du printemps;* Symphony in C; Symphony in Three Movements.

S. PROKOFIEV   Symphonies 5–7.

D. SHOSTAKOVICH   Symphonies 1, 5, 9.

A. COPLAND   ○● *El Salón México; Appalachian Spring;* Symphony 3.

W. SCHUMAN   ○● Symphony 3 (1941).

H. HANSON   ○ Symphony 2.

R. VAUGHAN WILLIAMS   Symphony 5.

LISTENING 7.25

Important works for concert band include the following, all available on recordings:

GUSTAV THEODORE HOLST   Suites for Band in E♭, F.

PERCY ALDRIDGE GRAINGER   *Lincolnshire Posy.*

R. VAUGHAN WILLIAMS   *Toccata Marziale;* ○ *English Folksong* Suite.

NIKOLAY YAKOVLEVICH MIASKOVSKY   Symphony 19 for Concert Band.

A. COPLAND   *An Outdoor Overture.*

D. MILHAUD   *Suite française.*

H. HANSON   *Chorale and Alleluia.*

P. HINDEMITH   Symphony in B♭.

A. SCHOENBERG   Theme and Variations for Band, op. 43a.

W. SCHUMAN   *Chester.*

V. PERSICHETTI   Symphony for Band.

H. OWEN REED   *La Fiesta Mexicana.*

R. R. BENNETT   ○ *Suite of Old American Dances.*

LISTENING 7.26

Here are selections from a burgeoning record list. Most recordings include technical information about how the sound was produced, and a reading of the notes accompanying the records will give the listener a clear idea of the ingenious ways technology is being put to artistic purposes.

The following pieces combine electronically produced sounds with traditional instruments and voice:

L. BERIO   *Differences* (with five instruments).

REMI GASSMANN   *Music to the Ballet* (with orchestra).

CHARLES HAMM   *Canto* (with soprano, speaker, chamber group).

K. STOCKHAUSEN   *Progression* (with gong, viola, piano); *Mikrophonie II* (with choir, Hammond organ).

V. USSACHEVSKY   *Creation-Prologue* (with multiple chorus).

H. EL-DABH   *Leiyla and the Poet* (with voice).

D. ERB   ○● *Reconnaissance* (with several instruments).

KENNETH GABURO   *Antiphony III: "Pearl White Moments"* (with sixteen voices).

O. LUENING   *Concerted Piece* (with orchestra); *Gargoyles* (with violin).

L. HILLER   *Avalanche* (with voices, player piano, percussion); Suite (with two pianos).

The following are composed entirely of electronically produced or manipulated sounds:

E. VARÈSE   *Poème électronique.*

TOD DOCKSTADER   *Eight Electronic Pieces.*

M. BABBITT   ○ *Composition for Synthesizer.*

DICK RAAIJMAKERS   *Contrasts.*

BULENT AREL   *Electronic Music No. 1.*

O. LUENING   *Piece for Tape Recorder.*

J. CAGE   *Fontana Mix; Cartridge Music.*

I. MIMAROGLU   *Agony.*

K. STOCKHAUSEN   *Kontakte.*

M. DAVIDOVSKY   *Electronic Study No. 1.*

OTHER SOUNDS OF MUSIC

During the past twenty to twenty-five years a new world of electronically produced and manipulated sound has been discovered. Technology has made it possible to record natural sounds and traditional musical-instrument sounds and then alter them endlessly to create entirely new tone colors to be used as the material for composing (this process is called *musique concrete*) and to generate new sounds electronically, these sounds then being used as the material for composing (Figure 7.12).

That sounds are produced by an electronic machine tells one nothing about what the music using those sounds will be. As we have seen in the *Switched-on Bach, Switched-on Rock,* and *Well-tempered Synthesizer* type of recording, electronic sound can be used to reproduce traditional music and to imitate traditional instruments; but most composers are not interested in such uses of electronic sounds. They want to explore the new expressive possibilities offered by the fantastically increased rhythmic, pitch, and tone-color capacities now available. So most music using electronic equipment is of an exploratory sort: both exploring what the new world of sound can do and exploring new areas of feeling by the creation of new sound conditions to arouse feeling. The music thus produced has posed some of history's toughest challenges to the listener, the music theorist, the aesthetician, the critic, and the music educator. All have had to rethink their notions of music, including in their conceptions a far different kind of expressive sound than has ever existed before.

What the effects of these new departures will be on the history of music is anybody's guess. It is safe to say, in any case, that electronically produced sound will continue to be used in creative ways by composers. The educated listener should be able to share these creations as much as he cares to. Our study of rhythm, melody, harmony, counterpoint, tone color, and form would be incomplete if it ignored this large and growing body of music; so examples and comments have been offered from the beginning of the book and will be continued to the end. Our focus now is on the sound itself—the tone colors of electronic music. Whether these can equal traditional tone colors in usefulness and expressiveness is probably beside the point. Something has been added to contribute new, exciting possibilities to music (LISTENING 7.26).

Dynamics (*amount of sound*)

Figure 7.12 • Electronic studio at the Cleveland Institute of Music.

Our discussion of tone color to this point has concentrated on the mediums of sound, the different qualities of sound that are an integral part of the expressiveness of rhythm, melody, harmony, counterpoint, and form. In addition to the *kind* of sound one hears, there is the factor of the *amount* of sound: No matter what kind of sound is being used, it must be present in some degree of volume. In music this loudness or softness is called "dynamics."

Loudness and softness may seem like such obvious qualities that they hardly need to be mentioned. It is true that the listener will naturally be aware of gross differences in dynamics; yet these differences are so essential to musical expressiveness and can be so endlessly subtle that sensitivity to them must be consciously improved, as is true of all complex musical components.

The amount of sound in music ranges from the barely audible to the deafening. The following traditional dynamic markings give a rough guide to the volume of sound:

ppp (*pianississimo*)	extremely soft
pp (*pianissimo*)	very soft
p (*piano*)	soft
mp (*mezzopiano*)	medium soft
mf (*mezzoforte*)	medium loud
f (*forte*)	loud
ff (*fortissimo*)	very loud
fff (*fortississimo*)	extremely loud

Obviously, soft and loud exist on a continuum with an infinite number of points between the extremes, the terms above only marking off large areas on the continuum. This richness of dynamic possibilities adds a great deal to musical expressiveness. A change of loudness from one statement of a melody to another will change the feeling of that melody, as is made clear when a melody is played very softly (*pp*) and then played very loudly (*ff*): The effect will be enormously different. The more subtle the difference in dynamics, the more subtle will be the effect. Composers and performers and conductors must be extraordinarily sensitive to

LISTENING 7.27

The following works use dynamics in either very subtle or very obvious ways. Some combine the obvious with the subtle. Try to focus your attention on changes in volume, whether sudden or gradual, slight or great. Each piece will give plenty of opportunity for you to sharpen your perception of these basic musical means. (These pieces are listed in a suggested order for listening.)

C. FRANCK   Symphony in d, I.
V. USSACHEVSKY   *Piece for Tape Recorder.*
H. BERLIOZ   ○● *Symphonie fantastique,* op. 14, V.
P. I. TCHAIKOVSKY   Symphony 5 in e, op. 64, I.
E. VARÈSE   *Ionisation.*
I. STRAVINSKY   *Le Sacre du printemps:* ○ "Ritual Performance of the Ancestors" and "Sacrificial Dance."
L. VAN BEETHOVEN   *Leonore* Overture 3 in C, op. 72*b.*
W. SCHUMAN   Symphony 3 (1941), IV.
A. SCHOENBERG   ○● *Pierrot lunaire,* op. 21.
M. RAVEL   *Bolero.*
THE MODERN JAZZ QUARTET   "Sketch," from *Third Stream Music.*
J. S. BACH   ○ Cantata 80, *Ein feste Burg ist unser Gott,* I.
F. J. HAYDN   Symphony 101 in D, I.
S. BARBER   ○● *Adagio* for Strings, op. 11.
F. F. CHOPIN   ○ Étude for Piano in E, op. 10, no. 3.
C. DEBUSSY   ○● *The Afternoon of a Faun.*

Tone color concluded

refined differences in volume because this is a crucial factor in the music's success as an expressive event. The listener should be able to perceive the differences in dynamics and react to their affective power. It is easy to hear an *fff* followed by a *ppp;* but it takes *listening* to hear slight but crucial changes in volume as they unfold during the course of a piece (LISTENING 7.27).

Some music moves from one dynamic level to another in a kind of step-by-step process, the changes being sudden even if small. (See especially the discussion of tone color in Chapter 10.) All styles have used sudden changes of volume to create a moving sequence of events.

In addition to a step-by-step, or "terraced," kind of dynamic change, there is the gradual increase or decrease of volume. When sound gradually gets louder, it is described as *crescendo* (*cresc.*, or $<$). Getting gradually softer is *decrescendo* or *diminuendo* (*decresc.* or *dim.*, or $>$). *Crescendo*s or *decrescendo*s can be very obvious, moving gradually from *ppp* to *fff* or in the opposite direction, either quickly or over the course of an entire piece. They can also be extremely subtle, involving such slight differences from moment to moment or over a long span of time that only the keenest ear can detect them. The composer can put a $<$ or $>$ mark in his score when he wants a gradual change of dynamics; but many such changes are too slight to be notated and must be added by the performer as he builds and relaxes tension in an unfolding piece by his control over tiny gradations of loud and soft. It is often such control (or the lack of it) that makes a piece come alive in one performance or seem dead in another.

Finally there is the matter of very sudden loud notes called "accents." In Chapter 4 we discussed accents as they function rhythmically, adding to the sense of movement as they occur in regular or irregular ways and in stronger or weaker amounts of sound. Accents can also be regarded for their sheer dynamic expressiveness. The sudden loudness is of itself an important musical quality, giving still another dimension to the many possibilities of musical dynamics.

The many details attached to musical color could be pursued much longer, but what has been covered in this chapter is sufficient for our purposes. Now it is time to put all the elements into the context of music as a structured whole: the context of form.

Chapter 8 ∘ *The expressiveness of form*

FORM (ORGANIZATION OF ALL ELEMENTS)

PRINCIPLES (ALL FORMS): UNITY AND VARIETY

PROCEDURES (ALL FORMS)

Repetition.
Contrast.
Variation.
Development.

FORMS

Repetition (AAA . . .): one-part song, round.
Repetition with contrast ($AB, ABA, ABACA$ . . .): two-part, three-part, rondo.
Repetition with variation ($AA_1A_2A_3$ . . .): theme and variations, continuous variation, fugue.
Repetition with development: sonata-allegro.
Free (all contain repetition, contrast, variation, and/or development): toccata, prelude, fantasia, étude, impromptu, rhapsody, nocturne, overture, symphonic poem, and the like; contemporary free forms.

COMBINATIONS OF FORMS

Instrumental: sonata, symphony, concerto, suite. Vocal: opera, oratorio, cantata, Mass, song cycle.

PREFORMED AND UNFORMED MUSIC

Principles: unity and variety

EVERY WORK OF ART, WHETHER A SYMPHONY, A PAINTING, A SCULPTURE, a dance, a poem, a building, a film, or a play, is a thing that has been formed to capture and display feeling. The feeling it produces in the perceiver results from the way he follows the tensions, resolutions, uncertainties, deviations, and fulfillments of expectation presented by the work. The feeling is not usually an "emotion": it cannot be named or described in words. Instead, it is an experience, a going through, a shaped episode in the flow of life. Such an experience seems significant because it heightens the sense of what living can be. It is a proof that what happens to human beings can be meaningful, coherent, and powerful rather than just meaningless, scattered, and dull. Every time we experience the shaped, formed qualities of a work of art, our experience has for that moment taken on a shape and a form. The human condition is one characterized by the ability to know oneself as a person—a series of experiences that constitute a personal life. Every experience adding to the shaped quality of that life adds to your depth as a person. A major reason for the existence of art is to contribute this dimension of "significant form" to people's experience.

Each art shapes experience in its own way—which is why each art offers its special insights into life. In music the shaping or forming process takes place through the use of rhythm, melody, harmony, counterpoint, and tone color. These elements create an ongoing, formed experience as they interact with one another, setting up probable events, resolving in expected or unexpected ways, holding back resolutions or introducing uncertainties—in short, presenting a musical composition, of which the parts are rhythm, melody, harmony, counterpoint, and tone color. The whole is the form, the sum total of every moment of shaped sound events.

We directed our attention in the previous four chapters to the parts of music out of which whole compositions are made. Now we can focus on the principles and processes by which the parts are formed into wholes. The marginal outline will guide our exploration.

The idea of unity, of wholeness, is one of the most powerful in human thought. Religion, whether traditional or nontraditional, is unthinkable without the idea of wholeness. Science also has been influenced at every point by principles of uniformity in nature and of unity of physical phenomena. Political and social systems, psychological theories, and philosophical positions have all depended in large degree on the concept of unity: Things are interconnected and interdependent rather than totally separate from one another. Human life has identity because human experiences seem to be related with one another, each experience contributing to the whole making each of us an individual.

Simple organisms, simple ideas, or simple events are small wholes, with few parts involved. As organisms, ideas, or events grow in detail and scope, the number of parts grows, making their wholes more and more complex. The body of a complex organism, such as a human being, has a great variety of parts and functions, each of which has its role in the unified organism to which it belongs. Complex theological, psychological, or social systems of thought, such as those of Paul Tillich, of Carl Jung, or of Karl Marx, are unified structures, but they contain within them many interconnected ideas. An operating political entity, say, the United States of America, is an enormously complex system of subunits, all adding up to a unified nation, however imperfect.

Unity and variety, wholes and parts, the one and the many—few concepts have had the long-lasting and penetrating implications of this one. We may suspect that it reaches so deeply into human consciousness (and unconsciousness) as to be a given, an inherent characteristic of the type of organism we are.

Of all human activities, art is perhaps closest to the underlying conditions of our common estate. It should not be surprising, therefore, that works of art are among the clearest examples of the principle of parts adding up to larger wholes. In works of art, as a basic condition of their existence, we find things that display unity and variety *to be experienced as such*. The work of art exists to be experienced. The experience—the going through, the perceptive reaction or reactive perception we have described as aesthetic experience—is essentially one of unity with variety, and seems significant to us because it illustrates the conditions at the core of our being.

In art the manifestations of unity and variety exist on a kind of continuum: Toward one end are works that are highly unified, with just the slightest bit of variety; toward the other, works that are extremely varied, with obscure unifying impulses. Within this range of differences is an infinity of combinations of unity with variety, not only from work to work but within single works. Of course, there is no easy way to measure the exact amount of unity and variety in a work of art and put it on the continuum in its proper place; and there is no way to generalize about the power of a work according to its blend of unity and variety. A work with very little variety can easily be boring. On the other hand some simple pieces seem so right that their effect can be profound. A few very complex works have created an entire world of artistic insights, a world we can explore again and again without ever discovering all that is there. Yet other such works seem merely bombastic—lots of sound and fury with little that engages our feelings. The successful works are those that have a kind of rightness in the proportions of unity and variety. It is this rightness, or convincingness, that the artist strives for anew in every work he creates.

At the very ends of the continuum are works totally lacking in variety (or at least they can be in theory) or totally lacking in unity (again, at least theoretically). Traditionally, any such works have been regarded as either bad works of art or not art at all. In recent years, however, genuine attempts have been made to create works that are, on the one hand, devoid of variety or, on the other hand, devoid of unity. These attempts have raised serious new problems for philosophers of art, other artists, and people who want to share art: What can we make of such works? Do they deserve the name ''art''? Are they merely put-ons? We shall comment on such works at the end of this chapter, in our discussion of preformed and unformed (random) music. Until that point we shall deal with those works (the vast majority) which contain both unity and variety in some created degree.

How does a composer create a set of sound events—a piece of music—that will give the impression that it is unified while a variety of interesting things are going on in it? The *materials* with which he works are rhythm, melody, tone color, harmony, and counterpoint, and four basic *procedures* exist for using these materials: repetition, contrast, variation, and development. Each contributes to the forming process by means of which the materials, while being interrelated and coherent, can produce an ongoing, diverse experience.

Procedures

REPETITION

The most basic procedure in musical forming is repetition, and indeed there are few pieces of music that contain no repetition. It is not hard to understand why it is important in music, for music takes place in time, and to experience a composition as a unity, you must remember at least some of what took place before, as the music moves along from point to point. Because this is not easy to do, a composer will constantly remind the listener of important sound events by repeating them. A repetition may come immediately after a first statement, or it may come later in the piece. A musical idea may be repeated just once, or it may be repeated over and over again. A repetition may be exact, or it may be altered in some way. An entire idea may be repeated, or only a part of it might be.

The procedure of repetition may sound like such a simple thing that not much need be said about it, but in actuality it is far more complex than you might think. First of all, there is the enormous number of things that can be repeated. In the previous four chapters we have explored a great many qualities of sound that composers use to create music; each one can be a candidate for repetition. For example, a simple kind of repetition might be that of a short melody; the melody is stated and then repeated. You can easily hear the repetition and feel the resulting unity because the two statements of the melody are identical twins. A little later in the piece the melody is repeated but in a different tone color—instead of by the original violins, it is played by flute and oboe. We hear the repetition and at the same time a change; our sense of unity has been strengthened, but that of variety has been added. A bit later we may hear something familiar: the pitches of the original melody in a different rhythm. Something is the same—again contributing to unity—but something is different—contributing to variety. Then we hear something else that sounds familiar: the rhythm of the original melody in different pitches. The sense of unity and variety grows. Later, we recognize the harmony that accompanied the original melody. It is being repeated, but with different melodic material. Then some of the intervals between the notes of the original melody are repeated but in different registers than they were at first. A scale passage from the end of the melody appears, repeated over and over in different instruments and different registers. Then the meter changes, and the melody is heard in triple meter rather than in the original duple. Some new notes are added to it, stretching its structure and adding a new rhythmic complexity. The notes become shorter than they were at first, then longer and smoother. The harmony becomes more active; the key changes;

Each of these pieces contains some very obvious repetitions, many of them exact. But even the simplest examples have subtleties of repetition that require some concentration and repeated hearings to share them. Try to spot as many repeated aspects as you can, recognizing the same ideas even if they have been altered in some way. Your powers of concentration and memory can get a good workout here.

    A. VIVALDI   Concerto for Violin and Orchestra in E, op. 8, no. 1, o I, III.

    J. S. BACH   Italian Concerto for Harpsichord Solo in F, S. 971, I, o● II.

    W. A. MOZART   *Eine kleine Nachtmusik* in G, K. 525, II; o● Symphony 40 in g, K. 550, IV.

    L. VAN BEETHOVEN   o● Symphony 3 in E♭, op. 55, III; o● Symphony 5 in c, op. 67, I; Concerto for Violin and Orchestra in D, op. 61, o II, III; o● Quartet for Strings in B♭, op. 130, IV.

    F. P. SCHUBERT   *Die schöne Müllerin,* op. 25, nos. 1, 2, 14.

    R. WAGNER   *Tristan und Isolde:* Prelude.

    C. DEBUSSY   "Clair de lune."

    A. COPLAND   o● *El Salón México.*

    D. BRUBECK   "Take Five," from *Time Out.*

    THE ROLLING STONES   "Sympathy for the Devil," from *Beggars Banquet.*

Many new electronic pieces contain repetition of ideas to a surprising degree. Such pieces are far from being collections of random sounds. The repetitions may not be of traditional melodies, metrical patterns, or harmonic progressions, but they are there nevertheless.

    M. BABBITT   o *Composition for Synthesizer.*

    H. EL-DABH   *Leiyla and the Poet.*

    O. LUENING   *Gargoyles.*

    I. MIMAROGLU   *Agony.*

the melody is heard against a second melody in counterpoint; a fragment from the middle of the melody is scatter-shot from high to low; the dynamics shift from the original soft to an ear-shattering loud and everywhere in between; accents are added in unexpected places; the melody shifts from major to minor—there is no end to the possibilities. Each of the foregoing ones uses repetition; something has remained the *same.* Yet something has also *changed:* contrast, variation, development—each has done its bit to make the repetition more than merely a literal repeat. With each change has come a sense of variety; but each change has retained a part of the original to give a strong sense of unity.

Repetition permeates all the other procedures. And every subtle quality of sound can be subtly repeated. It takes a keen ear to perceive all the kinds of repetition in even a simple piece, much more a complex one. To the degree you hear the use of repetition in a composition, you will be able to share the power of its unified yet varied structure (LISTENING 8.1).

CONTRAST

If music contained only repetition, we would get not only a strong sense of unity but also complete boredom. Anyone who has heard children repeat a simple play chant over and over, for what seems like hours on end, knows that there is primitive power in pure repetition. However, more is needed to explore the realm of feeling. The drive toward variety puts severe limits on the use of simple repetition.

Contrast is a basic means of providing variety while contributing to unity and essentially entails a musical idea followed by a differing one. The difference can be obvious: a *staccato,* fast, high section followed by a *legato,* slow, low section; or homophonic texture followed by polyphonic texture; or a theme in one key followed by a different theme in another key; or brass tone color followed by string tone color; or smooth upward-swooping electronic smears followed by a scattering of short, downward-moving blips. Every contrast adds variety to the piece, but it must be perceived as a contrast to something already heard and therefore as *related* to what was heard. So contrast can contribute to both unity and variety.

Contrast need not be so obvious as are the examples listed above. Often the slightest contrast occurs: a theme played by one violin and

LISTENING 8.2

In the listing accompanying Repetition were pieces containing obvious and subtle repeated ideas. Each of those pieces contains some obvious and subtle contrasts as well. Choose some you have listened to previously, and this time concentrate on the *differences* rather than the *similarities*. Remember that contrasts may be quite easy to hear but also so delicate as to require keen ears to perceive them.

In addition to the pieces in the previous list, the following contain contrasts ranging from much to little:

J. S. BACH   Suite for Orchestra in b, S. 1067, ○ IV, V.

G. F. HANDEL   ○● *Messiah:* "Hallelujah" chorus.

W. A. MOZART   *Eine kleine Nachtmusik* in G, K. 525, ○ I, II; ○ Symphony 36 in C, K. 425, I.

L. VAN BEETHOVEN   Symphony 5 in c, op. 67, III; ○● Symphony 3 in E♭, op. 55, I.

J. BRAHMS   Symphony 2 in D, op. 73, IV.

B. BARTÓK   *Music for String Instruments, Percussion, and Celesta,* ○● II, III.

THE MODERN JAZZ QUARTET   "Exposure," from *Third Stream Music.*

B. AREL   *Stereo Electronic Music No. 1.*

M. DAVIDOVSKY   *Electronic Study No. 1.*

LISTENING 8.3

The following theme-and-variations examples illustrate the many ways a musical idea can be varied. For now just get the flavor of unity and variety provided. Later we shall introduce other variation forms.

J. S. BACH   Aria with Thirty Variations for Harpsichord Solo in G, S. 988 (*Goldberg*).

W. A. MOZART   ○ Twelve Variations for Piano on "Ah, vous dirai-je, Maman," in C, K. 265 (300*e*).

L. VAN BEETHOVEN   ○● Sonata for Violin and Piano in A, op. 47, II; ○ Concerto for Violin and Orchestra in D, op. 61, II; Symphony 5 in c, op. 67, II; Symphony 3 in E♭, op. 55, IV.

then by two violins; a rhythm pattern with a subtle change of tempo; a melody in one key and then in a closely related key; a chord progression thickly spaced and then a bit more thinly spaced; a high-register passage followed by a middle-register passage. Here there may be strong elements of repetition mixed with contrasts; or to put it the other way around, the contrasts are slight ones to what are basically repetitions. When differences are slight, the two procedures begin to merge and blend. Both are in operation together, interdependent and intermixed, creating a "unified variety" or a "varied unity." Between the two extremes of obvious differences and subtle alterations the composer has available an enormous number of generative possibilities provided by the procedures of repetition and contrast (LISTENING 8.2).

VARIATION

In discussing repetition and contrast, we introduced the idea of making changes in musical material to give a sense of variety within unity. One important way of creating changes is called "variation." The term variation has a more technical, narrower meaning in music than does the word "variety": Variety is achieved by any change, such as those discussed above; variation is a particular procedure involving the restatement of an idea with some aspect altered, deleted, or replaced. For example, a melody may be stated. Then it is restated, but this time it is ornamented with notes added between the original notes. In a second variation the melody undergoes a change in rhythm—the pitches remain the same, but the durations are shortened. In a third variation the melody is turned upside down. This is followed by a variation in texture: the original homophonic setting has now become polyphonic, the original melody heard in counterpoint with a subsidiary melody. And so it goes; the original idea is presented again and again, but each time with something varied. Obviously, the procedure of variation depends on repetition, and yet each variation can be considered a contrast to the original.

We shall soon discuss the musical forms (the structures of whole pieces) based on each of the procedures explained here. Several forms depend on variation; but for the moment, the most obvious variation procedure, theme and variations (LISTENING 8.3), will serve to introduce the subject in the clearest way.

ERNŐ DOHNÁNYI   Variations on a Nursery Song, op. 25.

J. BRAHMS   Variations on a Theme by Haydn in B♭, op. 56a.

L. ARMSTRONG   "When the Saints Go Marching In," from *Louis Armstrong at the Crescendo, Vol. 2.*

THE MODERN JAZZ QUARTET   "Between the Devil and the Deep Blue Sea," from *The Modern Jazz Quartet.*

LISTENING 8.4

The clearest examples of development occur in the sonata-allegro form, which has a special section set aside for it and which we shall explain later. For now, listen to the beginning of the following pieces, where the ideas are stated, and then listen to the development section to get a sense of how the ideas are worked out. The approximate timings will help you find the development section (3.42 means 3 minutes 42 seconds).

F. J. HAYDN   Symphony 101 in D, I. Development starts about 3.42 from beginning and lasts about 1.31.

W. A. MOZART   ○ Symphony 36 in C, K. 425, I. Development starts about 5.59 from beginning and lasts about 0.55.

○● Symphony 40 in g, K. 550, I. Development starts about 4.10 from beginning and lasts about 1.17. IV. Development starts about 1.57 from beginning and lasts about 1.10.

L. VAN BEETHOVEN   ○● Symphony 5 in c, op. 67, I. Development starts about 1.26 from beginning and lasts about 1.27.

F. P. SCHUBERT   Symphony 8 in b, I (*Unfinished*). Development starts about 3.59 from beginning and lasts about 3.03.

B. BARTÓK   Quartet for Strings 4, I. Development starts about 0.57 from beginning and lasts about 2.24.

Musical forms

DEVELOPMENT

Like "variation," the word "development" has both a broad meaning and a narrower, more technical meaning. In the broad sense, every repetition develops or continues or adds to the unfolding piece of music, as does every contrast. And every variation helps build the formed whole that has developed from beginning to end. In the more technical sense, the procedure of development is a particular one, used most often in the center section of the sonata-allegro form (see later in this chapter). Here a musical idea is worked out: its implications are explored; its potential expressiveness is searched out, uncovered, and displayed.

The idea may be a theme that suggests within itself a number of possibilities for investigation. Usually its development includes breaking it up into parts, which are then manipulated separately for a while before they are put back together. When the whole theme is heard again, it sounds fresh, carrying with it the new insights that the fragmentation uncovered. Other common development devices operate to alter the order of events in a musical idea, to expand and contract the distance between pitches, to speed up and slow down the durations of the notes, to add many extra pitches to harmonies and to change harmonic progressions, to explore different textures for the same idea (such as to state a theme homophonically and later in a variety of contrapuntal settings), to change key frequently for a "scattershot" effect in the ideas, to combine several ideas previously separate, to vary dynamic levels dramatically, to leap from one register to another, or to present ideas in radically different tone-color settings.

The effect of all this and much more is one of exploring. Wherever development is found, whether in a specific section set aside for it, for a few moments here and there in an ongoing piece, or as the basic procedure for an entire composition, there will be repetitions, contrasts, and variations, along with a working out of possibilities for expanding the expressiveness of musical ideas (LISTENING 8.4). Development is a basic and exciting way of giving a sense of variety within a unified whole.

The four procedures discussed above have been used in several characteristic ways in the history of music. These ways of putting the proce-

LISTENING 8.5

The following examples are strophic songs. Each song has its inner phrase substructure. Listen to the repetitions of *A* first, and then see whether you can discern how each *A* is structured.

F. P. SCHUBERT   *Die schöne Müllerin,* op. 25, nos. 1, o 7–9, 12, 14, 16, 20; *Die Winterreise,* op. 89, no. 6: "Wasserflut" ("Floodtide").

J. BRAHMS   *Acht Lieder und Romanzen,* op. 14, no. 7: "Ständchen" ("Serenade"); *Fünf Gedichte,* op. 19, no. 2: "Scheiden und Meiden" ("Parting and Shunning").

PETER, PAUL AND MARY   "Stewball," "Don't Think Twice," "Freight Train," "Quit Your Lowdown Ways," "Long Chain On," from *In the Wind.*

BOB DYLAN   "Pledging My Time," "I Want You," "Leopardskin Pill-box Hat," from *Blonde on Blonde.*

LISTENING 8.6

In the following outlines the measure numbers in the left-hand column can serve as guides while you listen. They indicate when the small sections (small letters) and the large sections (capital letters) appear.

F. P. SCHUBERT   *Die schöne Müllerin,* op. 25, no. 1: "Das Wandern."

Measure

1	Piano introduction	
4	*a* "Das Wandern ist . . ."	
8	*a* repeated	*A*
12	*b* "Das muss ein schlechter . . ."	

The entire song is then repeated several times in strophic form.

F. P. SCHUBERT   o *Die schöne Müllerin,* op. 25, no. 18: "Trockne Blumen."

Measure

1	*a* "Ihr Blumlein alle . . ."	*A*
16	*a* repeated (different words: "Ach, Thränen machen . . .")	
30	*b* "Und wenn sie wandelt . . ."	

dures together according to established practice are called "forms." Each moment of a piece has been formed by the composer; and each formed moment contributes to the total shape of the work—that is, its form, its overall design or structure.

Some pieces have very clear form, easy to identify and easy to hear. Others are so loose and free in their form that they cannot be placed in any particular form category; so we simply call them "free forms" and let it go at that. In between are many pieces that belong to some form category but only in a rough sort of way. They have many of the characteristics of a particular category but are also different in important features. Even those pieces which are used as models for particular forms seldom follow the model exactly. So when we talk about a musical form's having such-and-such structure, we are talking about a kind of average. Of course, the average may not really exist; nevertheless, the guidelines roughed out by a description of an average form can help the listener find his way through many pieces related to that form. The danger lies in thinking that individual pieces must conform to the average although few pieces do. With this warning in mind, we can safely describe some of the major form categories to lead you to a grasp of whole musical compositions.

There are essentially five categories of musical forms, behind all of which stands the procedure of repetition, with the use of one or more of the other procedures—contrast, variation, development—as a major organizing device. These five basic categories are as follows:

1. Forms based on repetition alone.
2. Forms based on repetition with contrast.
3. Forms based on repetition with variation.
4. Forms based on repetition with development.
5. Free forms, which contain various combinations of repetition, contrast, variation, and development.

1. REPETITION ALONE (*AAA* . . .)

The number of forms based entirely on repetition is very small because only a limited amount of interest can be generated when there is a limited amount of variety. Some songs consist of a single melody repeated over and over, each time to different words (occasionally even

39   *b* repeated (same words; phrase extended *B*
       four measures)

52   Piano coda

J. S. BACH   Suite for Orchestra in b, S. 1067, VI: *Menuet.*

Measure			Measure		
1	*a*	*A*	17	*b*	*B*
9	*a* repeated		33	*b* repeated	

J. S. BACH   Suite for Orchestra in b, S. 1067, IV: ○ *Bourrée* I, *Bourrée* II.

Bourrée I

Measure			Measure		
1	*a*	*A*	17	*b*	*B*
9	*a* repeated		32	*b* repeated	

Bourrée II

Measure			Measure		
1	*a* (flute solo)	*A*	9	*b*	*B*
5	*a* repeated		17	*b* repeated	

Bourrée I is then repeated.

J. S. BACH   Cantata 80, *Ein feste Burg ist unser Gott,* VIII: ○ *Chorale.*

Measure		
1	*a* "Das Wort sie . . ."	*A*
5	*a* repeated (different words: "Er ist bei . . .")	
9	*b* "Nehmen sie . . ."	*B*

the words are repeated). If we label the melody *A*, the form of such music is symbolized as *AAA* . . . . The technical term is "strophic."

A simple example is the nursery tune "London Bridge," of which the melody falls into two phrases:

London Bridge is falling down, falling down, falling down, . . . (1)
London Bridge is falling down, my fair lady. . . . (2)

Both phrases together complete the song, which can be designated *A*. Within each *A* are two identifiable parts, the two phrases. If we want to pay attention to that level of the form, we have to recognize that phrase 2 begins just like phrase 1 but ends differently. Because of their similarity, we can call the first phrase *a* and the second a_1. (If phrase 2 were quite different from phrase 1, we could call it *b*.) The outline of "London Bridge" now becomes:

This little analysis is intended to raise one of the troublesome problems in perceiving musical form: Which *level* of the form are we talking about? In almost all cases music has different form levels, each a subdivision of a broader one. We shall try to make clear which one we are discussing. Our analyses will use capital letters for the large sections of pieces and small letters for the subdivisions within the large sections since the analyses will seldom go beyond these two broad levels (LISTENING 8.5).

One other repetition form should be mentioned, the *round*. In it a single melody is repeated over and over, each time overlapping the previous statement in contrapuntal texture. The form is thus a set of overlapping *A*'s, as diagramed in the margin. (Compare page 96.)

2. REPETITION WITH CONTRAST (*AB, ABA, ABACA* . . .)

Addition of contrasting material opens up many opportunities for building musical forms containing variety as well as unity. Alternation of

LISTENING 8.7

W. A. MOZART ○ Twelve Variations for Piano on "Ah, vous dirai-je, Maman" in C, K. 265 (300*e*). The theme of this piece is in the following form:

Measure		Measure	
1	*a*	17	*b*
9	*a* repeated	25	*a*

Each variation follows precisely the same form except for the twelfth and last, which doubles the length of the *b* and adds a coda. Listen to all, following the *aaba* form in each variation.

LISTENING 8.8

W. A. MOZART *Eine kleine Nachtmusik* in G, K. 525, III: *Menuetto*.

Menuetto

Measure		Measure		
1	*a*	16	*a₁*	
8	*a* repeated	24	*a₁* repeated	*A*

Trio

32	*b*	48	*b₁*	
40	*b* repeated	60	*b₁* repeated	*B*

Menuetto

72	*a*		
80	*a₁*	*A*	

W. A. MOZART Symphony 41 in C, K. 550, ○ III: *Menuetto*.

Menuetto

Measure		Measure		
1	*a*	33	*a₁*	
17	*a* repeated	76	*a₁* repeated	*A*

Trio

119	*b*	135	*b₁*	
127	*b* repeated	155	*b₁* repeated	*B*

Menuetto

175	*a*		
191	*a₁*	*A*	

repeated sections with contrasting sections is one of the most common ways to contruct a piece of music.

The simplest use of contrast is a musical idea, *A*, followed by a different but related idea, *B;* sometimes one or the other (or both) sections are repeated: *AAB* or *ABB* or *AABB* (LISTENING 8.6). The second idea usually completes the first, bringing the piece to a logical conclusion in a unified way. In this sense the *B* section is not so much a completely contrasting section as a complementary, rounding-off idea.

A common way to handle a contrasting section is to place it between the first section and a repeat of the first section to make the structure *ABA*. Any section can be repeated without alteration of the basic outline, and the usual way to do this is to repeat the first *A* to construct *AABA* (LISTENING 8.7). Many songs are in this form. Here are a few examples from familiar songs; hum them to yourself to get the feeling of this form:

"All through the Night"

Sleep my child . . .	*a*
Guardian angels . . .	*a*
Soft the drowsy hours . . .	*b*
I my loving vigil . . .	*a*

"Oh Susanna"

I come from Alabama . . .	*a*
It rained all night . . .	*a*
Oh Susanna . . .	*b*
I've come from Alabama . . .	*a*

"Home on the Range"

Oh, give me a home . . .	*a*
Where seldom is heard . . .	*a₁*
Home, home on the range . . .	*b*
Where seldom is heard . . .	*a₁*

"Swanee River"

Way down upon the Swanee river . . .	*a*
There's where my heart . . .	*a₁*
All the world . . .	*b*
Oh, dear ones, how my heart grows weary . . .	*a₁*

F. J. HAYDN   Quartet for Strings in C, op. 76, no. 3, III: *Menuett.*

Menuett

Measure		Measure		
1	a	40	a_1	
20	a repeated	76	a_1 repeated	A

Trio

112	b	128	b_1	
120	b repeated	164	b_1 repeated	B

Menuett

200	a	
220	a_1	A

Other minuets are:

W. A. MOZART   Symphony 36 in C, K. 425, ○ III; Symphony 40 in g, K. 550, ○● III.

F. J. HAYDN   Symphony 101 in D, III.

L. VAN BEETHOVEN   Symphony 3 in E♭, op. 55, ○ III; Symphony 5 in c, op. 67, III. These two movements follow the general form of the classic minuet but are more boisterous than the stately dance of the classic era. Beethoven called the movements "*scherzo.*"

P. I. TCHAIKOVSKY   Symphony 5 in e, op. 64, ○ III. This movement follows the classic form, but the minuet has become a waltz.

LISTENING 8.9

A. VIVALDI   Concerto for Violin and Orchestra in E, op. 8, no. 1, ○ I. In this movement all the *A* sections are played by full orchestra. The contrasting sections are played by a solo violin with orchestral accompaniment.

Measure		Measure		Measure	
1	A	31	C	59	F
7	A_1	41	A_1	66	A_1
13	B	44	D	70	E_2
28	A_1	56	A_1	76	A

J. S. BACH   Partita 3 for Violin Solo in E, S. 1006, V: *Gavotte en*

(continued on page 138)

Still another way to use a contrast in between repetitions is to extend sections by including two closely related ideas in each. An *A* section will then include an *a* and a_1, the second idea being an extension of the first; a *B* section will include *b* and b_1. Then the *A* section is repeated. With internal repeats of the *a*'s and *b*'s, the entire form is often arranged as follows:

A	B	A
aaa_1a_1	bbb_1b_1	aa_1

This structure is frequently found in pieces called "minuets" (or *menuet* or *menuetto*) of the eighteenth and early nineteenth centuries. The first *A* is the minuet, the *B* is called "trio," and the minuet is then repeated, but usually without the repeats of the *a* and a_1 (LISTENING 8.8). The third movement of many classic symphonies (see Chapter 12) is in this form.

One other major way to create a musical structure with the procedure of contrast is to state an idea, *A*, follow it with a contrasting idea, *B*, repeat the first idea, *A*, then state a totally new idea, *C*, and follow it with another repeat of the first idea, *A*. This alternation of contrasting material between a repeated section can be extended indefinitely: *ABACADA, ...*

The *A* section need not be identical each time it reappears; the *A* can become A_1, A_2, and so on. The contrasting sections can be similar to one another or very different, and each of the sections can itself be a short *ab* or *aba* form. So the simple idea of alternating contrasting and repeated material can become complex indeed in the hands of an adventurous composer. The general form, with all its alterations, is called "rondo" (LISTENING 8.9). It has been popular with composers for hundreds of years.

3. REPETITION WITH VARIATION ($AA_1A_2A_3 . . .$)

The variation procedure gives rise to several forms that composers have found useful for centuries. The most common of these is the theme and variations, in which a musical idea (theme) is stated clearly at the beginning so that the listener can get it firmly in mind and then is restated several times, each time being varied in some way. Each variation is intended to show the idea in a new light. The variations can range from simple ones, in which only a slight change has been made, to extremely complex treatments, in which the original idea has been *rondeau.* A guitar version of this piece is also available on record.

Measure		Measure	
1	*A*	48	*A*
8	*A* repeated	56	*D*
16	*B*	72	*A*
24	*A*	80	*E*
32	*C*	100	*A*

L. VAN BEETHOVEN   Sonata for Piano in C, op. 2, no. 3, III.

Measure	
1	*A*
16	Episode (extension material)
26	*B*
41	A_1
56	*C*
111	A_2
125	Episode
134	*B*
146	*A* ideas extended (a long coda)

Other rondos are:

W. A. MOZART   Quintet for Strings in E♭, K. 614, II; Rondo for Piano in a, K. 511.

F. J. HAYDN   Symphony 88 in G, IV; Symphony 101 in D, IV; Symphony 103 in E♭, IV.

L. VAN BEETHOVEN   Concerto for Violin and Orchestra in D, op. 61, III; Sonata for Piano in B♭, op. 22, IV.

B. BARTÓK   *Music for String Instruments, Percussion, and Celesta,* IV.

LISTENING 8.10

In the examples of LISTENING 8.3 try to keep the original theme in mind as it is subjected to variations. Feel the differently expressive character of each treatment of the theme as the composer explores its varied possibilities.

Some additional theme-and-variations compositions are:

W. A. MOZART   Sonata for Piano in A, K. 331, I.

so transformed as to be hardly recognizable (LISTENING 8.10). Each variation is a separate section of the piece so that the form can be outlined as $AA_1A_2A_3, \ldots$. Usually the sections are clearly distinguished from each other, but sometimes the change from one variation to another is more gradual. And often the form is not pure or simple, elements of other forms being mixed in as the music proceeds.

In addition to the theme-and-variations form, there is another procedure based on progressive repetitions with variations: *continuous variation.* In this procedure a musical idea is stated over and over; the idea itself is not changed, but the accompanying material is different each time. So the restatements of the idea are heard in a continually varied context.

Several descriptions exist for this kind of form: cantus firmus, passacaglia, chaconne, or ground bass (when the theme is always heard in the lowest part). We need not be concerned with the differences among them, for in each our ear recognizes the restated idea but hears it in a wide variety of contexts (LISTENING 8.11).

In the composition of polyphonic music there are several procedures related to variation, of which the most important is fugue. It is, however, impossible to outline a single form as the "genuine" fugue because fugue is less a set form than a loose combination of several procedures.

The crucial one is imitation. The beginning section of most fugues, called the "exposition," states a distinctive idea, the "subject." When the subject is over, the part that stated it goes on to another idea ("countersubject"). At the same time, a second part enters with the original idea. At that point two ideas are being set off against each other. A third imitation of the original idea can be stated, adding still another line of music to the texture. The use of imitation in a cumulative, contrapuntal way is the distinguishing characteristic of the fugue. After the exposition, the original ideas are varied, developed, and altered. The subject continues to be heard, but in different settings and interrupted by "episodes," which explore related material and heighten the action. Toward the end of the fugue the subject is often heard again in its original shape. Sometimes the fugue will close with the opening ideas tumbling over one another in quick succession (*stretto*) and a final statement of the original subject ending in a strong cadence in the original key.

The subject of a fugue is the key to its entire character since it is the basic material that pervades the piece. Each time the subject appears,

F. J. HAYDN   Quartet for Strings in C, op. 76, no. 3, II; Symphony 103 in E♭, II.

L. VAN BEETHOVEN   Quartet for Strings in E♭, op. 127, II.

B. BRITTEN   *Young Person's Guide to the Orchestra*, op. 34.

NORMAN DELLO JOIO   Sonata for Piano 3, I.

S. PROKOFIEV   Concerto for Piano and Orchestra 3 in C, op. 26, II.

I. STRAVINSKY   Octet for Wind Instruments, II.

LISTENING 8.11

J. S. BACH   Mass in b, S. 232: Crucifixus; Partita 2 for Violin Solo in d, S. 1004, VI: Chaconne (several guitar versions of this piece have been recorded); ○ ● Passacaglia and Fugue for Organ in c, S. 582.

J. BRAHMS   Symphony 4 in e, op. 98, IV.

B. BRITTEN   *Peter Grimes*, op. 33: Passacaglia.

W. SCHUMAN   Symphony 3 (1941), I: Passacaglia.

LISTENING 8.12

In the following fugues concentrate first on recognizing the subject as it keeps reappearing. After you are fairly secure at that, pay more attention to the other material and how it relates to the subject. Try to recognize the subject even when it has been altered in various ways.

J. S. BACH   ○ Fugue for Organ in g, S. 578; Passacaglia and Fugue for Organ in c, S. 582; Toccata and Fugue for Organ in d, S. 565; fugues from *The Well-tempered Clavier*, Books I, II; *Kunst der Fuge* (*Art of Fugue*) in d, S. 1080.

W. A. MOZART   ○ Requiem in d, K. 626, I: Kyrie section.

B. BARTÓK   ○ ● *Music for String Instruments, Percussion, and Celesta*, I.

I. STRAVINSKY   *Symphony of Psalms*, II. Double fugue, having two subjects.

P. HINDEMITH   Sonata for Piano 3, IV.

W. SCHUMAN   ○ ● Symphony 3 (1941), II: Fugue.

it is heard in a new light because of the other material accompanying it, and the subject itself is transformed in a variety of ways throughout the piece. All this must be kept track of by the listener—no easy job. The challenges of fugue are so intriguing, for composers as well as listeners, that it has been practiced for a long time. Whether old or new, fugue presents the listener with a unique combination of repetition with variation and a real test of the powers of skillful listening. (LISTENING 8.12).

4. REPETITION WITH DEVELOPMENT

In the discussion of development procedure we explained its usefulness as a means of musical exploration. Sonata-allegro form, or sonata form or first-movement form (which is misleading in that other movements are often in this form), is a particular structure that has evolved over the years to provide for development within a unified whole. The form had taken on its classic shape by the time of Haydn and Mozart and has been used, in expanded and altered ways, ever since. Given the freedom with which the sonata-allegro outline has been adapted to individual uses, you must take our explanation only as a broad guide.

There are three major sections in this form: exposition, development, and recapitulation. A slow introduction may precede the exposition; a coda may follow the recapitulation; but the three major sections are the essential characteristics of the form.

The exposition states, or exposes, the ideas that are to be the basis of the entire movement. There may be one, two, or several ideas. These ideas are customarily contrasting, both in overall character and in key. The drama of the exposition section lies in the contrast—the setting-off of ideas and keys. Especially in nineteenth-century music, the first theme, fast and in the tonic, is often aggressive and dramatic, whereas the second theme, in a different key and sometimes slightly slower, is more lyrical. If a third theme is present, it is highly individual, serving to conclude the exposition section. In small pieces the ideas in the exposition are short and easily recognized; in large works the ideas are not simply contrasting themes but contrasting idea clusters, each of which can be quite complex. In any event the exposition section ends in a key different from the opening tonic. Originally, the entire exposition section was repeated, but as the form became longer and more involved,

LISTENING 8.13

Listen again to some of the sonata-allegro movements in LISTENING 8.4. This time listen to the entire movement, noting as many features of the form as you can.

Other sonata-allegro movements are:

W. A. MOZART ○ *Eine kleine Nachtmusik* in G, K. 525, I; Symphony 41 in C, K. 551, I, ○ II, ○ IV.

L. VAN BEETHOVEN Sonata for Violin and Piano in A, op. 47, I, III; Concerto for Violin and Orchestra in D, op. 61, I; ○ Symphony 5 in c, op. 67, IV; Quartet for Strings in B♭, op. 130, I, III; ○● Sonata for Piano in c, op. 13, I.

F. J. HAYDN Symphony 104 in D, I, IV; Symphony 103 in E♭, I; Symphony 100 in G, I, IV; Symphony 94 in G, I, IV.

F. P. SCHUBERT Symphony 8 in b, I, II.

F. MENDELSSOHN Symphony 4 in A, op. 90, I.

B. BARTÓK ○● *Music for String Instruments, Percussion, and Celesta*, II.

J. BRAHMS Symphony 2 in D, op. 73, I, IV.

LISTENING 8.14

These pieces are generally in free form. The character of the music comes largely from its freely unfolding nature, which produces a sense of spontaneous generation of ideas.

J. S. BACH Toccata and Fugue for Organ in d, S. 565: Toccata; Chromatic Fantasy and Fugue for Harpsichord in d, S. 903: Fantasy; Fantasia and Fugue for Organ in g, S. 542: Fantasia.

W. A. MOZART Fantasy for Piano in c, K. 475.

F. P. SCHUBERT *Moments musicaux,* op. 94; Nocturne for Piano in E♭, op. 148.

R. SCHUMANN *Carnaval,* op. 9; *Fantasiestücke,* op. 12;

composers ceased to specify that the exposition was to be repeated.

The development section emphasizes exploration. Here the ideas from the exposition are subjected to the development techniques described previously. The overall pace of this section is more active than is the exposition, with quick changes of key, of rhythm, of melodic flow, or of texture. The predictability of the exposition gives way to uncertainty, fragmentation, imbalance. This section may last only a few moments in an early work, but with Beethoven and many later composers it became the major section of the form. Whatever the length, toward the end the key gradually centers around the dominant (the fifth note of the scale) as preparation for the return in the tonic of the first idea from the exposition.

With this return to the exposition the recapitulation section begins. Now the opening ideas are heard again, usually in their original order, but this time they are all likely to remain in the tonic key. The reintroduction gives the effect of viewing the ideas in a new light: We first heard them, new and fresh, in dramatic opposition; then their inner nature was explored; now we hear them very simply, not even with key changes, and they are no longer what they first seemed. Having glimpsed their expressive power under the surface, we hear them now as more significant than we would have at first imagined. The sonata-allegro form has served its purpose of musical discovery (LISTENING 8.13).

So we may outline sonata-allegro form as follows:

Introduction (if present)   Exposition   Development   Recapitulation   Coda (if present)

5. FREE

In the forms described so far it has been possible to characterize types and to assume that pieces of that type will be similarly structured. Many subordinate differences will exist among pieces of the same type, but the major characteristics can be identified because there is a degree of consistency. On the other hand, many pieces are characterized by a form that cannot be described so neatly as those above. All are formed in that they contain unified and varied sound events created by the composer, and they are far from being incoherent occurrences; they simply do not lend themselves to categorization in the traditional groupings.

Kinderscenen, op. 15; *Papillons*, op. 2.

J. BRAHMS   Ballades for Piano, opp. 10, 118, no. 3; Intermezzi for Piano, opp. 76, 116–119.

F. F. CHOPIN   Preludes for Piano, op. 28; Impromptus for Piano, opp. 29, 36, 51, 66; Études for Piano, opp. ○ 10, 25.

C. DEBUSSY   Preludes for Piano, Books I and II; Études for Piano, Books I and II; ○● *The Afternoon of a Faun.*

F. LISZT   *Les Préludes;* Hungarian Rhapsody 2.

M. RAVEL   *Gaspard de la Nuit; Jeux d'Eau.*

J. SIBELIUS   *Finlandia,* op. 26; *The Swan of Tuonela,* op. 22.

BEDŘICH SMETANA   *The Moldau.*

R. WAGNER   "Siegfried Idyll."

LISTENING 8.15

The following pieces use traditional instruments; so they have a built-in familiarity, at least in tone color. Listen for the procedures of repetition, contrast, variation, and development, freely used.

I. STRAVINSKY   Symphony in C; Capriccio for Piano and Orchestra; *Threni.*

CARLOS CHÁVEZ   Toccata for Percussion.

O. MESSIAEN   *Et exspecto resurrectionem mortuorum; Chronochromie;* Preludes for Piano.

GYÖRGY LIGETI   *Atmospheres.*

E. BLOCH   *Schelomo* for Cello and Orchestra.

C. T. GRIFFES   ○● *The White Peacock,* op. 7.

B. BARTÓK   *The Miraculous Mandarin.*

G. SCHULLER   *Seven Studies on Themes of Paul Klee.*

P. BOULEZ   *Le Marteau sans maître.*

The next group is partly or fully electronic. The forms are free in that they fit no traditional category; but the music depends just as much as does any other formed music on the four basic procedures to create unity and variety. Listen for repetitions of sounds, for contrasts between sounds, for variations to sounds, and for development or extension or drawing out of sound ideas. All these make the pieces "formed."

L. BERIO   ○ *Omaggio a Joyce.*

V. USSACHEVSKY   *Creation-Prologue.*

D. ERB   ○● *Reconnaissance,* I.

K. GABURO   *Antiphony III.*

O. LUENING   *Concerted Piece; Gargoyles; Piece for Tape Recorder.*

(continued on page 142)

When clarity and precision of form play a large part in the expressiveness of a piece, the music is usually described as classic. The classic period (Chapter 11) produced much music in which form *as such* had a major role. That is why so many of our examples of traditional form come from that period (for example, the works of Mozart, Haydn, and Beethoven). And much music of the twentieth century has been classic in its return to dependence on clarity of form (see the discussion of neoclassicism in Chapter 13).

The romantic period, that is, most of the nineteenth century (Chapter 12), and the baroque (Chapter 10) created music of a clearly formed sort but also a good deal in which orderliness of form was not striven for. Many baroque and romantic pieces are in "free form," in which the procedures of repetition, contrast, variation, and development are employed in unpredictable ways (LISTENING 8.14). When listening to such music, you do not get a sense of knowing just where you are in relation to an overall structure as you do, for example, in sonata-allegro form. There is, instead, an ongoing, flowing rise and fall of involvement as the music unfolds from beginning to end.

CONTEMPORARY FREE FORMS   Much music of this century continues to use the traditional forms described in sections 1 to 4 above. Repetition, contrast, variation, and development are so basic to music that, despite radical changes in such musical elements as rhythm, melody, harmony, and tone color, the forming of music remains largely a function of these time-honored procedures. A surprising number of contemporary works can be understood as extended and altered but recognizable rondos, fugues, sonata-allegros, and the like.

But several new versions of the traditional procedures have appeared (LISTENING 8.15). One of the earliest and most long-lasting is serialism, initiated by Schoenberg and his followers and taken up in various ways by a great number of composers ever since. We have explained some of the important characteristics of Schoenberg's twelve-tone system in other places (pages 18 and 77). The student interested in its details will find ample information in the books cited at the end of Chapter 13 and under "Serial Music" in *Harvard Dictionary of Music.* The ideas of serialism have led to some recent uses only remotely related, if at all, to traditional formal conceptions. Some comments about such music will be made at the end of this chapter.

Other modern compositions are more comparable to traditional free

H. EL-DABH   *Leiyla and the Poet.*
E. VARESE   *Poème électronique.*
D. RAAIJMAKERS   *Contrasts.*
M. BABBITT   ○ *Composition for Synthesizer.*
Y. XENAKIS   ○● *Pithoprakta.*

Combinations of forms

LISTENING 8.16

Following are some representative works from the hundreds that exist in each category; there are many exceptions to any sort of rule about overall formal structure.

SONATAS

W. A. MOZART   Sonata for Piano in D, K. 576.

forms. They use the four basic procedures in novel ways without abandoning the conception of music as a process of creative forming. No matter how unusual their rhythm, melody, harmony, counterpoint, or tone color, no matter how far from traditional tonal rules and regulations they may stray, they are formed sound events having unity and variety. In this they are traditional music. They may sound quite untraditional in many ways, but in their form they continue to create a unified experience of interrelated sounds—the basic condition, many would argue, for anything that is to be perceived as music (LISTENING 8.15).

INSTRUMENTAL

The forms discussed to this point have represented the overall structure of single movements or one-movement pieces. Large musical works consist of several movements, each of which is in one or another of the forms mentioned or in a free form. No rule requires a composer to assemble any particular group of forms for a multimovement work. However, so many composers have made similar choices that it is possible to state a few generalizations about the common types of multimovement compositions, which in instrumental music are the sonata, the symphony, the concerto, and the suite.

The sonata is usually a piece for a solo instrument, such as piano, or for a solo instrument (violin, flute, and so on) and piano. A typical classic sonata would be in four movements: the first in fast sonata-allegro form; the second in slow three-part, sonata-allegro, or other form; the third in fast or moderate minuet-and-trio form; and the fourth in fast sonata-allegro or rondo form. Many three-movement sonatas exist (usually in movements fast, slow, fast), and there are some with more than four movements. The basic conception is that of complementary movements, each of which has its own identity yet contributing to a larger whole.

This conception is the foundation of most string quartets, symphonies, and concertos, among which the major difference is the performance medium: a typical string quartet being a sonata for four string instruments; a symphony, a sonata for orchestra; a concerto, a sonata for solo instrument with orchestral accompaniment. All are made up of several movements in a more or less expected order of forms and tempos, the expectation naturally being often fulfilled in works of the

F. J. HAYDN   Sonata for Piano 52 in E♭.

L. VAN BEETHOVEN   ○● Sonata for Violin and Piano in A, op. 47 (*Kreutzer*); ○● Sonata for Piano in c, op. 13 (*Pathétique*).

J. BRAHMS   Sonata for Clarinet and Piano in f, op. 120, no. 1.

B. BARTÓK   Sonata for Violin and Piano 1.

QUARTETS

W. A. MOZART   Quartet for Strings in B♭, K. 589.

F. J. HAYDN   Quartet for Strings in C, op. 76, no. 3 (*Emperor*).

L. VAN BEETHOVEN   ○● Quartet for Strings in B♭, op. 130.

F. P. SCHUBERT   Quartet for Strings in d, D. 810.

M. RAVEL   Quartet in F.

SYMPHONIES

W. A. MOZART   Symphonies ○ 36, ○● 40, ○ 41 in C, g, C, K. 425, 550, 551.

F. J. HAYDN   ○● Symphony 101 in D.

L. VAN BEETHOVEN   ○● Symphonies 3, 5 in E♭, c, opp. 55, 67.

J. BRAHMS   ○● Symphony 2 in D, op. 73.

H. BERLIOZ   ○● *Symphonie fantastique*, op. 14.

P. I. TCHAIKOVSKY   ○● Symphony 5 in e, op. 64.

I. STRAVINSKY   ○● *Symphony of Psalms*.

W. SCHUMAN   ○● Symphony 3 (1941).

H. HANSON   ○ Symphony 2, op. 30 (*Romantic*).

CONCERTOS

A. VIVALDI   ○ Concerto for Violin and Orchestra in E, op. 8, no. 1; ○● Concerto for Two Flutes and Orchestra in C, F. VI, no. 2.

L. VAN BEETHOVEN   ○ Concerto for Violin and Orchestra in D, op. 61.

P. I. TCHAIKOVSKY   ○ Concerto for Piano and Orchestra in b♭, op. 23.

F. LISZT   ○ Concerto for Piano and Orchestra 1 in E♭.

SUITES

J. S. BACH   ○ Suite for Orchestra in b, S. 1067.

G. F. HANDEL   "Royal Fireworks" Music.

F. MENDELSSOHN   *A Midsummer Night's Dream*, op. 61.

G. BIZET   *L'Arlésienne* Suites 1, 2.

I. STRAVINSKY   ○● *L'Histoire du soldat*.

R. R. BENNETT   ○ *Suite of Old American Dances*.

R. VAUGHAN WILLIAMS   ○ *English Folksong* Suite.

classic period and less fulfilled from that time on. It would be unwise to bet on a modern sonata's being in classic order; but one could safely bet that the idea of independent yet related movements will have been retained (LISTENING 8.16).

Another multimovement instrumental type is the suite. In the baroque period the suite was a group of stylized dances, the most common being the allemande (in moderate tempo and duple meter), courante (faster tempo, triple meter), sarabande (slow, triple meter), and gigue (fast, compound meter). Several more dances—minuets, bourrées, gavottes, polonaises—could be inserted as the composer wished. This dance-suite type was the basis of many baroque chamber-music and orchestral compositions. Later, various assortments of movements strung out one after another became known as suites, the most popular of which were the descriptive suites of the nineteenth century. These, such as Tchaikovsky's *Nutcracker* suite, are series of pieces with descriptive titles, sometimes ballets but often only for listening (LISTENING 8.16). They follow no particular order of forms.

VOCAL

Just as many large instrumental works consist of several movements, each in some definite form, many vocal works are collections of movements. In Chapter 7 we discussed the major multimovement vocal types, opera, oratorio, cantata, mass, and song cycle, with examples of each. Our interest now is in the way such works are formed out of separate but related parts.

Opera, as a musical type, can easily take up an entire course of study by itself. Many controversies have surrounded it throughout its history, most stemming from its use of elements from many other arts—visual, dramatic, poetic, dance—than the musical. Some have argued that this makes opera better than other kinds of music; others have argued that it makes it worse. Many persons believe that opera should always be sung in the language for which it was originally composed to protect the close relationship between word sounds and musical sounds; others argue that performances should be translated into the language of a particular audience so that listeners can understand what the words mean. Controversy exists about whether opera is dead, having been replaced in modern life by operetta and musical comedy, or whether

OPERA

A part of Act I of Mozart's *Don Giovanni,* K. 527, has this structure:

Orchestra   An overture, of which the slow introduction contains a motive heard later in the finale. The fast section is in sonata-allegro form (exposition, development, recapitulation) and concludes with a half cadence, from which Act I promptly begins.

1. Four soloists and orchestra   A lengthy conversational singing section. The four solo voices are heard alone and in combination. Full orchestra accompanies.

2. Two soloists and continuo   Recitative. The continuo (harpsichord and cello) provides occasional accompaniment chords.

3. Two soloists and orchestra   Recitative, then a duet.

4. Two soloists and continuo   Recitative.

5. Three soloists and orchestra   An aria in *ABA* form for soprano. Two male soloists add occasional melodic fragments.

6. Three soloists and continuo   Recitative.

7. Soloist and orchestra   An aria in $\frac{4}{4}$, later changed to a lyric $\frac{3}{4}$ in which material is repeated several times.

8. Soloist and continuo   Short recitative.

9. Two soloists, chorus, and orchestra   A simple theme is repeated by the soloists, interrupted by the chorus.

10. Four soloists and continuo   Recitative.

11. Soloist and orchestra   An aria in free form.

12. Two soloists and continuo   Recitative.

13. Two soloists and orchestra   A duet. Two sections, the first in duple meter and the second in compound ($\frac{6}{8}$) meter.

14. Two soloists and continuo   Recitative.

15. Soloist and strings   An aria in free form.

16. Three soloists and continuo   Recitative.

17. Four soloists and orchestra   A quartet, four overlapping lines.

18. Soloist and continuo   Short recitative.

19. Two soloists and orchestra   Accompanied recitative followed by an aria, which is in *ABA* form.

Here is how Puccini's *La Bohème* is put together:

ACT I

1. Orchestral introduction   Only thirty-nine measures long, this material, with its thick opening chords in the lower register and contrasting following measures, is heard through the first scene.

2. The Bohemians in conversation   This section consists primarily of conversations between Rodolfo, Marcello, Colline, Schaunard, and Benoît. The style is recitative alternating with brief melodic passages. Occasionally the four men sing briefly together in quartet fashion. Heard in the orchestra is the introductory material, frequently alternating with a new waltzlike melody.

3. Rodolfo and Mimi in conversation   Recitative style alternating with brief melodic passages; becomes more legato in the duet between Rodolfo and Mimi, still in dialogue fashion.

4. ○ Aria, "Che gelida manina"   A solo by Rodolfo, through-composed in form and rather lengthy. The orchestra accompanies and frequently carries the melody of the soloist.

5. ○● Aria, "Mi chiamano Mimi"   Mimi presents her solo, the musical content of which is similar to Rodolfo's aria. The form is *ABA* (shortened), the orchestra frequently doubling the melody.

6. Cry from the streets   Bohemians call out and Rodolfo answers in recitative fashion. The rhythmic phrase (in lower strings) of the introduction is heard.

7. Duet, "O soave fanciulla"   A legato duet between Rodolfo and Mimi. The duet begins with Rodolfo alone; then Mimi enters on a unison high note. The duet continues, using brief fragments in alternating melodic and recitative style.

ACT II

1. A short orchestral introduction, consisting of a trumpet fanfare in accented ascending and descending chords, is followed by a lengthy section consisting of choruses, two- and three-voice dialogues, and brief arialike solos. There is much alternation between recitative style and melodic style. Several new melodies appear. The orchestral accompaniment frequently consists of material heard in the introduction to the act.

2. Aria, Musetta's waltz song   A soprano solo, which uses much rubato, in $\frac{3}{4}$ meter. The form is *ABA*. The orchestra frequently doubles the melody. Other voices are occasionally interjected.

3. Conversational section   Another dialogue section alternating in the use of recitative and legato melodic style. Familiar melodies are occasionally heard. The section closes with a chorus in animated march rhythm and thick harmony.

ACT III

1. Orchestral introduction   Of forty-eight measures, this introduction has thin overall texture. The lower strings play *tremolo* throughout while above them the woodwinds move in thin staccato chords that are later picked up by the harp.

2. Conversational section   This section consists of the dialogues characteristic of this opera. The orchestral material of the introduction is continued, frequently interrupted by women's small ensemble, men's small ensemble, and a brief statement of Mimi's aria "Mi chiamano Mimi." The section is closed by a return of the women's small ensemble and brief orchestral material.

3. Orchestral interlude   A brief orchestral section presenting the melody from "Mi chiamano Mimi." The texture is thin. This section closes with a thick chord.

4. Conversational section   Beginning with an unaccompanied soprano recitative, this section is comprised of several dialogues, brief arialike solos, new melodies, and brief phrases of music from Act I and the earlier part of this act. Both recitative and legato melodic styles are used in duet or trio fashion.

5. Aria, "Addio"   A soprano solo (Mimi) which is through-composed in form and modulates frequently.

6. Duet   A brief tenor solo introduces a duet for tenor and soprano (Rodolfo and Mimi).

7. Quartet   A soprano (Musetta) and baritone (Marcello) join to form a dynamic quartet to close the act. The quartet uses a mixture of dialogue and ensemble singing.

Preformed and unformed music

it is very much alive, changing with the times and showing continually renewed vitality. Whatever position you may take in these long-standing arguments, your enjoyment of opera can be enhanced in the same way as your enjoyment of any music: through perception of more of its expressiveness to share more of its power. The accompanying two outlines will give you a sense of how an opera unfolds through a succession of movements or parts (also see the discussion of Berg's *Wozzeck* in Chapter 13).

Outlines of oratorio, cantata, Mass, and song cycle (pages 146–149), like the preceding outlines of opera, will show how parts are strung together to make a whole. Of course, every composition is unique; so these outlines cannot be applied to the details of other works. The idea of successive parts, however, is common to most large vocal works.

The music we have discussed up to now has blended unity and variety. The major unifying force is repetition; contrast, variation, and development provide variety, and at the same time they add to the sense of a unified whole. As a composer works, making decision after decision about how a piece should proceed (forming the work), he is partly free to do anything he wants to do but is also partly limited by the decisions he has already made. For example, if he chooses to compose a piece with a strong key feeling (a strong sense of tonality), he must by necessity limit his choices of melodies and harmonies to those which emphasize tonal centers. If he chooses to compose a set of variations, he is free to create any variations he wishes, but he is not free to create a strophic song. Compositional decisions, like practically all other decisions, are made with some freedom and with some constraints; and most pieces reflect this condition, providing a sense of unpredictability, surprise, uncertainty, and the unexpected, balanced against a degree of predictability, probability, and expectedness. The combination of the unpredictable and the predictable lets us live through an experience that has both irregularity and order.

In recent years some composers have worked at the farthest reaches of predictability and unpredictability. At one end of the scale is so-called preformed music, in which the composer sets up some rules governing what can happen in a piece and then systematically plays out those

(continued on page 150)

ORATORIO

Only a part of the first section of Handel's *Messiah* is included in this outline. Arias, small ensembles, recitatives, and chorus passages alternate. Notice that certain forms within the oratorio fulfill the same purposes as they do in opera: Recitative tells the story quickly, whereas aria and chorus sections pause on certain aspects of the story and momentarily halt the action. Conductors of *Messiah* often do not use all parts of the work; so in any given performance do not be surprised if some of the following parts are left out or if a few different parts are inserted.

1. Orchestra An overture, for orchestra alone, in *AB* form. A slow homophonic *A* section is contrasted with a lively, polyphonic *B* section. A slow cadence concludes the overture.

2. Solo tenor and strings An arioso (small aria). Basically homophonic accompaniment with countermelody in motives. Ends with recitative.

Comfort ye my people. Prepare the way of the Lord.

3. Solo tenor and strings An aria for tenor. The orchestral introduction is repeated at the conclusion. Throughout the aria, the orchestra imitates the vocal line.

Every valley shall be exalted; every mountain and hill made low; the rough places plain; the crooked made straight.

4. Chorus and strings Polyphonic vocal texture. The orchestra provides harmonic accompaniment, sometimes doubling the voices. A homophonic, block-chord section appears frequently in the chorus.

And the glory of the Lord shall be revealed.

5. Recitative for bass solo and strings The orchestra provides only occasional chords at first. The vocal line is embellished twice. For the middle section, the orchestra provides a repeated-chord pattern.

Thus saith the Lord: I will shake all nations, the heavens, the earth, the sea, the dry land.

6. Aria for bass solo and strings Cast in *ABAB* form. The *A* section is homophonic, the orchestra providing block-chord accompaniment. The *B* section (*prestissimo*) has a fast repeated rhythmic pattern in the orchestra. The vocal line is in long phrases and often embellished. *A* is repeated briefly. The fast *B* section returns and concludes the aria.

But who may abide the day of His coming? For He is like a refiner's fire.

7. Chorus and orchestra (and oboes) A polyphonic texture. Much imitation between the voices. Momentary sections of block-chord harmonies.

And He shall purify the sons of Levi.

8. Recitative for alto solo and continuo A typical recitative: occasional chords from harpsichord and basses (continuo) support a very brief melodic line.

Behold a son shall be born and shall be called Emanuel—"God with us."

9. o *Aria for alto solo, violin, and continuo* The vocal line is generally set in short phrases, with its melodic content echoed by the violin. Occasional embellishments occur in the vocal line.

O Thou that tellest good tidings to Zion, get thee up into the high mountain. Lift up thy voice with strength. Say to the cities of Judah, Behold your God.

10. o● *Chorus and orchestra* Extended passages of imitation are offset by moments of block-chord declamation. The orchestra frequently supports with short, thin chords. For points of emphasis, a recurrent sixteenth-note figure is heard in the violins.

For unto us a child is born, and his name shall be called Wonderful, Counsellor, the mighty God, the everlasting Father, the Prince of Peace.

11. Orchestra A pastoral symphony cast in *da capo* form, that is, an *ABA* structure. It is characterized by smooth melodic motion set in $\frac{12}{8}$ meter.

CANTATA

Written for the Reformation festival of 1730, Bach's Cantata 80, *Ein feste Burg ist unser Gott* is constructed as follows:

1. ○ *Full orchestra and chorus* This long movement is made of several sections run together, each of which uses imitative polyphony. The chorale, in addition to being sung by the choir, is played by the trumpets several times.

God, a sure stronghold, will never fail us. He protects us from evil and trouble which assail us daily.

2. Sopranos with bass solo The chorale is carried by all the sopranos, against which the bass has a long spun-out countermelody.

Christ will uphold us. Those who follow Him will share in His victory.

3. Bass recitative A "song speech" for solo voice with simple accompaniment.

Christ rose triumphant for your sake. Let not sin take hold of you. Repent.

4. ○● *Aria for soprano and orchestra* The solo is supported by organ and cello only (continuo). The aria is set in ternary form, *ABA*.

Come Jesus and dwell in my heart. Bid evil depart; begone, sin—away, away.

5. Full orchestra and chorus The chorale theme is sung in unison by the entire chorus. The orchestra has an active, polyphonic texture.

Though evil persists all around us, we need not fear, for God shall smite the fiend.

6. Tenor recitative A song speech for tenor solo with simple accompaniment.

Stand with Jesus and trust His power. No foe can withstand you. Salvation is certain.

7. Duet for alto and tenor The two voices imitate each other throughout. The English horn and violin, also in imitation, weave a background of counterpoint as the accompaniment. The duet is in *da capo* form (at the conclusion of the movement, the beginning is repeated to make an *ABA*).

Blessed are those who carry God in their hearts.

8. ○ *Orchestra and chorus* A simple hymn arrangement of the chorale melody.

God will battle on our side; His might is all-prevailing.

MASS

This example is that of a particular kind of Mass, Mozart's Requiem in d, K. 626.

1. ○ *Requiem* (*soprano solo, chorus, and orchestra*)   Imitative polyphony. The orchestra contributes harmonic accompaniment figures. Near the end, a double fugue (two subjects) for chorus, doubled by the orchestra.

Grant them eternal rest. Lord have mercy, Christ have mercy, Lord have mercy.

2. *Dies Irae* (*full chorus and orchestra*)   Lively homophonic text setting. The orchestra doubles the chorus and adds rhythmic patterns.

Day of wrath and mourning. The Judge shall descend to pass sentence on all.

3. ○● *Tuba Mirum* (*four soloists and orchestra*)   Bass solo with countermelody in trombone. The other soloists enter one by one. A homophonic text setting and orchestral accompaniment conclude the movement.

The trumpet shall sound, calling all to the throne. All must answer the call. "What shall I plead, when even the just need mercy?"

4. *Rex Tremendae* (*chorus and orchestra*)   Trombones are prominent. A homophonic setting, with some imitation. The orchestra maintains a dotted rhythmic figure.

King of tremendous majesty, who sends us free salvation, save me, fount of pity.

5. ○ *Recordare* (*four soloists and orchestra*)   Contrapuntal imitation abounds, with some homophonic passages. The orchestra (strings and winds only) has a smooth countermelody throughout the movement.

[A lengthy text that asks for God's grace and mercy to save us from the undying fires of Hell.]

6. *Confutatis* (*full chorus and orchestra*)   Active two-part writing for men's voices in imitation, answered by two-part writing for women's voices in hushed, half-voice tones. A homophonic setting concludes the movement.

While the wicked are confounded in Hell, save me. Help me in my final condition.

7. ○ *Lacrimosa* (*chorus and orchestra*)   A homophonic setting, against which the strings weave a continually repeated motive.

Day of tears and weeping. Man must prepare for judgment. Spare him, God. Grant eternal rest.

8. *Domine Jesu* (*four soloists, chorus, and orchestra*)   Initially, the movement is in homophonic texture. A jagged fugal theme is then begun by the chorus. The four soloists then have a short passage in fugal imitation. The chorus follows with another theme, also treated fugally. The orchestra doubles the chorus, adding harmonic material. The trombones are prominent throughout.

Lord Jesus, deliver the faithful from Hell. Let the archangel Michael lead them to the sacred light, as Thou once promised Abraham and his children.

9. *Hostias* (*chorus and orchestra*)   Homophonic texture initially. The strings maintain a syncopated pattern. Then the final fugal

section from the Domine Jesu movement is repeated, supported by trombones.

We offer prayers and sacrifices of praise. Let the dead pass from death to life, as Thou once promised Abraham and his children.

Mozart died before completing the Requiem, and the following movements are thought to have been mostly composed by an associate, Franz Xaver Süssmayr:

10. ○ *Sanctus* (*chorus and orchestra*)   Homophonic texture at first, with strings in an active sixteenth-note pattern. The time signature changes to $\frac{3}{4}$, and the chorus begins a fugue, doubled by the orchestra.

Holy, holy, holy, Lord God of Hosts. Hosanna in the highest.

11. *Benedictus* (*four soloists, chorus, and orchestra*)   The four soloists sing overlapping lines, occasionally merging into a homophonic texture. The time signature $\frac{4}{4}$ is changed to $\frac{3}{4}$, and the full chorus repeats the Hosanna fugue from the Sanctus. The orchestra doubles and adds other melodic material.

Blessed is He that comes in the name of the Lord. Hosanna in the highest.

12. *Agnus Dei* (*soprano solo, chorus, and orchestra*)   Homophonic texture. The violins play a smooth, scalelike countermelody. The $\frac{3}{4}$ meter changes to $\frac{4}{4}$. The soprano repeats the same solo passage as in the Requiem (1), with new words. From this point to the end, the music is the same as it was in the Kyrie; only the text changes.

Lamb of God, who takes away the sins of the world, grant them eternal rest. Let perpetual light shine upon them.

SONG CYCLE

Schubert's *Die schöne Müllerin,* op. 25, is a typical *song cycle,* a series of songs (in various forms) of related thought and character designed to form a musical entity. Listen to this song cycle while following the words, using the indications given below as guides to the forms. (As we have seen, *strophic* refers to songs in which all stanzas of the text are sung to the same music; and *through-composed* refers to songs in which new music is provided for each stanza.)

1. *"Das Wandern"* (*"Wandering"*)   Strophic.
2. *"Wohin?"* (*"Whither?"*) $AA_1(ba_1)A_1$.
3. *"Halt!"* (*"Halt!"*)   Through-composed.
4. *"Danksagung an den Bach"* (*"Thanksgiving to the Brook"*)   ABA.
5. ○ *"Am Feierabend"* (*"At Leisure"*)   ABCDA (codetta).
6. *"Der Neugierige"* (*"The Questioner"*)   Through-composed.
7. ○ *"Ungeduld"* (*"Impatience"*)   Strophic.
8. *"Morgengruss"* (*"Morning Greeting"*)   Strophic.
9. *"Des Müllers Blumen"* (*"The Miller's Flowers"*)   Strophic.
10. *"Tränenregen"* (*"Rain of Tears"*) $AAAA_1$ (modified strophic).
11. *"Mein!"* (*"Mine!"*)   ABA.
12. *"Pause"* (*"Pause"*) $ABCA_1A_2$.
13. *"Mit dem grünen Lautenbande"* (*"With the Green Lute Ribbon"*)   Strophic.
14. *"Der Jäger"* (*"The Hunter"*)   Strophic.
15. *"Eifersucht und Stolz"* (*"Jealousy and Pride"*)   Through-composed.
16. *"Die liebe Farbe"* (*"The Beloved Color"*)   Strophic.
17. *"Die böse Farbe"* (*"The Hateful Color"*) $ABACA_1$.
18. ○ *"Trockne Blumen"* (*"Wither'd Flowers"*)   AABB.
19. ○ *"Der Müller und der Bach"* (*"The Miller and the Brook"*) ABA_1.
20. *"Des Baches Wiegenlied"* (*"The Brook's Lullaby"*)   Strophic.

rules. Schoenberg had made the first step in this direction when he set up some rules for the order in which pitches could be sounded in a piece, and other composers have gone even further, ordering (or "serializing") not only pitches but also rhythms, dynamics, tone colors, densities, or registers. Once a composer has decided the order in which events are to take place, composing consists in simply following the rules until they have all been accomplished. The composer Ernst Křenek describes such a process in one of his works:

> In my oratorio for voices and electronic sounds, Spiritus intelligentiae, sanctus, there is a section without voices (so to speak an "instrumental" interlude). The material of this section is a tempered scale of thirteen tones. From the continuum of this scale, groups of tones were selected to form alternatingly disjunct and conjunct heptachords of equal and symmetrical structure. A seven-tone pattern (seven-tone row) meanders through this system of pitches constantly retaining its principle of progress: from any tone on which it starts it goes up to the third and fourth, then back to the second, up to the sixth, back to the fifth, and it stops on the seventh tone of the network of pitches. Since the pattern always progresses conjunctly (which means that the first tone of its next appearance is identical with the last of the preceding) while the pitch system is based on the alternation of conjunct shapes, the internal intervallic configuration of the pattern is always different, although its general outline remains the same. After thirteen appearances the pattern lands again on the tone from which it started, and the "rotation" has come to an end.*

Curiously, neither the composer nor the listener can predict how the carrying out of the predetermined rules will actually sound. So while a totally serialized piece is *technically* predictable, in its sound it may lack any order for the ear. As Křenek explains:

> It may be stated that whatever occurs in this piece at any given

*Ernst Křenek, "Extents and Limits of Serial Techniques," in Paul Henry Lang (ed.), *Problems of Modern Music*, W. W. Norton & Company, Inc., New York, 1962, p. 81. © G. Schirmer, Inc., 1960. Students interested in controversies about contemporary music will find this a useful book.

point is premeditated and therefore technically predictable. However, while the preparation and the layout of the material as well as the operations performed therein are the consequence of serial premeditation, the audible results of these procedures were not visualized as the purpose of the procedures. Seen from this angle, the results are incidental. They are also practically unpredictable because the simultaneous progress of highly complex rhythmic patterns at various relative speeds together with the corresponding transpositions of equally complex pitch patterns creates situations that defy precise visualization. *

Preformed music, then, is "composed" according to formulas chosen by the composer but in practically all cases sounds chaotic because the formulas cannot be heard when the music is performed. Many persons will argue that such music is not composed at all because it lacks the ongoing, intimate interaction between sounds and the creator of them, in which the composer shapes and molds and forms the sounds in a creative interplay. And the point is made that, no matter how well organized in theory a composition may be, the criterion for whether it can be considered music is that at least *someone* can *hear* it as organized. Advocates of preformed music argue that it is indeed meaningful, reflecting in sound the condition of life as both ordered and chaotic (**LISTENING 8.17**). (See Chapter 13 for further comments.)

In traditionally composed music and in preformed music the composer assumes that he is responsible for choosing which aural events will take place. The performer must contribute some decisions to the music, but the composer has stipulated, as precisely as notation or machine manipulation allows him, just what is to take place at every moment.

Recently, some composers have used chance in their works (as have painters, poets, dancers, novelists, sculptors, and dramatists). Chance, or random, or aleatoric, music involves complete unpredictability in composition or performance. For example, tape recorders can be set up at various street corners, picking up whatever sounds happen to occur; then these tapes can be fed simultaneously onto a single tape, further mixing up the sounds; and added to the master tape can be several radios tuned to different stations, several phonographs playing a variety of records, assorted noises from the recording studio, and so

Ibid., p. 83.

LISTENING 8.17

Some degree of "predetermined" events exists in the following:

Y. XENAKIS ○● *Pithoprakta* (see the discussion of this work in Chapter 13); *Acchoripsis; ST/10-1, 080262; Akatra.*

E. KŘENEK *Spiritus intelligentiae, sanctus; Sestina.*

P. BOULEZ *Structures for Two Pianos; Le Marteau sans maître.*

K. STOCKHAUSEN *Zeitmasse; Gruppen; Kontakte.*

M. BABBITT *Philomel; Composition for Twelve Instruments.*

on. The result is unorganized, unformed sound. One can throw dice to select from a variety of possible events (an idea used as early as the eighteenth century as a kind of musical parlor game) or use sticks or coins thrown to the ground in the manner of the *I Ching* (the ancient Chinese *Book of Changes*) or develop mathematical formulas to generate random tones. Whatever the method, the result is music in which unpredictability plays a major part.

Chance music can also occur at the level of performance. For example, a composer might tell ten performers to play in any order or all together, sounding whatever notes come to mind. Or he could provide each performer with a dozen pages of music, instructing him to shuffle the pages and then play them in whatever order happens to result. Or a musical score can be divided into segments, the performer making the choices of which segments to play when.

In all of this the attention of listeners is called to a *process* rather than a *product*. Random music offers an alternative to the age-old idea that experience, to be meaningful, must be formed. If life is a chaotic, undetermined process, then this process can be experienced through chaotic, unpredictable sounds (or paintings or poems or dances or theater events). Composer and performer are to be guided by forces outside their control, allowing the flux and freedom of life to find expression in the unordered events they produce. Needless to say, this view has caused endless debates between those who agree and those who disagree. Some are totally devoted to randomness as a valid principle of creation, while some are totally opposed to the entire idea. Some persons, composers included, have taken a position toward the middle, recognizing that formed experience produces significant meaning but that some degree of chance can add a new dimension to experience. Several composers therefore, leave only a few things to chance at carefully selected moments, the rest of the time forming the music in the usual ways. In such music the formed and the unformed both play a part to provide experiences in which both the predictable and the unpredictable can exert their power (LISTENING 8.18).

Whatever the future of chance music, it is very much with us today. Whatever opinion you may have of it should be based on unprejudiced experience of the music and open debate of the issues. The goal should not be a position about unformed (or preformed) music but the free sharing of whatever significance such music may add to your experience.

LISTENING 8.18

J. CAGE ○ *Variations IV* (see the discussion of this work in Chapter 13); *Music of Changes; Indeterminacy; Atlas Eclipticalis; Cartridge Music; Fontana Mix.*

K. STOCKHAUSEN *Klavierstück; Zyklus.*

MAURICIO KAGEL *Transición II; Sonant; Improvisation ajoutée.*

HELLMUTH CHRISTIAN WOLFF *Duo for Violinist and Pianist; Summer,* for String Quartet.

L. FOSS *Time Cycle (Improvised Interludes); Echoi.*

MORTON FELDMAN *Out of "Last Pieces."*

LARRY AUSTIN *Improvisations for Orchestra and Jazz Soloists.*

W. LUTOSŁAWSKI *Three Poems of Henri Michaux.*

K. PENDERECKI ○ *Passion According to St. Luke* (see the discussion of this work in Chapter 13).

Part 1 of this book introduced the persons and processes involved in the experience of music. Part 2 explored the ways that sound is used for expressive purposes. In Part 3 we shall discuss the social and historical context of music and study specific pieces as examples of the major musical styles. Our concern now is to see the large picture: the flow of history, of which music has been a part, and important works that exemplify the many ways music has served its function as an art. The understandings and skills developed in Parts 1 and 2 can now be applied to this broad level of study.

The Ideas and Arts . . . sections, which discuss cultural and intellectual backgrounds for each period, are necessarily interpretive. With the vastness of the material and the brevity of the sections, the discussions must be taken as tentative, introductory essays, which will raise as many questions as they answer; nevertheless, they will give a flavor of the thought and action of each major historical period. You cannot predict what the art of a period will be like just from reading about the important events, major figures, and pervading ideas of a particular time, for much of what takes place in art stems from sheerly artistic matters, which, however influenced by other things taking place, are to a large extent determined by the art form itself. But a sense of the world surrounding art can give an added perspective—a dimension of context—that can enhance the experience of art.

In the musical-style sections is an overview of the characteristic ways the elements of music were used at each particular time in history. Here the broad historical context is focused into the ways that rhythm, melody, harmony, counterpoint, tone color, and form were actually used to create musical events. The sense given by these sections is of the general style of music you can expect to hear from each period.

In the sections on representative pieces the background material is applied to specific, important pieces of music. Now we are at the level of the particular, the unique, the distinctive. The discussion at this level concerns the work as it is experienced musically, with some background information about it as a means of placing it in the period. This is the level of musical experience, toward which the broader levels aim. For each piece discussed in these sections there is a detailed analysis in the Listening Charts. The combination of the text discussion of the work and the Listening Chart analysis should give ample means for experiencing the work with perception and therefore with enjoyment.

The remaining sections of each chapter introduce materials for supplementary listening and study: The Other Important Music sections call attention to additional compositions of interest, which may serve as further entries into the music of each period; and Further Readings offer highly selective bibliographies. The student wishing to expand his understanding of history and of art can use these sections as a guide for his explorations.

Chapter 9 ∘ The Middle Ages and renaissance

EVERY AGE STANDS ON THE SHOULDERS AND IN THE SHADOW OF THE PAST. The twentieth century is no exception. In spite of remarkable technological advances, which have dramatically transformed our modes of living, we have not changed entirely from what our ancestors were like. The religious arguments of St. Thomas Aquinas (*ca.* 1225–1274) find modern expression in the efforts of today's theologians to build convincing views of man and his nature. The political realism of Niccolò Machiavelli (1469–1527) is matched by Herman Kahn's rationalizations for a "credible first-strike capability." The simple purity of St. Francis (*ca.* 1182–1226), can be found in the impulses of young idealists to scorn worldliness in favor of the simple life. The sophisticated ribaldry of François Rabelais (*ca.* 1490–1553) has its counterpart in those modern plays and movies which frankly explore the sexual foibles of men and women. There are differences in style and content, but modern man shares many of the concerns of his ancestors, including the fears of life as well as death. Each age seems to give its own expression to the underlying needs and hopes of man.

In medieval and renaissance men you can find counterparts of modern thinkers: cynics, idealists, realists, pessimists, optimists, and fools, the last, if one were to believe Desiderius Erasmus (*ca.* 1466–1536), outnumbering all the others by a very wide margin. The more we know about earlier cultures, the more we realize that stupidity and vice are not limited to our present generation, nor does all the brain power belong to the man of the 1970s, who cannot escape the influences of his own past even when he deliberately closes his eyes to it.

Ideas and arts of the Middle Ages and renaissance

The term "Middle Ages" was perhaps invented by Petrarch (1304–1374) to refer to that vast stretch of time between the breakdown of the Roman empire and his own "brilliant age" (as he fondly characterized it). However artificial, incorrect, and arbitrary it might be, the name is still used as a convenient label for hundreds of contradictions and contrasts. It embraces the complex overlappings of classical Greek, Christian, and barbarian mentalities over a number of centuries. It includes elements of Judaic, Byzantine, and Islamic civilizations to the extent that they affected western Europe. Feudalism, monastic learning, scholastic philosophy, growing confrontations of Church and state, artistic creations ranging from miniature-illuminated manuscripts to vast epic poems and gothic cathedrals—all are covered by the single name Middle Ages.

Like Middle Ages, the term ''renaissance'' was first used after the fact although renaissance man often claimed unusual distinction for his times, acutely conscious of living in a ''new age''—at least as he saw it. Voltaire and other eighteenth-century philosophers used the word *rinascimento* (renaissance) to indicate the period from about 1450 to 1600. To them this was a time much to be admired, unlike the preceding medieval period, which they disdained. For such nineteenth-century scholars as Jacob Burckhardt (*The Civilization of the Renaissance,* first published in 1860) and John Addington Symonds (*The Renaissance in Italy,* 1875–1886), the renaissance was viewed as a sharp contrast to the Middle Ages, that is, as a period when thinkers and artists consciously divorced themselves from the teachings of the medieval Catholic Church as they became more aware of the spectacular achievements of classical Greece. Although the mainstream of writing about the renaissance in our own century has largely taken the same course, several historians, such as Étienne Gilson (*Héloïse and Abélard,* 1960), Charles Homer Haskins (*The Renaissance of the Twelfth Century,* 1927), and Johan Huizinga (*The Waning of the Middle Ages,* 1919), have challenged that view. The differences between the periods are now thought to be less clear-cut than was formerly believed: There seem to be subtle interactions between these periods, medieval ideas carrying over into the renaissance and renaissance attitudes and behaviors being found in the midst of the medieval world. As Haskins notes, ''Modern research shows us the Middle Ages less dark and less static, the Renaissance less bright and less sudden, than was once supposed.''

If in the following paragraphs we talk about the two periods together, we must recognize the fiction and the amount of error involved. But we may also remind ourselves that history is the study of continuity as well as change, that past prejudices exist alongside budding new beliefs. To trace all the differences and similarities in this six-hundred-year period would be impossible: Symonds takes seven volumes to discuss the Italian renaissance alone. Our purpose here is to spread before you only a brief picture to give you some sense of the world in which medieval and renaissance music existed.

The Roman Catholic Church dominated the medieval and renaissance scene even though its influence waxed and waned. Practically all western

Figure 9.1 • The gothic cathedral at Chartres, France, constructed mainly from about 1194 to 1260, with details dating from both earlier and later periods. (French Government Tourist Office.)

Europeans paid allegiance to the Church and acknowledged the pope as their spiritual leader. Scholasticism, that is, philosophical and theological thinking dominated by assumptions concerning the authority and rationality of ecclesiastical dogma, attempted answers to what Crane Brinton in *Ideas and Men* calls "the Big Questions"; but the subtleties of scholastic logic seldom intervened in the daily lives of people, being content to serve the Church well in defense of its postures. Men were born into, lived, and died in the Church, which provided the rules and regulations covering almost all threads of life. No man escaped entirely from the sphere of its power: political, physical, social, intellectual, and psychological.

Nevertheless, secular interests caused constant friction. Since Christianity had stated its beliefs with certainty and for long, it now had to defend itself against increasingly strong attacks from inside and outside its walls: Leaders from outside the Church began to develop theoretical arguments that ran counter to Church dogma, and confrontations became typical of the times as peasants, merchants, scholars, and nobility tried to come to grips with the increasing tensions between secular society and the sway of the Church. New views about the universe began to emerge from budding sciences, and these contradicted traditional doctrines. Money, culture, and learning more and more fell into secular hands in the late Middle Ages. This led to new rules for daily living and, at the highest philosophical level, new views in opposition to Church teaching.

Yet hundreds of factors gradually changed life: the growth of cities, the establishment of great banking houses, the breakdown of feudalism, the opening of commerce through exploration, and in the realm of art, the sharpening of appetites for the styles of Greek and Roman antiquity. Questioning began in earnest as a result of a period of upheaval in the Church from 1378 to 1417, when there were two or sometimes three candidates claiming to be the true pope. The Black Death, a form of bubonic plague, swept through Europe in the fourteenth century, killing something like a quarter of the population. The revolutionary doctrines of reformers like Martin Luther (1483–1546) contributed to the destruction of the old order of things. The world was changing in basic ways, never to be the same again.

But the majority of men, however confused they may have been at given moments, generally believed in the meaningful and purposeful "Christian epic": the idea that the universe was the scene of a great drama, with God and His magnificent order locked in a titanic struggle with the Devil. Although the latter won most of the battles, he must certainly lose the war because God and the Church had so ordained it. Given these conditions, the epic drama was always exciting, especially since the Devil, ever alert to opportunity, plotted to trap men into evil ways, while on another scale he fought mightily against God, with appropriate lighting and sound effects, in the immensity of the heavens above and the earth below. Medieval men may have sometimes doubted this view of the world; but until fairly late in the period they were firm believers, reassured that, regardless of their human condition, life throughout the universe had some ultimate meaning defined by God Himself even if His purposes temporarily seemed difficult to understand.

The democratic ideal of the twentieth century, which argues that all human life should be treated as of equal value, would have sounded

Figure 9.2 • Filippo Brunelleschi's Pazzi chapel at Florence, Italy. Built from around 1429 to 1451, this renaissance structure shows classical influence in its formal balance. (Alinari—Art Reference Bureau.)

Figure 9.3 • Detail of the principal tympanum at Chartres cathedral. Small differences in detail unified by hierarchical treatment and an imposing central figure reflect the social structure of the Middle Ages. (Archives Photographiques, Paris.)

strange to men reared in the social structure of the Middle Ages, for they took human inequality for granted. The Church said that all persons were equal in the sight of God, but this was lip service to a kind of democracy seldom practiced. Although a pope could arise from lowly origins, generally the Church nourished and sanctioned the "establishment" of its time, a strictly graded social, political, and religious system of unequals. Peasants were ministered to, but leadership was kept strictly to the nobility. Except at the lowest levels of society, all found it useful to stick to this rigid, ordered system of "separate and unequal."

The Middle Ages and renaissance left us a collection of conflicting ideas. They also left lasting monuments of art, some of which will perhaps never be surpassed as testimonials of dedication and craft.

If the Church represented the spirit of the Middle Ages, gothic cathedrals (Figure 9.1) captured that spirit in stone. Between the eleventh and fourteenth centuries, at the height of their construction, cathedrals blended the worldly and the sacred, sometimes effortlessly, at other

Figure 9.4 • *Antonio Pollaiuolo:* Hercules and Antaeus (ca. 1475). In its 1½ *feet of height, a powerful expression of the renaissance interest in classical antiquity and human anatomy.* (Gabinetto Fotografico della Soprintendenza alle Gallerie, Florence.)

times with restless tension; as they reached toward the heavens, their feet rested in the earth, close to squalid hovels. The medieval cathedrals were at the very center of life. Stonecutters, masons, sculptors, engineers, and laborers, supported by the entire community, carefully balanced stone against stone as they built these miracles in which their love of God fused with enormous civic pride. For the ''glory of God'' their cathedrals stood, and they wanted to make the most of them. Here peasants, merchants, and nobility listened to sermons, knelt and prayed together, witnessed impressive ceremonies, heard music, marvelled at the inspiring narratives suggested by stained-glass windows, empathized with statues of saints, and trembled at the pictured torments of the damned, which were intended, as one writer put it, ''to scare the hell out of [the] beholders.'' While religious drama, through the Mass and other services, was being acted inside, the cathedral exterior witnessed the beginnings of modern secular entertainment, with mystery plays, minstrels, dances, and jugglers. Visual counterparts of the theological system of St. Thomas, cathedrals served man from cradle to grave.

Architecturally, cathedrals summed up the world view of the late Middle Ages. But changing times brought a surge of interest in secular buildings, especially in those palaces designed to satisfy renaissance nobility who pursued worldly, intellectual, or artistic pleasures. Renaissance architects, following Greek and Roman models, preferred balance, symmetry, harmonious proportion, and clean lines (Figure 9.2). The gothic cathedral had beckoned and invited mystery, aspiration, and yearning in its dizzy heights, its dark recesses, and its asymmetrical patterns; the renaissance palace, on the other hand, stood self-contained, enclosing a neatly laid out, well-proportioned space. The cathedral *aspires;* the palace simply *is*—a masterpiece of controlled composition.

Sculptors throughout both periods created graven images in the service of the Church. They not only chiselled scenes of the apostles, early Church fathers, popes, and saints (Figure 9.3) but also dared to set pagan philosophers and scientists embarrassingly close to revered Christian figures. Most sculpture, however, dealt with the Annunciation, Crucifixion, Entombment, Adam and Eve, the Virgin Mary, and other religious scenes and symbols. It presented moral and religious lessons, served artistic purposes, and at the same time functioned as an integral part of the structure of a building. Then largely through the efforts of Donatello (*ca.* 1386–1466), Antonio Pollaiuolo (1429–1498), and

Figure 9.5 • *Giotto di Bondone:* Death of St. Francis (ca. 1320). *In the Church of Santa Croce, Florence, this early-renaissance (or late-medieval) fresco combines didactic, spiritual intention with human expression of grief.* (Alinari—Art Reference Bureau.)

Andrea del Verrocchio (1435–1488), the carving of free-standing statues imitating those of classical antiquity was revived in fifteenth-century Italy, and a change of artistic ideals became noticeable. Because of their interest in classical Greece and Rome, these and other artists studied human anatomy as carefully as had their Greek and Roman predecessors. Donatello's *Gattamelata,* Pollaiuolo's *Hercules and Antaeus* (Figure 9.4), and, later, the *David* of Michelangelo (1475–1564) owed much to ancient models. It is not surprising, therefore, that renaissance sculptors often portrayed Christian themes in forms associated with pagan antiquity.

Painting during the Middle Ages was not of the oil-paint, canvas, and easel variety common in later periods but concentrated mostly on wall painting, frescos (Figure 9.5), panels, and manuscript illuminations, exquisitely beautiful, charming, decorative, and frequently instructive miniatures; and at the very end of the medieval period we find one of the greatest examples of this last art, the *Très riches heures du Duc de Berry,* a book of hours (prayer book) with illustrations by Pol de Limburg and his brothers (Plate 1*a*).

Roughly contemporary in the early fifteenth century were Hubert (*ca.* 1366–1426) and Jan van Eyck (*ca.* 1370–*ca.* 1440), traditionally credited with the invention of oil painting. But the main thrust of renaissance painting soon moved south to Italy, to Andrea Mantegna (1431–1506), Sandro Botticelli (*ca.* 1444–1510; Plate 1*b*), Leonardo da Vinci (1452–1519), Michelangelo, Titian (1477–1576), and Raphael (1483–1520), to that enormous outpouring of great pictorial art which caused Burckhardt and others to see a remarkable "new world" rising out of the earlier, darker period.

The history of the Italian renaissance—its joyfulness, religious self-denial, perversions, ideals, personalities—can be found on thousands of painted canvases and walls. As sculpture, the art of painting also revealed its debt to classical antiquity, depicting pagan themes (Figure 9.6) and presenting Christian subject matter in pagan dress or undress (Figure 9.7). The nude regained its ancient artistic importance, finally losing its medieval connotations of shame. Renaissance painting exalted man by often picturing him just a "little lower than the angels" and crowned with "glory and honour" (as in Figure 9.8). Having accepted dominion over all the works of God's world, renaissance man asserted that he was the measure of all things, a creature who now chose his

Figure 9.6 • Raphael's School of Athens. *Dating from around 1508 to 1513, this large fresco (18 by 26 feet) in the Vatican exhibits the classical influence on the renaissance in restrained, balanced, and planned style.*

own destiny. The painters caught the strutting actors in their play. Yet they were far too wise to see merely the outward appearance. Instead, they made sensitive visual impressions of man's dual qualities: sensuality lurking under outward piety, grossness within simplicity, pride in humbleness, and goodness beneath immorality. Their keen eyes penetrated behind the players' masks, and they handed down a telling record of humanity in all its brilliance and folly.

In literature we can observe trends similar to those in other arts. Aquinas's *Summa theologica* and the gothic cathedral had struck a delicate balance, momentarily resolving conflicting tensions both in theology and in architecture. The *Divine Comedy* of Dante (1265–1321) also tried to effect a sublime unity, for it was at one and the same time an encyclopedia, a spiritual sermon, an epic poem, and a stirring drama of Christian faith.

Only a generation later, Chaucer (*ca.* 1340–1400) was describing much more believable people in down-to-earth terms. By the end of the renaissance, Shakespeare (1564–1616) was immortalizing not God and His judgment, but man. Provided with a magnificent gift of subtle language, pictured in moods ranging from thoughtful reflection to impulsive action, *man* occupies the center of Shakespeare's stage.

The world was also changing in other, more practical ways. In an age of exploration, adventurers like Marco Polo (1254–1324) and Columbus (1446–1506) expanded the knowledge of distant lands; Copernicus (1473–1543) and other scientists studied the universe. Gradually their findings began to substitute logically argued theories based on man-made observations for the long-cherished explanation that God's power determined everything.

Centuries of study—of debunking, classifying, defining, and clarifying—have not yet illuminated all the mysteries surrounding the Middle Ages and the renaissance. Historians continue to interpret data and to debate the impact of these formative periods on later history. At the risk of oversimplification, we can reasonably assume that most of them would agree to some broad generalizations: We might safely say that according to the God-centered medieval world view man lived in a meaningful and purposeful universe, for God not only ruled, He also cared about His world and His special creation, man. In the man-centered renaissance the same conditions prevailed, but there was some shift in emphasis. Man himself became more active in the divine drama;

Figure 9.7 • *Andrea Mantegna:* Crucifixion (ca. 1459). *Although movingly Christian in theme, this painting is handled in a typically static classicizing fashion.* (Musée du Louvre; cliché des Musées Nationaux.)

Figure 9.8 • Michelangelo's Creation of Adam (1511) *from the ceiling of the Sistine chapel at the Vatican. Here the renaissance virtuoso style, which catches the most dramatic moment, begins to pass over into the exuberance of the baroque.*

he moved, he worked, he fashioned, he organized, he created, and he often defined his purpose by his all-too-human lights.

In *Main Currents of Western Thought*, Franklin Baumer includes three subdivisions under the larger heading "The Age of Religion": "The Medieval Christian World-View," "The Renaissance," and "The Confessional Age" (signifying the age of Luther, Calvin, Loyola, and their contemporaries). As he notes, most renaissance thinkers were sincere Christians even when they severely criticized the blunders of the Church (as did Erasmus in *The Praise of Folly*). These men might not have belonged to the Middle Ages, but emotionally they had roots there. Intellectually, culturally, and artistically, they rejected much of their heritage. Yet the ties were not completely cut; the decisive break was to come later.

Musical style

RHYTHM

Until the late twelfth century no satisfactory system of notating rhythm had been developed in the various musics that had contributed to that of the Middle Ages in the West. Up to that time the theoretical writings and the musical manuscripts themselves had only hinted at what the rhythms should be; the rhythms may have been free, or they may have been measured. Consequently, the problem of what is authentic Gregorian-chant rhythm vexes scholars to this day, as does the rhythm problem in early secular monophonic music. Respectable scholars have advanced theories, but many of the questions remain unanswered.

With the establishment of a modal rhythm notation in the thirteenth century, more exact communication of rhythms became possible. The new system was basically dependent upon two note values: long and short (*longa* and *brevis*). Combinations of various sorts lent some variety, but the entire system, with all its subtleties, was quite restrictive.

Early in the fourteenth century there became established a system of measuring rhythm that permitted the notation and practical use of both triple and duple meter. For the next three centuries this system remained basically the same. Perfectly suited to the needs of the music, it could handle syncopations, polyrhythms, and other rhythmic complexities. A steady overall pulse characterized renaissance music. However, much of the rhythmic interest resided in the remarkably free life of each part: different rhythm patterns were combined in seemingly inexhaustible ways, each part stressing its own accents through its text, its high notes, and its notes of longer duration. Bar lines found in modern editions were absent from the original manuscripts. Their presence today often obscures (both visually and musically) the rhythmic flexibility and independence of each polyphonic part.

MELODY

As we have implied, over a period of many centuries the musical influences of ancient Greek, Hebrew, Byzantine, and other cultures merged in the Middle Ages. By that time several characteristics had evolved that continue today. One was the idea of an ascending scale in which the octave and fifth played primary roles; so certain tones of each scale were more important than others. (A complete "democracy of tones" did not make an appearance until the twentieth century.) A set of internal relationships existed within the scale so that individual tones stood at fairly determined distances from each other. Means of rearranging these internal relationships had also evolved to create a system of scales, or "modes," that gave a variety of flavors to melodies composed in them.

A period of roughly a thousand years elapses between 604, the date of the death of Pope Gregory, whose name attaches to a body of melodies called "Gregorian chant," and 1600, a round terminal date for the renaissance. During much of that time musical traditions were transmitted orally; yet it is possible to make a few generalizations about melodies during that millennium in spite of many uncertainties and much variety. The initial development, Gregorian chant, was monophonic. The range seldom exceeded an octave, and the melodic motion emphasized steps rather than leaps. The melodies were sung in various combinations of male choral group and solo voice. Over the centuries innovations occurred, one of the most important being the modification of some tones through raising or lowering by a half step. These "chromatic" notes may have been introduced to facilitate singing, to avoid an awkward melodic interval, to avoid a harsh harmonic sound, and for other reasons, including the one that some of these "foreign" notes simply sounded good.

In the later centuries of the period (the fourteenth through the sixteenth) melodies became slightly more complex: the range was extended, more leaps were used, and chromatic notes were introduced more boldly. Secular influences, increasing employment of instruments, and developing taste for nuance account for these gradual changes.

HARMONY AND COUNTERPOINT

As we have stated, early medieval music was entirely monophonic. Performed by a solo voice or a small group of singers, sacred music was probably unaccompanied. Quite possibly secular music, under certain circumstances, was sung with some kind of instrumental accompaniment, but the evidence is scanty and unreliable. If instruments were used, they probably played the melody in unison or at the octave with the singer(s), played a bagpipelike drone, provided a rhythmic accompaniment (percussion instruments), or combined some of these possibilities. By the later Middle Ages instruments were adding colorful accompaniments, for both pictorial and literary sources document their presence. The use of monophonic texture lasted well into the thirteenth century although other developments were gradually replacing it.

As a rough generalization, two-part writing became prominent between 900 and 1200. From 1200 to 1450 three-part writing prevailed. From 1450 to 1600 four- and then five- and six-part writing became the norm. Exceptions, of course, abound: for example; four-part writing encountered in the thirteenth century and monophonic Gregorian chant still performed in the sixteenth century.

In two-part textures the parts can move together, note sung against note (*punctus contra punctum*—from which the term "counterpoint" is derived); or one voice (usually the lower) can move in a relatively sustained way, singing notes of long duration while another voice, more agile, sings a rapid series of notes. Usually the sustained part is a chant melody.

One of the voices in three-part texture is also often built on a preexistent Gregorian chant. This voice, called "cantus firmus," usually proceeds more slowly than the other voices do, imparting solemnity through dignified movement. Where all three parts are freely composed, their activity yields a busier texture.

In four-part music of the late fifteenth and sixteenth centuries the most sophisticated composers tend to vary textures, not keeping all parts moving and active all the time. Frequently the parts enter imitatively one after another; or the voices may be paired, two entering at one moment and two others in imitation later, with the first two sometimes resting or sometimes continuing; less common are three voices set against one. By means of a liberal sprinkling of rests throughout all parts, the composer colors his music by changing textures and exploiting contrasting vocal qualities (for example, soprano and alto against tenor and bass).

Although used extensively, contrapuntal imitation of the kinds just described does not exclusively characterize renaissance style. Many compositions are written in completely chordal style, where all the parts move simultaneously, with no attempt at independently moving contrapuntal lines. Other compositions, although primarily polyphonic, include sections in chordal style for purposes of contrast, as suggested by appropriate text changes.

As multiple-part writing became more frequent in the sixteenth century, composers sought novel methods of overcoming constraints, for in general, the more parts, the less freedom of movement for each. So composers seldom used all the voices all the time, diversifying their style by setting two parts against four, three against three, and so on. Under these conditions parts tend to echo or to oppose the others. The concept of antiphonal music, in which one part responds to another, found much favor in the latter part of the sixteenth century. With its acceptance came an increasing participation of instruments, which either doubled the voices or substituted for a certain group of voices. The possible combinations gave composers almost unlimited opportunity in their handling of textures and tone colors.

As over the centuries the number of musical parts grew from a single part in unison or at the octave to many parts sung on different notes, the combinations of pitches became more complex. The first combination of two pitches used was that of two voices singing along at the intervals of a fourth or fifth. From about 1200 to 1450 thirds and sixths crept in, fourths being used less and less. Once it became popular, three-part music often utilized the 1–3–5 triad, which later formed the basis for harmony as we now know it. From about 1450 to the end of the renaissance triads on all notes of the scale became common: 1–3–5, 2–4–6, 3–5–7, and so on. In compositions of more than three parts one or more of the notes in a triad must be doubled—which allows many subtle shadings of pitch relations. At its best, renaissance harmony is a beautifully balanced interplay of factors: the use of triads, the doubling of notes in triads, the manipulation of subtle dissonances between pitches, the movement from triad to triad, and finally, the interaction of all these with the polyphonically conceived melodic motion.

TONE COLOR

It is almost impossible to reconstruct accurately the tone colors heard by people in the Middle Ages although paintings, sculpture, and written works offer clues and the relatively few surviving instruments from that period provide some evidence. Visual records picture a wide variety of instrumentalists playing singly and in groups, with and without singers. Much music was apparently accompanied by instruments capable of producing drones, like the medieval hurdy-gurdy and bagpipe. Portative organs and certain kinds of stringed instruments could also sound drones; so this must have been a frequently heard tone color. And various written documents support the belief that a nasal quality in instruments and in the human voice was much admired. Percussion instruments also are shown in woodcuts and similar sources. Instruments were produced by individual craftsmen and no doubt differed from one another in kind and quality. In matters of pitch, length of tubing and placement of the holes in wind instruments, thickness of wood, and countless other details, standardization was almost nonexistent. Any grouping of such variable instruments surely would have resulted in a wild assortment of timbres and pitches. The evidence suggests that music making was as riotously colorful as were some costumes and paintings of the time.

If tone color in the Middle Ages tended toward variety, unified sounds were generally preferred by renaissance musicians. During the renaissance definite families of instruments developed, each family consisting of like instruments in a series ranging from high to low pitches. Although the ideal ensemble in a particular piece might have been an "unbroken consort," that is, only one instrumental family or a group of voices alone (a cappella), in actual practice a variety of tone colors appeared. One example may suffice: For the wedding of Francesco de' Medici and Giovanna of Austria, in 1565, the finale to an allegorical play was sung "very loudly and cheerfully" by sixteen voices (four on each part),

accompanied by two cornetts, two sackbuts, a dolcian, a treble cro-
morne, a lirone, a treble rebec, and two lutes. This festivity may have
demanded exceptional musical resources, but festive occasions were
common in renaissance life. Very likely music making under normal
circumstances was accomplished by whatever instruments and voices
happened to be available.

FORM

Since most of the music of the period was vocal, it is obvious that
textual considerations largely controlled musical form. Punctuation
determined musical cadence points, where the part or parts came to
a temporary halt. At such a point, a singer literally took a breath, the
motion of the music momentarily stopped (often because of a long note
value and a rest), the sonority arrived at, or suggested, some sort of
break, or the texture itself changed. Because text plays such a vital role,
familiarity with it increases understanding of early music, for melody,
rhythm, and harmony and texture usually collaborate to heighten the
meaning of a text and in turn contribute to the formation of a musical
phrase. The structure of musical phrases of the period may be regular
or irregular, the latter in spite of frequent regularity of poetic text. By
linking series of phrases, composers built extended compositions.

From form-building processes, we move now to common forms in
medieval and renaissance music. In the earlier period, organum, motet,
and various fourteenth-century secular forms were most important.
Stages of development can be observed in organum and motet, organum
reaching its peak probably in the twelfth century and motet in the
thirteenth. Three-voiced gothic motets frequently combined different
texts (all Latin or Latin and French) sung simultaneously. Of renaissance
vocal forms, it was the Mass, motet (different from the gothic motet),
chanson, and madrigal that captured the attention of composers. The
Mass, usually set in four or more polyphonically conceived parts, consisted of five sections, or movements: Kyrie, Gloria, Credo, Sanctus, and
Agnus Dei. The motet, likewise for four or more polyphonic parts, was
based on sacred Latin texts, was sung by an unaccompanied choral
group, and was heard chiefly at Vespers in the Catholic service. The
French chanson, the German Lied, and the Italian and English madrigal
were secular counterparts of the motet. Contrapuntally imitative, these

forms often had more clearly defined sections than did the motet. They were less somber sounding because of their lively rhythms and used homophonic textures frequently.

Of renaissance instrumental forms, the prelude, toccata, *canzona*, ricercar, and suite stand out. Keyboard preludes and toccatas, short but remarkably free in conception, contrasted sharply with the more strictly imitative, polyphonic vocal style. During the sixteenth century, *canzone* split into two branches: one for keyboard, the other for instrumental ensemble. Both types were modeled after the vocal *chanson*. They adopted various textures (contrapuntal and homophonic), generally preferred active motion, and characteristically opened with three repeated notes, one long followed by two short. The term "ricercar" covers a number of related types and styles, not always clearly differentiated. One kind of ricercar for instrumental ensemble or for organ resembled the vocal motet, being imitative, sectional, multithematic, and somewhat more somber in spirit and "learned" in style than were the *canzona* types. The nonimitative ricercars—for instruments, lute, organ, or voices—bore no resemblance to the vocal motet, the style generally being free, with scale passages, chords, and improvisatorylike sections. During the sixteenth century the suite, which reached its peak in the later baroque, consisted primarily in combinations of dances. Two dances were often put together, one in duple time followed by another in triple time. The pavane and galliard, for example, was a favorite combination. Especially in lute books three or more dances were to be played in succession, such groupings being forerunners of the baroque suite of dances.

Instrumental music made enormous progress. Partly because of improvements in instruments and partly because an instrumental repertory became available, instrumental music began to offer serious competition to the popularity of vocal music.

Representative pieces

The compositions discussed in this and parallel sections in later chapters are musically valuable in their own right and representative of important practices and trends in the era under examination. They should be regarded as entry points into the rich and diverse musical literature of each period, for an acquaintance with these representative pieces can provide a base for continuing explorations.

For most of the compositions discussed here, separate Concentration Charts are provided in the Listening Charts. Most are recorded on the appropriate records accompanying the Listening Charts. The combination of reading about the pieces in each chapter, listening to them with the aid of the analyses provided in the Concentration Charts, and rehearing them at leisure, as often as time permits, should make you quite able to share the musical enjoyment that each composition will offer.

1. GREGORIAN CHANT (NINTH CENTURY)

Almost 3,000 Gregorian melodies, based mostly on prose texts, still exist today. "Veni Creator Spiritus" is one of the most famous of the 120 or so Latin hymns in current use. It has been employed as a cantus firmus in polyphonic compositions by numerous composers, especially in the renaissance.

○ "Veni Creator Spiritus" is set in iambic tetrameter ("*Veni Creator Spiritus*") and has seven verses arranged in four-line stanzas. The scale is modal, the melody moving mostly in small steps.

Come, O Creator Spirit,
And within our hearts make thy home:
Give thy celestial Grace to us,
Who of thy breathing move and live.

Veni Creator Spiritus,
Mentes tuorum visita:
Imple superna gratia
Quae tu creasti pectora.

2. GREGORIAN CHANT

Whereas Gregorian hymns such as "Veni Creator Spiritus" were syllabic, each syllable having a separate note, this alleluia, ○● "Alleluia vidimus stellam," is *melismatic,* many notes being sung to a single syllable. As part of the Mass, the alleluia belongs to the Proper, where the texts and chants change daily according to the church season (in the Ordinary—Kyrie, Gloria, Credo, Sanctus, and Agnus Dei—the texts are virtually always the same). The range of this chant is only an octave, one note wider than the preceding hymn; but its exuberant nature and melismatic style give the impression of a more expansive range. After an opening solo "Alleluia," the chorus sings an identical passage but continues with a long melisma on the last syllable ("-ia").

Alleluia, alleluia.
We have seen His star in the east
and are come with gifts
to worship the Lord. Alleluia.

King of the Heavens, Lord of the wave-sounding sea,
Of the shining sun and of the squalid earth.
Thy humble servants, venerating Thee with pious accents,
Entreat Thee that Thou wilt command them freed from manifold ills.

Alleluia, Alleluia.
Vidimus stellam ejus in oriente,
et venimus cum muneribus
adorate Dominum. Alleluia.

3. EARLY ORGANUM

The first kind of polyphonic music was organum, the earliest examples dating from the ninth century. The simplest type merely paralleled an original chant at the interval of a fourth or fifth.

In this example, ○● "Rex coeli, Domine," the two parts move primarily in parallel fourths, except at the beginning and end of each line, where they meet at the same note (unison). The text is set with each syllable to a separate note.

Rex coeli, Domine maris undisoni,
Titanis nitidi squalidique soli.
Te humiles famuli modulis venerando piis,
Se jubeas flagitant variis liberare malis.

4. GIRAUT DE BORNEIL (GUIRAUT DE BORNELH; died *ca.* 1220)

Many secular poems sung to music during the twelfth and thirteenth centuries have come down to us, but the music for most of them has been lost. About 300 troubadour and about 800 trouvère melodies survive, probably only a small percentage of the original repertory. Of 80 poems by Giraut de Borneil, only 4 have survived with melodies, of which ○ "Reis glorios" is one.

In secular monophonic styles the melodic range seldom exceeded an octave. The tune was probably sung by a solo voice, with or without instruments. If an instrument was used, played by the singer or another person, it most likely duplicated the tune, with occasional interludes by the instrument alone to allow the singer to rest.

Since the rhythm of this kind of music is uncertain, at least five different rhythmic solutions of "Reis glorios" have been suggested by scholars. Three of these can be examined in A. I. Davison and W. Apel, *Historical Anthology of Music* (Harvard University Press, Cambridge, Mass., 1949), vol. I, no. 18c.

Glorious King, true light and brightness,
Almighty God and Lord, for our sake

Grant faithful help to my friend,
For I have not seen him since the night came,
And soon it will be dawn.

They all saw.

The form of "Reis glorios" is *aab;* a first section repeated (lines 1, and 2, below) followed by a longer *b* section (lines 3, 4, and 5). The last part of the *b* section (line 5) is a refrain for the following stanzas (not given here). This refrain is a repeated warning that dawn nears.

Reis glorios, verais lums e clartatz,	*a*
Deus poderos, Senher, si a vos platz,	*a*
Al meu companh sias fizels aiuda,	
qu'eu non la vi, pos la noitz fon venguda	*b*
Et adés sera l'alba.	

5. LÉONIN (LEONINUS; *fl.* 1150)

○ "Viderunt omnes," in organum *duplum* style, is one of a cycle of over eighty pieces. Based on a Gregorian cantus firmus, the lower melody, except for one section, moves in extraordinarily long notes identical with those of the original chant.

The section where the *tenor* cantus firmus also adopts even, measured notes is called a *clausula,* the upper part (*duplum*) having been moving in a measured rhythm from the beginning of the piece. *Clausula* sections, where both parts were measured rhythmically, became important forerunners of the medieval motet, the most characteristic form of the gothic period. Scholars still disagree about the exact interpretation of rhythmic values for this music.

Viderunt omnes.

6. THIRTEENTH-CENTURY MOTET

As *clausula* sections expanded, they eventually broke away to become independent pieces. In two parts, the upper part came to be called *motetus.* When a third voice was added above the *motetus,* it was called the *triplum.* The lowest voice (*tenor*) continued to be extracted from a chant, but it was treated with increasing freedom.

For about half of the present example (○ "Ave, Virgo—Ave gloriosa Mater—Domino") the *tenor* moves in three equal notes followed by a rest. Then the pattern changes, with five unequal notes and a rest

Hail, royal Virgin, mother of mercy,
Hail, thou full of grace, queen of glory,
Surpassing mother of an exalted offspring,
Who sittest in the glory of the heavenly land,
In the court of the True King, Mother and daughter,
Abode of virtue and guiding star,
On the throne of justice stay;
Let all the army of the heavenly host
Run to meet you. And to you
Let their harmonious and manifold songs go before.

. . .

Hail, glorious mother of the Saviour,
Hail, beautiful Virgin, flower of chastity,
Hail, happy light, bride of splendor,
Hail, precious deliverance of sinners,
Hail, road of life, chaste, comely, pure,
Sweet, gentle, faithful, happy creature.

. . .

Lord.

sounded in the same amount of time as in the original pattern. This thirteenth-century motet, which combines different texts and rhythms, is an attempt to blend contrasting, conflicting or opposing elements.

Owing to the length of the texts, the quotations below give only a portion of the *triplum* and *motetus* parts.

Triplum

Ave, Virgo regia, Mater clemencie,
Ave, plena gracia, Regina glorie
Genetrix egregria Prolis eximine,
Qui sedes in gloria Celestis patrie
Regis veri regia, Mater et filia,
Castrum pudicicie Stellaque previa,
In trono justicie Reside obvia
Agmina milicie Celestis omnia
Occurunt milicie Que tibi previa
Cantica simphonie Tam multipharia

Motetus

Ave gloriosa Mater salvatoris,
Ave, speciosa Virgo, flos pudoris,
Ave, lux iocosa, Thalamus splendoris,
Ave, preciosa Salus peccatoris,
Ave, vite via, Casta, Munda pura,
Dulcis, mitis, pura, Felix creatura.
. . .

Tenor

Domino.

7. GUILLAUME DE MACHAUT (1300–1377)

Musician and poet, Guillaume de Machaut was a towering figure in fourteenth-century France. Composer of about thirty motets, he is also remembered as the first to write a complete polyphonic setting of the Mass. But most of his output consisted of secular music in various forms, such as the *lai, rondeau, virelai,* and *ballade*.

In Machaut's time a *virelai* was used to accompany dancing, and the present example, ○● "Plus dure que un dyamant," has the following form:

Refrain	Stanza 1	Refrain	Stanza 2	Refrain	...
a	*bba*	*a*	*bba*	*a*	

The music is divided into two sections, *a* and *b*. In the refrain (lines 1 to 7) the music and text remain constant; and in each stanza (*bba*) lines 8 to 10 and 11 to 13 are set to *b* music, lines 14 to 19 to *a*. "Plus dure" is one of seven *virelais* by Machaut with an instrumental *tenor*, in this instance a lute and a vielle (an early bowed string instrument).

Refrain
  Plus dure que un dyamant
  Ne que pierre d'ayment
  Est vo durte,
  Dame, qui n'aves pite   *a*
  De vostre amant,
  Qu'ocies en desirant
  Vostre amitie.

Stanza 1
  Dame, vo pure biaute
  Qui toutes passe, a mon gre,   *b*
  Et vo samblant,

  Simple et plein d'umilite,
  De douceur fine paré,   *b*
  En sousriant,

  Par un accueil attraiant,
  M'ont au cuer en resgardant
  Si fort navré   *a*
  Que jamais joie n'avré,
  Jusques a tant, que vo grace
  Qu'il atant m'aures donné.

Harder than a diamond
Or than a lodestone
Is your hardness,
Lady, who have no pity
For your lover,
Who dies longing for
Your friendship.

Lady, your pure beauty,
Which to my taste surpasses all,
And your appearance,

Simple and full of humility,
In delicate sweetness decked,
Smiling,

With an attractive welcome
Have in the heart
So deeply wounded me
That I shall never be joyful
Until your grace
Shall have been granted me.

8. ANONYMOUS (FOURTEENTH CENTURY)

This example, ○● "Trotto," shows that instrumental music of the late Middle Ages and early renaissance could very well have been vigorous, stimulating, and lively. The work is performed by rebec (a violinlike instrument with only three strings), tenor violin, lute, sopranino recorder, buysine (an early slide trombone), drum, and tambourine. After the opening drum beats, the buysine sounds a fanfare motive, the last note of which becomes a sustained pedal point. Against this note the upper instruments frolic with the tune. The tambourine provides rhythmic emphasis.

9. FRANCESCO LANDINI (1325–1397)

Francesco Landini, the foremost Italian composer of the fourteenth century, was a blind organist who wrote a considerable amount of secular music. He preferred the *ballata*, of which ○ "Chi più le vuol sapere" is an example, over the madrigal and *caccia*, the two other popular forms in his country. The Italian *ballata* followed the same form as the French *virelai: abbaa* . . . (see the notes for 7. Guillaume de Machaut).

The lower instrumental part in this example moves in fairly regular quarter and half notes against a much more rhythmically free vocal line. The range of each melody remains within an octave span, with one exception. Periodically the parts converge to a unison or arrive at an octave, where cadences occur. The accompanying instrument is a viola da gamba, a bowed string instrument.

Who desires to know them more
Will know them less,

And he little knows them
Who imagines
That he will ever have
One that is perfect.

Then foolish indeed is he
Who sees pleasure
And takes it not,
Saying he will do better.

For seldom will good fortune
Return.

Chi più le vuol sapere,
Quel men' le sa,   a

Colui sa poco'l
Qual credo potere
Alcun bochon aver   b
Gianmai perfecto.

Dunque stolto è
Qual buon vede'l piacere
Et nol prende,   b
Per dire'il vo' più netto

Chè rado un dolce caso,
Tornerà.   a

Who desires to know them more
Will know them less.

Chi più le vuol sapere,
Quel men 'le sa.   *a*

10. JEAN LEGRANT (FIFTEENTH CENTURY)

o "Entre vous" probably dates from the early part of its composer's century. The work is in three parts, to be sung or played. In this example it is played by three instruments: *pardessus de viole* (a treble viol), lute, and tenor violin, with the addition of a drum. The drum provides a steady, thumping rhythmic background to the three melody instruments. "Entre vous" contains some syncopations, especially in the upper two parts.

Basically a binary form (*ab*) in duple meter, the composition is lengthened by repeats of the *a* section, as follows: *aabaab* plus a short *codetta* (ending) of four measures in triple meter. All parts in the original score have text, the poetry being a kind of warning to newly married men, but no text is sung in this purely instrumental performance.

11. GUILLAUME DUFAY (*ca.* 1400–1474)

The original manuscript for o ● "Ce jour de l'an," a three-part piece, characteristically gives little indication as to performance medium. In this performance three voices and three instruments participate in a lively realization. Bassoon, recorder, and viola enter successively before the voices are introduced. (Only the refrain is given below.) "Ce jour," in the Dorian mode, moves in a sprightly $\frac{6}{8}$ meter.

This New Year's day I will be joyful,
To sing, dance, and hold good cheer,
To keep the agreeable custom
That all lovers must.

Ce jour de l'an voudray joye mener,
Chanter, danser, et mener chiere lie,
Pour maintenir la constume joyle
Que tous amans sont tenus de garder.

12. JOANNES OKEGHEM (1430–1494)

The two principal forms of religious music in the fifteenth century were the motet and Mass. Okeghem's extraordinary *Missa prolationum*, from which the o ● Sanctus example has been taken, consists entirely of double canons: two parts written, the other two "derived" by entering later as imitations at designated points. The large work, a display of con-

(a)

Examples of late-medieval and renaissance techniques and styles of painting: (a) *Pol, Hermann, and Jan de Limburg's miniature of the Annunciation from the* Très riches heures du Duc de Berry. *Detailed representations of celebrating angelic musicians surround and accompany the principal scene.* (Musée Condé, Chantilly; phot. Bibl. nat., Paris.) (b) *Sandro Botticelli:* The Birth of Venus (ca. 1480). *A revival of a theme from pagan antiquity and of interest in depiction of the nude.* (Uffizi Gallery.)

(b)

Plate 1

Peter Paul Rubens: The Garden of Love. *This vibrant and lavishly painted allegory is a splendid baroque hymn to sensuality.* (Museo del Prado.)

Plate 2

trapuntal virtuosity, nevertheless stands as an expressive musical composition.

In the Sanctus the imitation takes place at the interval of a sixth above. If you listen carefully to the alto at the beginning, you will later hear exactly the same sequence of notes a sixth higher when the soprano voices enter. At that point the tenor voices also enter and sing a sixth higher exactly what the basses sang in the opening measures.

The individual melodic lines are smooth flowing and lengthy. The density, of course, increases from the original two parts to four where the canonic imitation begins. The general impression is of a complete mastery of technique; the flow of the melodic lines, the harmonic fabric, and the steady rhythms all blend to catch the listener up in an experience far larger than the sum of the common devices used.

Holy, holy, holy,
Lord God of Hosts.

Sanctus, sanctus, sanctus,
Dominus Deus Sabaoth.

13. ANONYMOUS (SIXTEENTH CENTURY)

The *tordion* was popular in mid-sixteenth-century Spain, Italy, and France. A fairly fast dance, it was usually in triple meter and binary (*ab*) form. Its melodies were mostly modal, with much stepwise motion. Since the dance served as secular entertainment, it was most likely performed with whatever instruments were at hand.

In this example of a ○● tordion, a tambourine provides a background rhythm for the viol, which plays the tune. On each of the repeats, a recorder is added an octave higher than the viol, and a lute is plucked at the same pitch level as the viol.

14. JOSQUIN DES PRÉS (1450–1521)

Many scholars would rank Josquin as the greatest of renaissance composers. As a contemporary of Michelangelo, Leonardo, and Raphael, of great aristocratic families like the Medici, Sforza, and Este, and of flamboyant renaissance popes like Alexander VI, Julius II, and Leo X, Josquin came into contact with renaissance life at its height. Like Michelangelo and Raphael, the qualitative level of his work seldom dropped below superior, with the result that his music served as a model for composers throughout the entire sixteenth century. Unlike the fate of many of his musical colleagues, neither Josquin nor his music fell into oblivion after his death.

The motet ○● "Ave Maria" was built by freely adapting a Gregorian melody. Listeners who were familiar with the chant could follow its general outlines in the motet in much the same way that modern listeners can sense the underlying popular tune in a free arrangement by a jazz group.

Josquin treated each phrase of the text with new material and in different ways. Typical of his motet style, the texture often shifts between two and four parts. But it is kept continuous by overlappings so that a new section begins just before the previous one ends. Melodic motion is primarily stepwise, with skips usually compensated for by step motion in the opposite direction from the skips. Because of the many imitative entrances, at certain moments four different portions of text are being heard. Yet the music sounds controlled, unified, and expressive. Roughly two-thirds of the way through the motet, Josquin changes to triple meter, but for the last section he returns to the original duple meter. Each of the Latin lines below is set to new thematic material.

Hail, Mary, full of grace,
The Lord is with thee;
Blessed art thou among women,
And blessed the fruit of thy womb,
Jesus Christ, Son of the living God.

Ave Maria, gratia plena,
Dominus tecum,
Benedicta tu, in mulieribus,
Et benedictus fructus ventris tui
Jesus Christus Filius Dei vivi.

And blessed be
Thy breasts
That have suckled The King of Kings

Triple meter
Et benedicta sint
Beata ubera tua
Quae lactaverunt regum regum

And the Lord our God.

Et Dominum Deum nostrum.

15. CLAUDE LE JEUNE (1528–1600)

French humanism, among other things, sought to purify and codify the French language. In pursuit of this goal it recommended close examination of the much-admired classical models. One result was a musical style in which rhythmic patterns in music were determined by the text: Long and short syllables in the poetry were reflected by long and short notes in the music, generally on the basis of two to one;

for example, long syllables became half notes in the music and short syllables quarter notes. At its worst, the procedure produced dry, sterile musical compositions; at its best, as in the example ○● "La bel'Aronde," the music conveyed a light grace brought about mainly by a remarkable flexibility of rhythm.

The refrain ("La bel'Aronde . . .") is in six parts. In between each refrain are verses in four-part writing. On the recorded example, only the first two of five original verses are heard.

Refrain
La bel'Aronde or' acourant
Mene la gaye saison,
On la void folasstrant,
Qui vole la mouchelette,
Qui vole le moucheron.
Je reviens de la voir
Je reconois le dos noir
Je l'y voy le ventre blanc,
Ja je l'y voy chaque flanc,
De deca la void on,
Qui vole la mouchelette,
Qui vole le moucheron.

Verse 1
Gentille Aronde tu viens
Avec l'émable Printans,
Apres l'été tu t'en vas,
Onques hyver ne sentis.

Verse 2
Quand nou quitant tu depars,
Aronde, mais ou vas-tu?
La ou revient le dous tans
D'oules orages s'en vont.

The beautiful Swallow, now swooping,
Ushers in the joyous season;
We see her frolicking,
Catching flies,
Seizing gnats.
I have just seen her again,
I recognize her black back,
I see her white breast,
I see her sides already;
From afar we see her,
Catching flies,
Seizing gnats.

Pretty Swallow, you come
With the pleasant Spring;
After the summer you fly away,
Never a winter do you feel.

When, leaving us, you depart,
Swallow, where do you go?
There where pleasant climes return,
And whence storms depart.

16. GIOVANNI PIERLUIGI DA PALESTRINA (1525–1594)

Perhaps the greatest composer for the Catholic Church, Palestrina wrote about 100 polyphonic Masses and about 350 motets. His poly-

phonic technique is well illustrated in a five-part piece, the second ○●
Agnus Dei from *Missa Brevis*. Careful listening will detect that the two
cantus (soprano) parts are in exact imitation. Thus only one soprano
part need be written, the other singing exactly the same notes two measures later.

In this movement, much of the melodic direction is downward, the
parts starting high and gently moving to lower pitch levels. The canon,
of course, provides a series of literal imitations, but the other parts are
also imitative. The texture, five-part and generally thick, is thoroughly
polyphonic. Attention shifts from one part to another as they weave in
and out. At the opening "Agnus Dei," the "Qui tollis," and the "Dona
nobis pacem" sections, all parts have successive imitative entrances.

Lamb of God
Who takest away the sins of the world,
Grant us peace.

Agnus Dei,
Qui tollis peccata mundi,
Dona nobis pacem.

17. ANDREA GABRIELI (1510–1586)

The pageantry that surrounded St. Mark's cathedral and its square in
sixteenth-century Venice may well have inspired works like this ○●
"Ricercar del duodecimo tuono." Written for *cantus* (soprano), *altus*
(alto), tenor, and bass, the composition does not precisely specify a medium of performance. So the medium no doubt varied, depending on
the performers available for any given occasion and on the financial resources of the supporting agent. For this recording, instrumentation is
for brass ensemble: two trumpets, horn, and trombone.

Imitative entrances abound in the ricercar. Most often the entrances
are in one individual part after another, but there are instances where
two parts playing a musical motive are echoed by another two. At a
few points strong harmonic cadences can be heard, even though the
texture is polyphonic. The work contains almost no chromaticism.

Like most ricercars, the form is sectional. The first and second parts
are in duple meter. The third part is in a contrasting triple meter, followed
by a very brief fourth part in duple. The third and fourth parts are
repeated; then the first part returns to complete the piece. So the entire
form can be outlined as *abcdcda*, or 2, 2, 3, 2, 3, 2, 2, where 2 stands
for duple meter, and 3 for triple.

18. ORLANDO DI LASSO (ROLAND DE LASSUS; 1532–1594)

A prolific composer, Orlando di Lasso is credited with over 1,250 sacred and secular works. He set to music Latin, French, Flemish, Italian, and German texts.

o● "Selig ist der, auf Gott sein Hoffnung setzet," the little German sacred song presented here, was originally published in 1583 and dedicated to the young Prince Maximilian of Bavaria. It was to be played on "all sorts of instruments" or to be sung.

In this example, sung a cappella, Lasso's mastery of polyphonic style is evident. In only twenty measures, the composer combines two separate melodies in pairs of voices ("Selig ist der"), sets parts in syncopation ("Wo nit noch mehr"), adopts a new rhythmic motive ("Und ihn anrufet"), plays with melismas ("in betrübter Zeit"), and elsewhere introduces various other kinds of contrapuntal devices.

After a somber and stately opening, regular in pulse, the motion of the music increases. Notes become successively quicker at "Und ihn anrufet" and at "als in betrübter Zeit." The ending is particularly interesting as the two inner voices continue the quick movement against more slowly moving outer voices. A plagal, "amen"-type cadence brings the piece to a quiet close.

Blessed is the man who puts his hope in God
And calls upon Him as much in good fortune and joy—
If not then even more—as in time of trouble,
And who values human aid as trifling and worthless.

Selig ist der, auf Gott sein Hoffnung setzet,
Und ihn anrufet, sowohl in Glück und Freud,
Wo nicht noch mehr, als in betrübter Zeit,
Auch ring und schlechte menschlichen Beistand schätzet.

19. LUCA MARENZIO (*ca.* 1560–1599)

A gifted Italian madrigal composer, Marenzio exhibited such versatility that his style is hard to characterize: It can be highly dramatic, poetically expressive, lyrical, light-hearted, or serious. He preferred to write in five parts, and his style moves freely from homophonic to polyphonic passages. Considerable chromaticism often appears, especially where the text is dramatic.

Published in 1594, the madrigal o "S'io parto, i' moro" treats its text phrase by phrase, the end of each line often being marked by a harmony sufficiently sustained to permit the entry of a new musical motive and text. The technique resembles that described under 14. Josquin des Prés, but actually the styles are quite dissimilar in sound.

Although the texture is five-part in some places, at times only two parts are present, such as at "Quei che conguins' Amor." So Marenzio varies texture constantly by having individual parts rest frequently. The rate at which the harmonies change (harmonic rhythm) is rather slow.

If I depart, I die,
And yet I must leave thee;
I shall die then, my dearest,
And this my sad departing
Which takes me from thee
Takes from me my being.
O cruel departure that will kill me,
How can those whom love has joined—
Ah, how—be divided?

S'io parto, i' moro,
E pur partir conviene
Morò dunque il mio bene,
E questa mia partita
Che mi ti toglie
Mi terà la vita.
Dolorosa partita che m'uccidi,
Quei che conguins' Amor perche,
Perche dividi?

20. JOHN MUNDY (DIED 1630)

o ● "Mundy's Joy," a short piece for virginal (a sixteenth-century type of harpsichord), is an example from an enormous output of keyboard music by Elizabethan composers. Basically a dance, "Mundy's Joy" displays strong rhythmic vitality; it is in triple meter. The overall form is binary, with a variation reprise at the end of each section: *AaBb*. Although virginal music of the period was often heavily ornamented, this piece is somewhat less so. However it requires a sure, deft touch and accurate technique. Many such pieces are either programmatic or hint at a program. "Mundy's Joy," accordingly, is in an appropriately light-hearted mood.

21. WILLIAM BYRD (1543–1623)

Byrd, the distinguished Catholic composer who served Queen Elizabeth at the Chapel Royal, wrote extensively in every medium: keyboard and other instrumental music, Masses, motets, Anglican anthems, madrigals, and solo songs. Of his Masses three are preserved: one in three, one in four, and one in five parts. The *Mass for Four Voices*, from which we have selected the ○ Agnus Dei, dates from around 1588 to 1591 (that is, from a period when Elizabethan England was reaching a peak) and consists of the usual five sections of the Ordinary: Kyrie, Gloria, Credo, Sanctus and Benedictus, and Agnus Dei. In all movements Byrd's mastery of counterpoint is evident.

The Agnus Dei begins with a duet between soprano and alto. The two parts are treated imitatively and arrive at a temporary cadence on the syllable ''-bis'' of ''nobis.'' At this point the tenor and bass enter in close imitation, followed by the soprano. Three-part texture prevails until the alto enters after the other parts have another cadence on the syllable ''-bis.'' All parts participate with entrances on the words ''Agnus Dei,'' the motion becoming more active.

In the last section, starting with ''dona nobis pacem,'' the movement gradually comes to a quiet close on a bright major triad rather than the expected minor. Throughout this movement Byrd frequently compensates for melodic leaps in one direction (up or down) by stepwise motion in the opposite direction.

Lamb of God, who takest away the sins of the world, have mercy upon us.
Lamb of God, who takest away the sins of the world, have mercy upon us.
Lamb of God, who takest away the sins of the world, grant us peace.

Agnus Dei, qui tollis peccata mundi, miserere nobis.
Agnus Dei, qui tollis peccata mundi, miserere nobis.
Agnus Dei, qui tollis peccata mundi, dona nobis pacem.

Other important music

For some additional pieces by medieval and renaissance composers, see the Music Index. However, because the time covered by this section is long and includes a wide variety of forms and styles, we are here suggesting anthologies of recorded music rather than individual compositions.

Archive Production Research Periods I–IV, Deutsche Grammophon Gesellschaft History of Music Division. These first four periods cover the growth of Western European music from Gregorian chant to the end of the renaissance. About fifty LP records have been issued—which makes this the most complete by far of all the recorded anthologies.

The History of Music in Sound, vols. II–IV, RCA Victor. This set consists of ten boxed albums covering music from chant to the twentieth century. Accompanying booklets for each album provide some background material and often a partial score for each item recorded. Volume II, *Early*

Medieval Music up to 1300, contains examples of early Byzantine, Ambrosian, Mozarabic, and Gregorian chant, liturgical drama, medieval songs, and early polyphony. Volume III, *Ars Nova and Renaissance,* has secular and sacred music in fourteenth-century France and Italy, music in fifteenth-century Burgundy, the Netherlands, and England, and organ and instrumental ensemble music of the fifteenth century. Volume IV, *The Age of Humanism,* includes Italian madrigal and French *chanson,* English, German, and Italian church music, solo song literature, and keyboard and instrumental ensemble music.

History of European Music, Orpheus. Three LP records, with more to come, contain excellent performances of music found in printed score in A. J. Davison and W. Apel, *Historical Anthology of Music,* vol. I: early chant, French troubadour and trouvère music, German minnesinger works, Italian *lauda,* Spanish *cantiga,* English song, German master-singer music, and early polyphony at various stages of development (organum, motet, *clausula,* and *conductus*). Thirty-two consecutively numbered items from the *Historical Anthology* are recorded.

Historical Anthology of Music in Performance, Pleiades. Four LP's in a continuing series, like the preceding one, record items from the *Historical Anthology,* vol. I, starting where the previous set ends and continuing through no. 120. They cover, therefore, late medieval music, keyboard music, the entire fifteenth century, and the early sixteenth.

Masterpieces of Music before 1750, Haydn Society (distributed by W. W. Norton & Company, Inc., New York). Three LP records contain fifty items from Gregorian chant through the music of Bach and Handel, with an accompanying book of descriptions and complete scores for every piece. The first twenty-nine items cover music through the renaissance. This set, easily accessible and not overdetailed, provides an excellent introduction to major composers and important forms.

A Treasury of Early Music, Haydn Society (distributed by W. W. Norton & Company, Inc., New York). In exactly the same format as the preceding set, this contains four LP records and a book. Thirty-six items cover music to the end of the renaissance. A complement to *Master-pieces, Treasury* fills in some gaps by providing examples of additional forms and music by other composers. Together, both sets constitute a practical package of one hundred recorded pieces, with two books complete with scores and informative descriptions.

Music of the Middle Ages, Musical Heritage Society. Seven LP records cover the following topics: troubadour and trouvère songs, organum at Notre Dame, *Las Cantigas de Santa Maria,* English polyphony of the thirteenth and early fourteenth centuries, English medieval songs, English polyphony of the fourteenth and early fifteenth centuries, and French *ars antiqua.*

The Treasury of English Church Music, Odéon. Of four LP's, the first two cover music through the end of the sixteenth century. Very early examples are given, along with later English composers like Dunstable, Thomas Tallis, Byrd, and Richard Farrant.

The Art of Ornamentation and Embellishment in the Renaissance and Baroque, Bach Guild. Two LP records present fascinating juxtapositions of the same pieces—vocal and instrumental—first performed "straight" (that is, as they more or less stand in manuscript or print) and then with authentic elaborations consistent with our present knowledge of actual performance practices of early music.

L'Anthologie Sonore, Haydn Society. These records are LP reissues of an earlier sixteen-volume set of 78-rpm recordings. Not all the original 155 works have been included in the LP series, but many pieces have been added. Covering the period from around 1200 to 1800, the performances and authenticity of style are at times somewhat uneven; nevertheless, the set has recorded items unavailable elsewhere.

The History of Italian Music, RCA Italiana. This very expensive set consists of forty LP records in four large volumes. Each volume includes a beautifully illustrated book with excellent color plates of paintings, buildings, instruments, composers, and music. Also included are descriptions and texts of the music. Volume I is entitled *From Gregorian Chant to Giacomo Carissimi.* Although the performances are uneven in quality, the volume contains a comprehensive picture of Italian renaissance music and musical styles.

Further readings

HISTORIES OF MUSIC

For the student who wishes to purchase a single book that covers the *entire* history of music, the following are recommended:

BORROFF, EDITH   *Music in Europe and the United States: A History,* Prentice-Hall, Inc., Englewood Cliffs, N.J., 1971. A comprehensive, readable history in an attractive format, beautifully illustrated. Useful at different levels of study. Unusually wide coverage of musical developments in the United States, especially of popular styles.

CANNON, BEEKMAN C., ALVIN JOHNSON, AND WILLIAM WAITE   *The Art of Music,* Thomas Y. Crowell Company, New York, 1960. Subtitled as a "short history of musical styles and ideas," this book is divided into eighteen chapters, each of which begins with an exposition of the intellectual and cultural background before an examination of musical developments. The authors have chosen to present relatively few musical compositions, but each of these is worked into a larger musical context. Well written, accurate, and dependable. A lengthy appendix describes and defines basic musical terms used throughout the book.

GROUT, DONALD JAY   *A History of Western Music,* W. W. Norton & Company, Inc., New York, 1960. Since its first appearance, this study has been enthusiastically endorsed by scholars and widely accepted as a standard undergraduate textbook and reference work. Clearly written, well organized, and in an excellent format, with detailed bibliography and index (with subdivisions of entries) and a useful chronological table of music against the background of history. For a single volume the book contains an enormous amount of information. A short edition is available; a new, revised edition is being planned.

LANG, PAUL HENRY   *Music in Western Civilization,* W. W. Norton & Company, Inc., New York, 1941. Less technical than Grout, Lang's extensive survey (over 1,000 pages) is more narrative and descriptive. Profoundly erudite and scholarly, the author integrates the art of music within a total cultural, intellectual, social, economic, and political setting. Students who want to see the whole picture cannot afford to pass up Lang.

Two series of books—one hardcover only, the other both hardcover and paperback—survey the history of music: a series published by W. W. Norton and addressed primarily to advanced students and music scholars; one from Prentice-Hall, less extensive and detailed but offering excellent introductions to special fields of study. Not all volumes in the Prentice-Hall series have yet been published. The listings below give authors and titles only; individual volumes are discussed later in appropriate chapters.

The volumes in the Norton series are:

AUSTIN, WILLIAM   *Music in the 20th Century.*
BUKOFZER, MANFRED   *Music in the Baroque Era.*
EINSTEIN, ALFRED   *Music in the Romantic Period.*

REESE, GUSTAVE   *Music in the Middle Ages.*
REESE, GUSTAVE   *Music in the Renaissance.*
SACHS, CURT   *The Rise of Music in the Ancient World.*
SALAZAR, ADOLFO   *Music in Our Time.*

The titles for the Prentice-Hall History of Music Series (under the general editorship of H. Wiley Hitchcock) are:

BROWN, HOWARD   *Renaissance Music.*
CHASE, GILBERT   *Music of Latin America.*
HITCHCOCK, H. WILEY   *Music in the United States: A Historical Introduction.*
LONGYEAR, REY M.   *Nineteenth-century Romanticism in Music.*
MALM, WILLIAM P.   *Music Cultures of the Pacific, the Near East, and Asia.*
NETTL, BRUNO   *Folk and Traditional Music of the Western Continents.*
PALISCA, CLAUDE V.   *Baroque Music.*
PAULY, REINHARD G.   *Music in the Classic Period.*
SALZMAN, ERIC   *Twentieth-century Music: An Introduction.*
SCHWARZ, BORIS   *Two Hundred Years of Russian Music, 1770–1970.*
SEAY, ALBERT   *Music in the Medieval World.*

The individual and collected studies given in the following sections are useful in supplying further information about the development of institutions and art in European civilization. They range from introductory to sophisticated, from pleasurable background reading to reference works for advanced research projects; and they present panoramic views of the Middle Ages and renaissance through literature, art, religion, politics, and other human activities.

BACKGROUND FOR THE MIDDLE AGES

ARTZ, FREDERICK B.   *The Mind of the Middle Ages,* A.D. *200–1500,* Alfred A. Knopf, Inc., New York, 1958. For years one of the standard textbooks on the subject.
COULTON, G. G.   *Life in the Middle Ages,* Cambridge University Press, London, 1928. A great scholar presents translations, together with his own commentaries, of medieval chronicles, letters, and other documents. Included is everything from ridiculous and entertainingly told folk

tales to moving religious writings, thus giving the reader a sense of the color and flavor of the period.

DURANT, WILL   *The Story of Civilization,* Part IV: *The Age of Faith,* Simon and Schuster, New York, 1950. Subtitled "A History of Medieval Civilization—Christian, Islamic and Judaic—from Constantine to Dante: A.D. 325–1300." A historian who writes interestingly, Durant also provides extensive documentation: original sources have been consulted, along with later studies by authoritative writers. Fourteen pages of bibliography. The "Index" is occasionally subdivided for quick reference.

FLEMING, WILLIAM   *Arts and Ideas,* Holt, Rinehart & Winston, Inc., New York, 1955 and later editions. A popular study that avoids the format of a continuously developing history. The author chooses only isolated but distinguished periods—limited by time and place—and then discusses significant ideas in the arts. Profusely illustrated and very readable.

FREMANTLE, ANN   *Age of Faith,* Time-Life Books, New York, 1965. From the twenty-volume Time-Life series, *Great Ages of Man,* this volume covers the Middle Ages. Like companion volumes in the set, it presents certain aspects of the medieval scene through expository essays, while color prints, black-and-white drawings, maps, and other illustrative materials make it an attractive volume. The text is not documented. The bibliography is short but excellent. Each volume in the series contains a chronological table.

ROSS, JAMES BRUCE, AND MARY MARTIN MCLAUGHLIN (EDS.)   *The Portable Medieval Reader,* The Viking Press, Inc., New York, 1960. Available in hardcover or paperback, this little volume (in size, not content) is part of a series of "portables," for example a Greek reader, Roman writings, the Age of Reason. A wise purchase for the student, it contains translations of letters, chronicles, statutes, addresses, poetry, and other contemporary source materials. Medieval wit, cynicism, resignation, hope, mysticism, and love pour forth in short, readable excerpts.

The following three volumes are special. They are expensive but beautifully illustrated and well-written presentations.

EVANS, JOAN (ED.)   *The Flowering of the Middle Ages,* Thames and Hudson, London, 1966. A detailed study of various aspects of medieval society by a group of contributing British scholars. Lengthy essays, profusely illustrated, explore religious life, court life, architecture, universities and learning, craftsmen and their art, and the like.

JACOBS, JAY (ED.)   *The Horizon Book of the Great Cathedrals,* American Heritage Publishing Co., Inc., New York, 1968. After a lengthy introduction by Zoé Oldenbourg and a four-page glossary of terms relating to cathedral construction, five chapters follow on the great cathedrals of France, Germany, England, Spain, and Italy. Each chapter, illustrated with long views and detailed closeups, contains informative essays. The last section takes the reader on a ''tour'' of 113 great cathedrals of Western Europe, including those already dealt with in the main text.

KOTKER, NORMAN (ED.) *The Horizon Book of the Middle Ages,* American Heritage Publishing Co., Inc., New York, 1968. Companion volume to the preceding book, that is, same general treatment of pictorial materials. No bibliography or internal documentation, but a good index. Sample chapter headings: ''The Noble's Life,'' ''Knights in Battle,'' ''An Age of Faith,'' ''The Life of Thought.''

MUSIC OF THE MIDDLE AGES

Relevant sections of the Cannon, Grout, and Lang books on music history (see the first section, above) plus the following special studies may be useful:

HUGHES, DOM ANSELM (ED.) *New Oxford History of Music,* vol. II: *Early Medieval Music up to 1300,* Oxford University Press, London, 1954. Eleven comprehensive chapters by six contributing scholars. Useful bibliography and detailed index.

REESE, GUSTAVE *Music in the Middle Ages,* W. W. Norton & Company, Inc., New York, 1940. The definitive single volume in English, a model of scholarship. Because of its age, some aspects need to be updated, yet the Reese book remains incomparable as a detailed source of information, including an enormous bibliography.

SEAY, ALBERT *Music in the Medieval World,* Prentice-Hall, Inc., Englewood Cliffs, N.J., 1965. A useful, up-to-date study. Appended to the end of each chapter is a selective bibliography.

STRUNK, OLIVER *Source Readings in Music History,* W. W. Norton & Company, Inc., New York, 1965. Also available in paperback edition in five volumes. Translated excerpts from original writings by philosophers, music theorists, and composers.

BACKGROUND FOR THE RENAISSANCE

ARTZ, FREDERICK B. *From the Renaissance to Romanticism,* University of Chicago Press, Chicago, 1962. Subtitled ''Trends in Style in Art,

Literature, and Music, 1300–1830,'' this book is useful as a quick survey or general reference. Excellent bibliography on the arts. Available in paperback.

BURCKHARDT, JACOB   *The Civilization of the Renaissance in Italy* [S. G. C. Middlemore (trans.)], Harper and Brothers, New York, 1929. Since its first appearance in German over one hundred years ago (1860), Burckhardt's interpretation of the renaissance has fascinated and challenged historians. The book, now available in paperback, remains ''must'' reading for all students and scholars of the period.

DURANT, WILL   *The Story of Civilization,* Part V: *The Renaissance,* Simon and Schuster, New York, 1953. This and the succeeding volume, below, cover mainly the fifteenth and sixteenth centuries. *The Renaissance* is almost exclusively concerned with the Italian renaissance. The organization and format are the same as other books in the series; good and readable.

DURANT, WILL   *The Story of Civilization,* Part VI: *The Reformation,* Simon and Schuster, New York, 1957. Subtitled ''A History of European Civilization from Wyclif to Calvin: 1300–1564,'' this volume completes Durant's picture of the renaissance. Religious controversy, therefore, is not the only subject matter, even if it is central. Music, painting, and the other arts are also treated.

HALE, JOHN   *Renaissance,* Time-Life Books, New York, 1965. See remarks under the section Background for the Middle Ages, above. Same general format and organization as the Fremantle book but here applied to the renaissance. Centers mainly on Italy, with a brief glance at northern countries.

ROSS, JAMES BRUCE, AND MARY MARTIN MCLAUGHLIN (EDS.)   *The Portable Renaissance Reader,* The Viking Press, Inc., New York, 1960. See remarks under the section Background for the Middle Ages, above. Same general format and organization as *The Portable Medieval Reader* but here applied to the renaissance.

SIMON, EDITH   *The Reformation,* Time-Life Books, New York, 1966. Companion volume to Hale's *Renaissance,* above. Life and times in a sixteenth-century Europe torn by religious dissension. A balanced, dispassionate view of a difficult subject is presented.

SYMONDS, JOHN ADDINGTON   *The Renaissance in Italy,* Modern Library, Inc., New York, n.d. A not-quite-so-famous contemporary of Burckhardt, Symonds provides an exhaustive survey of the Italian renaissance.

The books listed below are expensive publications, beautifully illustrated and well written.

CHASTEL, ANDRÉ   *The Age of Humanism: Europe, 1480–1530* [Katherine M. Delavenay and E. M. Gwyer (trans.)], McGraw-Hill Book Company, Inc., New York, 1963. Highly specialized study of one of the most important half centuries in history. Over 40 color plates and 400 illustrations, most of which avoid the frequently found, obvious, popular types, are drawn from woodcuts, paintings, drawings, miniatures, frontispieces, maps, and other sources. Sophisticated, suggestive, and scholarly.

HAY, DENYS (ED.)   *The Age of the Renaissance,* McGraw-Hill Book Company, Inc., New York, 1967. See the Evans volume under Background for the Middle Ages for a companion volume. Eleven contributors examine various aspects of the renaissance in a series of scholarly essays on, for instance, Italian art from Masaccio to mannerism and English society under the Tudors. Over 600 illustrations: 180 color and 420 photos, drawings, woodcuts, and maps. Select bibliography and a useful index.

KETCHUM, RICHARD M. (ED.)   *The Horizon Book of the Renaissance,* American Heritage Publishing Co., Inc., New York, 1961. Attractive organization contains biographical essays as central features for nine chapters flanked by an opening and closing chapter. Individual scholars contribute sketches on Petrarch, Machiavelli, Michelangelo, Lorenzo de' Medici, Pope Pius II, and other renaissance figures. Good index, but no bibliography.

LONGNON, JEAN (ED.)   *The Très Riches Heures of Jean, Duke of Berry, of the Musée Condé, Chantilly,* George Braziller, Inc., New York, 1969. A magnificent, spectacularly beautiful publication of the famous calendar of the seasons by the Limburg brothers. This volume is the next best thing to viewing the original fifteenth-century manuscript itself. This book of hours catches all the nuances of life at the threshold of the renaissance.

MUSIC OF THE RENAISSANCE

ABRAHAM, GERALD (ED.)   *New Oxford History of Music,* vol. IV: *The Age of Humanism, 1540–1630,* Oxford University Press, London, 1968. Companion volume to the following book but covering a later period. Additional scholars contribute authoritative chapters dealing with their special fields, as German secular song, Protestant church music, and solo instrumental music. Well documented, practical, detailed. Good bibliography and index.

HUGHES, DOM ANSELM, AND GERALD ABRAHAM (EDS.)   *New Oxford History of Music,* vol. III: *Ars Nova and Renaissance,* Oxford University Press, London, 1960. Companion volume to the Hughes one under Music of the Middle Ages, above. Individual scholars contribute detailed, well-documented studies on various subjects. Sophisticated writing, but informative.

REESE, GUSTAVE *Music in the Renaissance,* W. W. Norton & Company, Inc., New York, 1954. An overwhelming, scholarly study, representing immense erudition. All music studies of the renaissance start (and sometimes end) with Reese. The bibliography alone consists of sixty-three small-print pages.

STRUNK, OLIVER *Source Readings in Music History: The Renaissance,* W. W. Norton, & Company, Inc., New York, 1965. A sequel to the Strunk volume mentioned under Music of the Middle Ages.

Chapter 10 ○ The baroque era

LIKE SO MANY OTHER DESCRIPTIVE TERMS, THE WORD "BAROQUE" HAS changed in meaning throughout its long history. The term was originally used in the writings of scholastic logicians in the late Middle Ages. Gradually it came to be applied to a type of art that was considered to be overelaborate, tasteless, perverse, contorted, decadent, bizarre, corrupt, exaggerated, or even ridiculous. By the eighteenth century, French philosophers such as Jean-Jacques Rousseau and neoclassic writers such as Roberto Milizia, who preferred the more restrained art of Leonardo and Raphael, expressed their disdain for much art of the late sixteenth and seventeenth centuries by means of "baroque," viewing that art as a decline from the dizzy summits of the high renaissance. Later, two typical nineteenth-century views of the baroque were "grotesque Renaissance" (John Ruskin) and "a corrupt dialect of the Renaissance" (Burckhardt). But in 1948 Manfred Bukofzer's *Music in the Baroque Era* established the notion of a period, roughly 1580 to 1750, whose stylistic unity was sufficient to be called by a single term; and in that book and others of our century the baroque is recognized as an independent style as worthy in its own right as was the renaissance in earlier views. Thus there have been several meanings of the term "baroque," its beginning and ending dates vary from art to art and country to country, and opinions differ on the role of the period in the shaping of our modern society.

Ideas and arts of the baroque

What kind of world was the baroque that it causes so much confusion? The question cannot be answered with certainty, for it involves many complex matters that scholars have still not completely sorted out. Our intention is not to belabor the difficulties, but we must acknowledge their presence in order to avoid painting a simple picture of a complex subject.

Let us divide our question and examine only the first part: What kind of world was this? We find that the number of events, discoveries, developments, and changes in all domains of human activity is staggering. So much happened in the baroque that still affects our lives that many thinkers regard that time as the beginning of modern history.

Consider the consequences of the following developments in the sciences alone: the gradual acceptance of Copernicus's explanation of the solar system; Johannes Kepler's observations on the motions of the planets; Galileo's work with the telescope; William Gilbert's discoveries in magnetism; Evangelista Torricelli's work on the barometer; John Napier's method of logarithms; the explorations of Blaise Pascal and Christian Huygens in the calculus of probabilities; studies on protozoa and bacteria by Anton van Leeuwenhoek; Robert Hooke's discovery of the cellular structure of plants; William Harvey's work on the circulation of the blood. These mentions single out only one contribution of the many made by each of these scientists, to say nothing of thousands of advances made by others. Their contributions caused revolutionary changes, which eventually affected all aspects of life in Europe and America, and came in such abundance, especially in the seventeenth century, that Alfred North Whitehead called that century "The Age of Genius."

As scientists were challenging old ways of thinking, so were philosophers and humanists, for the bankruptcy of the old scholasticism was recognized by all except the most conservative thinkers. The chief purpose of the new philosophy, although it continued in its own way to

Figure 10.1 • Tintoretto (Jacopo Robusti): Last Supper (ca. 1592–1594). Typically baroque in its movement, passion, and agitation and its avoidance of neat, formal balance and a sense of serenity, this painting also exhibits a characteristic domestication of sacred subjects and their symbology. (Alinari—Art Reference Bureau.)

Figure 10.2 • El Greco's Adoration of the Shepherds *is an example of Spanish baroque mysticism, an intense and mannerist treatment of a tranquil theme contained within a formal structure.* (Museo del Prado.)

glorify God, was to bring traditional beliefs into line with the new frontiers of scientific knowledge. The concept of the universe as a fabulous, dependable machine became increasingly attractive; the role of God was diminished, and His importance minimized. The older philosophy came to be regarded as an inferior partner to the youthful and strongly developing scientific outlook, which argued that the entire natural system is based on laws that, one after the other, can be revealed by scientific observation and study. Man must then bring himself to live in harmony with nature (usually capitalized) and permit his life to flow in accordance with these laws.

Stated in various ways by a number of writers, that beautiful theory was destined to stumble over two nasty little facts that succeeding centuries fully brought out: Man himself has proved to be so unpredictable that observations about his true nature have become hazardous undertakings at best; and the study of Nature has multiplied rather than reduced the number of problems facing humanity. Nevertheless, Pandora's box had been opened, and a new kind of inquiry based on scientific methodology emerged—for both good and evil ends. Philosophy, political theory, historiography, education, religion, law, social customs, and the arts—all felt the pull of the new scientific spirit.

Spinoza's *Ethics*, with its series of definitions, axioms, propositions, and demonstrations, is in the flavor of its organization strangely reminiscent of ancient Euclid's geometry. Thomas Hobbes, under the spell of mathematical studies and rationalist philosophies, attempted to structure a mechanistic political and social system. The historians of the seventeenth and eighteenth centuries began to write histories, essays, and critiques with the systematic thoroughness of a Newton. Countless scholars compiled enormous collections of sources (still usable), which served the talents of David Hume, Voltaire, and Edward Gibbon.

Changes in education occurred also, for the needs of an increasingly technological and democratic society were not those of the previous theologically and classically oriented aristocracy. In the field of religion there was open warfare, denunciation of others' beliefs, suspicious intolerance of church by church—all stemming from the growth of

Figure 10.3 • The pompous rhetoric of the baroque: Baldassare Longhena's Church of Santa Maria della Salute (ca. 1631–1656) at Venice. (Italian Government Travel Office.)

Figure 10.4 • Giovanni Bernini: The Rape of Proserpina *(1621–1622). A dramatically violent and virtuosic expression of a classical theme.* (Borghese Gallery, Rome.)

rationalism. This spread a healthy skepticism about religion among those who survived the verbal and real wars. Yet it is noteworthy that many churchmen, Catholic as well as Protestant, adopted the new scientific methods of biblical criticism and historiography to bolster their various claims. Others, of course, continued to write the more traditional eloquent and rhapsodic ''proofs'' to defend their brand of Christianity.

Social customs also began to change with the times. There were movements away from trying to solve problems spiritually toward an attempt to better external, material circumstances, away from a religious basis of morality toward one based on utility and situation, away from a view of man in the image of God toward the ''real'' or ''natural'' man, in short, away from absolutes and transcendentals toward the relative and observable. These changes permeated society, transforming views on women, sex, marriage, honor, eating, drinking, dress, and manners. But change comes hard, and the period was rich in sermons damning innovation.

The arts too reflected the times: Precision-oriented works based on ''scientific principles'' can be found along with uninhibited, emotional utterances; clean, classical lines, along with extravagantly diffused colors; secular themes, along with divine symbols (Figure 10.1); rules of ''correct taste,'' along with expressions of individuality; closed artistic structures, along with open ones. The period was one of brilliant contrasts. Within one single work or between two works contemporary with each other there can be sensed a love of harmonious balance and symmetry characteristic of the renaissance simultaneous with a dynamic exuberance, color, and ornamentation typical of the baroque (Figure 10.2). At times these different artistic strands merged without conflict; but more frequently they aroused inner tensions that the great baroque artists found challenging as aesthetic problems.

The Counter-Reformation enlisted the aid of the arts in its efforts to fight heresies and religious skepticism. Architecture, sculpture, painting, literature, and music were employed as religious propaganda through which appeals were made to the senses. In some cases the appeals were subtle; in others, as blatant as certain television commercials. But

Figure 10.5 • Peter Paul Rubens: Crucifixion (*altar, ca. 1620*). *A unified religious drama emphasizing emotional extremes and other contrasts.* (Royal Museum of Fine Arts, Antwerp.)

they were effective, and they helped stem the rising flood of the wavering and the disenchanted. Architecture was meant to be awe-inspiring and overwhelming (Figure 10.3); sculpture, to be restless movement (Figure 10.4); painting, impressive and monumental; literature, powerfully eloquent and rhetorical; and music, a study of colorful contrasts in tempo, sonority, and texture. Blended in the service of the Roman Catholic Church, the result was great theater, where religious ideals and sensuous qualities were linked in a series of dramatic acts of hedonistic mysticism (Figure 10.5). It is not out of order, therefore, to imagine the baroque as a kind of dramatic ensemble, colossal and complicated, full of action, motion, and sound, accompanied by grand gesture, lighting, and scenery. Designed to create illusion, it juxtaposed and merged opposites (Figure 10.6). But above all it tried to engage the spectator and listener in active participation through sensory as well as mental contact with art.

Baroque musicians also participated in this quest for theatricality. They did so by writing dramatic music, especially opera, which became the period's most typical artistic genre. Opera tried to accommodate all the arts in one large and extravagant show: Drama, poetry, architecture, painting, sculpture, dancing, music, history, and myth—with their attributes of climax, rhyme, perspective, color, form, motion, sound, and illusion—were mingled in abundance. To this mixture were added elaborate stage machinery as complicated as the plots themselves, the settings outside and inside the opera houses, the colorful costumes of expectant audiences, and the unrestrained enthusiasms of those audiences for their favorite singers—the result was baroque opera.

It is little wonder that almost all composers were involved in opera. Even those few who did not write opera were influenced by techniques of composition associated with it. In constant search for musical devices that could catch the spirit of the play, opera composers created new tonal expressions, which naturally carried over to their keyboard, chamber, and church music. The dramatic musical language of opera infiltrated even the generally conservative church music, where the dividing line between secular and sacred often became blurred, if not obliterated. Cantatas, motets, and other vocal forms felt the influence, as did almost all instrumental music, for composers were intent on making music "move the passions of the soul."

From somewhat tentative beginnings in Florence, opera spread to other

Figure 10.6 • Balthaser Neumann's chapel at the Würzburg Residenz. Dating from around 1719 to 1744, this baroque, theatrical piece of ornamental architecture and decoration looks forward to the playfulness of the rococo style. (Verlag Gundermann, Würzburg.)

musical centers in Italy, notably Rome, Venice, and Naples; then the Italian operatic style soon penetrated all countries of Western Europe, and every court or city aspiring to cultural recognition had to take into account the dominant popularity of Italian opera. Hundreds of dramatic works by hundreds of composers were seen, heard, and enjoyed in hundreds of productions. Although most of these have been relegated to the attics of music history, one fact clearly emerges: These entertainments fascinated popes, cardinals, kings, dukes, merchants, and artisans. In the minds of those who held the pursestrings, opera and its many branches (English masque and French *comédie-ballet*, to name but two) seemed to be at the highest level the art of music could reach even though, as a form, opera often violated the integrity of its individual arts in the interests of a massive unification, a unification not always satisfactory and not always dramatic.

If some aspects of the baroque were marked by theatricality, other portions, particularly in France, stressed the earlier admiration for correctness, proper form, good taste, adherence to authoritative artistic rules, urbanity, and self-discipline. Under the influence of Nicolas Boileau-Despréaux, the Académie française launched a determined effort to purify the French language, which—at least according to members of the Académie—needed it badly: One reads of "impurities," of "bad usages," of "freeing the language from obscurity," of making it "friendly to elegance." Grammar, syntax, rhetoric, and poetics were to be organized according to exacting rules, and a dictionary was to be issued standardizing spelling and setting forth precise definitions. In spite of all this, France produced a Molière.

Other academies attempted to recruit, mobilize, and mold artistic dispositions. The Academy of Painting and Sculpture under Charles Le Brun, the Academy of Architecture under Jules Hardouin-Mansart, and the Academy of Music under Lully more or less controlled their respective art. To receive appointments, commissions, prizes—in fact to have almost any door opened for study or exhibition—the architect, sculptor, painter, and musician had to cultivate those artistic techniques which were in accord with the aesthetic ideals of the powerful. The pervasive influence of the new science is evident here too. In setting pictorial standards, for example, the controllers demanded demonstrable relationships based on scientific laws such that formal design, color combinations, and even thematic treatment could be explained through logi-

Figure 10.7 • Not all the baroque was untrammeled: Nicolas Poussin's Et in Arcadia Ego (ca. 1638) *shows its classic side, with formal patterns, order, careful design, and interest in the ideal, the typical, and the general. (Musée du Louvre; cliché des Musées Nationaux.)*

cal, rational analysis. Under Louis XIV a degree of artistic freedom was therefore lost, but we must also observe that during his reign (1643–1715) France became the artistic center of Western Europe, partly because of the number and quality of highly skilled technicians produced by the academies and partly because of imposing figures like Mansart, Jean Racine, Lully, and Boileau.

Of course, the art of music did not entirely escape the tendencies to reducing things to rules and regulations. Operatic forms naturally drew attention to relationships between music and speech, and by observing such parallels, writers began to view music as a kind of rhetoric, closely allied to language in regard to syntactical principles. Certain musical patterns were believed to be capable of presenting particular moods or emotional states, or "affections." Although lacking clear definition, the patterns nevertheless assumed some level of literal meaning. For the sophisticated listener of the time, they contributed to the total affect of a composition (for an instance, see Handel's "Perfido!" from *Radamisto,* under Representative Pieces, where the opening motive reflects the natural speech rhythm of the word "Perfido"). Various writers, especially in eighteenth-century Germany, formulated elaborate aesthetic theories to deal with problems of musical metaphor, simile, expression, and ultimately meaning. Referred to today as the "doctrine of affections" (*Affektenlehre*), this body of writings, with its focus on methods whereby music can arouse specific emotions in well-determined ways, reveals the strong influence that the philosophical rationalism of the time exerted on the arts.

As Friedrich Blume remarks in *Renaissance and Baroque Music,* "not everything about Baroque works of art is necessarily Baroque." Nicolas Poussin's attraction to high-renaissance designs (Figure 10.7) is in vivid contrast to Peter Paul Rubens's sprawling, voluptuous figures (Plate 2). Francesco Borromini's approach to architecture is not that of the classically oriented Le Brun. Baroque and classic elements contend for supremacy in John Milton as well as in J. S. Bach. Each of these artists was profoundly aware of the delicate balancing of emotion against intellect, of unhindered expression against problems of proportion, of sonority against sensible meaning, of exultation checked by restraint. The baroque artist, if we can generalize, created and worked in a flux of ideas, from which he drew his inspiration: rationalism, scientific method, authoritative politics, religious controversy, to name only a few.

Figure 10.8 • *Rembrandt:* Self-portrait with Saskia. *Probably created shortly after Rembrandt's marriage to his first wife in 1634, this painting summarizes the virile, robust side of the baroque.* (Staatliche Kunstsammlungen Dresden—Gemäldegalerie alte Meister.)

According to his own art, he painted kings, glorified God in sound, or damned unbelievers in words; but whatever he did, he did with verve and spirit (Figure 10.8).

Musical style

RHYTHM

After some experimentation at the beginning of the seventeenth century, the mainstream of baroque rhythm became marked by continuity of flow, very frequent repetition of rhythmic patterns, and regularity of beat. The relentless motion was a musical counterpart of the baroque ideal of space filled with dynamic motion and energy: time, likewise, was to be filled with pulsation and active movement.

The practice in rhythm was not uniform, for at least one other important method can be found. In recitative and some *arioso* passages the rhythm is relatively free in that it is influenced mainly by the movement of the words; the beat is irregular if not altogether absent. Rhythmic motion (when it is felt) constantly changes by *accelerando*s and *ritardando*s according to the meaning of the text. To some extent, instrumental forms like the fantasia and toccata used these typically vocal expressions in short passages that sound like recitatives or *arioso*s for instruments.

A natural source for rhythms, which served baroque instrumental and vocal composers alike, was the dance. Dance rhythms, regular out of necessity, were adapted, modified, transformed, and extended into lengthy and serious pieces, these artistic transformations growing into *concerto grosso* movements, suite movements, or even in some instances arias expressing great tragedy. Such transformations only hint at origins in the physical movements of rustic or courtly dances.

MELODY

During the baroque period, composers necessarily worked—as they have in all periods—within limitations: the physical limitations of the human voice, the limitations imposed by available instruments, and the restrictions of the existing practices for using rhythm, melody, harmony and counterpoint, and form.

Compared with renaissance melody, baroque vocal melody considerably extended the range of the voice. Especially was this so in long, flowing, *cantabile* melodies (such as would be found in arias) and in the more

Allegro

Example 10.1 • *A. Vivaldi: Concerto for Violin and Orchestra in e, F. I,*
no. 208, I (Il Favorito).

dramatic lines of recitative (an imitation of speech) and *arioso* (a vocal
style midway between aria and recitative). Recitative writing used jagged
melodic lines with large leaps, sudden changes of direction, unequal
phrase lengths (determined, in part, by the natural flow of language),
and in the case of *parlando* recitatives, a series of repeated notes on
a single pitch. In the aria, however, we find baroque melody in its most
characteristic form: relatively predictable and emphasizing continuity and
smoothness. On the other hand, there was one type, strongly influenced
by instrumental composition, that contained many motivic patterns,
rapid scale passages, arpeggios, and spun-out phrases with decorative
embellishments and ornaments. This kind of melody demanded the
technique of a virtuoso singer, capable of execution typical of such agile
instruments as the flute or violin.

Instrumental melodies ranged from purely lyrical to intensely dramatic
types. The lyrical type, found at its best in a composer such as Corelli,
is like a vocal melody in smooth, continuous, almost effortless lines,
with small-step motion, clear phrase structure, regular melodic goals,
and moderate registers. Other instrumental melodies, more dramatic,
give a sense of active motion by contrasting vigorous triadic motives
and short rhythmic fragments. The former are often hammered out in
straightforward *staccati;* the latter, in steady, machinelike melodies of
short, equal notes, as in Example 10.1.

Melodic writing of the nineteenth century, as we shall see, often gradually worked toward a single big climax, after which the section or movement quickly came to an end. Baroque melody appears to have been
more controlled by form in that overall design and mood are primary.
Although baroque melodies also rise and fall, climaxes tend to appear
in each large or small section and are not ''saved up'' for one big
moment in the piece.

In a change from earlier practice, composers began to write especially
for the various instruments, taking advantage of the particular properties

of each: We find melodies for organ in polyphonic texture, harpsichord melodies calling for brilliant technique (arpeggios, scale passages, trills), wind-instrument melodies that seem to be ''natural'' (fanfares for trumpets, highly elaborate melodies for flutes), and melodies to reveal the expressive range of the string family of instruments.

HARMONY AND COUNTERPOINT

The general trend during the baroque was toward the establishment of a homophonic texture at least equal to that of the older polyphony. Polyphonic and homophonic textures were often contrasted and mingled in a single composition, although many works used only one texture or the other.

The commonest texture resulted from the most characteristic stylistic feature of baroque music: the figured bass (often called ''thorough bass'' or similar names). If you look at the score for a baroque trio sonata (a work for four performers, two playing solo treble instruments and two—a low-string player and a keyboard player—''realizing'' the thorough-bass accompaniment), such as the portion of one in Example 10.2, you will see three staves of music: two for the treble parts and one for the bass. What next catches the eye are the Arabic numbers and occasional symbols (4+, ♮, ♭, ♯) under certain notes of the printed bass. The numbers and accompanying symbols constitute a kind of musical shorthand for a keyboard player (harpsichord or organ), whose

Example 10.2 • *A. Corelli:* Sonata da chiesa *in d, op. 3, no. 5, I.*

job it is to realize the figured bass; from the clues provided by the figures and the upper printed parts, he is expected to provide an appropriate texture. He may select one or more of several options: thick or thin sonorities, broken chords in arpeggiated fashion, short imitative entrances in polyphonic style, changes of register, or various combinations of these and other possibilities suited to the composition. The bass line of the keyboard instrument was intended to be reinforced by a low string or wind instrument, such as a cello or bassoon. In larger ensembles (for example, a *concerto grosso*) it was customary to have more than one string or wind instrument on the bass line and two harpsichordists, one realizing the bass for the soloists, the other realizing the bass for the orchestral players.

Another texture using figured bass is found in recitative, *arioso,* arias, and songs for solo voice with accompaniment. Here the music appears on two staves: one for the vocal line and the other for the figured bass. Again, the bass notes are to be played by a bowed string instrument and the left hand of a harpsichordist or organist, who at the same time is to realize the code provided by the written symbols by filling in with chords, arpeggios, melodic imitations, and various other inventions.

Because of the extraordinary emphasis placed upon the upper vocal line (or, in the case of the trio sonata, two upper instrumental lines in counterpoint with each other) and the figured bass, much music of the time is polarized as soprano-bass. The attention, therefore, constantly focuses on the interplay of soprano and bass, with the bass serving as a foundation for the melody above it.

Although soprano-bass polarization is abundant, fuller textures are also common. Three-, four-, and five-part writing in both homophony and polyphony is often found. In homophonic textures sonorities may be thick or thin, and the series of harmonies may or may not blend or contrast with a vocal or instrumental line; in polyphonic textures lines may or may not be presented in various tone colors. For example, a vocal solo may be supported by sustained chords played by the entire string family of instruments; or the solo voice may, as a single contrapuntal line, compete with other contrapuntal lines in a thick, imitative texture with contrasting colors. In most cases the *basso continuo* is there, being realized by a keyboard performer, and by attentive listening you can hear the sound of an organ or harpsichord.

Numerous writings on the rules of musical composition appeared in the baroque period. Rules for harmony were brought together mainly between 1722 and 1762, when, in a series of works, J.-P. Rameau codified the theory that chords, the building blocks of harmony, are based on "nature," that is, the harmonic series. This theory was to dominate musical thinking until the twentieth century.

Baroque harmonic practices, derived in part from continuo, or thorough-bass, playing, gradually led to new ideas about the handling of dissonance, the establishment of keys, the movement from one key to another (modulation), and the development of a strong sense of tonality. It was tonality—the strong tonal center with its various structural supports—that established a basic sense of aesthetic unity in much baroque music. Certain chords helped to establish tonality; and to create tensions, others forced harmonic progressions to move away from points of stability and rest. Baroque harmony thus became "functional," each chord functioning within a key in its agreed-upon capacity.

Polyphonic textures tended to be increasingly governed by principles of functional and tonal harmony. Cadences in polyphonic textures were often very weak; but in homophonic textures, where harmony served primarily as accompaniment to melody, cadences were clearly defined, strong, and often predictable. In both polyphonic and homophonic writing the pace of harmonic change was generally fast, with more chord changes per measure or phrase than one might find in the music of Haydn and Mozart, in the following era. At its height, baroque harmony became so completely integrated with polyphony that each was governed by the other; a sense of harmonic progression emerged from a web of moving polyphonic lines, and the interweaving polyphonic lines were controlled by harmonic progression. This synthesis of vertical (harmony) and horizontal (polyphony) is one of the great achievements of the period. But it was not always sought after: Many composers, content to meet the pressing needs of the moment, did not labor to bring it about.

TONE COLOR

During the baroque many technical improvements were made in existing instruments (the organ and harpsichord, for example), and newer instruments, like the violin family, clarinet, and piano, were developed. Composers, at the same time, began to take advantage of the particular qualities associated with each instrument. Combined with a search for dramatic effect, these factors influenced baroque composers' awareness of tone color as an important element in music. Renaissance composers, you will recall, had generally contented themselves with writing excellent part music—two, three, four, or more polyphonic lines—which could be performed by whatever voices and instruments happened to be at hand. Although this practice did not completely disappear during the baroque, it was much weakened as composers came to depend on the expressive potentialities peculiar to certain instruments and began to contrast vocal sound with instrumental, brass with string, flute with violin, and so on. The *concertato* principle of ''musical rivals'' was established, juxtaposing contrasting sonorities, large and small ensembles, loud and soft dynamics, and other combinations. But whereas many composers exploited the expressive possibilities of tone color, the old practice of optional instrumentation (the use of any available instruments suited to the range of a part) continued well into the later eighteenth century.

One of the most challenging problems in performing baroque music today is the difficulty—in some cases the impossibility—of reproducing the tone colors employed by baroque composers and heard by their audiences. Some baroque instruments have simply disappeared and are not available even in modern reconstructions; others were gradually replaced during the period itself to suit changing tastes. But some continued to be used and to be mechanically improved, thereby perpetuating their existence. Some instrument makers today are making and selling modern versions of baroque instruments like the cornett, viola da gamba, recorder, harpsichord, and other important types. As musicologists continue to study and solve problems relating to performance, they create and revive needs for authentic instruments. So we have in the past few decades witnessed a strong resurgence of interest in baroque music played on modern baroque instruments. Completely absent from modern performances, of course, is the most spectacular vocal sound of the baroque: the *castrati,* male sopranos and altos who captivated audiences with their extraordinary vocal powers.

The term ''flexibility'' best describes instrumental groups or orchestras of the period. In the beginning neither the quantities within the groups nor the participating instruments were standardized. Gradually, however, the nucleus of the orchestra became a grouping of violins, violas, cellos, and double basses plus continuo, the last including the appropriate keyboard instrument and one or more low-pitched instruments. Later, in the seventeenth century, with the string nucleus established on a firm basis, flutes, trumpets, and other wind instruments were added by Lully and his contemporaries. The art of orchestration had been born.

Because of many factors, physical as well as aesthetic, dynamic levels tended to alternate between loud and soft or some intermediate stage rather than gradually increase or decrease in volume. For example, the harpsichord could not easily produce variations in dynamics as the piano was later able to do, nor was the organ equipped with a swell box. Such limitations among others together with the baroque preference for vivid, sharp contrast (the *concertato* principle again) produced music in which dynamic levels moved by terraced steps rather than graded swells and falls. Thus the art was the aural equivalent of the visual arts of architecture and painting, which often utilized strong juxtapositions of brightness and shadow, lightness and heaviness, and similar decisive contrasts. It was not until the mideighteenth century that the extended *crescendi* and *diminuendi* that became characteristic of nineteenth-century music began to be adopted.

FORM

Many musical forms were used in the baroque: binary, ternary, rondo, variations, chorale prelude, toccata, fugue, motet, sonata, cantata, *concerto grosso*, suite, Mass, opera, oratorio, to name only some of the more important ones. Certain forms, such as the toccata, fantasy, and prelude, were more or less free, not necessarily fixed in some preexisting mold. Others, such as most movements of a suite, could be counted on to be binary. The da capo aria of later Italian baroque opera was ternary by definition, first presenting an opening section (*A*), followed by a contrasting section (*B*) and then directions to return to the beginning for a repeat of *A* or most of it.

Unity and variety were provided mainly by repetition, contrast, and variation. (The development procedure did not become widespread until the classic and following periods, when composers such as Mozart, Beethoven, and Brahms worked with sonata-allegro form.) Three major forms in the baroque combine repetition with contrast: binary (basically *AB*), ternary (basically *ABA*), and *rondeau* (later called ''rondo''; basically *ABACADA* . . .). Good examples of binary forms can be found in the dance movements of harpsichord suites; the aria ternary form has just been described; and of *rondeau* movements, the harpsichord music of Couperin, Rameau, and other French composers offers clear examples.

Although baroque composers enjoyed playing with oppositions of tone color, dynamics, and ensembles (loud-soft, high-low, string-wind, vocal quartet–large choir), they thought relatively little in terms of thematic contrast, in which two themes of different character are set off against each other. In baroque binary, ternary, and *rondeau* forms the contrast between sections is usually in key or rhythm or texture, not in theme.

Finally, a good example of free form is the fantasy (prelude) section of the Bach Prelude and Fugue for Organ in g, S. 542. Although we can analyze the structure of this remarkably dramatic piece, the fantasy primarily builds its own form as it goes, instead of being cast into the more highly organized forms discussed above. In fact, some of the free forms of the baroque strongly suggest that their origin lay in the popular practice of improvisation, for many toccatas, capriccios, and fantasies sound as if they were being spontaneously created, or at least are meant to give that impression. This same spontaneity of form is found in vocal music in recitatives and *ariosi*.

Representative pieces

1. CLAUDIO MONTEVERDI (1567–1643)

In the Orpheus legend, a favorite theme of baroque composers, one great tragic moment occurs when Orpheus is informed of the death of his wife, Eurydice. His disbelief gradually shifting to impassioned outburst as the reality of his loss becomes apparent, Orpheus decides to abandon earth, to follow Eurydice to the underworld to rescue her, or failing that, to remain in Pluto's realm with her forever.

In his opera *Orfeo* (1607) Monteverdi sets this scene, ○● "Tu se' morta," in recitative and captures the spirit of tragedy. Whereas Verdi or Wagner might need from 10 to 30 minutes and a large orchestra to express a lament, Monteverdi takes $2\frac{1}{2}$ minutes and calls for "Un organo di legno e un chitarone," that is, a small reed organ and a long-necked lute. The power of music to move the minds and hearts of men can be accomplished equally, it seems, with modest as well as imposing means.

Monteverdi at times deliberately sets the vocal line of Orpheus in dissonance against the harmonic background. Near the beginning one noticeable example occurs on the words ''se' da me partita'' and at the immediate repeat of the phrase. Near the end of the excerpt, Monteverdi typically chooses to set his melodic line in a low register for the texts ''in compagnia di morte'' (''in the company of the dead'') and ''addio, terra'' (''farewell, earth'') but quickly moves upward for the words ''cielo'' (''heaven'') and ''sole'' (''sun'').

''Tu se' morta'' is an illustration of the early declamatory recitative style, in which there is an almost complete absence of lyrical, flowing, rhythmically propelled melody. There is considerable flexibility of tempo and rhythm, the accompanying instruments adjusting their playing to the declamation of the singer. In addition to a rather irregular rhythmic pulse, it is often difficult to anticipate the next harmony. Monteverdi's harmonies do not function as do those of Corelli or Vivaldi, which often suggest an inevitability quite lacking in the earlier composer.

Thou art dead, my life, and yet I breathe?	*Tu se' morta, mia vita, ed io respiro?*
Thou hast from me departed	*Tu se' da me partita*
Nevermore, nevermore to return, and I remain?	*Per mai più, mai più non tornare, ed io rimango?*
No, no, for if [my] verses can do anything,	*No, no, che se i versi alcuna cosa ponno*
Then I shall surely go to the deepest abysses,	*N'andrò sicuro a più profundo abissi,*
And having softened the heart of the king of the shades,	*E intenerito il cor del Re de l'ombre*
I will bring you back with me to see the stars again:	*Meco trarotti a riverder le stelle:*
Or if this be denied me by cruel destiny,	*O se ciò negherammi empio destino*
I shall stay with thee in the company of the dead.	*Rimarrò teco in compagnia di morte.*
Farewell, earth; farewell, heaven, and sun, farewell.	*Addio, terra; addio cielo, e sole, addio.*

2. HEINRICH SCHÜTZ (1585–1672)

The motet **o** ''Anima mea liquefacta est'' (from the first part of *Symphoniae Sacrae*) is the first of two based on the Song of Solomon. It is scored for two tenor voices, two *fiffari* or cornetts, and continuo. The *fiffari* or cornetts, obsolete renaissance instruments, have been replaced by English horns for this example.

The motet is in two unequal parts, the first having seventy-three measures and the following having thirty-one. Each part begins with an instrumental section, after which voices and instruments perform together. The instruments can be heard playing together and in imitative conversations with each other. Schütz treats the voices in like manner, with frequent imitations balanced by simultaneous singing in similar rhythms. On the next-to-last syllable of the first part, both tenor voices engage in a long, decorated passage.

My soul failed when my beloved spoke;
His voice is sweet, and his countenance comely.

His lips are like lilies, dropping sweet-smelling myrrh.

Anima mea liquefacta est, ut dilectus locutus est,
vox enim eius dulcis, et facius eius decora.

Labia eius lilia stillantia, myrrham primam.

3. PIETRO FRANCESCO CAVALLI (1602–1676)

As of May 6, 1637, when the San Cassiano opera house in Venice opened its doors, opera moved from the relatively restricted court to the public marketplace. The newly developing dramatic entertainment no longer had to conform to the tastes of nobility; it now had to survive the overtly voiced challenges of the approbation and disapproval of the people. One expedient was to provide virtuoso singers capable of performing sustained lyrical passages and brilliant technical feats; another was to dazzle the audience with spectaculars, feasts for the eye as well as the ear. Venetian opera, then, depended upon beautiful singing and ingeniously contrived stage productions for some of the successes it enjoyed. If Claudio Monteverdi was the first to bring distinction to opera in Venice, Francesco Cavalli kept the standards sufficiently high to make that opera the envy of Europe during the last half of the century. Composing over forty operas in less than a thirty-year span established his fame, a fame which was unequalled in his day but which vanished shortly thereafter.

A few of his works are available in recordings. One is *L'Ormindo* (1644) on Argo ZNF 8-10, from which we shall discuss ''No, no, non vo' più amare'' (on the beginning of side 4). The plot of *L'Ormindo*, like most of the plots of that time, is complicated, but the commonplace trinity is central to the story: an aging king (Ariadeno), his young wife (Erisbe), and the man in love with her (Ormindo). A saucy, pert maid (Mirinda) provides some comic relief. Ten characters in all appear in the opera. The recorded version is in three parts: (1) *ritornello*, aria, and *ritornello*; (2) a recitativelike section; (3) aria plus added voice, and *ritornello*.

The first part opens with a purely instrumental *ritornello* in the strings and continuo. With the entrance of Erisbe (sung here by a mezzo-soprano), the emphasis is on *bel canto* singing, and the accompaniment is lightened accordingly. Note that the first line of text, sung twice, is balanced musically by the second line. The opening instrumental *ritornello* reappears immediately following the full cadence of the voice on the syllable ''-re'' of ''ingannare.'' The meter hitherto has been triple.

For the second section the string orchestra remains silent, and only continuo instruments (harpsichord, cello, and harp) are heard. In contrast to the first section, the rhythm here is much freer, the vocal line not quite so lyrical, and the accompaniment more improvised in character. A full cadence occurs on the word ''lego.'' The first syllable (''le-'') is treated melismatically, at the end of which the singer employs a *trillo* (not a modern trill but a rapid measured tremolo on the same note). Ornaments of this sort were commonly improvised by opera singers in the seventeenth century.

The third part begins with the voice, the opening *ritornello* being omitted. Like the first section, the first line is repeated, with the music identical with that of the first section. But the music heard at ''un core'' (line 2) differs, partly to accommodate the entrance of a second voice (Mirinda, a mezzosoprano), which enters with the text of line 1 (''No, no, non vo' più amare''). The two voices conclude on a full authentic cadence followed by an ending *ritornello* in the strings.

No, no, I will not cherish
A lover who could stoop to such dissembling.

To you alone I consecrate
All my being, Ormindo;
The other love I banish,
And with stronger fetters to you I bind me.

No, no, I will not cherish
A lover who could stoop to such dissembling.

No, no, non vo' più amare
un core assuefatto ad ingannare.

A te solo consacro
l'anima intera, Ormindo,
l'altr'idolo rinnego,
con più forte catene a te mi lego.

No, no, non vo' più amare
un core assuefatto ad ingannare.

4. JEAN-BAPTISTE LULLY (1632–1687)

Although Lully was the dominant musical figure in seventeenth-century France, few of his works are heard today. His establishment of the

French overture, a piece intended to be played by the orchestra before an opera began, merits recognition because of its enormous influence; even late-baroque composers like Bach and Handel followed the overture model provided by Lully. In its characteristic form the French overture begins with a slow, stately section in dotted rhythms followed by a quick, lively section in polyphonic texture. This *allegro* either broadens out at its end or, in the most developed versions, is succeeded by a third section that resumes the stately pace of the opening.

Our example, the ○● overture to *Armide* (1685), requires, typically, a string ensemble and continuo; and its texture tends to be thick, especially when the entire ensemble is playing. The first (slow) section is repeated. At the beginning of the second (fast) section, the first and second violins, playing together in thirds, introduce a little ascending motive of four notes: long, short, short, long. In turn, the first and second violas enter and finally the lower strings and continuo. This fast section merges into a concluding slow section, at the end of which the players are instructed to repeat the second section. The tempos slow, fast, slow suggest a ternary division; the repeat marks, however, mark off a binary division. So the form unfolds as ‖:slow:‖: fast, slow :‖, that is, slow, slow, fast, slow, fast, slow.

5. HENRY PURCELL (1659–1695)

Taken from Virgil's *Aeneid*, the libretto of Purcell's *Dido and Aeneas* (1689) recounts a tragic love affair mainly through the role of Dido, who sings her famous lament, ○● "When I am laid in earth," near the end of the opera, as the ship of Aeneas sails out to sea.

The lament is based on a five-measure ground bass, which is repeated seven times. (The basic problem in handling such a repeated pattern is to disguise the obvious repetitions by expressive qualities strong enough to keep the music from getting monotonous; on the other hand, the technical procedure, fundamentally a simple series of notes presented in different contexts, can produce a strong sense of unity with variety.) Purcell's bass begins with the notes moving downward in small steps followed by four cadence notes. The small-step motion gives Purcell an opportunity to create a series of different and unusual harmonies above the constantly repeated ground. In addition, the vocal line is not the same length as the bass pattern. Phrases of various lengths thus contribute such flexibility and contrast that listeners are often quite unaware of the ground bass. It is also easy to miss the narrow range of the melody, most of which is confined to the interval of a fifth; but at the climax (the last ''Remember me''), where the highest notes occur, the effect is as powerful as if the range had been considerably wider and the orchestra considerably larger (the air is scored only for strings and continuo).

When I am laid in earth, may my wrongs create no trouble in thy breast. Remember me, remember me, but, ah, forget my fate.

6. JOHANN PACHELBEL (1653–1706)

The baroque toccata, perhaps the most typical keyboard form of the time, was usually a free composition, a style of imaginative playing rather than a fixed structure. It was designed to sound like an improvisation. The toccata suggested spontaneity and freedom and a kind of wandering from chord to chord for the sheer sensuous pleasure of the sounds.

This example, ○● Toccata for Organ in e, opens on a descending arpeggiated e chord. With the entrance of the long note E, the texture changes and continues to change until one figuration appears, to dominate about the last half of the piece. In the first half of the piece, interest centers on the changes in texture, the dissonances, the short motivic imitations, and the restless harmony. Later, over a slow-moving bass, the more elaborate figuration is tossed about in the upper parts. Characteristic pedal points, first on the dominant and then on the tonic, conclude this short toccata.

7. ARCANGELO CORELLI (1653–1713)

Near the end of the seventeenth century two types of ''sonata'' existed: the *sonata da chiesa* (church sonata) and the *sonata da camera* (chamber sonata). Church sonatas, as one might expect, were somewhat more sombre, conservative, and serious than were chamber sonatas. They favored polyphonic textures and avoided dancelike movements—although such movements can be found. Church sonatas typically had four movements: slow, fast, slow, fast. The first movement generally set a grave introductory mood; the second movement, brisk and polyphonic, was followed by a slower, more lyrical third movement; and the last movement frequently used livelier rhythms to provide a suitable finale. Chamber sonatas, closely related to suites, were intended as entertainment for home and court. Consisting of a series of dance movements, their mood was lighter than that of church sonatas. After an introductory movement entitled *Preludio* or *Sinfonia*, a series of dance movements, *Allemanda, Sarabanda,* and *Giga,* usually followed.

The Corelli ○● *Sonata da chiesa* in e, op. 3, no. 7, exemplifies the baroque trio sonata, a common instrumental combination in both types of sonata. In performance the trio sonata was usually played by four (two treble parts—in this instance, two violins—plus two for the continuo).

Two movements of the original four are heard in the recording. The opening *Grave* contains imitative entrances (for example, first and second violins and cello in the first three measures) and very characteristic Corelli dissonances, usually between the two violins as they playfully maneuver around each other. Taken out of context, many of the dissonances are sharp, but rather clear harmonic directions will lead you to anticipate the resolution of these dissonances. The second movement, *Allegro*, also contains imitations, this time at greater distances (first violin in measure 1, second violin in measure 4, and cello in measure 7). Later the imitative entrances are separated by only one measure.

The *sonata da chiesa* and *sonata da camera* in both solo and trio form represent the most common chamber music of the late seventeenth and early eighteenth centuries. The usual combination was two violins plus continuo for the trio sonata, but scoring for other treble instruments such as flute and oboe became increasingly common.

8. FRANÇOIS COUPERIN (1668–1733)

From the grand baroque of Louis XIV French taste gradually shifted to the more intimate rococo of Louis XV. The miniature, emphasizing grace, delicacy, charm, polish, wit, and even frivolity, became fashionable. French music, particularly that for harpsichord, mirrored these sentiments in pieces that were usually small in form, highly ornamented, and suggestive in title. As composers sought to echo the "gallantry" of court life, their music became refined and elegant.

Dated around 1717, ○ "La Galante" is an excellent example of a simple binary form (*AB*) with each part repeated, that is, *AABB*. Immediately noticeable is a two-part texture, to which notes are added freely in order to fill out the harmony. The score of this piece is visibly sprinkled with specific signs (*agréments*) to indicate the kind of ornament to be performed. This French system of notating ornaments spread to other countries, where it was modified to suit differing national tastes.

Many of Couperin's harpsichord pieces that stem from dance movements (for instance, allemande, courante, sarabande) were given fanciful titles; "La Galante" is a gigue.

9. ANTONIO VIVALDI (1675–1741)

One of the most productive composers of all time, Antonio Vivaldi was an important figure in the development and establishment of the baroque concerto. The concerto form had been brought to one level by composers like Corelli and Torelli, but the concertos of Vivaldi represent a different stage. He preferred three movements, usually fast, slow, fast, to four, and he experimented with varied combinations of winds and strings to get more contrast in sonorities, the players in his *concertino* groups (small groups of soloists) being often heard more distinctly than were the *concertini* in earlier *concerto grosso* compositions. This procedure led to the independence of the soloists in later concertos.

In the ○● Concerto in C, F. VI, no. 2, Vivaldi calls for two transverse flutes (the flutes we know today) rather than the older *flauti dolci,* or *Blockflöten* (recorders), plus strings and continuo. In the recorded first movement the first violins and the first flute often play identical parts, especially in *tutti* (full-orchestra) passages. Similarly, the second-violin and second-flute parts are the same. When the flutes are used as solo instruments, the texture often becomes that of the trio sonata (see the remarks on 7. Arcangelo Corelli).

Once the *Allegro* begins, there is constant pulsation as the music moves with machinelike regularity. The more rapid melodic figures are heard in the solo flutes and upper strings while the low strings provide steady eighth notes, broken occasionally by slower note values and rests. Dynamic contrast mainly follows texture, that is, *tutti* passages are loud, solo passages soft. Vivaldi's range of keys in this movement is restricted to those closely related to C and, in two notable changes of mood, to the tonic minor (c).

Although in an overwhelming number of concertos Vivaldi calls for a string *concertino* group accompanied by string orchestra and continuo, in this movement he provides us with an illustration of the use of wind instruments in an eighteenth-century concerto; the listener is thus given an opportunity to grasp more clearly the concerto idea, that of contrast between *concertino* group and larger ensemble.

10. GEORGE FRIDERIC HANDEL (1685–1759)

A monumentally conceived masterpiece and unquestionably Handel's most frequently performed work, *Messiah* (1741) places Handel in the company of other great baroque artists whose ideas were big and who had the craftsmanship to carry them out: Milton, Bernini, Rubens, Bach.

To illuminate his text, Handel divides fifty separate movements into three large parts: Advent and Christmas; the Passion; and the Resurrection. On this epic canvas he obtains variety by employing typical baroque movements: chorus, aria, *arioso,* duet, air and chorus, accompanied and *secco* recitative, and two instrumental movements (the opening *Sinfonia* and the so-called pastoral symphony). *Concertato* style, homophonic and polyphonic writing, and fugal texture (as in the "Hallelujah" and "Amen" choruses) show Handel's choral composition at its best. His amazing versatility in writing arias can be heard in "The people that walked in darkness" (a unison aria), "Why do the nations" (da capo aria), and the familiar *bel canto* aria "I know that my Redeemer liveth."

The recorded excerpt, ○● "For unto us a Child is born," will show us Handel stealing his own ideas, for this movement is a rearrangement of material originally composed by him for the first movement of an Italian chamber cantata for two sopranos and continuo. What had been a light, flexible duet Handel transformed into a powerful chorus by an important insertion at the words "Wonderful, Counsellor, The Mighty God, The Everlasting Father, The Prince of Peace" and other changes. Thus secular music was transferred into the domain of the religious.

Imitative entrances and two-part textures are heard in the vocal parts up to the first outburst on the word "Wonderful." Being aware of the movement's origins, you will appreciate the elaborate coloratura passages demanded from each section of the chorus. Three basic musical ideas dominate this chorus: that which accompanies the opening text, that at the words ''and the government . . .,'' and that at the words ''Wonderful, Counsellor, ...'' The first might be described as light and agile in style; the second, as rhythmic; the third, as massive and chordal.

Handel's choral music almost always ''sounds,'' as musicians put it. What they mean is that it is gratifying to play, inspiring to sing, beautifully constructed, and ennobling to listen to. As with Alexander Pope, so with Handel: ''One truth is clear, Whatever is, is right.''

For unto us a Child is born, unto us a Child is given: and the government shall be upon his shoulder: and his name shall be called Wonderful, Counsellor, The Mighty God, The Everlasting Father, The Prince of Peace.

11. GEORGE FRIDERIC HANDEL (1685–1759)

In the solo vocal pieces discussed earlier (see 3. Pietro Francesco Cavalli and 5. Henry Purcell) the tempos were slow to moderate and the vocal lines lyrically expressive. In o ''Perfido!'' from Handel's *Radamisto* of 1720 we have an example of the agility sometimes demanded in baroque arias. Originally conceived for a *castrato* voice, the aria in the recorded excerpt is sung an octave lower than it was in Handel's day.

Radamisto, his cruel and treacherous brother-in-law, Tiridate, and his old father, Farasmane, propel the action in Act I. Tiridate has captured Farasmane, whom he threatens to execute unless Radamisto himself capitulates. (To this customary complicated plot, Handel and his librettist, Niccolò Haym, provided a happy ending, when Radamisto and Zenobia are reunited.) Radamisto's *bravura* aria ''Perfido!'' breathes defiance, perhaps even youthful indiscretion. In the eighteenth century, the timbre and range of the *castrato* captured this fresh spirit of heroism.

The overall design of the aria is ternary, that is, *ABA*, the third part constituting a literal return to the beginning (da capo). The *A* sections, much longer than the *B* section, are set from the first two lines of text. After a vigorous opening in the orchestra, the voice enters alone on the word ''Perfido!'' Note that the rhythm (''*per*-fi-do'') has already been anticipated in the instrumental introduction and is heard immediately following the first vocal ''Perfido!'' The vocal line changes back and forth from this strong rhythmic motive to rapid scale passages, most of the time being heard with only a continuo accompaniment. Occasionally, however, the orchestra bursts in with the "Perfido!" rhythm. The first section closes, as it began, in the orchestra and in the major key. With the *B* section (lines 3 and 4 of the text) the mood changes. Starting in c, the section finally works its way to an *Adagio* close in g. Rhythmic contrast is also present; except for one *tutti* passage of two measures, the *A* rhythmic motive has largely disappeared although the rhythm itself can occasionally be heard in an unobtrusive way in the bass part. This section is mainly voice with continuo accompaniment up to the second *forte tutti*, after which the upper strings softly fill in the harmonies. After the *Adagio* close of section *B*, a full repeat of section *A* is heard, according to the instructions in the score. The scoring is for strings and continuo.

Traitor! Say to that pitiless tyrant
That great souls are not afraid.

They know how to live and die bravely,
The noble son and his great father.

Traitor! Say to that pitiless tyrant
That great souls are not afraid.

Perfido! di a quell'empio tiranno
Che l'alme grandi non hanno timor.

Che viver forti e morir forti sanno
Il nobil figlio, il gran genitor.

Perfido! di a quell'empio tiranno
Che l'alme grandi non hanno timor.

12. JOHANN SEBASTIAN BACH (1685–1750)

As the German church cantata developed in the baroque, it increased in overall size. By Bach's time it consisted of several movements calling for varying musical resources: solo arias, *ariosi*, choral movements, recitatives, independent instrumental passages (occasionally entire movements), and frequently a Lutheran chorale to underlie the whole cantata.

As early as 1715, in Weimar, Bach had fashioned a cantata based on Luther's "mighty hymn," *Ein feste Burg ist unser Gott*. Shortly after his appointment to the St. Thomas Church in Leipzig, he reworked and enlarged the Weimar version into o Cantata 80, our recorded example. To gain some understanding of the magnificence of Bach's achievement, you should familiarize yourself with the hymn tune and its harmonization by listening to movement VIII (a chorale, the last movement of the cantata) a few times before hearing the cantata from beginning to end.

Bach's orchestra in the huge first movement calls for three trumpets, two oboes, timpani, first and second violins, violas, and a continuo consisting of cellos *and* double basses and organ. Added to these forces is a four-part chorus (sopranos, altos, tenors, and basses). The opening portion of the movement, which concerns us most, presents a series of imitative entrances, whose melodic contours are derived from the chorale melody itself: The first entrance of the trumpet states the hymn in a high register; in the measure after the trumpet entrance violone and organ, the lowest instruments of the orchestra, begin a canon by sounding exactly the same notes. If you review the whole movement, you can sense Bach's superb craftsmanship in manipulating musical ideas.

''Komm in mein Herzenshaus,'' for soprano and continuo, is an aria. Among the characteristic features are a motto opening (in the continuo), a basic two-part texture (between the bass of the continuo and the soprano) to which harmonies are added by the organ, long decorated passages in the voice, and a repeat of the opening text.

In the last movement the chorale is presented in a simple hymnlike manner. It is typical of Bach's church cantatas that their last movements are essentially unadorned chorales. Since they were intended to precede sermons, they no doubt anticipated mood and content. In larger, two-part, cantatas the second half followed the sermon.

A stronghold sure is our God, a strong warrior and arm;
He keeps us free from all the troubles that assail us.

Come dwell within my heart, Lord Jesus, my beloved.
Drive the world and the Devil out, and let Thine image ever shine within me.
Away, base sin!

The Word of God will firm abide [against our foes].
He is with us on the battlefield with His Spirit and Grace.
Though they take from us life, treasure, honor, child, and wife,
They will gain nought, for the Kingdom remains to us.

Ein' feste Burg ist unser Gott, ein' gute Wehr und Waffen;
Er hilft uns frei aus aller Not, die uns jetzt hat bestroffen.

Komm in mein Herzenshaus, Herr Jesus, mein Verlangen.
Treib Welt und Satan aus, und lass dein Bild in mir erneuert
  prangen.
Weg, schnöder Sünden graus!

Das Wort sie sollen lassen stahn und kein Dank dazu haben.
Er ist bei uns wohl auf dem Plan mit seinem Geist und Gaben.
Nehmen sie uns den Leib, Gut, Ehr, Kind und Weib,
Lass fahren dahin, sie habens kein Gewinn; das Reich muss uns
  doch bleiben.

13. JOHANN SEBASTIAN BACH (1685–1750)

Vivaldi's instrumental concertos had unquestionably impressed Bach, as demonstrated by the latter's many arrangements of the older master's music. The later virtuoso-type concerto, in which a solo performer dominates the scene, was in its infancy in Bach's day. Rather, the notion of contrasting equals, similar to that in seventeenth-century consort ensembles, was more in style, for it meant a balance in the distribution of melodic, thematic, and other musical interests among the participating soloists and concerted units.

In our recorded example, the "derivative" ○ ● Italian Concerto in F, S. 971, Bach's imagination creates with a single harpsichord what might have been an orchestral work.

It opens with an *Allegro* movement, has a middle *Andante* movement, and a closing *Presto*. The *Allegro* contains identical passages at the beginning and end; the *Presto* has the same design. These passages, if this were an orchestral work, would be played by the full orchestra, whereas the middle sections of the *Allegro* and *Presto* would feature either the solo instrument or the solo with instrumental accompaniment. In the second movement you can hear, with little imaginative effort, a broadly conceived, lyrical violin solo with string accompaniment. Bach has, in sum, realized the "idea of the concerto" in a work for harpsichord solo, the effect resulting from textural changes, contrasting musical ideas, and dynamics, for Bach has indicated, by his employment of the terms *forte* and *piano*, various combinations of solo, solo with accompaniment, and *tutti*.

With Johann Sebastian Bach and George Frideric Handel the music of the baroque reaches dazzling heights. Its end, however, is near, and perhaps historical necessity as well as aesthetic wisdom caused Bach's own sons to write in a style different from that of their father. Musical changes were already taking place during Bach's lifetime, but he preferred to sum up the baroque rather than to drift into the fashionable and the new. The achievements of Bach and Handel stand as enduring monuments, as if to say that the baroque could go so far but not beyond.

Other important music

For additional music by composers of this period, see the Music Index. Five recorded anthologies will also provide the interested listener with a broad survey of baroque music. Each anthology includes music before and after the baroque but the listings below cover only the period from around 1600 to 1750.

Archive Production Research Periods V–X, Deutsche Grammophon Gesellschaft History of Music Division. Each research period is divided into a series of recordings: for example, Research Period VI contains *German Baroque Music:* (*Series A*) *Heinrich Schütz,* (*Series B*) *Clavier, Organ, and Lute;* (*Series C*) *The Ensemble Suite;* (*Series D*) *The Lied;* (*Series E*) *The Sonata;* and (*Series F*) *Spiritual Concerto and Church Cantata.* The number of recordings in Research Period VI alone approaches twenty LP's. Each record is carefully documented with historical and other information about the music and the performing groups.

The History of Italian Music, RCA Italiana. This set consists of forty LP recordings in four volumes (see also Chapter 9, Other Important Music). Volumes II and III deal with Italian music of the seventeenth and eighteenth centuries. Each volume contains a booklet of about a hundred pages, which explores various categories of Italian music by describing developments in a given genre and is illustrated with color reproductions of works by contemporary artists.

The History of Music in Sound, RCA Victor. See also Chapter 9. Volumes IV (*The Age of Humanism*), V (*Opera and Church Music*), and VI (*Growth of Instrumental Music*) deal with baroque music and its immediate predecessors.

Masterpieces of Music before 1750, Haydn Society (distributed by W. W. Norton & Company, Inc., New York). See also Chapter 9. Items 30 through 50 deal with the baroque.

A Treasury of Early Music, Haydn Society (distributed by W. W. Norton & Company, Inc., New York.) See also Chapter 9. Items 37 through 50 deal with the baroque.

The preceding collections do not begin to exhaust the possibilities, but they will organize for the listener a coherent picture of baroque music. For music by J. S. Bach and Handel in particular, you can consult Archive Production Research Periods IX and X, *The History of Music in Sound,* Volumes V and VI, and *Masterpieces of Music before 1750,* items 43 to 50. Both composers have been extensively recorded; a quick perusal of the Schwann catalogue will confirm how popular their music is. Out of their enormous output it would be rash and arbitrary to signal here only a few additional compositions.

Further readings

GENERAL BACKGROUND

BARNES, HARRY ELMER   *An Intellectual and Cultural History of the Modern World,* 3rd rev. ed., Dover Publications, Inc., New York, 1965. Originally published in 1937, this survey in its second volume treats the period from the renaissance through the eighteenth century. For the beginning student seeking orientation to almost every aspect of life (economics, politics, sociology, arts, science, technology) during the baroque. Index-glossary in the third volume only.

BLITZER, CHARLES   *Age of Kings,* Time-Life Books, New York, 1967. Popular presentation of various aspects of seventeenth-century life: the Thirty Years War, Louis XIV and court life at Versailles, Bernini and the baroque spirit in the arts, the rise of scientific thought, and the like. Beautifully illustrated.

BRINTON, CRANE (ED.)   *The Portable Age of Reason Reader,* The Viking Press, Inc., New York, 1956. An anthology of writings from Descartes to Immanuel Kant, Adam Smith, and Gibbon in the late eighteenth century. In short excerpts from poetry, drama, essays, philosophical works, and other documents, a wide range of commentary on human existence is presented.

DURANT, WILL, AND ARIEL DURANT   *The Story of Civilization,* Part VII: *The Age of Reason Begins,* Simon and Schuster, New York, 1961. Thorough, detailed, documented study of the period from 1558 to 1648. Very readable, with excellent index.

DURANT, WILL, AND ARIEL DURANT   *The Story of Civilization,* Part VIII: *The Age of Louis XIV,* Simon and Schuster, New York, 1963. Covers the period from 1648 to 1715. A model of organization and readability.

DURANT, WILL, AND ARIEL DURANT   *The Story of Civilization,* Part IX: *The Age of Voltaire,* Simon and Schuster, New York, 1965. Covers the period from 1715 to 1756, with "special emphasis on the conflict between religion and philosophy." "Bibliographical Guide," "Notes," and "Index" alone cover a hundred pages.

GAY, PETER   *Age of Enlightenment,* Time-Life Books, New York, 1966. A companion volume to Blitzer's *Age of Kings.* Deals primarily with eighteenth-century Europe.

GAY, PETER   *The Enlightenment: An Interpretation.* Alfred A. Knopf, Inc., New York, 1966. A brilliantly written, provocative examination of the origins and development of those critical eighteenth-century ideas expounded by Voltaire, Hume, and other such personalities. In his search for a common denominator, Gay shows their debt (as an alternative to Christian faith) to classical antiquity and hence his subtitle "The Rise of Modern Paganism."

SMITH, PRESERVED *A History of Modern Culture,* Henry Holt and Company, New York, 1930. Critical, provocative, but readable survey of the period from 1543 to 1776. A must reading for any beginning student.

MUSIC

BLUME, FRIEDRICH *Renaissance and Baroque Music* [M. D. Herder Norton (trans.)], W. W. Norton & Company, Inc., New York, 1967. Eight chapters on baroque. Sophisticated and rich in ideas. Contents and style of writing require a good background of intellectual history, aesthetic criticism, and music, but useful to students who enjoy wrestling with ideas.

BUKOFZER, MANFRED F. *Music in the Baroque Era,* W. W. Norton & Company, Inc., New York, 1947. A work of monumental scholarship, unsurpassed as a single study although subsequent writings have argued for modification of some of Bukofzer's positions or correction of some of his facts. The first source to consult in seeking further information about music of the period. Excellent, exhaustive bibliography.

GROUT, DONALD J. *A Short History of Opera,* 2nd ed., Columbia University Press, New York, 1965. Indispensable for those who wish to examine more closely the development of baroque opera. Dependable scholarship. Exhaustive bibliography.

PALISCA, CLAUDE V. *Baroque Music,* Prentice-Hall, Inc., Englewood Cliffs, N.J., 1968. A considerably shorter but worthy companion to Bukofzer's book. Systematically organized, this volume contains up-to-date information offered by recent scholars. No composite bibliography, but each chapter concludes with brief, useful suggestions for further study.

Chapter 11 ○ *The classic period*

BY THE MIDDLE OF THE EIGHTEENTH CENTURY MOST THOUGHTFUL MEN BELIEVED that through the application of reason, or "rationalism," man could solve most, if not all, of his problems as his knowledge of the external world increased. This idea had grown slowly from the early seventeenth century on. Until the upheaval caused by the French Revolution (1789–1799) this view was held by some of the most able minds in Europe: historians like Edward Gibbon, economists like Adam Smith, religious and political thinkers like Thomas Paine, painters like Sir Joshua Reynolds, and no doubt a number of composers. The composers, of necessity, came into contact with rationalistic influences in everyday life and, even more directly, in musical essays inspired by such thinking.

What did the term "reason" mean, and what consequences followed from its acceptance as a way of life? As usual, precise definition raises difficult problems, for it is no easier to define reason than Christianity. Once beyond a few core beliefs, disagreements quickly develop. Basic differences occur among the various Christianities of St. Thomas Aquinas, Martin Luther, Søren Kierkegaard, and Teilhard de Chardin. Basic differences also exist in the thought of a much more unified group (in time as well as in geography): Voltaire, Jean-Jacques Rousseau, Denis Diderot, and Baron d'Holbach—all "rationalists." Yet some common assumptions about reason existed in the period we are examining: Man depends upon a set of senses that are fairly standard and uniform throughout the world; appealed to through his rational faculties, man will respond by acting in accordance with the logic of reasoned argument. The first assumption sets the stage; the second provides the drive toward change and action.

Ideas and arts in the classic period

Characteristically, the rationalists set up an "ought." If men uniformly (and normally) have two eyes, they see similar colors, shapes, and patterns. It follows logically and reasonably that they *ought* to appreciate the same kind of art, to hold somewhat similar ideas about what is beautiful, pleasing, ugly, and distasteful. If men normally have two ears, they hear sounds within a relatively fixed range of frequencies; it follows that they *ought* to like the same kind of music.

Applied to personal relationships and human institutions, reason would eventually display and distinguish right from wrong, reality from appearance, the natural from the unnatural, and in the case of art the beautiful from the ugly. In its extreme form this philosophical view led to an indefensible position, a position that caricatured man's very humanity, for the one-sided picture too often neglected to take into account man's powerful instinctual and emotional drives; it represented an outlook that events like the imminent French Revolution were later to sweep away completely.

In the eighteenth century the belief in reason led to the establishment of "canons of good taste": those rules which any reasonable man, given proper education and enlightenment, would find acceptable. In the last half of the century reasonableness in art frequently came to be equated (in a somewhat forced way) with a famous phrase of Johann Winckelmann (1717–1768): "noble simplicity and quiet grandeur." (That Winckelmann, who had never been in Greece and had based his theories on Roman copies, and his followers misjudged and misread the temperament and art of the ancient Greeks is a matter of record. However, as the eminent American historian Charles A. Beard once remarked, "The world is largely ruled by ideas, true *and* false.") So an idea swept over Europe, the notion that the much-admired art of Greek antiquity exhibited the ideals usually considered to be the essence of "classicism": universality, refinement, simplicity, harmonious proportion, objectivity, permanence, serenity, cleanly delineated lines and forms, and of course a restraint on expression imposed by reason. The conception of Greek classicism that developed in the 1760s encouraged the historical fiction that ancient art almost exclusively expressed those qualities; even Hellenistic works like the magnificently wild Laocoön group were forced to fit into the scheme. In effect, the classicists of the late eighteenth and early nineteenth centuries, disregarding wider historical truth, adopted those aspects of classic antiquity which best suited their purposes. They then developed appropriate aesthetic theories, usually founded on rationalistic principles, to justify themselves. Thus the neoclassicism of the period was made of many things: remaining bits of renaissance classicism, seventeenth-century French classicism, contemporary English and German archeological findings, the study of Greek and Roman artifacts and literature, and, needless to say, eighteenth-century rationalism.

The arts of the time were naturally affected. "One should never put anything in a building for which one cannot give a solid reason," declared Laugier, a French priest, in his *Observations on Architecture*

Figure 11.1 • Jacques Germain Soufflot: The Paris Pantheon (ca. 1764–1790). Here the classic ideal is expressed in clean lines and balanced proportions, with discreet references to ancient decorative motifs. (Éditions Chantal.)

Figure 11.2 • Antonio Canova's Pauline Borghese as Venus *of 1808. A lifesize celebration of a member of the ruling family, Napoleon's sister, in a neoclassically careful imitation of ancient style.* (Borghese Gallery, Rome.)

(1775). In the spirit of Laugier architects like Jacques Ange Gabriel (1698–1782), Jacques Germain Soufflot (1713–1780), and Carl Gotthard Langhans (1732–1808) adapted classic building principles with some disregard for purity of style, including a monumentality foreign to the more modest size of the originals. Gabriel's Place de la Concorde and Soufflot's Pantheon (Figure 11.1) in Paris and Langhan's Brandenburg Gate in Berlin were influenced by the classic ideal as understood (and practiced) at the time. Their conceptions reveal many Greek and Roman structural principles: straight lines; geometric, planned, and balanced space enclosures; relatively undecorated surfaces; and an overall appearance of permanent, cool inertia. Some of the aesthetic principles found in these neoclassic buildings later became the standard for post offices, state capitols, courthouses, and other public buildings in the United States, a standard that was especially observed in the nineteenth century.

Architecture had to serve contemporary needs and therefore could not literally reproduce ancient buildings; painting had no Greek examples to copy. But the art of sculpture in the eighteenth century could, by the nature of the medium itself, imitate with ease the many existing classic models. Implied in Winckelmann's "noble simplicity and quiet grandeur" was a moral undercurrent: By assimilating the ideals expressed in Greek art, modern art could rejuvenate a spiritually tired Europe. Accordingly, the sculptor sought to portray in his faces and bodies an inner dignity and a controlled restraint, a harmonious blending of physical charm and spiritual integrity. French revolutionaries and subsequently Napoleon and his followers looked to ancient Rome in particular for inspiration. The Roman republic and empire yielded many symbols relating to patriotism, government, heroism, dress, manners, and various other aspects of sociology and politics. It became fashionable, for example, to adopt certain poses; for if a man dressed and acted like a noble Roman, it was assumed that he thought like one. No doubt such gestures served politically useful ends, but we can never be sure how far appearances were separated from reality, how completely expediency covered truth. The most famous sculptor of the period, Antonio Canova (1757–1822), created a series of statues for Napoleon and his family. Classic gestures and postures in his *Cupid and Psyche, Napoleon,* and *Pauline Borghese as Venus* (Figure 11.2) clearly reveal Canova's debt to two concepts: Winckelmann's Greece and Napoleon's

Figure 11.3 • François Boucher: **The Toilet of Venus (1751).** *The rococo's delicately provocative view of a classic theme was to be superseded by a self-important seriousness at the end of the century.* (The Metropolitan Museum of Art; bequest of William K. Vanderbilt, 1920.)

Rome. Realistic portraiture, especially in the face, harks back to the realism of Roman busts. The naked or half-draped bodies frequently imitate the more graceful, idealized lines of Greek models. Canova's Napoleon and Napoleon's sister thinly disguised as Venus exemplify the sculptor's compromise between Greek idealism and Roman realism; especially in comparison with the capricious rococo (Figure 11.3) of only a few decades before, the statues also exude a slickness almost too reasonable to be true.

The neoclassic style, dominated by the French Academy and officially supported during the Napoleonic era, had thus allied itself with politics. The artist was frequently a man with his ear close to the shifts of political fortune. For example, of the painters, Jacques Louis David (1748–1825) managed to survive a period of royal patronage, the hardships of revolution, the Napoleonic era, and finally the Bourbon restoration. Throughout most of those times he painted scenes capable of being interpreted as idealizing nobility, virtue, and other useful abstractions. The titles alone tell the story: *Oath of the Horatii, The Death of Socrates* (Plate 3), *Battle of the Romans and Sabines*. Since nearly every government in its quest for self-perpetuation pays lip service to such vague concepts, David's themes were popular until his style was finally assimilated into the romantic spirit. David's immediate follower, Jean Auguste Dominique Ingres (1780–1867), painted *Apotheosis of Homer* (Figure 11.4). This work shows Homer surrounded by the world's great figures from both classic and modern times and crowned by Victory, with personifications from the Iliad and Odyssey at his feet. Noticeably absent from this assembly of greats are Milton and Goethe, whose styles were not sufficiently classic to pass Ingres's (or his patrons') admission standards.

As observed earlier, admirers of reason and the classic usually tried to justify their tastes by formulating rules and models that pretended to universality. Sir Joshua Reynolds (1723–1792), in his famous discourses before the Royal Academy, flatly insisted: "Take the world's opinion rather than your own: you must have no dependence upon your own genius." This view was echoed in somewhat different words by his friend, the imposing Dr. Samuel Johnson: "The business of a poet is to examine, not the individual, but the species; to remark general properties and large appearances; he does not number the streaks of the tulip, or describe the different shades of the verdure of the forest."

Figure 11.4 • Apotheosis of Homer, *by Jean Auguste Dominique Ingres, is perhaps the culmination of the utilization of motifs from antiquity in a neoclassic work.* (Musée du Louvre; cliché des Musées Nationaux.)

When under the sway of neoclassic thought, the artist distills essences: David does not naturalistically depict a particular oath sworn by particular members of the Horatii but, rather, incarnates an idea, general civic duty exalted over personal sympathies and love; it is not so much Pauline Bonaparte who is sculptured by Canova but the idea of Venus, or lovely womanhood, individualized. The idea, then, dominated the art, submerging the particular and the personal in what was thought to be the universal essence.

Musicians also came into contact with rationalistic thinking. They too were influenced by classicism, both as historical phenomenon and aesthetic position. Christoph Willibald Gluck (1714–1787), in typical fashion, chose classic themes, as in his operas *Orfeo ed Euridice* (1762) and *Alceste* (1767). He sought a "beautiful simplicity" and produced works that, in their balance, grace, and grandeur, were at their best reminiscent of ancient classic tragedy.

The two great composers of the classic period were Franz Joseph Haydn (1732–1809) and Wolfgang Amadeus Mozart (1756–1791). Their enormous output consistently reflected an internal musical logic, a balanced blending of all musical factors that can be characterized as classic. Their most passionate music seldom, if ever, exceeded the boundaries of good taste, a position eloquently stated by Mozart in a letter to his father dated September 26, 1781: "Passions, whether violent or not, must never be expressed in such a way as to excite disgust; even in the most terrible situations, music must never offend the ear, but must please the hearer, or, in other words, must never cease to be music." In this we are reminded of Robert Conway's meeting with the High Lama in James Hilton's *Lost Horizon* (1933); blessed with an extraordinarily long life and with the intelligence and wisdom to make the most of it, the High Lama, in commenting upon the art of music, remarks, "Mozart has an austere elegance which we [in Shangri-La] find very satisfying. He builds a house which is neither too big nor too little, and he furnishes it with perfect taste."

With Ludwig van Beethoven (1770–1827), we arrive at a monumental figure like Michelangelo. Hard to categorize conveniently, both geniuses were products of their time yet seem to stand above it: Michelangelo is something more than high renaissance in the manner of Raphael; Beethoven, something more than classic in the manner of Mozart. Beethoven's debt to his immediate predecessors can be pointed out,

Figure 11.5 • Antoine Watteau: The Music Party *(ca. 1719). Although early rococo in its graceful style, the undercurrent of melancholy in this painting (as with others of Watteau) points to the sentimental romanticism of the last years of the eighteenth century.* (Reproduced by permission of the Trustees of The Wallace Collection.)

but he is best viewed today as a transitional figure, whose style encompassed both worlds—the classic and early nineteenth-century romanticism.

However important the ideas of classicism and rationalism were in eighteenth-century art, they did not stand alone. Many other currents vied for popularity, among which were hints of that new view, romanticism, which eventually was to sweep over the arts. Preferences for naturalism, sentimentality, and emotion broke out in late eighteenth-century poetry, novel, and drama although they had been foreshadowed many years previously in painting (Figure 11.5) and other visual arts. Subject matter dealing with unclassic themes and treated in unclassic ways became increasingly popular in the sentimental novels of Samuel Richardson (1689–1761), whose *Pamela* (1740), which was quickly translated and imitated in France and Germany, led to the writing of novels that minutely analyzed emotions and motives. The so-called gothic novels of Horace Walpole, Ann Radcliffe, and Matthew Gregory Lewis, the mystical poems of William Blake, *Sturm und Drang* (storm and stress) writings in Germany, and the novels of "naturalness" of Rousseau in France—all were indicators of a new time soon to come.

Musical style

RHYTHM

Generally, regularity of rhythm is the rule in classic music. Rhythmic pulses, once set in motion, often continue without interruption so that time beating and foot tapping is quite easy. Gradual changes and abrupt breaks in the steady beat seldom occur. But when they do, the attentive listener rarely misses the effect.

Of the three great composers of the period—Mozart, Haydn, and Beethoven—Mozart is perhaps the most conventional in his treatment of rhythm. Regularity of beat and meter, symmetry of phrase, and a proportional rhythmic order make his compositions models of the classic ideal in music. Rhythmic departures in Haydn and Beethoven take many forms: sudden changes of dynamic stress, unexpected holds and rests that break the continuity, prolonged syncopations, and irregular phrase groupings, in which an 8-measure period might consist of 5 + 3 measures instead of the usual 4 + 4. Odd groupings, because of their imbalance, inhibit rhythmic expectations. Yet the overall effect of rhythm in all three composers is one of easily anticipated steady beats.

MELODY

Owing to improvements in instruments, to actual changes in musical style, and to numerous nonmusical factors, instrumental music became more important than vocal music during this period. Instruments, as it were, began to sing, with the result that, regardless of medium, interest centered upon the melody, which was to be pleasant, attention-getting, tuneful, entertaining, simple, and amusing. It was to conform to accepted taste, usually meaning the taste of a musically educated and cultivated patron or of a money-paying, middle-class audience.

In general, 4-measure phrases are the norm in classic melodies: they may outline the principal tones of major or minor scales, be based on rather clear progressions of harmonies, follow fairly simple rhythm patterns, be basically diatonic rather than chromatic in scale passages, and set up clear expectations in developments and a sense of finality at cadence points. Complete musical ideas usually result from a combination of two or more phrases.

Many melodies are built around the tonic (1) and dominant (5) pitches of a scale (see Chapter 6), or they literally sound the tonic triad (1–3–5 or some combination of 1–3–5) or the dominant triad (5–7–9). Classic harmonies bear so clear a relationship to each other as they progress that the melodies attached to them strongly reflect the harmonies. A classic melody, by itself, often suggests precisely which chords must support it. (Similarly, the rhythmic impulse of a melody is often so definite that, if we are given only two measures of a classic melody, we can often guess the rhythms of the next two with a high degree of accuracy.)

Where scale passages occur in a melody, diatonic notes (those belonging to the scale in question) usually come at points of rhythmic stress, chromatic notes tending to fall between stresses. Analogous to literature or speech, classic melody proceeds by commas, semicolons, periods, and paragraphs. Each section has a contour that suggests either that it will continue or that it will arrive at a point of rest. For expressive purposes classic melodies may have unusual intervals (diminished sevenths, augmented seconds, and so on) and feminine endings, where the cadence falls on a weak rather than on a strong beat. But it is mostly the dissonance of the appoggiatura (the sounding of a note not belonging to the underlying harmony but heard on a strong beat) that figures prominently in the music of Haydn and Mozart to give their melodic lines a sharp flavor, for the appoggiatura usually resolves in a more or less expected manner although it provides a bite to the melody. Where chromaticism appears through the use of appoggiaturas and chromatically altered notes, it might be said to be "accidental" rather than "essential," even though the style would lose much of its appeal if it were to be weakened by eliminating chromatic notes in either the melody or the harmony. Dance rhythms can also affect melodies since they call for regularity and periodicity.

So melody, harmony, and rhythm each reinforce the others in the classic style. There is a clear relationship among the three factors even though it is mainly melody that appeals to the listener.

HARMONY AND COUNTERPOINT

The classic style is basically tonal and diatonic. It rests firmly on triads (1–3–5, 2–4–6, and the like) and seventh chords (1–3–5–7, 2–4–6–8, . . .), whose functions support the unfolding of tonality. With emphasis on certain relationships, harmonic tensions are set up, coming to resolution only when appropriate harmonic expectations have been fulfilled. The tonic (1) of a key, the center of the tonal universe, determines a complete hierarchy of notes in which each note functions as an individual or as part of a chord; the tonic is home base, the static point, the point of rest. Next in importance is the dominant (5), the tension-producing agent, with its own satellite notes and chords. Then follows another important element, the subdominant (4) and *its* subsidiary notes and chords. These three, tonic, dominant, and subdominant, are the pillars upon which classic harmony is founded. Much of the music of the period can be reduced to manipulation of fundamental harmonies.

But a composition entirely in one key, limited to the notes found in that key, could hardly satisfy the demands of even naive listeners. So foreign elements began to intrude upon the basic diatonic harmonies. To establish the dominant key as a temporary contrast to the tonic, a composer necessarily had to introduce at least one sharp (and most often two sharps); for the subdominant, one flat; and for other, more distant keys, additional chromatic notes. Modulation to other keys became a vital part of classic harmony. The power of the music came from relationships between keys as well as from melodic and rhythmic factors.

Even staying within a key, classic composers introduced daring harmonic effects: simple harmonies could be made more colorful by modifying certain notes of a chord, not for purposes of modulating to another key but for embellishing the harmonic flavor of the principal key. Such alterations—types known as diminished-seventh chords, augmented sixths, Neapolitan sixths—were used effectively but with discretion and restraint. They enhanced the flavor of harmony without destroying its fundamental nature.

Again, distinct differences separate the three major composers in their handling of harmony, but all three pay full allegiance to a major-minor and triadic tonal system.

Although homophonic textures had existed in music history prior to the classic period, it was with the music of Haydn, Mozart, and Beethoven that one voice supported by a chordal accompaniment became the principal method in composition. In contrast to polyphonic textures, where there is a kind of equality of parts, homophonic texture draws attention to the melody, whether the latter is in an upper part or in a middle or lower part. The melody gains its prominence mainly because of texture, for the texture subordinates all accompanying parts, high or low. Polyphonic textures, however, continued to be found in the classic period, especially in types of music deemed to be traditional or "learned," such as church music, or where a certain quality of expression demanded that condition, such as the later string quartets of Haydn and Mozart and the chamber music of Beethoven.

Textures, then, vary from piece to piece and even within compositions. Yet, where polyphonic textures are to be found, the flow of parts is usually determined by tonal considerations. So counterpoint and harmony, strictly in keeping with classic ideals, are held in a delicate but firm balance.

In the *late* works of Beethoven frequent textural changes can be found to threaten the balance of classicism in Haydn, Mozart, and *early* Beethoven. But to be understood they must be examined in the light of a developing highly personal style and in relation to other musical factors: Beethoven, ever the innovator, began the bridge between the classic and romantic periods.

TONE COLOR

In classic composition the string section asserted its position as the heart of the developing symphony orchestra. Members of the older viol family were definitely replaced by the violin family, which in the usual orchestra was divided into five units: first and second violins, viola, violoncello, and double bass. This grouping, established on a firm footing and confirmed by the practical experience of classic composers, has remained essentially the same to the present day. The string section was able to provide full range in a unified tone color, to play contrapuntally upon demand, and to play melodic lines with complete harmonic accompaniments within the section. Thus it provided the composer with a nucleus around which other instrumental colors could revolve.

As the style developed and matured, independent string writing grew. Among early symphonists of the Mannheim school (a midcentury German group of orchestral composers) and in many works of Haydn and Mozart, doublings (identical parts) at the unison or octave were frequent, for example, second violins doubling first violins, violas doubling violins or cellos, and double basses doubling cellos. But increasingly each of the unit groups asserted its independence so that in the late works of Haydn, Mozart, and Beethoven doublings, when they occurred, were turned to special effect. The sole exception might be considered to be the cello–double bass combination, where the double-bass part continued either to duplicate the cello part or to strongly resemble it.

The next most important tone colors were produced by the woodwinds. From relatively insecure beginnings, this group gradually became standardized. In the early works, a pair of oboes, an occasional flute, and one or two bassoons (written in the score or assumed to have been there in accordance with the prevailing optional instrumentation of the period) added color. Often these parts merely doubled or occasionally echoed the strings. But, like the strings, independence developed. During the later stages of the period, a standard grouping of two flutes, two oboes, two clarinets, and two bassoons became more common (the clarinets, less frequently found, were the latecomers to the woodwind section). If the string section is roughly equivalent to the vocal ranges, as soprano (first violin), alto (second violin), tenor (viola), and bass (cello and double bass), so also in a general way does the woodwind grouping allow for a complete range. As solo instruments, the woodwinds approximate the vocal ranges of soprano (flute), alto (oboe), tenor (clarinet), and bass (bassoon) although the instrumental range in both woodwind and string groups exceeds that of the corresponding voices. In combination woodwind instruments during the period lost some independence, the parts frequently doubling each other or doubling string or brass parts.

The brass section consisted usually of two French horns and occasionally of two trumpets. A notable omission was the trombones, which, except at the opera and in the church, did not become standard members of the orchestra until about the middle of the nineteenth century. They appeared in Mozart's music (*Don Giovanni* and elsewhere), but their first use in a symphony was in the finale of Beethoven's fifth, first heard in performance on December 22, 1808. Horns and trumpets during the classic period had limited melodic possibilities; so they frequently sounded fanfares and other militarylike calls. They also pointed up rhythmic figures and fundamental harmonies.

Percussion was almost exclusively limited to the timpani. In some ways the use of percussion paralleled that of horns and trumpets: to reinforce certain harmonic sounds in full-orchestra passages, thereby adding to the volume of sound, and to provide additional rhythmic accents. Used in pairs, timpani of the period were tuned to tonic and dominant pitches.

For well over a century the harpsichord had been a favorite instrument for solo keyboard performance. It also had participated in small instrumental ensembles, had accompanied the voice in recitative and solo song, and had served as a continuo instrument in orchestras. But the younger piano, capable of producing gradual as well as sudden dynamic changes and of sustaining tones and having various other features, rapidly (between around 1770 and 1790) became the more popular instrument. The early pianos and the mature harpsichords did not differ greatly in sound so that much of the keyboard music written during the transitional years could be played on either instrument, although some music clearly called for one or the other, and it was not until the early decades of the nineteenth century that the grand piano, with its enormous tonal resources, developed into what we recognize today as the modern instrument. Typically, the Viennese piano of Mozart's day had lighter strings, dampers, and action and a thinner soundboard than do our modern instruments. The general tone quality, therefore, was more delicate, less heavy and ponderous, brighter but thinner. Owing to different stringing, the bass sounded more distinct, the individual tones of chords in low registers being more cleanly separated than they are on a modern grand. Extreme loudness, however, was not possible. Because of the simpler action of the Viennese piano, it was not so easy to repeat notes rapidly as it is on a modern piano.

For home and smaller private or public gatherings, various combinations of instruments were assembled to provide entertainment: The piano (or harpsichord) frequently played in small ensembles with strings, where the common groupings were the piano trio (violin, cello, and piano) and the piano quartet (violin, viola, cello, and piano); important string combinations were the string quartet (two violins, viola, and cello) and the string trio (two violins and cello or violin, viola, and cello); and combinations also existed for wind instruments alone or for mixed strings and winds, in which the frequently participating instruments were the flute (for instance, the quartet for flute and strings), oboe, clarinet, bassoon, or French horn. Once again we must point out that the actual sound of these instruments was not exactly that of modern instruments, for each of the types changed and developed, especially during the nineteenth century.

The organ was heard mainly in connection with music in the church. Since what was musically permissible in religious services varied widely, the use of the organ likewise varied. Organists playing on large and small instruments contributed solo music (preludes, postludes, and so on), lent support to chant and congregational singing, and accompanied choirs. Because of the relative permanence of church-installed organs and the financial problems of keeping up with almost continuous mechanical improvements and changes, one probably could have heard a wild variety of sounds—tuned, untuned, squeaky, massive—in the various organs of the late eighteenth century.

We know little about the quality of vocal sound most sought after by classic singers and conductors. So most performances of the vocal music of that period that we hear today reflect the tastes of voice teachers or, in the case of choruses, conductors. While the latter may scale down the size of their choral forces to match those of eighteenth-century groups, they can only guess at the *quality* of sound actually produced in earlier performances. So modern realizations may or may not be accurate reproductions of what eighteenth-century ears heard.

FORM

Musical ideas, resulting from a combination of melodic, harmonic, rhythmic, and tone-color factors, are given coherence through form. When you describe something as "chaotic," that something does not have a discernable organization. Its parts have little relationship to each other or to the whole, continuity seems absent, and random events abound. Music of the classic period is not chaotic. The forms are quite ordered yet flexible enough to allow for interesting departures.

The sonata became the most important instrumental form of the period. It commonly consisted of three or four movements. If three, the usual combination was fast, slow, fast, with at least the first movement cast in a particular form called "sonata-allegro." If four, the usual combination was fast, slow, a dance, fast. Again, the first movement was conventionally sonata-allegro although (like the three-movement type) other movements could also be in sonata-allegro form. Sonata-allegro, then, can describe the form of one or more of the movements of a sonata. As explained in Chapter 8, sonata-allegro form has a well-defined internal structure. At its best, as in Haydn, Mozart, and Beethoven, it proved to be a flexible organization that in no way inhibited the free exercise of great composers' musical imaginations; but at its worst, it provided merely a convenient set of rules for some less gifted composers to fill with sterile thoughts.

Other important forms include rondo, theme and variations, and ternary design. Various hybrid forms can also be found that usually show the dominance of sonata structure.

The principle of rondo form (review pages 135–137) lies in the more or less regular return of an opening theme ("refrain") in the tonic key as it alternates with episodes. The episodes usually contain new melodic material and contrast with the refrain by being in keys other than the tonic. Rondos are most frequently found as final movements in classic sonatas, symphonies, and concertos, with often lively rhythm.

The theme-and-variations form (review pages 137–138) is frequently encountered in the second movements of three- or four-movement sonatas. The theme itself, usually binary in form (basically *AB*), is a complete musical idea, with a clearly defined melody, a pattern of harmonies, and a rhythmic basis. Any one or all of these are then varied.

Jacques Louis David's neoclassic The Death of Socrates (1787): *noble theme, sculptural poses and gestures, and clean delineation.* (The Metropolitan Museum of Art; Wolfe Fund, 1931.)

Plate 3

Eugène Delacroix: The Death of Sardanapalus *(1827). A huge (about 13 by
16 feet) romantic explosion, with its exotic theme, writhing bodies, and
fascination with violent emotions.* (Musée du Louvre; cliché des Musées
Nationaux.)

Plate 4

The form is a challenge for both the listener and the composer: If the variety is too great, the form may become impossible to follow; if the variations are too easily grasped, their simplicity may become monotonous. Some unity, then, must be imposed upon the variations, but not so much as to cause dullness. In successful variations sufficient musical elements are altered to arouse uncertainty while adequate connection with the original theme is kept to provide security.

In four-movement sonatas the third movement is most often in ternary design (review pages 135–137). Basically *ABA*, this form contains one major section (*B*) often contrasting by key, thematic material, texture, and almost always instrumentation. The outer sections, designated *A*, either are identical or differ in relatively minor details. Customarily, all repeat marks are disregarded when *A* returns, thus shortening it. The form is psychologically satisfying in that the return is welcomed after the contrast *B* but is sufficiently curtailed to avoid possible boredom. Usually such a third movement betrays its dance origin, for it is choreographic in feeling, is in triple meter, and is most frequently labelled as a minuet and trio, the trio being the *B* part. Beethoven later established a scherzo, trio, scherzo movement in place of the minuet.

All these forms, as explained in Chapter 8, are only descriptions of averages. Sonata-allegro form did not burst forth complete; rather, a number of stages can be traced. Nor did it remain static, for it passed on from Beethoven into the hands of composers whose fundamental musical language differed from his. Modifications of the form, therefore, have continued down to the present day. Beethoven sometimes mixed rondo and sonata-allegro elements; and Haydn and Mozart also wrote hybrid forms as well as other forms not easily definable. Yet most sonata movements fall into sonata-allegro, theme-and-variations, binary, ternary, and rondo forms.

The forms we have been discussing exist as patterns, or schemes, common to a number of works, and at least in the past they produced aesthetically satisfying results. But, as always, it was the particular application that separated genius from mediocrity.

Representative pieces

1. FRANZ JOSEPH HAYDN (1732–1809)

That Haydn is credited with one hundred four symphonies, Mozart with forty-one, and Beethoven with nine indicates that the writing of a symphony during the approximately 60 years separating Haydn's first and Beethoven's ninth gradually changed in character, a change due in part to reciprocal interactions among those composers. Mozart died in 1791, but he had developed so rapidly as a symphonist that his older friend Haydn, notably in his so-called Paris symphonies (82 to 87), came to be influenced by his younger contemporary, just as Mozart as a young composer had learned much from Haydn. In Haydn's twelve Salomon symphonies (of which our example, ○● Symphony 101 in D (*Clock*), is one) Mozart's influence is no longer so evident.

Scored for two flutes, two oboes, two clarinets, two bassoons, two horns, two trumpets, timpani, and strings, Symphony 101 was first performed on May 4, 1795. Its title, *Clock,* refers to the regularity of the rhythm in the second movement. In G this *Andante* is an example of ternary form: an *A* main section, a *B* middle section in the contrasting keys of g and B♭, an *A* third section, which is an elaborated return to the main section, and a coda.

After an introductory measure (bassoons and *pizzicato* strings) that sets the clocklike rhythm in motion, the first violin enters with the principal theme, characterized by dotted rhythms. The theme outlines the key of G by skips, after which the melody moves by steps. The texture is homophonic, a clear division being made between melody and the steady pulse of the accompaniment. Throughout section *A,* Haydn stays close to his tonic key. Strings are predominant, woodwinds providing a touch of color. There is fairly constant use of accompanying bassoons, and in two instances, where solo oboe and then solo flute play a melody, they play in unison with the first violins.

In *B,* the middle section, the key changes from major to minor. At the opening of this part the entire orchestra enters *forte.* A new tune is heard. Throughout section *B* the steady pulse continues, along with dotted rhythms carried over from section *A.* Motion increases as note values become smaller, and this entire section reaches a dynamic peak of *fortissimo* about halfway through. Here the dynamic, rhythmic, and melodic elements are intensified, and the full orchestra is present. A brief interlude played by first violins prepares for the return of section *A.*

The return, in G, is unmistakable even though it is embellished (mainly by solo flute and oboe). This entire section is remarkable for its unusual orchestration. Haydn begins by using only first violins and three solo woodwinds (flute, oboe, and bassoon). The solo bassoon, accordingly, carries the entire weight of the bass line; the first violins, the tune, with accompanying commentaries by solo flute and oboe. The result is a texture in which three high treble instruments are combined with one bass instrument, the middle registers hardly being touched at all. After a typical Haydnesque pause of one measure, the composer unexpectedly starts off in E♭. Beginning in the strings only, this section becomes louder. With the entrance of trumpets and kettledrums, the main melody, at a *forte* level, is heard with a rapidly moving triplet accompaniment. A *fortissimo* for the full orchestra introduces the melody for the last time and marks the beginning of the coda.

2. WOLFGANG AMADEUS MOZART (1756–1791)

Nicknamed the *Jupiter*, ○ Symphony 41 in C, K. 551, is Mozart's last. It belongs, together with Symphony 39 in E♭ and Symphony 40 in g, among the greatest of all symphonic works. Miraculously composed during a period of about seven weeks in the summer of 1788, these three completely independent works are as surely different from one another as they are the work of a single composer.

This symphony typically contains four movements, of which three (I, II, and IV) are in sonata-allegro form. The third movement has the usual ternary design (minuet, trio, minuet).

The finale, one of the most famous movements in all symphonic literature, unfolds in heavily contrapuntal sonata-allegro form. Five separate themes participate, as shown in Example 11.1.

In the *exposition*, themes 1 and 2 are heard in succession. Then a little fugato appears in which theme 1 enters five times (second violin alone, first violin, viola, cello and bass together, and then upper winds). This short passage develops from a one-voiced texture to a *forte* passage for the entire orchestra. Themes 3, characterized by an upward *staccato* scale with a noticeable trill, and 4, jagged and *staccato*, begin a modulating bridge passage. Near the end of this, theme 2 is heard in quick imitations. After a half-measure rest, theme 5, in the contrasting key of G, enters. Almost immediately themes 2 to 4 contrapuntally join in. From this point to the end of the exposition, contrapuntal and homophonic textures can be heard. Theme 2 is important, making appearances in its original form and ''upside down,'' that is, beginning at the

Example 11.1 • Themes of Mozart's Symphony 41 in C, K. 551, IV.

bottom of the scale and rising to the top. Near the end of the exposition the dynamic level drops to *piano*, and a solo oboe followed by a solo bassoon sound theme 2.

The *development* begins with theme 1 in the upper strings against a repeated note in the cellos and basses. In this section Mozart skillfully moves themes 1 and 2 through a series of keys. Horns, trumpets, and timpani add rhythmic touches occasionally by playing the first three notes of theme 2.

The *recapitulation* follows in somewhat normal fashion, if anything in this movement can be considered normal. All five themes participate as they did in the exposition, and the overall key scheme in this section emphasizes the tonic key, as standard practice would dictate. The section closes as the solo bassoon plays an inversion of theme 2, followed by the solo flute's playing it as originally stated.

What follows is a remarkable display of virtuosity, for Mozart has written a coda of incredible contrapuntal complexity. In earlier sections of this finale, themes had been used in combinations; but in the coda all five on occasion are sounded simultaneously. Yet the music gives the impression of effortlessness and of balance, proportion, and clarity. Mozart has fused complex webs of counterpoint into a classic form to make them sound natural and inevitable.

3. WOLFGANG AMADEUS MOZART (1756–1791)

During the early part of the eighteenth century, the established *opera seria* was seriously challenged by the novel *opera buffa*. The formality of opera based on figures from antiquity, like Orpheus, Alceste, and Dido, now vied with opera based on the human comedy, opera peopled with clever servants, witty mistresses, foolish husbands, and various buffoons. Because of realistic plots and the use of more natural voices, *opera buffa* steadily gained in popularity.

One device typical of this new form was the ensemble finale at the end of each act. Here most or all of the characters participated in a large, dramatic, musical movement that was unbroken and sequential. In a finale a composer would avoid recitative but did attempt to merge many styles of singing and exploit a variety of vocal combinations. As may be imagined, librettists lamented the problems inherent in such operatic finales. Lorenzo da Ponte (1749–1838), one of the most accomplished of eighteenth-century librettists complained: ". . . in defiance of his judgment, of his reason," the poet must "find some way of making the plot allow for it," that is, the "theatrical theology," as he puts it, that requires all singers to appear on stage in the finale!

Happily, da Ponte himself not only was extremely adaptable but also possessed writing talent and a keen dramatic sense. Coupled with Mozart's musical skills and some last-minute assistance by the Don Juan of his day, Giacomo Casanova, one of his most important librettos came to life in ○● *Don Giovanni,* K. 527 (1787). This combination of talents produced a masterpiece that goes far beyond the merely comic situation opera or the sentimentalizing or moralizing operatic entertainments popular in their day. In its own way Mozart's opera touches profundities comparable to the greatest literary and artistic achievements that have used Don Juan as a subject. Interpretations of this opera abound. Søren Kierkegaard's *Either/Or* (1843) being one of the most extensive and certainly one of the most controversial. With his usual deep insights, the Danish philosopher praises the work in a series of intricate arguments whereby he arrives at the idea that the person Don Giovanni "does not fall under the [usual] ethical categories." Something like Faust, Don Giovanni stands apart from normal humanity; "he desires," but "he does not seduce." In Kierkegaard's view he is desire incarnate.

Although da Ponte and Casanova had contributed to *Don Giovanni*, the guiding hand was that of Mozart, who had always insisted that in opera "the poetry must be altogether the obedient daughter of the music." Donna Anna, the aristocrat, Donna Elvira, the respectable *bourgeoise*, and Zerlina, the peasant girl, are given musical characterizations that suit not only their stations in life but also their different personalities, and each soprano sings arias appropriate to a given dramatic moment. Likewise, the tenor, Don Ottavio, Donna Anna's fiancé, is a conventionally nice young man but ineffectual; his lyrical arias reflect that role in the drama. The aristocratic Commendatore and the peasant Masetto are both basses; yet even the most naive listener cannot fail to distinguish between their respective characterizations. Leporello, the comic servant of Don Giovanni, grumbles and chatters as a basso buffo servant should. Overshadowing all is Don Giovanni, Kierkegaard's desire incarnate, a personality so forceful that it carries all before it—until he himself is carried off by demonic forces.

The finale to Act II (the last act) takes place in the palace of the noble Don Giovanni. As he awaits dinner guests, Donna Elvira, one of the many women he has loved and discarded, arrives unexpectedly. Mocked by him, she tearfully rushes off stage and then screams. Leporello, sent to investigate, returns in terror, for the statue of the Commendatore, whom Giovanni had earlier murdered, is at the door. Refusing to submit to this ghostly presence, Giovanni, perhaps in a spirit of bravado and perhaps in an insistent last effort to be true to himself, grasps the outstretched hand of his "stone guest" and is flung into hell. As he sinks into the abyss, the other principal characters of the opera arrive to join in a final section. Each exclaims over the end of Don Giovanni and then offers brief plans for the future. In a *tutti* ensemble they turn to the audience and sing a moral exhorting the living to mark the dismal fate of Don Giovanni, the sinner.

The present recording contains only the opening section of the big finale and ends shortly after the entrance of the Commendatore. The music begins *forte* in the full orchestra, its emphasis on tonic and dominant harmonies and straightforward rhythms in $\frac{4}{4}$ meter serving to establish D as the tonal center. This section is scored for two flutes, oboes, clarinets, bassoons, horns, and trumpets, plus timpani and the usual strings. In the fifth measure the orchestra announces the melodic line that Don Giovanni will sing about twelve measures later. The general character of the music assigned to the Don reflects his character: vigorous, assertive, and secure. A strong cadence in the tonic, in the vocal part and the orchestra, closes this opening section, which moves without interruption into $\frac{6}{8}$ meter (in the seventh measure of which Leporello sings an isolated "Bravi! *Cosa rara!*"). The orchestra here is reduced mainly to oboes, clarinets, bassoons, horns, and cellos. Only in the last six measures of this section do the upper strings and basses enter (where Leporello sings "Piatto!" and the Don echoes "Servo!") to close on a cadence in D.

Note that the next section, an *Allegretto* in $\frac{3}{4}$, immediately assumes a new key, F, and a new melody. A steady quarter-note pulse (in horns and cellos) persists throughout this third section. With an instrumentation similar to that of the second section, this one also concludes with the entrance of the upper strings and basses (marked *piano* and followed by a hold).

Following the hold, a new key (B♭), a new meter (¢), and a familiar melody (Mozart's own "Non più andrai" from *Le Nozze di Figaro*) are heard immediately. Clarinets in this fourth section engage in figurations, especially sweeping descending scale passages.

As the Don quotes the music from *Figaro*, the music merges into a fifth section, during which Donna Elvira enters. The meter is now $\frac{3}{4}$. Donna Elvira's melody generally moves in even quarter notes and avoids stepwise motion in favor of skips. While the lady and the Don wrangle, Leporello provides a few musical asides. String figurations, sustaining harmonies in the winds, and numerous *forte-piano*s can be heard. The last occur mainly after the exit and reentrance of Donna Elvira and the evident fright of Leporello.

The sixth section, in the key of F again and marked *Molto Allegro*, opens ("Ah, Signor! per carità") and closes with Leporello. Notice the long sustained octave pedal point for fourteen measures in the horns at the opening of the section. These same measures are also characterized by chromaticism in the voice and instruments (flutes, bassoons, and violins) as Leporello splutters out to Giovanni the news that the statue has arrived. The faster tempo also contributes to the sense of agitation and terror.

The last section opens *fortissimo* on two dissonant chords in the full orchestra. With the entrance of the Commendatore's bass voice, the orchestra quickly drops to *piano*, with dotted rhythms in the strings and sustained chords, also *piano*, in the trombones (heard for the first time) and later in other winds. Seven measures later the first violins play a syncopated figure; then the second violins begin a rapid sixteenth-note passage. Note that the music assigned to the Commendatore is similar to, but not identical with, that given the Don at the opening of the entire finale. It consists of strong intervals (fourths, fifths, and octaves) and uncomplicated rhythms. It also suggests power, security, and vigor, but the mode is now minor, not major, and the tonal scheme avoids the neat tonic-dominant relationships that open the finale.

4. LUDWIG VAN BEETHOVEN (1770–1827)

After two earlier symphonies, which were similar in style to the music of Haydn and Mozart, Beethoven literally moved in new symphonic directions with his ○● Symphony 3 in E♭. op. 55. The development section of the first movement alone would be capable of engulfing some complete movements by earlier composers, and besides being conceived on a vast physical scale, the symphony also introduced a number of formal innovations: a second movement *Marcia Funebre,* a large-scale finale in the form of theme and variations, and a third movement—a big, powerful scherzo—that went far beyond the traditionally graceful minuets of Haydn and Mozart.

Throughout all the movements Beethoven manipulated rhythmic, harmonic, and melodic factors in a highly individual manner. Because of this unique treatment of purely musical elements, the impression is one of overwhelming proportions. Yet Beethoven's orchestra exceeds the typical Haydn-Mozart orchestra by only one horn; the symphony is scored for two each of the woodwinds (flutes, oboes, clarinets, and bassoons), *three* French horns, two trumpets, timpani, and strings. All participate in the third movement, which is our example.

This movement, marked *Allegro vivace*, has a ternary design: section *A* (scherzo), section *B* (trio), section *A* (return of the scherzo), and coda. Although smaller divisions of form within each part can be analyzed, the principal contrast in the large *ABA*-coda design comes with the *B* section, where three horns literally mark the beginning of the trio.

The *A* section of the movement opens *pianissimo* and *staccato* in the strings. The $\frac{3}{4}$ meter moves so rapidly in quarter notes that conductors set the pulse by beating one, not three, to the measure. Above the restless motion and mutterings of the strings a tune appears in the oboe, but the main impression of this opening section is that of a musical rumbling produced by flashes of melody, relentless rhythmic impulse, sudden outbursts of sound from the entire orchestra, and a series of syncopations (marked *sforzando*—with special stress) that momentarily shift the weight of the measure to the second, normally weak, beat of the measure. Echo (antiphonal) effects between woodwinds and strings, rising chromatic lines, and *staccato* harmonies also help to generate excitement in the scherzo.

By contrast, the opening of the trio and much of what follows involve a lighter texture. The three horns are given the most important thematic material, their sounds relieved by antiphonal play between woodwinds and strings. Trumpets and timpani are silent in the trio.

At the return of the scherzo Beethoven reverts to both the mood and the music of section *A*. But at one spot the energy of the movement literally bursts from its meter as four measures of *fortissimo* intrude with all instruments at the unison or octave. Antiphonal effects between woodwinds and strings follow, and eventually the entire orchestra arrives at another *fortissimo*.

The coda begins with an abrupt change to *pianissimo*, opening with the timpani alone. After a rapid *crescendo*, Beethoven hammers out tonic and dominant harmonies at a *fortissimo* level to conclude the movement.

The first performance of Symphony 3 took place on April 7, 1805, with Beethoven himself conducting. Nothing like it had ever been heard before, and it was not exactly well received, one critic observing that "the work often seems to lose itself in confusion." As often happens, time has revealed the profundity of what was once so original that it seemed chaotic.

5. LUDWIG VAN BEETHOVEN (1770–1827)

Because of its well-known opening motive, Symphony 5 in c, op. 67, is probably the most famous of all symphonies. In common with other celebrated works of art, it is surrounded by stories, true, false, and uncertain. One thing is certain, however: It was first heard in performance on December 22, 1808, in Vienna, where it was falsely recorded as the sixth symphony. Regardless of how the work came into existence, what inspired it, or what stories are told about it, the symphony holds its popularity mainly because it makes powerful musical sense.

For this remarkable work, Beethoven chose to enlarge his orchestra. In addition to the usual pairs of woodwinds (flutes, oboes, clarinets, and bassoons), the score calls for one piccolo and one double bassoon. The two French horns and the two trumpets are traditional, but the three trombones required in the finale mark the first appearance of those instruments in symphonic music. Two timpani and the usual string section complete the orchestra.

The symphony consists of four movements: ○ ● I, a sonata-allegro movement; II, a theme and variations; III, a scherzo; and ○ IV, a sonata-allegro. The keys of the respective movements are c, A♭, c, and C. This is the first of Beethoven's symphonies to be mainly in a minor key even though the composer chose to write the finale in C.

The first movement, our initial recorded example, opens *fortissimo* with the very well-known motive consisting of four notes (𝄾 ♫| ♩). Although each of the first two statements ends with a *fermata* and other temporary holds appear in the movement, the general impression is one of constant rhythmic drive and energy principally owing to the frequent use of the opening motive. Strong orchestral contrasts, sudden dynamic changes, abrupt changes in registers, and occasional biting dissonances also suggest a sense of power and vitality.

The movement provides a clear example of sonata-allegro form. After statements of the opening motive, a transition containing a series of *sforzando*s reaches a *fortissimo* in the full orchestra. A strong unison passage in the French horns introduces a second thematic group in E♭, the relative major key to c. This horn theme and subsequent passages in the exposition are derived from the initial motive.

The development section, opening with the same motive as the exposition, is tonally more restless: Near the end the four-note rhythmic pattern is abandoned in favor of modulatory chords heard in different registers and dynamic levels.

The beginning of the recapitulation can be recognized as similar, but not exactly identical, to the opening measures of the movement. Two holds confirm the reentry. Later the horn theme, now in C, is heard. A lengthy coda, initially resembling a development in character, strongly establishes the tonic minor key and brings the movement to a close.

The entire symphony contains numerous distinctive touches in matters of harmony, rhythm, melody, orchestration, and form. One highly original example takes place at the end of the third movement, where the whole musical fabric dissolves over long pedal points (tonic, dominant, then tonic) in the timpani. Instead of stopping to conclude the third movement, Beethoven extends this suspenseful passage and uses it as a direct transition to the finale so that these innovative measures join the two movements without a break.

The finale, our second example, bursts forth *fortissimo* in the entire orchestra. The main theme of the movement outlines a C triad (1–3–5) followed by a stepwise progression back to the tonic (1). A second part of this section, still in C and played *forte* by woodwinds and horns, also outlines a C triad but in a different way (1–5–3). Strong tonic-dominant harmonies, ascending scale passages, and full texture dominate the music up to the entrance of the second theme, in G. This theme is characterized by rising triplet figures. The entire exposition closes with a four-note descending melody, the last note of which is heard three times.

Throughout the exposition, development, recapitulation, and lengthy coda, Beethoven depends upon fairly simple musical means to accomplish monumental effects. Perhaps the dominating aspect is his powerful rhythms, which are sometimes as straightforward as steady hammer beats, at times syncopated by accent markings, and at other times derived from the famous rhythmic figure of the first movement, three short notes followed by a longer one. Harmonically, Beethoven works mainly with triad outlines or with motives encompassing a fourth or fifth and filled in with diatonic scale passages. The whole movement, one of the most powerful and effective in the symphonic literature, is based on relatively simple resources. It took a remarkably talented composer to mold those resources into a significant musical form of such large dimensions.

6. LUDWIG VAN BEETHOVEN (1770–1827)

Written between 1822 and 1825, the last five quartets of Beethoven presented so many novel ideas that his contemporaries were generally alarmed. Innovations in form, harmony, tonal range, and other technical aspects lifted these works far above the musical standards of the day. Even now they remain in the class of the not easily accessible, known by name perhaps but seldom heard and, if heard, not always enjoyed or understood. In this respect they resemble monuments of imagination like Cervantes's *Don Quixote* and Milton's *Paradise Lost,* also known by name but seldom read. The last quartets were regarded by some contemporaries as indicating a decline in Beethoven's creative powers; they were characterized as ''unplayable'' and ''problematic,'' terms of disapproval that continued to sprinkle the pages of critics long after Beethoven's death. Yet today the quartets are firmly established in the chamber-music repertory as testimonies of Beethoven's greatness.

To the question of what makes these quartets difficult a number of answers can be suggested: daring instrumental effects, wide leaps, fragmented motives, extreme ranges, unusual modulations, striking dynamic effects, syncopations, abrupt changes in tempo, hybrid forms, contrapuntal textures, uncommon key relationships, and underlying all these, innovations in rhythm that went far beyond the music of Beethoven's time. Beethoven, handling form and rhythm with the uncanny certainty of a genius, left to music lovers in this series of works, each unique and individual, a rich fund of music to be examined, analyzed, discussed, argued over, and written about. Above all, they should be heard, for they are stamped with the character of Beethoven, whose unmistakable signature is to be found on every page.

The works are in E♭, op. 127, in B♭, op. 130, in c♯, op. 131, in a, op. 132, and in F, op. 135. A sixth quartet, the ''grand fugue'' in B♭, op. 133, should be included in the list since, although it originally formed the finale of op. 130, it was later withdrawn in favor of the present finale to that quartet and now stands as an independent piece.

Opus 130 was also one of three quartets commissioned by, and dedicated to, Prince Nikolai Galatsin, the others being opp. 127 and 132. Written late in 1825, it was first performed on March 21, 1826. Reception of the quartet, as we might expect, varied. Among the immediately appealing movements in this six-movement work (two beyond the customary number) was the fourth, ○● *Alla danza tedesca* (''in the style of a German dance'').

The movement, in G, is in triple meter. The opening musical idea consists in a classically formed 4 + 4 measures, the entire 8 being repeated. The melody outlines a G triad (5–3–5–1) against a simple accompaniment in the lower three strings. After a contrasting 8 measures (*B*), the opening melody (the 4 + 4 *A* section) returns, and these two parts are then immediately repeated. The classic symmetry is already clouded by the ranges and registers that Beethoven employs: Near the end of the *B* section, the first violin and cello move in contrary motion to high and low registers simultaneously, and the melody is flung about at the octave rather than remaining in a more restricted range.

Following this, Beethoven breaks up his textures, introduces a new tune in the first violin, changes his dynamic level (*crescendo* to *forte*), and yet retains a sense of formal symmetry, in this case 8 + 8 measures. The key changes, and the cello picks up the tune just heard. Other ideas follow, but although Beethoven toys with his musical ideas, the underlying symmetrical structure holds.

Eventually the original melody returns in the first violin for 8 measures, but the accompanying voices are more active. Then for another 8 measures these accompanying voices impose a duple rhythmic pattern against the basic triple meter, a bit of rhythmic humor that recurs after an intervening 8 measures. Near the end of the movement Beethoven again plays with his original melody, this time completely shattering the texture with impish solos in all instruments. This is also the only section in the movement where the regularity of phrases breaks down. A final 8 measures in four-part texture complete the movement.

The *Alla danza tedesca*, with its slightly suggestive waywardness, is reminiscent of *Delight in Disorder* by Robert Herrick (1591–1674): "A sweet disorder in the dresse / Kindles in cloathes a wantonnesse: . . ."; and it may be that Beethoven's good-natured eccentricities in this movement "Doe more bewitch [us], then when Art / Is too precise in every part."

Other important music

For some additional pieces by composers of this period, see the Music Index.

The following two anthologies will give the best and most balanced view of the whole period, for they include otherwise unavailable recordings of excerpts and complete works by a number of contemporaries of Haydn, Mozart, and Beethoven.

Archive Production Research Periods XI, XII, Deutsche Grammophon Gesellschaft History of Music Division. Together these two research periods total over thirty LP records. The first, *German Pre-Classics (1700–1760)*, covers that period when new modes of musical expression began to compete with the established baroque. The following titles indicate the kinds of music offered: *Music of Georg Philipp Telemann* (born before and died after Bach and Handel); *Music at the Court of Frederick the Great; Music for Domestic Entertainment;* and *Orchestral and Chamber Music in Transition.* The second, *Mannheim and Vienna (1760–1800)*, passes through the various stages of the developing classic style from the early efforts of Stamitz to its full establishment in Mozart. Subdivisions of this set are as follows: *The Mannheim School; Divertimento and Serenade; The ''Galant'' and ''Empfindsamer'' Styles; C. W. Gluck;* and *W. A. Mozart.*

The History of Music in Sound, RCA Victor. See also Chapter 9. Volume VII is *The Symphonic Outlook, 1745–1790;* VIII, *The Age of Beethoven (1790–1830)*. As with other volumes, each consists of LP records (two and three respectively) and accompanying booklet to describe the music heard and with printed thematic materials. Representative and typical music is presented: neither the greatest nor the most frequently heard works by the three major composers and good examples by their contemporaries. Gluck, Stamitz, C. P. E. Bach, Muzio Clementi, von Weber, Étienne Nicolas Méhul, Giacomo Meyerbeer, and other important musical figures can be heard. The ten sides provide an excellent coverage from the early antecedents of the classic style, through its flowering in Mozart, to the beginnings of romanticism.

No attempt is made to pass qualitative judgment on the following selected lists of compositions by Haydn, Mozart, and Beethoven. Each work stands on its intrinsic merits and will be measured, no doubt, against the preferences of the listener. Each has stood the test of time and, together with the other compositions listed, may contribute to a balanced picture of each composer's gift to the art of music.

F. J. HAYDN

MASS

Missa solemnis in B♭ (*Theresien-Messe*).

SYMPHONIES

45 in f♯ (*Farewell*).

102 in B♭.

103 in E♭ (*Drum Roll*).

104 in D (*London*).

QUARTETS FOR STRINGS

In D, op. 50, no. 6 (*Frog*).

In D, op. 64, no. 5 (*Lark*).

SONATAS FOR PIANO

30 in A.

34 in e.

36 in c♯.

49 in E♭.

51 in D.

W. A. MOZART

OPERA

Die Entführung aus dem Serail, K. 384

MASS

In c, K. 427.

CONCERTOS FOR PIANO AND ORCHESTRA

In d, K. 466.

In A, K. 488.

In c, K. 491.

OTHER CONCERTOS

For Violin and Orchestra in A, K. 219.

For Flute and Orchestra in D, K. 314.

For Clarinet and Orchestra in A, K. 622.

SYMPHONIES

29 in A, K. 201.

35 in D, K. 385 (*Haffner*).

39 in E♭, K. 543.

QUARTETS FOR STRINGS

In G, K. 387.

In d, K. 421.

In C, K. 465.

OTHER CHAMBER MUSIC

Quintet for Strings in g, K. 516.

Quintet for Clarinet and Strings in A, K. 581.
Trio for Piano and Strings in E, K. 542.
SONATAS FOR PIANO
In a, K. 310.
In c, K. 457.

L. VAN BEETHOVEN

CONCERTOS FOR PIANO AND ORCHESTRA
In G, op. 58.
In E♭, op. 73 (*Emperor*).
SYMPHONY
6 in F, op. 68 (*Pastoral*).
OTHER ORCHESTRAL MUSIC
Egmont Overture, op. 84.
Leonore Overture 3, op. 72*a*.
QUARTETS FOR STRINGS
In F, op. 59, no. 1.
In e, op. 59, no. 2.
In f, op. 95.
In c♯, op. 131.
OTHER CHAMBER MUSIC
Trio for Piano and Strings in B♭, op. 97 (*Archduke*).
SONATAS FOR PIANO
In c♯ op. 27, no. 2 (*Moonlight*).
In C, op. 53 (*Waldstein*).
In f, op. 57 (*Appassionata*).
In B♭, op. 106 (*Hammerklavier*).
In c, op. 111.
OTHER MUSIC FOR PIANO
Variations in E♭, op. 35 (*Eroica*).

Further readings

GENERAL BACKGROUND

Almost all the references listed at the end of Chapter 10 apply in some measure to the classic period. In turn, many of the references in Chapter 12 will also have relevance, primarily because the French Revolution (1789–1799) is often an ending as well as a beginning point for historians. Those few years fall within the classic period if we set its rough boundaries as 1750 and 1830; so no single volume neatly covers the musical period insofar as general history is concerned.

The following books are recommended from Chapter 9 or 10 and consequently are cited here only in short form:

ARTZ, FREDERICK B. *From the Renaissance to Romanticism.*

BARNES, HARRY ELMER *An Intellectual and Cultural History of the Modern World.*

BRINTON, CRANE (ED.) *The Portable Age of Reason Reader.*

DURANT, WILL, AND ARIEL DURANT *The Age of Voltaire.*

FLEMING, WILLIAM *Arts and Ideas.*

GAY, PETER *Age of Enlightenment.*

GAY, PETER *The Enlightenment: An Interpretation.*

Additional useful items are the following:

BERLIN, ISAIAH (ED.) *The Age of Enlightenment,* Houghton Mifflin Company, Boston, 1956.

COBBAN, ALFRED *In Search of Humanity: The Role of the Enlightenment in Modern History,* George Braziller, Inc., New York, 1960.

DURANT, WILL, AND ARIEL DURANT *The Story of Civilization,* Part X: *The Age of Rousseau,* Simon and Schuster, New York, 1968.

FRANKEL, CHARLES *The Faith of Reason: The Idea of Progress in the French Enlightenment,* King's Crown Press, New York, 1948.

HAVENS, GEORGE R. *The Age of Ideas,* Henry Holt and Company, New York, 1955.

SCHÖNBERGER, ARNO, AND HALLDOR SOEHNER *The Rococo Age: Art and Civilization of the 18th Century,* McGraw-Hill Book Company, Inc., New York, 1960.

TORREY, NORMAN L. (ED.) *Les Philosophes,* G. P. Putnam's Sons, New York, 1960.

WILLEY, BASIL *The Eighteenth Century Background,* Beacon Press, Boston, 1961.

MUSIC

Useful sections dealing with musical developments can be found in the Cannon, Lang, and Grout volumes (see Chapter 9, Further Readings). Also see Grout's *A Short History of Opera,* under the Further Readings for Chapter 10. Three volumes dealing specifically with music of the classic period are listed below:

BLUME, FRIEDRICH   *Classic and Romantic Music,* W. W. Norton & Company, Inc., New York, 1970. Reflective, stimulating essays dealing with definitions, concepts, and ideas in music. Seven chapters are devoted to classic music, from its earliest to its most mature stages.

PAULY, REINHARD G.   *Music in the Classic Period,* Prentice-Hall, Inc., Englewood Cliffs, N.J., 1965. An excellent survey treating the transition from late baroque and rococo to the established styles of Haydn and Mozart. The book systematically examines the main musical categories of the period: symphony, sonata, concerto, chamber music, opera, and sacred music. Beethoven and his music are not dealt with in this volume except for a brief final chapter, which discusses the transition from classicism to romanticism. Good, selected bibliographical references are found at the end of each chapter.

ROSEN, CHARLES   *The Classical Style,* The Viking Press, Inc., New York, 1971. This brilliantly written book describes the musical language of Haydn, Mozart, and Beethoven in advanced technical terms. Many illuminating insights and extensive musical illustrations and analyses. The author examines principal genres developed during the period.

STRUNK, OLIVER   *Source Readings in Music History: The Classic Era,* W. W. Norton & Company, Inc., New York, 1965. Similar to other volumes in the series: translated excerpts by writers contemporary with Haydn, Mozart, and Beethoven on various aspects of music, such as performance practices and opera.

Chapter 12 ∘ *The nineteenth century*

MORE THAN ANY PREVIOUS PERIOD, THE NINETEENTH CENTURY PRESENTS SUCH a profusion and confusion of ideas that a precise definition of romanticism, its most characteristic movement, is difficult; single definition can never hope to capture the many nuances of romanticism or the century of which it was a part. Whatever spiritual unity an era seems to have at one level of examination dissolves under the microscope of the specialist historian, for the profound scholar becomes all too aware of subtle differences in a culture that at first sight had seemed to display a striking uniformity in style, mood, feeling, and technique. Thus romanticism is perhaps better described than defined: One writer will concentrate upon its "sincerity, spontaneity, and passion" (Runes); another, upon its search for "an ideal of beauty through emotional expression" (Dannreuter); "its longing for the infinite" (Lang); "its remoteness and boundlessness" (Grout); "its necessity of originality" (Cannon); "its revolutionary tendencies" (Einstein); its emphasis upon the "organic," that is, seeing things as wholes and in relationships (Artz); or, as in Longyear's reluctant acceptance of Victor Hugo's statement about it, "a certain vague and indefinable fantasy." (See Further Readings for more information about some of these sources.)

Ideas and arts in the nineteenth century

For G. W. F. Hegel (1770–1831), one of the German philosophers of the period, all history is the history of thought. Whereas the scientist more properly investigates the tangible, phenomenal world of matter, the historian, according to Hegel, deals with ideas and concepts. But thoughts fuse, merge, and amalgamate; they are fluid, flexible, and fleeting. Even in the most disciplined minds, logical thinking is constantly bombarded by flashes of ideas, sparks of insight, annoying irrelevancies. Being a part of mind, history is never complete, never finished, always becoming. This conception of history strongly resembles some contemporary existentialist notions of man as an unfinished "ever-defining-himself" creature. A "true" history, then, must include *everything* (an impossible goal even for the most persistent seekers): The statement "In 1815 Napoleon was defeated at the Battle of Waterloo," which most accept as historical fact, obviously tells an incomplete story, for this fact (really the crystallization of thousands of other facts) tells us very little unless the year 1815, the man Napoleon, the term "defeated," and the location Waterloo are illuminated with innumerable

Figure 12.1 • Francisco Goya: Executions of the Third of May, 1808. *The romantic emphasis on the nationalistic and the background details of actual history.* (Museo del Prado.)

further bits of all sorts of information (Figure 12.1), a process never to be fully realized.

Hegel's conception of history as a dynamic process suited the temperaments of romantic personalities. As echoed in their own lives, writing, and arts, life was in constant flux and consisted in never-ending desires that cried for resolution, in searches for unattainable goals (like Hegel's complete history), and in a sense of incompleteness, which would have led many of them to sell their souls to the devil, like Faust, for more time on earth.

Bearing in mind that the following terms "suggest" (like the reference above to Napoleon and Waterloo) rather than define, we set forth below in roughly parallel columns some of the contrasting emphases attributed to classicism and romanticism:

Classicism	Romanticism
Universality	individuality
Simplicity	complexity
Form	content and substance
Reason	fancy
Absolute standard	relative standard
Objectivity	subjectivity
Sein (essence)	*Werden* (becoming)
Norms and canons of taste	individual differentiation
Permanence	growth, change, fleetingness
The essential	the accidental
"Apollonian"	"Dionysian" (Friedrich Wilhelm Nietzsche)
Typified perfection	personal character
Inertia	motion, action
Limitation	boundlessness
Craft	imagination
Closed structure	open structure
Organization	capriciousness
Purity of arts	merging of arts
Flat, "given" dimensions	perspective and "illusion"
Additive unification	organic unification
Impassivity	suffering

Figure 12.2 • The Church of Sainte-Clotilde (ca. 1846–1857). A nostalgic revival of medieval architectural ideals. (Éditions Chantal.)

Plainness	picturesqueness
Serenity	passion
Standardization	uniqueness

Of course, no single work of romantic art embraces the entire right-hand column; but may embrace much of it and, in fact, may embrace terms from the opposite column.

Given François Christian Gau's and Théodore Ballu's Church of Sainte-Clotilde (Figure 12.2), François Rude's *Departure of the Volunteers of 1792* (Figure 12.3), Eugène Delacroix's *The Death of Sardanapalus* (Plate 4), and Wagner's "Liebestod" from *Tristan und Isolde,* how can we interpret these evidences of romanticism? As products of human activity, they represent internal experiences externalized in different artistic ways. The classicist wanted to examine objects critically and analytically. The romanticist took the position that, if deprived of "inner meaning" (that is, ideas, images, feelings, emotions, volitions, values), Sainte-Clotilde is merely a collection of stones, the *Departure of the Volunteers* chiselled surfaces, the *Sardanapalus* lines and colors on a two-dimensional surface, and the "Liebestod" purely acoustical sound. The romanticist prefers, in other words, not only to examine the objects but to understand the cultural, artistic, and intellectual milieu of the works. For the romanticist Sainte-Clotilde embodies an allegiance to a past whose Gothic cathedrals symbolized a spiritually unified Europe. The *Departure* captures the idea of heroic patriotism. The *Sardanapalus* (influenced by Byron's play) expresses the mood of massacre and total renunciation by an exotic king bent on suicide. And the "Liebestod" implies that love's fulfillment comes only through death. Each interpretation represents, of course, only one of many that are possible, but each shows that, for the romantic spirit at least, we must look beyond surfaces, lines, and sounds if we seek understanding. Among other things, we must set each work of art in some sort of historical context, see it as part of an historical process: a task that, of course, is never-ending.

In the following pages we plan to survey briefly six aspects of the romantic movement: medievalism in the arts and crafts, the emergence

Figure 12.3 • *François Rude:* Departure of the Volunteers of 1792 (*stone relief on the Arc de Triomphe de l'Étoile, Paris). A typically romantic hodgepodge of motifs, national, medieval, and Roman, combined in a blood-stirring and passionate visual appeal.* (Archives Photographiques, Paris.)

of the ''romantic hero,'' the theme of *la femme fatale*, gloom and pessimism, escape to dream worlds and nature, and *Götterdämmerung*—the ''twilight'' of romanticism. Historically they overlap in chronology within their time range from the late eighteenth to the very early twentieth century, but for purposes of this brief explanation, we may roughly combine them in the following synopsis: One early display of the romantic spirit resulted from a revival of interest in history, especially the history of the Middle Ages. In glamorizing history, the romantics created certain types of heroes and often strongly identified themselves with the heroes. Characteristically the heroes (like many romantics) were victimized by determined, strong-willed women. Feelings of disillusionment, gloom, and pessimism and sometimes thoughts of suicide resulted from these experiences; so poets, painters, writers, and musicians tried to find peace in wild, tempestuous, but relatively safe ''nature.'' Finally some minds began to dream of art as a means of salvation—a way of fusing mankind into some mystical experience beyond that offered by traditional religion.

ARTISTIC MEDIEVALISM

Early versions of romanticism can be found in those eighteenth-century forms where sentimentality and the portrayal of passionate emotions are expressed: the English ''sentimental'' novel and poetry, the *Sturm und Drang* movement in Germany, the *empfindsamer Stil* (''sensitive style'') in music (from about 1750 to 1780, with music of C. P. E. Bach, Johann Joachim Quantz, and others), and the beginnings of a gothic revival. Of these the last had widespread influence, continuing into the late nineteenth century. Many factors contributed to its popularity, among them a renewed interest in human history, including secular traditions, a lively curiosity about medieval Christianity, a frequent identification with nationalistic movements, which required some knowledge of a country's heritage, and a cross-fertilization of thought encouraged by an enormous outpouring of translations of literature.

Today most of us take it for granted that history and tradition play vital roles in shaping individual and collective destinies. In almost all argument and debate men cite, for supporting evidence and documentation, the authority of the past: Politicians call upon the Founding Fathers to embellish their rhetoric, churchmen invoke the minutes of councils and the actions of saints to justify their precepts, and judges look to legal precedent for guidance. During the period we are considering men began to view themselves not as static essences but as the results of dynamic historical process; they became conscious of history. It followed that the condition, the strength, the vitality, of institutions and social customs and personal beliefs were to be understood from the standpoint of their historical development. Institutions and individuals, ever-changing and becoming, were to be viewed as the fascinating outcomes of their pasts.

Renaissance man had turned to the past of classical antiquity. The early and later romantics found more inspiration in the medieval world. Partly in revolt against the excesses of classic "enlightened" thought, they were attracted to medieval art and life, which had centered around a Christian ideal. They viewed that period—its spiritual unity, its metaphysical mysteries, and its primitive naturalness—as an ideal world. Today we may fault them for their misinformation and misinterpretation but not for their exuberance and enthusiasm.

The more the romantic looked to history and to the Middle Ages in particular, the more aware he became of his own cultural heritage. French history, Italian history, and especially German history now began to fascinate the minds of historians, poets, writers, and musicians. They naturally turned to the past, but it was the past of their own great ancestral heroes, the great strivers and achievers, those half-legendary giants of their culture who were shrouded in romance and mystery.

During the last decades of the eighteenth century many translations started to appear. Shakespeare revivals, Dante enthusiasms, and other fads and fashions based on some "foreign" literature became very popular in French, English, and German intellectual circles. This cross-breeding of ideas, through translated poetry and literature, also stimulated the already fertile romantic imagination by providing additional legendary figures from the past.

The lure, then, was to the strange, the miraculous, the mysterious, the foreign and exotic. Away from the control of neoclassic academicians, the artistic movement was toward a study of native folklore, legend, and superstition, national mythology, a love of wild and forbidding natural landscapes, and the gothic past. Works like James Macpherson's *The Poems of Ossian* (1765), Thomas Percy's *Reliques of Ancient English Poetry* (1765), and Thomas Chatterton's poems attributed to Thomas Rowley (1765) stimulated interest in early ballads, folksongs, and poems, which quickly inspired others in France and Germany to examine their own distant past. With Horace Walpole's *The Castle of Otranto* (1764), the gothic novel became an important force. Walpole (1717–1797), an ardent but decidedly amateur medievalist, actually had a gothic mansion (Strawberry Hill) built for himself; other enthusiasts followed in imitation, and gradually a gothic revival got under way in architecture as well as literature. The British Houses of Parliament and the Gau and Ballu Church of Sainte-Clotilde, both products of the nineteenth century, provide excellent examples, as does the late interpretation in Figure 12.4. American universities and churches, in attempts to attain academic and religious respectability, were often so constructed as to exhibit medieval flavor.

But it was the Gothic novel that most caught hold, enjoying an amazing popularity, first with Mary Ann Radcliffe (1764–1823) and Matthew Gregory Lewis (1775–1818) and then with Sir Walter Scott (1771–1832), the author of *Ivanhoe, Quentin Durward, The Betrothed, The Talisman,* and *Castle Dangerous.* Medievalisms also appear in works like Coleridge's *Christabel,* Byron's *The Prisoner of Chillon, Manfred,* and *The Lament of Tasso,* and Shelley's *Zastrozzi* and *The Rosicrucian.* In France, Victor Hugo (1802–1885), riding on a crest of French romanticism, made a sensation with his *Notre Dame de Paris* (1831). Alfred de Vigny (1799–1863) and Prosper Mérimée (1803–1870) likewise turned to historical settings. In Germany, Novalis (1772–1801) espoused the Middle Ages in *Christianity or Europe* (1799), a kind of German equivalent to *Mont-Saint-Michel and Chartres* (1904) of Henry Adams (1838–1918). Both men, Novalis and Adams, writing over a century apart, were alike impressed by a time past when religion had acted as the source and hub of all human activity. That their enthusiasms were somewhat misguided and uncritical is now common knowledge, the poetic beauty of their ideas spoiled by the nasty fact that life in the Middle Ages was hardly a bed of roses.

Opera from the early nineteenth century on was peopled with medieval and historical figures. If we stretch the term medieval to embrace what many romantics themselves called medieval, the list of operas and tone poems based on earlier periods can be staggeringly long: such historical personages as Belisarius, Richard the Lion-Hearted, Joan of Arc, Vasco da Gama, Alfred the Great, Dante, Petrarch, Ann Boleyn, and St. Francis

Figure 12.4 • *King Ludwig II's castle, Neuschwanstein, in the Bavarian Alps. Begun in 1869, this structure is an idealized romantic revival of a secular medieval style.* (Studio Tanner, Nesselwang.)

of Assisi all appear in operas, along with fictional or legendary figures like Parsifal, Lohengrin, Faust, and El Cid.

THE ROMANTIC HERO

Each age, no doubt, creates its own heroes; the hero image may be as necessary to a functioning society as religious impulse and political organization. Hero worship has included the ridiculous and the sublime,

Figure 12.5 • *Théodore Géricault:* Mounted Officer of the Imperial Guard (ca. 1812). *A romantic expression of interest in strong movement and the hero type.* (Musée du Louvre; cliché des Musées Nationaux.)

its objects ranging from the heroes of drama, fiction, and legend to persons as disparate as Alexander the Great and St. Francis.

The gothic novel had recreated a past—a highly romanticized past. Its characters, especially male, displayed qualities designed to spark excitement and curiosity (Figure 12.5). Their souls, deep, mysterious, enigmatic, rumbled with Faustlike characteristics. If Beethoven cried, "I shall seize Fate by the throat," these men, like Manfred in Walpole's *The Castle of Otranto,* intended to "seize *life* by the throat." They hungered for an experience-filled life, not some abstractly drawn picture, system, or scheme of life suited to a rationalist. Although Walpole, Radcliffe, Lewis, and Scott had created a variety of popular hero types in their novels, it was ultimately Lord Byron (1788–1824) who stamped his name on the hero of the age. Byron had steeped himself, of course, in the gothic novel. He seemed destined to create in his poems and dramas men who were mirrors of his own ego. A mass of contradictions, conflicts, and paradoxes, Byron's own life was wildly romantic and typically tragic. To what extent he brought his troubles on himself, to what extent he "posed" deliberately, and to what extent external events and internal turmoil tore at his personality baffle biographers.

In his works he created heroes who were in revolt against society—men who, like Byron himself, were sure of themselves but never quite sure exactly what they believed in. Like Faust, they were often men with an enormous appetite for life, but frequently lonely, haunted, pessimistic, weary, and disillusioned, they pressed forward without hope and, as the exile in Schubert's song *Der Wanderer,* often gazed back wistfully to times, places, and people no longer in existence. In the poems *The Bride of Abydos* (1813), *Giaour* (1813), *The Corsair* (1814), and *Lara* (1814), Byron depicts heroes who feel a deep spiritual isolation from conventional behavior and morality, and with *Manfred* (1817), his hero becomes positively Satanic, choosing deliberately to effect evil and to combat goodness. Intelligent, cunning, powerful and determined, Byron's heroes struggle in vain against superior forces, heroically striving to attain questionable goals.

LA FEMME FATALE

Although he had many imitators, Byron had created hero types whose actions and attitudes resembled Prometheus, Faust, Don Juan, or even

Satan himself. Later writers, however, found themselves attracted to a female counterpart of the Byronic hero—*la femme fatale*, the deadly woman. Gradually the emphasis switched from Manfredlike heroes to strong-willed heroines who bent men to their wills. Théophile Gautier (1811–1872), Gustave Flaubert (1821–1880), Algernon Charles Swinburne (1837–1909), Oscar Wilde (1856–1900), Gabriele d'Annunzio (1863–1938), and other poets, novelists, and dramatists searched historical sources for female types to suit their purposes: Cleopatra, Semiramis, Medusa, Scylla, the Sphinx, Phaedra, Venus, Salome, Nyssia, the Sirens, Imperia, Rosamond, Lucrezia Borgia, Cressida, and Lilith. These are formidable women or half monsters, as the case may be. They destroy men in various ways. Driven by strong physical lust, by jealousy, by revenge, by hatred of all things male, by the compulsion to kill the things they love, they dominate situations by striking physical presence and force of personality. Their loves and hates transcend normal codes of conduct. Coming from all walks of life, young and occasionally old (H. Rider Haggard's She has some two thousand years of experience), they stand even further removed from the usual norms than do Byronic heroes.

ROMANTIC GLOOM AND PESSIMISM

With love, disillusionment is always a possibility. With romantic love, such as that which fills the pages of romantic novels, dramas, poetry, and opera, it becomes a fairly safe bet. And with disillusionment, pessimism follows. Whereas Dr. Pangloss in Voltaire's *Candide* (1759) may have maintained that "this is the best of all possible worlds," romantic writers like Giacomo Leopardi (1798–1837), Gérard de Nerval (1808–1855), and Charles Baudelaire (1821–1867) disagree.

Bitterness and ennui
Is life, never anything else; and mud is the world.

*Amaro e noia
La vita, altro mai nulla; e fango è il mondo.* (LEOPARDI.)

I am the Dark, the Bereft, the Unconsoled.

Je suis le Ténébreux,—le Veuf,—l'Inconsolé. (DE NERVAL.)

Hope,
Vanquished, weeps, and fierce, despotic Anguish
Plants his black banner upon my drooping skull.

*L'Espoir,
Vaincu, pleure, et l'Angoisse atroce, despotique,
Sur mon crâne incliné plante son drapeau noir.* (BAUDELAIRE.)

As we have implied, for one reason or another many romantic figures led troubled lives. Their personal frustrations, yearnings, and despairs were reflected artistically through expressions of melancholy, self-pity, bitterness, weariness, hopeless love, contemplations of suicide, and other kinds of pessimism. Although some undoubtedly brought troubles upon themselves, outside forces were almost always contributing factors: inhumane upbringing, unhappy love affairs, physical infirmities, mental illnesses—to name but a few. Their lives, both practical and artistic, were touched by melancholy, for they created as they lived. They provide eloquent testimony for the Latin adage *ars longa, vita brevis* ("art is long, life is short"): their art has long outlasted the brevity of their earthly lives.

ROMANTIC ESCAPE

One source of peace for unhappy romantics was provided by "nature," or at least through their conception of it as tutor of men. William Wordsworth (1770–1850) in 1798 articulates an early romanticism:

One impulse from a vernal wood
May teach you more of man,
Of moral evil and of good,
Than all the sages can.

Placing oneself in the hands of nature is very different from the "enlightened" efforts earlier in the century to analyze and classify the phenomena of nature. Unlike the man of the baroque, the romantic did not seek to understand nature and to impose human order upon it. Rather, Wordsworth and his contemporaries sought to enjoy nature—to let their lives, when they could afford the time, flow in harmony with it. But they also tended to view nature as something beyond its purely objective existence: Trees, rivers, mountains, birds, and other aspects of the natural countryside offered refuge from the evils of men and society; but it was the undefinable force, the spirit behind these objects, that, as Wordsworth notes, taught and instructed men. Conceived in this fashion, nature constantly refreshed, revitalized, counseled, and consoled even though it remained unfathomable, mysterious, terrifying, yet beautiful.

GÖTTERDÄMMERUNG: THE END OF AN ERA

Eventually romanticism, through its own excesses, lost its attraction as a powerful artistic force. Its achievements as well as its exaggerations provoked reaction to sweeping gestures, rich colors, and emotional extremes. Changing times began to demand a change in aesthetics. From midcentury we can perceive the twilight of the romantic gods, as realism in literature, impressionism in painting, and nationalism in music modified the aims of Wordsworth, Delacroix, and Berlioz. Yet it was precisely during this half century or so that many of the arts and especially music were placed on high pinnacles by various writers and philosophers. In their efforts to praise art, they stated ideas that were not fully understood although uncritically believed by both laymen and artists. At best, the situation developed novel aesthetic thought; at worst, a confusion that may have led to the decline of romanticism.

As early as 1819, Arthur Schopenhauer (1788–1860) had maintained in *The World as Will and Idea* that music was the "copy of the will itself." He adds, "This is why the effect of music is so much more powerful and penetrating than that of the other arts, for they speak only of shadows, but it speaks of the thing itself." Somewhat later the English art critic Walter Pater (1839–1894) remarked, in a line most musicians have memorized, "All art constantly aspires towards the condition of music." In turn, Friedrich Wilhelm Nietzsche (1844–1900) rhapsodized about folksong ("the musical mirror of the world") and melody ("primary and universal") in his famous essay *The Birth of Tragedy* (1872). Music, the art of emotion (a notion perfectly in tune with ideas held by romantic musicians), symbolized for Nietzsche a "sphere which is beyond and before all phenomena," an art capable of transforming—or at least capable of redeeming—mankind.

For Richard Wagner (1813–1883) the purpose of music was to function as a catalytic agent to synthesize all arts into one grand *Gesamtkunstwerk* (total work of art), a drama with music that perfectly fused all the contributing arts. If one believes that certain arts had reached peaks of attainment and full maturity in past cultures (for example, sculpture in ancient Greece, painting in renaissance Italy, drama in Shakespeare, and music in Beethoven), what else remains but to merge them into one glorious art form, the music drama? For Wagner the participating arts were not to be merely additive, accidental, or ornamental but were to be completely amalgamated into some organic unity. At its highest level, according to its most ardent believers, this kind of art was life itself. Caught in the grip of a total context, the listener-viewer, his senses overwhelmed, loses his psychic distance and becomes a participant rather than an observer. He worships at the intoxicating, spirit-freeing altar of music drama. As expounded by Wagner, Nietzsche, and their followers, music drama, uniting all the arts it could embrace, approaches religious experience: In the beginning was Art, not the Word. Wagner and Nietzsche inevitably came to disagree—violently. But they had by then burdened the art of music with philosophical and extra-musical trappings.

But no one-to-one relationship existed between Wagner the philosopher and Wagner the practicing artist. As is often the case, the beliefs of the composer faded into irrelevance while his creations remain powerful in and of themselves. Wagner's music is still heard primarily because of its intrinsic merit and because it represents the essence of musical romanticism.

Yet his time was out of joint. The philosophical and religious roots of ancient Greek drama, which had provided inspiration for Wagner's ideas, were simply not present in late-nineteenth-century Europe. The last extremes of the romantic spirit probably occurred in the music of Alexander Nikolayevitch Skriabin (1872–1915), a mystical visionary who composed numerous piano pieces and a few colorful symphonic works. His proposed *Mysterium,* existing only in sketches, would have involved drama, poetry, costume, dance, instrumental music, solo singing, choral music, colored lights, and perfumes. To become a Skriabinite, if not a Wagnerite, one figuratively applies for admission, is baptized and initiated as a member of the cult, joins the congregation, and takes communion. Seeking to understand Wagner and Skriabin on purely musical grounds may miss the point entirely, for in them music and idea are wedded; for this reason objectivity is harder to maintain. If we listen only to the music—without scenery, action, and all the rest—we lose some of the dimensions. If we should choose to immerse ourselves in all the nonmusical trappings, however, we must be a believer in what can no longer be believed. It is perhaps a tribute to the power of music that we can acknowledge this problem and still be moved by the expressiveness of works that were intended to embrace more than music alone.

CONCLUSION

As we noted at the beginning of this essay, romanticism is many-sided. It defies definition. The romantic mind is viewed at its characteristic best in the individualized situation and not the collective state. When each artist is devoted to originality and uniqueness, to lump all artists under one heading denies their differences and becomes the unkindest cut of all. The sum total of all the different creations during that century is romantic, when that label allows uniqueness to be as important as similarity.

Musical style

RHYTHM

As music of the nineteenth century increasingly attempted to express programmatic ideas, its moods grew in flexibility. Composers sought to portray fleeting and complicated emotional states, and the rhythms they adopted reflected this search: Complete breaks in the music, by either prolonged rests or lengthy holds, momentarily halted the rhythmic pulse; the flow was also slackened or quickened by frequent use of *ritardando* and *accelerando* and *rubato* sections; abrupt changes in mood also brought about unexpected slow passages in fast movements and the converse. Contrasting moods often caused changes of meter within a movement to a much greater degree than could be found in music of the classic period. Yet many movements, of course, maintained a fairly steady pulse, a basic meter, and a relatively uninterrupted motion.

Highly distinctive musical motives are given recognizable form through rhythmic patterns. Although melodic shape and harmonic structure help create motives in Schumann, Brahms, and Tchaikovsky or in the leit-motifs of Wagner, rhythm often provides a motive with its essential character and personality. All three musical elements necessarily contribute, but identification can often be confirmed through the rhythmic element.

MELODY

Nineteenth-century composers continued to demand virtuosity from instrumentalists, with the result that melodic ranges considerably widened. As the art of orchestration expanded, composers sharpened their knowledge of the unique expressive possibilities of each instrument. In view of the prevailing aesthetic, it was natural that composers eagerly sought to be original. Exploiting the capabilities of instruments through novel melodic patterns was one way of realizing that goal.

In the early part of the century Beethoven, Schumann, Chopin, and Berlioz wrote melodies that became increasingly chromatic. From mid-century on, Wagner, Liszt, Franck, and other composers accepted this chromaticism and carried it further. In a rough way, taking a group of characteristic melodies (1) from the period of Haydn and Mozart, (2) from the first half of the nineteenth century, and (3) from the last half, we can generalize that melodies of the first group strongly oriented themselves to tonic and dominant outlines, were primarily diatonic, exhibited a modest range, used scale passages that were mainly diatonic, contained relatively few leaps (almost all of which leaped to a strong harmonic note or to a clearly defined substitute), strongly implied an underlying harmonic background, and displayed a phrase structure that was mostly regular and predictable. Melodies of the early nineteenth century (the second group) became more individualized. Not only did they reflect more idiomatic writing for particular instruments, but the characteristic melodic traits of the Haydn-Mozart style grudgingly yielded to increased chromaticism, a looser phrase structure, and various kinds of melodic innovation. Unlike the melodies of Haydn and Mozart, those of Wagner and many late-nineteenth- and early-twentieth-century composers (group 3) did not strongly orient themselves around the tonic and dominant notes of a scale. By being heavily chromatic, the melodies often obscured the fundamental notes of the tonal system. More was demanded of instrumentalists, almost all of whom were required to play chromatic melodies, to roam around in extreme ranges, and to articulate (that is, phrase, attack, breathe, bow, and the like) in a variety of ways. Melodies of this kind taken out of context and standing alone do not always give clues to the underlying harmonic background, nor are they very predictable because of their somewhat looser and less regular phrase structure. With Wagnerian melodies and those of composers like César Franck, the outer limits of melodies based on traditional procedures seemed to be reached. The next step was to find some organizing principles to replace the major-minor system. It was this quest that resulted in the experiments of such early-twentieth-century composers as Stravinsky, Schoenberg, Milhaud, Hindemith, and Bartók.

Vocal melodies of the period also reflected some of the changes observed above. In songs by Schubert, Schumann, Brahms, Hugo Wolf, Strauss, and Mahler and in the operas of Wagner and Strauss, vocalists were pressed into singing melodies with wide ranges, difficult melodic intervals, tricky rhythms, and irregular phrases—all this against a complicated series of harmonies in the piano or orchestra. In Italian opera more conservative practices persisted. But even there, where lyrical melodies were much appreciated, increasingly greater demands were made upon singers.

HARMONY AND COUNTERPOINT

In a style where melody is enhanced by harmony, it follows that much attention is given to the latter. Basically diatonic in its early years, romantic harmony grew greatly in chromaticism. Not content with diatonic triads and seventh and ninth chords, composers experimented and then adopted many alterations of those basic chords. Chromatic changes in the structure of a harmony provided rich, lush, and often exotic flavors; and the harmonic changes influenced the kinds of melodies written. As a result of chromatic alterations, suspensions, *appoggiature,* more complex chords, the use of pedal points, and pitches sometimes grouped in seemingly nonfunctional ways, the basic feeling of romantic harmony is one of restlessness, movement, instability, unpredictability, and strong tension. Harmonic direction is not always perfectly clear, and frequently one knows where he is only after he gets there. The surer harmonic guidelines of the classic period dissolved into colorful romantic harmonies of considerable uncertainty of function and direction.

From Beethoven on, composers employed clashing and dissonant chords. Seventh and ninth chords, plain or altered, create tension by demanding resolution; one technique common to romantic composers is to avoid that resolution as long as possible by moving from one tension-producing chord to another. The listener's expectations are therefore thwarted. Under such circumstances, it is understandable that a strongly oriented tonal system, with clear-cut harmonic goals, should gradually disintegrate under the impact of many measures of unpredictable harmonic movement leading only to unresolved dissonances.

Modulation was extended to remote keys. Distantly related keys require additional sharps or flats, and the gravitational pull of the tonic weakens. Yet a reasonably strong sense of tonality permeated most music of the romantic period. Composers almost always returned to the tonic key even after they had made lengthy excursions into many other and often remote keys.

Wagner's *Tristan und Isolde* (1859) provoked the earliest crisis for traditional harmony. By the last decades of the century the young Richard Strauss (1864–1949) and Claude Debussy (1862–1918) were writing music that shocked more conservative minds even though their styles were almost completely dissimilar. Strauss, more in the Wagnerian tradition, often used harsh-sounding harmonies appropriate for his programmatic tone poems. Debussy introduced complex, nonfunctional harmonies, which, even more than those of Strauss, broke away from the major-minor, functional harmonic system. In their music modern harmony makes its appearance.

Because much of the music is complicated and involved (listen to Wagner, Mahler, and Strauss), textures tend to be heavy. Essentially homophonic, the music in its simplest form (some Verdi, for example) sets a melody against a chordal accompaniment. Seldom, however, is the melody simple and the accompaniment straightforward: Melodies may be passed from voice to voice in high, middle, or low ranges; and chordal accompaniments are made more complicated by arpeggiated patterns, seventh and ninth chords, suspensions, nonchord tones, pedal points, doublings of chord tones at the octave, and heavy orchestration.

The age was not one to encourage a composer to develop his contrapuntal skills. There exist, of course, passages in which contrapuntal textures are in evidence; but the sense of contrapuntally combined lines is more the result of harmonic action than it is of independently conceived counterpoint, and although imitative entrances, a trademark of renaissance and baroque polyphony, appear in fuguelike passages, such sections usually move quickly into music controlled by harmonic considerations.

TONE COLOR

For centuries music had been associated with, and supported by, the church, an educated nobility, and in later ages small groups of dedicated amateurs and an increasingly rich middle class. With the romantic era, music shifts into large concert and recital halls. Except in the more intimate atmosphere of the salons, the emphasis was on size, even—or perhaps especially—in opera houses.

Technical advances have always affected the art of music. Larger halls resulted in a search for larger instruments, capable of carrying power sufficient to reach the most remote corners. So almost every instrument underwent some changes to increase its sound. Apart from size, the most important advances came from additions and improvements in the key systems of woodwind instruments and in the valve systems of horns and trumpets. Mechanisms that permitted percussionists to change the pitch of the kettledrums quickly meant an increase in the expressive possibilities of those instruments. In sum, increased sonorities and greater flexibility, including the possibility of playing quick chromatic notes on winds and brasses, made composers especially sensitive to dynamics and tone color, elements of orchestration on which the brilliant Berlioz wrote a major treatise in 1843. Later, Strauss, another great orchestrator, revised and enlarged his predecessor's book. In the Berlioz-Strauss edition there are described and discussed not only the standard orchestral instruments but also the piccolo, English horn, bass clarinet, contrabassoon, harp, guitar, organ, saxophone, and numerous percussion instruments. Music based on exotic ideas or on nationalistic and historical programs required colorful instrumentation. Solo sounds were exploited as well as instruments used in various combinations. From Berlioz through Strauss and Mahler sonority and color were elements to be carefully worked out by the composer. How sounds were made was often as important as what the sounds were doing.

As composers became more tone-color conscious, subtleties of performance became more crucial. Scores were more carefully marked, not only with tempo designations—*adagio, allegro,* and so on, with qualifiers such as *meno* (less) or *assai* (very)—but also with expressive terms like *morendo* (dying away), *con fuoco* (with fire), *lagrimoso* (tearful), *risoluto* (resolute), *misterioso* (mysterious), *con amore* (with love), and, of course, *con expressione* (with expression). Numerous terms and symbols indicating types of touch, bowing, phrasing, intensity, and other subtleties sprinkle the pages of romantic music.

Of all instruments it was the piano—the new pianoforte with a single cast-iron frame (after about 1825)—that became the dominant romantic instrument. Whether used as a solo instrument, a member of a chamber ensemble, or as a solo instrument in a concerto with orchestra, the piano seemed to be an ideal instrument for the emotional style. With mechanical improvements in its action, frame construction, pedals, and stringing, it gained significantly in power of sound and in range. The piano reached what is essentially its present form about midcentury, shortly after the death of Chopin, probably the greatest composer for the instrument.

FORM

Romantic forms range from miniature songs and piano pieces to gigantic music dramas like Wagner's *Die Meistersinger* (1862–1867) and enormous symphonies like Gustav Mahler's eighth (1906).

Naturally, enough, the salon and small recital hall were appropriate homes for small forms like the "character piece" for piano and the song with piano accompaniment. Character pieces, often short, usually related a programmatic idea or expressed a particular mood in typical romantic fashion. Nocturnes, impromptus, songs without words, intermezzos, preludes, capriccios and many other types stand as individual pieces although they were often published in groups. Other piano pieces, especially groupings by Schumann, were meant to be played successively as a unified cycle that suggested a program. Almost all the pieces mentioned above are ternary in form (*ABA*), the middle section usually providing a decided contrast to the two outer sections.

The art song reached a peak in the *Lieder* of Schubert, Schumann, Brahms, Wolf, and Strauss. Such an intimate relationship exists between text and music in these songs that the dictum *traduttori, traditori* ("translators [are] traitors") still holds for most music lovers in that the precise meanings and inflections of one language cannot be captured in another. Three types of song treatment can be distinguished: (1) a strophic type, where the musical setting remains the same for each of the several stanzas of the poetry; (2) a modified strophic, where some stanzas require changes in the music for dramatic or expressive reasons; and (3) the through-composed type (*durchkomponiert*), where the form and other musical elements are molded by the poem. The first two types usually exhibit a fairly well-defined phrase syntax, with balance, regularity, and cadence being very much in evidence. The third type is much freer in all respects, for the composer attempts to capture the spirit and meaning of the poem as it unfolds, as well as its natural rhythmic cadence and lilt.

Among large forms, we find sonata, symphony, concerto, tone poem, concert overture, opera, and chamber music, plus some hybrid forms like the program symphony and symphony with chorus. Those forms which relate to the sonata almost invariably became works of grand dimensions. The symphony (a sonata for orchestra) generally keeps to the traditional four movements, each movement of which is extended. The concerto (a sonata for soloist and orchestra) generally retains the three-movement plan of the late eighteenth century, the individual movements usually being longer. The piano sonata, the violin-and-piano sonata, the string quartet (a sonata for four stringed instruments), the piano trio (a sonata for piano and two strings), and chamber music in general tend to continue the four-movement plan.

In the romantic sonata, the first-movement sonata-allegro form remained in outline what it had been in Beethoven's works: exposition, development, recapitulation, with optional introduction and coda. However, more striking contrasts in keys and in thematic material appealed to romantic composers, and a more continuous unfolding of potentially useful materials takes place. Frequently added to the first group of themes (in the tonic) and the second group (in another key) is a third group, which closes the exposition, thus giving the composer more options for his development section. Many questions are posed in the definition and analysis of some large sonata-allegro forms in the nineteenth century, and most, but not all, of the romantic composers found themselves more at home in small forms (*Lieder* and character pieces). The sonata in its various guises presented problems of form and style that were not always compatible with those composers' creative dispositions, nor were these problems always solved satisfactorily. The prevailing lyrical quality in the music of the times did not lend itself naturally to the rigorous demands of development sections or to the hard integrity of competing contrapuntal lines.

Many tried various adaptations of the sonata idea by writing programmatic sonatas and symphonies, of which the most significant were one-movement works that incorporated in various orders the *allegro, adagio,* scherzo, and rondo sections of typical four-movement symphonies. These forms came to be called ''symphonic poems.'' The symphonic poems of Franz Liszt are based mainly on some poetic or literary idea that permitted Liszt freedom enough to create a number of changes of mood, tempo, and musical material within a single movement. Thematic material was transformed according to the dictates of the program; so each work literally created its own form. Of the twelve written by Liszt, *Les Préludes* is the most popular.

Near the end of the century Richard Strauss composed a series of *Tondichtungen* (tone poems) based on titles like *Don Juan, Don Quixote, Also sprach Zarathustra* (*Thus Spake Zarathustra*), *Tod und Verklärung* (*Death and Transfiguration*), *Ein Heldenleben* (*A Hero's Life*), and, perhaps the best known of all, *Till Eulenspiegel's lustige Streiche* (*Till Eulenspiegel's Merry Pranks*). Strauss was a virtuoso in handling his orchestra, and his skills in working with large one-movement forms matched other aspects of his talent. His tone poems, shaped by programmatic ideas, are cast in some formal, if very freely treated, design: *Till Eulenspiegel* is rondolike; *Don Quixote*, a series of variations; *Ein Heldenleben*, sonatalike. Other pieces are sectional but always based on musical logic as well as some external idea.

The rondo and theme and variations sometimes formed the basis for a single movement, either as part of a multimovement sonata (including symphony, concerto, and string quartet) or as a complete composition, as in the works of Strauss, Brahms's *Variations on a Theme by Haydn,* Liszt's *Totentanz,* or Schubert's Rondo in b, op. 70.

During the nineteenth century, composers also modernized the older baroque suite and the classic divertimento and serenade. The sequence of movements was no longer necessarily a set of dances. In most instances a program was suggested: Tchaikovsky's *The Sleeping Beauty,* Bizet's *L'Arlésienne* Suites 1 and 2, Grieg's *Peer Gynt Suites 1 and 2,* and Mussorgsky's *Pictures at an Exhibition* are examples.

Opera, of course, flourished, as in the Italian operas of Verdi and the music dramas of Wagner. Formal patterns gradually gave way to more flexible structures in an attempt to achieve dramatic continuity.

The Mass and oratorio did not exactly thrive, but important contributions like Mendelssohn's *Elijah,* Brahms's *Ein Deutsches Requiem,* Verdi's *Requiem,* and Bruckner's *Masses* are still performed. In the Mass and oratorio (both based on a series of individual movements) solo voices, solo ensembles, and choruses sing against moderate-sized to extremely large orchestras. The *Grande Messe des Morts* (Requiem) and *Te Deum* of Berlioz require enormous orchestras with large choruses to balance. Schubert, Liszt, and Bruckner, among others, contributed Masses and other religious vocal music, not all of it suitable for church service. Almost all composers produced some secular choral music, among which the *Schicksalslied* (*Song of Fate*), for chorus and orchestra, by Brahms is outstanding.

During the romantic period, the formality of a Mozart—precise, well conceived, cleanly articulated, and fairly predictable—was replaced with the sweeping gesture of a Liszt—dramatic, effusive, bold, colorful, and often unpredictable. As we have seen, many of the older forms of music continued to be found in the nineteenth century, but they have an expansiveness and freedom characteristic of their close association with extramusical ideas.

Representative pieces

1. FRANZ PETER SCHUBERT (1797–1828)

If Beethoven, the giant, seems to stand above any convenient classification, Schubert, who at age 31 died only a year after Beethoven, surely belongs with those composers labelled romantic. In a short life he poured forth an amazing number of symphonies, piano sonatas, chamber works, Masses, and over six hundred songs. Bedevilled by grim everyday necessities, unacknowledged by the public, and plagued by sickness and poverty, he constantly turned his thoughts to composing music, much of which is still performed today.

It is in his songs that Schubert's range of musical expression is most characteristic. The solo song with piano accompaniment provided Schubert with the greatest opportunity to use his incomparable gift for writing melodies with colorful harmonic accompaniments—beautiful melodic line, carefully attentive to the spirit of the text, is supported by an entirely appropriate piano part, the result being a perfect blend of all contributing elements. The spirit of the songs varies from simple folklike to highly dramatic. Some songs are in simple strophic forms, with literal or slightly modified repetitions of the music for each stanza. Others, like our example, ○● *Der Wanderer,* op. 4, no. 1, capture the poetic subtleties by continual changes in the various musical elements.

Written in October, 1816, and first published in 1821, *Der Wanderer* deals with a typical romantic theme, the longing of a wanderer far from his beloved home. The mood is immediately set in the piano introduction, with the triplet patterns and dissonances in the right hand and the recurring pedal point in the left. Within six measures the dynamic level moves from very soft through a *crescendo* to a *sforzando* (sudden stress) and a return to soft. Over a sustained chord the voice enters and ascends in recitativelike fashion. The mood of the opening persists, but by the words "Ich wandle still" ("I wander silently") the key has shifted from minor to major. Quickly Schubert returns to the minor key, ending the first section with a hold on the text "immer wo?" ("Always where?").

The following measures, marked *pianissimo,* are set to a steady chordal accompaniment. At "Wo bist du" the rhythmic pulse accelerates moderately. The strong beat of each measure is followed by a brief four-note motive in the accompaniment. As the wanderer remembers the pleasures of his own land ("Das Land"), the meter changes to a fast § and the key to major. At "O Land, wo bist du?" the original tempo is reestablished, and shortly thereafter Schubert returns to material heard before ("Ich wandle still").

The final words of the text, " 'Dort, wo du nicht bist, dort ist das Glück!' " (" 'There where you are not, there is happiness!' "), announce a tragic sentiment frequently echoed by Baudelaire, Alfred de Musset, Leopardi, and many other romantically inclined minds. Schubert has given it musical expression in this song.

I come from the mountains,	*Ich komme vom Gebirge her,*
The valley mists, the sea roars.	*Es dampft das Tal, es braust das Meer.*
I wander silently with little joy,	*Ich wandle still, bin wenig froh,*
And always my sighs ask: Where? Always where?	*Und immer fragt der Seufzer: wo? immer wo?*
The sun seems so cold here,	*Die Sonne dünkt mich hier so kalt,*
The flowers faded, life old,	*Die Blüte welk, das Leben alt,*
And what people say, empty sound;	*Und was sie reden, leerer Schall,*
I am a stranger everywhere.	*Ich bin ein Fremdling überall.*
Where are you, my beloved land?	*Wo bist du, mein beliebtes Land?*
Sought, dreamed about, but never found!	*Gesucht, geahnt, und nie gekannt!*
The land, the land so green with hope,	*Das Land, das Land so hoffnungsgrün,*
The land where my roses bloom,	*Das Land, wo meine Rosen blühn,*
Where my friends go roaming,	*Wo meine Freunde wandelnd gehn,*
Where my dead are resurrected,	*Wo meine Toten auferstehn,*

The land where my language is spoken—
O land, where are you?

I wander silently, with little joy,
And always my sighs ask: Where? Always where?

A ghostly whisper answers me:
"There where you are not,
There is happiness!"

Das Land, das meine Sprache spricht,
O Land, wo bist du?

Ich wandle still, bin wenig froh,
Und immer fragt der Seufzer: wo, immer wo?

Im Geisterhauch tönt's mir zurück:
"Dort, wo du nicht bist,
Dort ist das Glück!"

2. HECTOR BERLIOZ (1803–1869)

Berlioz, like many of his fellow romantics, lived life to the hilt. Volatile, passionate, imaginative, and talented, he sought relief for his abundant energies by fiercely fighting for his ideals, by writing letters, memoires, criticism, and a book on orchestration, and by composing music inspired by extramusical ideas. His was an intriguing personality, so much so that who he was, what he believed, and what he did as a person and the intrinsic musical qualities in his compositions are not cleanly separated. His detractors, like Heinrich Heine, may cynically remark that Berlioz did not possess sufficient talent for his genius; his admirers assert his originality, pointing to many imaginative passages.

Surrounded by painters, writers, and musicians excited by romantic themes. Berlioz composed his *Symphonie fantastique (Fantastic Symphony)*, op. 14, in 1830 at the height of the French romantic movement. Like his other works the symphony has a program: An "episode in the life of an artist," it depicts a young man, disappointed in love, who takes an overdose of opium and is then subjected to nightmares in which his beloved, represented by a musical *idée fixe* (a recurring theme), appears in various guises. The first four movements are called "Reveries and Passions," "A Ball," "In the Country," and "March to the Scaffold." Our recorded excerpt, finale, is o "Dream of a Witches' Sabbath." The program illuminates Berlioz's intention: "He sees himself at a Witches' Sabbath. . . . Unearthly sounds, groans, shrieks of laughter . . . The melody of his beloved [*idée fixe*] is heard, no longer noble, but base and vulgar. . . . It is She who comes to the Sabbath. . . . She joins the diabolical orgy. . . . The funeral knell, burlesque of the *Dies Irae* . . . Dance of the Witches . . . The dance and the *Dies Irae* are combined."

With such a program in mind, Berlioz, intentionally or not, raised an interesting problem in aesthetics: the deliberate use of the dissonant, the ugly, the grotesque, the disagreeable, and the hideous in a work of art. This is most striking when the ancient and solemn religious plainchant, the Dies Irae, is heard with wild and satanic sounds.

To achieve his effects Berlioz used a large orchestra. Added to the standard Haydn-Mozart orchestra are such instruments as piccolo, E♭ clarinet, two additional bassoons, two additional horns, two cornets, two trumpets, three trombones, two tubas, additional timpani, a bass drum, and two bells. Berlioz not only uses a larger orchestra than does Beethoven but also handles his instrumental resources differently, mainly in his efforts to achieve colorful effects. For example, he requires a muted horn to play *pppp* (two stages softer than *pianissimo!*) and throughout the score carefully specifies exact details about how each instrument is to articulate the music it plays. In this work the element of tone color becomes a crucial one in the total musical impact.

3. FRÉDÉRIC FRANÇOIS CHOPIN (1810–1849)

In Chopin we find a musical specialist. Composers before him had tended to write music of various kinds: symphonies, concertos, operas, chamber music, and songs. Chopin, on the contrary, wrote almost exclusively for the piano: études, *ballades,* scherzos, nocturnes, waltzes, impromptus, mazurkas, polonaises, and other individual pieces in addition to three sonatas and two piano concertos. His style has a distinct flavor, one more readily identifiable than that of many other composers. Like Schubert, he had a magnificent melodic gift, but it was tied closely to the piano instead of the voice. Rich, sometimes spectacular, harmonies in his music resulted from his exploitation of triads and seventh and ninth chords and his daring modulations. Finger technique, touch, use of pedals, dynamic changes, shifting textures, much use of *rubato,* and rhythmic variety all contribute to Chopin's general style. At another level, there are many Chopin styles: intimate, improvisatory, introspective, dancelike, brilliant, vigorous, and virtuoso.

The recorded example is the well-known ○● Fantaisie-Impromptu in c♯, op. 66, no. 4; written in 1834, it represents music of the kind enjoyed in French salon society of the period. Cast in a large *ABA*-coda ternary form, both the melodic and harmonic elements are highly chromatic.

Two themes dominate, one pianistic and the other a lyrical tune that, transformed into popular idiom, became ''I'm Always Chasing Rainbows.''

Technical problems abound for the pianist, not the least of which relate to rhythm: In the opening section a fast 4 against 3 is demanded, but in the B section (*moderato cantabile*) a slower 2 against 3; in the first section a steady pulse should be maintained, whereas in the second the performer must fight a tendency to drag, to sentimentalize the lyrical theme. The Fantaisie-Impromptu, long a favorite recital piece, combines within its form some very typical Chopin traits. It may not represent the most profound piece he wrote, but it has had an undeniable appeal for almost a century and a half.

4. RICHARD WAGNER (1813–1883)

Another specialist appears with Wagner, whose name is inseparable from opera, or, as he preferred to call it, ''music drama.'' Wagner was a man of controversial ideas on art and life in general and seemed never to hesitate to express his opinions. He wrote, pamphleteered, cajoled, argued, and won and lost many friends throughout a long, stormy life. Ruthless and tenacious in the pursuit of his artistic goals, he seized every possible opportunity if he thought it would further his career.

Along the way he managed to create eleven large-scale music dramas, which he hoped would raise the theater to the level of German symphonic music. Too long had French and Italian opera influenced a solid Germanic operatic tradition; Wagner determined to erase these foreign intrusions by creating an art form worthy of his Teutonic ''race.'' True art must be an expression of a people, an objectification of a communal spirit, and it must also be, according to Wagner, a totality, a participation of various arts united in a single drama: Music and poetry were to be joined; through them and the total environment in which the work unfolded, a drama expressive of a race was to emerge.

To realize his theories, Wagner called upon legend and myth, setting his music dramas in the heroic Teutonic past. Figures like Tannhauser, Lohengrin, Tristan, Siegfried, and Parsifal, reborn in his operas, would symbolize the aspirations of his people. Melody, by closely following speech accents, was to flow naturally and uninterruptedly, a procedure that struck at the traditional operatic ''set aria.'' Repetition, balance, and symmetry of phrase had to give way, in Wagner's code, to a never-ending melody, which attempted to capture the emotional nuances of the poetry. Harmony, instead of being a series of chord progressions, was to arise out of polyphony, a combination of melodies. Like melody, this harmony was to be flexible, as fluid as thought itself, often avoiding any suggestion of symmetry or inevitability. Moreover, Wagner's music was conceived in a different scope of time from that, for example, of a Beethoven piano sonata. His operas nevertheless depend upon tonality to help unify large structures. The drama inherent in a 30-minute sonata is now stretched over a 3-hour period or so. The drama and the entire tonal structure moves, accordingly, at a different pace than the sonata does. Yet another means of unification is the use of *leitmotifs,* which musically identify a person (Siegfried, for example), a thing (Valhalla), a state of mind (love), or an abstraction (fate). Each leitmotif, generally short, has its own distinct melodic shape and is also associated with a distinct rhythm, with a set of two or three chords, and occasionally with a particular orchestral tone color. Wagner's leitmotifs provide extra insights into the literal and external situations on stage at any given moment.

For special effects Wagner increased the size of the orchestra. In requiring wind instruments like the English horn, bass clarinet, contra-bassoon, serpent, bass trumpet, contrabass trombone, and ophicleide, he also needed a larger string group to balance the additional winds. Kettledrums, the standard percussion unit of the classic orchestra, now shared honors with the triangle, cymbals, tambourine, bass drum, snare drum, and bells.

Between 1848 and 1874 Wagner labored to complete the gigantic *Der Ring des Nibelungen,* a series of four unified music dramas: *Das Rheingold, Die Walküre, Siegfried,* and *Götterdämmerung.* He interrupted work on this project to write two of his greatest masterpieces: *Tristan und Isolde* (1859) and *Die Meistersinger von Nürnberg* (1867).

Tristan und Isolde exemplifies Wagner's attraction to legend and medieval epic. Like many of his other efforts, it demonstrates his philosophical belief in the power of symbolic figures and things. As such, he is dealing more with ideas and forces than with believeable, real people. In *Tristan* (as elsewhere) Wagner interweaves ideas—redemption by love, renunciation, honor, fate—into a complicated plot.

The recorded excerpt is one of the great moments from this opera:

the song of Isolde, the lament that closes the work after Tristan, her lover, dies in her arms. The pathos of the ○● "Liebestod," a supreme scene in romantic music, may well be compared to Dido's famous lament from Purcell's *Dido and Aeneas* (see Chapter 10). The seventeenth-century composer portrays his tragedy over a ground bass, in one key, with a small string orchestra and continuo, whereas Wagner calls for a large orchestra: his viola section is divided into two parts and the cello section into four parts in the opening measures (it is unlikely that Purcell had four cellos in his entire orchestra). Key changes, chromatic harmonies, deceptive cadences, chords of the seventh and ninth, close attention to tone color, and thick texture characterize Wagner's music. In the "Liebestod" voice and orchestra blend, instruments being given important thematic material and the voice at times merging into the orchestral fabric. The rise and fall of emotional tension is effected by changing dynamic levels. Wagner chooses to end his most passionate of music dramas by an extended plagal ("amen") cadence. As Isolde joins Tristan in death, the music slowly and quietly whispers the final chord.

See how he smiles, softly and gently,	*Mild und leise wie er lächelt,*
how fondly he opens his eyes—	*wie das Auge hold er öffnet—*
do you see, friends? Do you not see it?	*seht ihr's, Freunde? Seht ihr's nicht?*
See how he shines, always brighter,	*Immer lichter wie er leuchtet,*
glowing in starlight, does he not soar high?	*stern-umstrahlet hoch sich hebt?*
Do you not see	*Seht ihr's nicht?*
how his heart bravely swells,	*Wie das Herz ihm mutig schwillt,*
how it throbs full and calm in his breast?	*voll und hehr im Busen ihm quillt?*
How his lips, blissfully mild,	*Wie den Lippen, wonnig mild,*
how his sweet breath softly flutters?	*süsser Atem sanft entweht—*
Friends! See! Do you not feel and see?	*Freunde! Seht! Fühlt und seht ihr's nicht?*
Is it only I who hear this melody—	*Hör' ich nur diese Weise*
one so wonderful and gentle—	*die so wundervoll und leise,*
bewailing an ecstasy, saying all,	*Wonne klagend, alles sagend,*
sweetly reconciling, sounding from him,	*mild versöhnend aus ihm tönend,*
piercing me, rising upward,	*in mich dringet, auf sich schwinget,*
fondly echoing, around me ringing?	*hold erhallend um mich klinget?*
More clearly sounding, around me drifting,	*Heller schallend, mich umwallend,*
are they waves of gentle breezes?	*sind es Wellen sanfter Lüfte?*

Are they clouds of delicious perfumes?
As they swell and rustle around me,
shall I breathe, shall I listen?
Shall I sip, plunge under?
In their sweet fragrances breathe my last?
In the wavy flood, in the resounding noise,
in the world-spirit's infinite all—
to drown, sink down,
unconscious—
highest bliss!

Sind es Wogen wonniger Düfte?
Wie sie schwellen, mich umrauschen,
soll ich atmen, soll ich lauschen?
soll ich schlürfen, untertauchen?
Süss in Düften mich verhauchen?
In dem wogenden Schwall, in dem tönenden Schall,
in des Welt-Atems wehendem All—
ertrinken, versinken—
unbewusst—
höchste Lust!

5. FRANZ LISZT (1811–1886)

Perhaps the greatest pianist who has ever lived, Franz Liszt was also one of the most fascinating personalities of the nineteenth century. A dazzling virtuoso, a famous conductor, a prolific composer, and a darling of a fickle public, he later took minor orders and became an abbé in the Roman Catholic Church. His life was filled with contradictions in attitudes, playing, and creative work.

As a composer, Liszt's strong point was not his melodic invention but his sense of harmony, for often his melodies are derived from rich and daring harmonies. Unusual relationships in chord progressions, many deceptive cadences, a preference for the sound of the diminished seventh chord, and an extensive use of nonharmonic notes distinguish his powerful harmonic vocabulary.

Like Berlioz, Liszt was attracted to program music. A man of many musical ideas, he sometimes seems to introduce and then abandon one idea after another within a single work—a procedure not conducive to tightly knit, well-organized compositions. Because of the abundance of themes and their transformations, his works often give the feeling of spontaneous improvisation. Nevertheless, he made important contributions to musical form: (1) the refinement of the symphonic tone poem, (2) successful attempts to create sonatas and concertos in one continuous movement, and (3) the idea of transformation of theme: changing the character of a theme melodically, harmonically, and rhythmically (often because of programmatic ideas). Following leads given by Beethoven and Berlioz, he also used the chorus in his *Dante* and *Faust* symphonies.

Liszt's orchestral style in the symphonies, concertos, and tone poems can be colorful and brilliant although sometimes extravagant. He prefers a large orchestra and heavy brass and percussion sections and often uses small groups of solo instruments. The treatment of dynamics is romantic, extremes of loud and soft, long swells and diminutions, *sforzandi*, and *subito piano* (very suddenly soft) generally making for exciting listening.

This glamorous pianist naturally wrote well for his instrument. The recorded example is from the ○ Concerto for Piano and Orchestra in E♭, which took shape over a number of years, a first version being ready by 1849, with alterations in 1853 and 1856. The entire concerto is about 18 minutes long. Only the first movement is on our record.

The form can best be characterized as loose, capable of description but not fitting any of the standard structures. The rhythm is sometimes strict, sometimes free, the latter resulting from holds, *rubato,* cadenzas, and similar devices. Melodies tend to be emotional, with extensive ranges. Liszt's writing for the solo instrument makes strong demands on the pianist. Spectacular octave passages, difficult arpeggiated patterns, and wide leaps, together with the rhythmic flexibility and the contrasting lyrical parts, have made the concerto a popular work. Virtuoso pianists have enjoyed the challenges, and audiences seem to have enjoyed the pianists—perhaps as much as, or even more than, the music!

6. JOHANNES BRAHMS (1833–1897)

Brahms, unlike Berlioz, Liszt, and Wagner before him, was conservative. A romantic by nature and given to introspection, he nevertheless admired classic ideals to such an extent that he successfully handled and mastered those forms which Mozart and Beethoven had naturally adopted. Careful workmanship is always evident in his music. His symphonies, concertos, chamber music, songs, and piano and choral music continue to find favorable reception in recital and concert halls.

Melody in Brahms is varied: folksong influences, lyrical tunes, and simple triadic melodies are encountered. Frequently the phrase structure is complicated by being unexpectedly shortened or extended. Combined with Brahms's intricate rhythms, this type of flexible phrase structure makes for challenging listening. It is not uncommon to find the normal accents within the measure completely displaced. Texture tends to be thick, in part because of doublings either at the octave or at the third or sixth and in part because of his contrapuntal fluency, which results from concern for the movement of the inner voices. Orchestration is not the colorful, sparkling element that it is in Berlioz. In Brahms, the craftsman precedes the colorist, the idea outweighs the medium.

o *Ein deutsches Requiem* (*A German Requiem*), a choral work of the fully mature composer, dates from 1868. Brahms, whose songs show sensitive poetic insights, here worked in similar fashion with German text, with the result that this setting, like that of many of his songs, loses some of its finer qualities when sung in English translation.

After a brief orchestral introduction, the fourth movement, which is our recorded excerpt, opens with a beautifully contoured melody sung by the sopranos, the other three parts providing independent contrapuntal lines. This phrase is 9 measures long; after a brief orchestral interlude, an 8-measure phrase follows. The next choral entrance begins with the tenors alone, and 9 measures later the basses enter in imitation, quickly followed by altos and sopranos entering simultaneously. Having established two patterns of writing for his choral forces, Brahms switches back and forth between full, four-part, homophonic-polyphonic mixed texture (like the opening) and imitative entrances in contrapuntal style (the second pattern).

The middle section of the movement, beginning with the words "Meine Seele verlanget," develops his ideas through modulation. The opening melody returns in the tonic key, the same 9-measure phrase this time followed by a different 8-measure phrase. A few measures later Brahms begins a double fugue: Two subjects, one of which moves in more rapid notes, are heard at the same time; first the sopranos and basses and then altos and tenors enter in pairs with the words "die loben dich immerdar." These and the succeeding measures reveal Brahms's mastery of counterpoint. Phrases are lengthened and shortened, cross rhythms complicate the motion, and the harmonies create a sense of unrest through their avoidance of a cadence until the melody descends, the motion subsides, and the dynamic level becomes *piano*. The climax is followed by a short coda.

How lovely are thy dwellings, thou Lord of Hosts!
My soul hath a desire and longing to enter into the courts of the Lord;

Wie lieblich sind deine Wohnungen, Herr Zebaoth!
Meine Seele verlanget und sehnet sich nach den Vorhöfen des Herrn;

My heart and my flesh rejoice in the living God;
Blessed are they that dwell in thy house, they will always be praising thee.

Mein Leib und Seele freuen sich in dem lebendigen Gott,
Wohl denen, die in deinem Hause wohnen, die loben dich immerdar.

7. GIUSEPPE VERDI (1813–1901)

While Wagner was attempting to establish his theories of music drama in a series of stage works, most Italian operatic composers continued to work in the traditional number opera, consisting of separate arias, duets, solo ensembles, choruses, and recitatives. Strung together, such numbers provide a kind of dramatic continuity, each constituting a more or less self-contained unit. Under this method of composition, arias taken out of context and sung as individual pieces—in a vocal recital, for example—can make good musical sense. Generally, the plot of the opera is unfolded in the recitatives, which usually move the action along to some particular situation, at which point the aria, duet, ensemble, or chorus, by reflective commentary in lyrical song, portray some emotional state of an individual or group. In effect, then, the drama moves by stops and starts, almost suspended at times during an extended aria but moving rapidly during the recitatives. There are relatively few continuous dramatic scenes, owing partly to the organization just described and partly to the voice's being the center of attention. During the last half of the century, Italian opera was dominated by Verdi and Puccini, both of whom seem to have been more selective in their choice of stories than were some of their predecessors and contemporaries. In pursuit of their own dramatic goals, these two composers also modified, sometimes radically, the number-opera concept: Verdi's *Aida,* for example, is not a typical number opera although ○● "Celeste Aida" (and other sections) can bear isolation, as our recorded example demonstrates. Verdi's texture is primarily homophonic, in which the dramatic quality of the human voice is intensified by careful orchestral support; so vocal melody predominates while the harmony supports and accompanies. Even in Verdi's later operas, where there is less emphasis on melody and more important characterization of the text in the orchestral instruments, the voice is never submerged. Dramatic recitative is accompanied by the orchestra, which enhances the stage action through devices like string *tremolo* or outbursts of chords or highly colorful and suggestive instrumentation. In Verdi's aesthetic, characterization of persons and events plus good dramatic continuity are essential. Because his figures live the human condition and his vocal melodies are simple, direct, and easily remembered, most of his operas have been enormously popular.

Verdi was at the height of his career when he wrote *Aida,* first performed in Cairo on December 24, 1871. Set in ancient Egypt, the story centers around the mutual love of Radames, captain of the Egyptian army, and Aida, an Ethiopian princess who has been enslaved by Amneris, also in love with Radames. Jealousies and tormenting conflicts between love and duty plague all the principal figures: Although Radames is about to march against Aida's father, who leads the Ethiopians, he hopes to return victorious and lay his laurels before the enslaved princess. His sentiments are expressed in "Celeste Aida," a solo tenor aria considered to be one of the greatest in all operatic literature.

Heavenly Aida, beauty resplendent,
Mysterious twining of flowers and light,
Queen of my soul who reignest transcendent,
Thou of my life art the splendor bright.

To thy bright skies once more I'd restore thee,
To the soft air of thy native land;
With garlands imperial would I crown thee,
Raise thee a throne near the sun to stand, ah!

Celeste Aida, forma divina,
Mistico serto di luce e fior,
del mio pensiero, tu sei regina,
tu di mia vita sei lo splendor.

Il tuo bel cielo vorrei ridarti,
le dolci brezze del patria suol;
un regal serto sul crin posarti,
ergerti un trono vicino al sol, ah!

[First four lines repeated with same music.]

[Second four lines repeated with different music.]

8. PIOTR ILYICH TCHAIKOVSKY (1840–1893)

Along with the urge to explore the romantic past, the unusual, and the exotic, composers in the latter half of the nineteenth century self-consciously began to promote the cultural heritage of which they were a part. Folksong, folkdance, natural landscape, and national legends provided immediate sources of inspiration. Since this nationalistic music relied heavily on local color, orchestration in which special timbres were needed became very important. Orchestras grew quite large, containing at least two each of the woodwinds (flutes, oboes, clarinets, bassoons), four horns, three trumpets, three trombones, timpani, and strings. Additional instruments of special tone color were added: piccolo, English horn, bass clarinet, contrabassoon, and percussion instruments such as cymbals, triangle, bass drum, snare drum, and various noisemakers. With highly colorful orchestration, strong, vibrant rhythms, tuneful melodies, and rich, chromatic harmonies, it is little wonder that music of this kind has had such wide appeal.

The art of Tchaikovsky is now regarded as distinctly Russian in flavor, even though some of his contemporaries thought him to be ''too Western.'' A composer who sought to emotionalize music to the extreme, Tchaikovsky indulges in huge climaxes by blaring brasses, cymbal crashes, strings and winds in high registers, and dynamic levels as loud as possible. At the other extreme, somber, melancholy melodies in low registers will slowly move in a whisper. Whether gay and dancelike, lyrical, pensive, or sorrowful, his melodies are set to harmonies, rhythms, and orchestration to match the momentary mood.

Of the six symphonies written by Tchaikovsky only the last three are performed regularly. ○● Symphony 5, in e, op. 64, completed in 1888, precedes his last symphony, the *Pathétique,* by 5 years. The first and fourth movements are sonata-allegro forms with introduction and coda. The second movement is a large-scale *ABA* (ternary) form.

Our recorded excerpt is the third movement, a waltz; it also is ternary, with an extensive coda. Its main section is based on a lyrical theme heard first in the violins and later in the bassoons. The melody is mainly diatonic, in stepwise motion and in the opening two measures descending. The contrasting trio section, in f♯, is characterized by violins playing *spiccato* (bouncing bow). After the return of the main waltz section, a coda, which continues to rely on the waltz rhythm, completes the movement.

Near the end of this movement, Tchaikovsky introduces the ''motto'' theme found in all four movements of the symphony (*pianissimo* in clarinet and bassoon). Based on a distinctive rhythmic pattern, this motto theme helps to unify the entire symphony and to set a prevailing mood of resignation and pessimism. Intruding at this point in the otherwise gracious waltz movement, the motto serves to remind the listener of the first two movements.

Tchaikovsky's compositional technique in this movement is worth comment. The initial waltz is set simply: a melody harmonized in a waltz rhythm. The second section introduces sixteenth-note patterns that are tossed about, fragmented, and given to contrasting groups of instruments. In the third section, where the waltz theme returns, this pattern continues only through the statement of the first phrase of the waltz, after which the rest of the section is practically a literal repetition of the opening section. With the coda, chromatic harmonies are heard prior to the *pianissimo* motto theme. The movement ends with six *fortissimo* chords in full orchestra.

Other important music

For some additional pieces by composers of this period, see the Music Index.

Two volumes in RCA Victor's *The History of Music in Sound*, VI, *The Age of Beethoven (1790–1830)*, and VII, *Romanticism (1830–1900)*, contain six LP records covering the period from early romanticism to its gradual disappearance around 1900. The recordings are accompanied by two booklets descriptive of the background of the music heard. (See also Chapter 11.) Besides Beethoven and Schubert, there were many important composers writing in the first three decades of the century. Excerpts from the music of Luigi Cherubini, Méhul, Gasparo Spontini, Louis Spohr, Rossini, and Weber are included and a composer every young pianist has probably encountered, Clementi. But how many have heard of Jan Ladislav Dussek, Johann Rudolf Zumsteeg, Johan Nepomuka Hummel, and Jaroslav Tomášek? The wide range of selections will assist any student in capturing the flavor of the Napoleon-Talleyrand period. Volume VII covers the height of romanticism to its last stages at the end of the century. Some very important composers are missing, for example, Wagner and Brahms, presumably in an effort to provide music by other representative romantics like Meyerbeer, Heinrich August Marschner, Paganini, Mikhail Ivanovich Glinka, Henri Duparc, and Ernest Amédée Chausson. More familiar composers include Berlioz, Liszt, Schumann, Mendelssohn, and Grieg. Like Volume VI, this volume records a panorama of typical music composed during the period that we have been discussing.

The following pages divide music of the nineteenth century into the most important genres. The listener will find it most instructive to trace the development of a single type of composition under the hands of different composers. (To include a complete list of works still forming part of present-day repertories would unduly extend this book.) *Compositions already referred to in the body of the text are not listed here.*

OPERAS

C. M. VON WEBER
Der Freischütz (1821).

VINCENZO BELLINI
Norma (1831).

H. BERLIOZ
Les Troyens (1856–1858).

C. GOUNOD
Faust (1869).

G. VERDI
La Forza del Destino (1869).
Falstaff (1893).

PIETRO MASCAGNI
Cavalleria rusticana (1890).

RUGGIERO LEONCAVALLO
Pagliacci (1892).

R. STRAUSS
Salome (1905).
Elektra (1909).
Der Rosenkavalier (1911).

CHORAL MUSIC

F. LISZT
Christus (1865).

C. FRANCK
Les Béatitudes (1879).

E. W. ELGAR
The Dream of Gerontius (1900).

SONGS

F. P. SCHUBERT
"Gretchen am Spinnrade," op. 2 (1814).
"Erlkönig," op. 1 (1815).

"Heidenröslein," op. 3, no. 3 (1815).

"Der Tod und das Mädchen," op. 7, no. 3 (1817).

"Die Forelle," op. 32 (1817).

"Du bist die Ruh'," op. 59, no. 3 (1823).

R. SCHUMANN

"Die Lotusblume," op. 25, no. 7 (1840).

"Du bist wie eine Blume," op. 25, no. 24 (1840).

"Die beiden Grenadiere," op. 49, no. 1 (1840).

F. MENDELSSOHN

"Neue Liebe," op. 19*a*, no. 4 (*ca.* 1832).

"Nachtlied," op. 71, no. 6 (1847).

F. LISZT

"Die Lorelei" (1841).

"Wanderers Nachtlied" (1848).

ROBERT FRANZ

"Für Musik," op. 10, no. 1 (*ca.* 1850).

J. BRAHMS

"Die Mainacht," op. 43, no. 2 (*ca.* 1868).

"An die Nachtigall," op. 46, no. 4 (*ca.* 1868).

"O wüsst' ich doch den Weg zurück," op. 63, no. 8 (1873–1874).

"Sapphische Ode," op. 94, no. 4 (1884).

"Der Tod, der ist die kühle Nacht," op. 96, no. 1 (1886).

H. WOLF

"Im Frühling" (1888).

"An die Geliebte" (1888).

"Auf ein altes Bild" (1888).

"Anakreons Grab" (1890).

R. STRAUSS

"Cäcilie," op. 27, no. 2 (1893–1894).

"Morgen," op. 27, no. 4 (1893–1894).

"Traum durch die Dämmerung," op. 29, no. 1 (1894–1895).

SONG CYCLE

M. P. MUSSORGSKY

Songs and Dances of Death (1875).

CONCERTOS

F. F. CHOPIN

For Piano and Orchestra in e, op. 11 (1830).

F. MENDELSSOHN

For Violin and Orchestra in e, op. 64 (1844).

R. SCHUMANN

For Piano and Orchestra in a, op. 54 (1845).

For Cello and Orchestra in a, op. 129 (1850).

F. LISZT

Totentanz for Piano and Orchestra (1859).

For Piano and Orchestra 2 in A (1839, revised 1849–1861).

E. H. GRIEG

For Piano and Orchestra in a, op. 16 (1868).

J. BRAHMS

For Piano and Orchestra in d, op. 15 (1858).

For Violin and Orchestra in D, op. 77 (1878).

For Piano and Orchestra in B♭, op. 83 (1881).

P. I. TCHAIKOVSKY

For Violin and Orchestra in D, op. 35 (1878).

C. FRANCK

Variations symphoniques (1885).

A. DVOŘÁK

For Cello and Orchestra in b, op. 104 (1895).

SYMPHONIES

R. SCHUMANN

3 in E♭, op. 97 (*Rhenish*) (1850).

A. BRUCKNER

4 in E♭ (*Romantic*) (1874).

J. BRAHMS

1 in c, op. 68 (1876).

A. P. BORODIN

2 in b (1877).

A. DVOŘÁK
5 in e, op. 95 (*From the New World*) (1893).
G. MAHLER
5 in c♯ (1902).

PROGRAM SYMPHONY

H. BERLIOZ
Harold en Italie, op. 16 (1834).

SYMPHONIC POEMS

P. I. TCHAIKOVSKY
Romeo and Juliet (1870).
M. P. MUSSORGSKY
A Night on the Bare Mountain (*ca.* 1872).
CAMILLE SAINT-SAËNS
Danse macabre, op. 40 (1874).
A. N. SKRIABIN
Symphony 3, op. 32 (*The Divine Poem*) (1905).
The Poem of Ecstasy, op. 54 (1908).
Prometheus, op. 60 (1911).

OTHER SYMPHONIC MUSIC

F. LISZT
Mephisto Waltz (1858–1860).
J. BRAHMS
Academic Festival Overture, op. 80 (1880).
N. A. RIMSKY-KORSAKOV
Scheherazade, op. 35 (1888).
A. P. BORODIN
Prince Igor: Polovetsian Dances (1889).
P. I. TCHAIKOVSKY
Casse-Noisette (*Nutcracker*) Suite, op. 71 (1892).
E. W. ELGAR
Variations on an Original Theme (*Enigma*), op. 36 (1899).
G. MAHLER

Das Lied von der Erde (1907–1910)

CHAMBER MUSIC

R. SCHUMANN
Quartet for Strings in A, op. 41, no. 3 (1842).

F. MENDELSSOHN
Quartet for Strings in f, op. 80 (1847).

B. SMETANA
Quartet for Strings in e (*Aus meinen Leben*) (1876).

C. FRANCK
Quintet for Piano and Strings in f (1879).

J. BRAHMS
Quintet for Piano and Strings in f, op. 34*a* (1864).
Trio for Piano, Violin, and Horn, op. 40 (1865).
Sextet for Strings in G, op. 36 (1867).
Quartet for Strings in B♭, op. 67 (1876).
Sonata for Violin and Piano in A, op. 100 (1886).
Trio for Piano and Strings in c, op. 101 (1886).

A. DVOŘÁK
Quartet for Strings in F, op. 96 (*American*) (1893).

PIANO MUSIC

F. P. SCHUBERT
Der Wanderer Fantasia, D. 760 (1822).
Sonata for Piano in B♭, D. 960 (1828).

R. SCHUMANN
Fantasiestücke (1837).
Davidsbündlertänze (1837, revised 1850).

F. MENDELSSOHN
Variations sérieuses in d, op. 54 (1841).

F. F. CHOPIN
Scherzo in b, op. 20 (1831–1832).
Ballade in g, op. 23 (1831–1835).
Prelude in D♭, op. 28, no. 15 ("Raindrop") (1836–1839).
Sonata in b♭, op. 35 (1839).
Impromptu in F♯, op. 36 (1839).

Nocturne in E♭, op. 55, no. 2 (1843).
Sonata in b, op. 58 (1844).

M. P. MUSSORGSKY

Pictures at an Exhibition (1874).

J. BRAHMS

Rhapsodie in b, op. 79, no. 1 (1879).
Pieces from opp. 116, 117, 118, or 119.

C. FRANCK

Prelude, Chorale, and Fugue (1884).

Further readings

IMMEDIATELY USEFUL

BURCHELL, S. C. (ED.)   *Age of Progress*, Time-Life Books, New York, 1966. In the Time-Life series *Great Ages of Man*. This volume presents, in eight essays with numerous illustrations, underlying ideas of the nineteenth century. Its science, technologies, arts, politics, and wars are compared with "progress." Little attention is given to music.

HUGO, HOWARD E. (ED.)   *The Portable Romantic Reader*, The Viking Press, Inc., New York, 1957. Similar to companion volumes in the Viking Portable series. Unequalled as a single book that captures, through extracts from romantic writers themselves, the spirit and variety of romanticism. Brief selections give readers the flavor of poetry, drama, novel, confessional autobiographies, letters, manifestoes, and critical essays. An excellent book to browse through, it confirms the idea of a movement into which composers like Berlioz, Liszt, and Schumann fit.

LOVEJOY, ARTHUR   "On the Discrimination of Romanticisms," in *Essays in the History of Ideas*, The Johns Hopkins Press, Baltimore, 1948. This essay, now considered a classic, was written by the former editor of *The Journal of the History of Ideas*. Profound and searching in his analysis, the writer probes the question of definition and concludes that romanticism, a collection of sometimes conflicting and opposing elements, may be apprehended other than by some neat definition.

WEBER, EUGEN (ED.)   *Paths to the Present*, Dodd, Mead & Co., New York, 1960. Subtitled *Aspects of European Thought from Romanticism to Existentialism*, the collection provides an excellent survey of typical writings from Wordsworth, Hugo, Baudelaire, Zola, Wilde, and Nietzsche to Malraux, Sartre, and Camus. Length of the extracts ranges from a page or so to over twenty. The editor has selected typical and controversial readings and has divided them into seven sections ("Romanticism," "Positivistic Reaction," "Consciousness and Confusion,"

"Social Awareness," "Literature of Disillusions," "New Individualism"), each of which is chronologically ordered. The first section is especially useful for our Chapter 12, the other sections presenting ideas that mainly postdate romanticism. In this respect the volume traces the development and evolution of many twentieth-century ideas.

OTHER STUDIES

ATKINS, STUART P. *The Testament of Werther in Poetry and Drama,* Harvard University Press, Cambridge, Mass., 1949. The influence of Goethe's enigmatic and tragic hero, imitated and adapted in many subsequent literary efforts, is traced in this scholarly study.

BABBITT, IRVING *Rousseau and Romanticism,* Houghton Mifflin Company, Boston, 1919. A standard study to be read with some caution today, for some of the views expressed have been modified by later scholarship. Babbitt's work, however, remains a major critical examination of Rousseau's relationship to the romantic movement.

BARZUN, JACQUES *Romanticism and the Modern Ego,* Little, Brown and Company, Boston, 1944. Reprinted in a paperback edition as *Classic, Romantic and Modern,* this thoughtful study probes relationships of ideas and traces influences on modern life and thought.

EASTLAKE, CHARLES *A History of the Gothic Revival,* Longmans, Green & Company, Ltd., London, 1872. Detailed examination of architecture in the nineteenth century. The author discusses some 343 buildings erected between 1820 and 1870 that reveal gothic influences.

KERMODE, FRANK *The Romantic Image,* Routledge & Kegan Paul, Ltd., London, 1957. Kermode's study deals with literary criticism.

RAILO, EINO *The Haunted Castle,* E. P. Dutton & Co., Inc., New York, 1927. A study of the gothic novel.

RAYNAL, M. *The Nineteenth Century: New Sources of Emotion from Goya to Gaugin,* Skira Art Books, New York, 1952. An excellent introduction to nineteenth-century painting.

RUDWIN, MAXIMILIAN *The Devil in Legend and Literature,* Open Court Publishing Co., La Salle, Ill., 1931. A good companion volume to those sections of Praz's *The Romantic Agony* which deal with "Satanism" in literature of the nineteenth century.

SUMMERS, MONTAGUE *The Gothic Quest,* Fortune Press, London, 1938. A standard study of the gothic novel.

TALMON, J. L. *Romanticism and Revolt,* Thames and Hudson, London, 1967. Well-written intellectual history covering 1815–1848.

THORSLEV, PETER *The Byronic Hero.* University of Minnesota Press,

Minneapolis, 1962. Thorslev takes to task some writers (Railo, Birkhead, and others) and insists that careful distinctions must be made between the villainous type in gothic novels (Walpole, Radcliffe, Lewis) and the rebel type of true hero created by Lord Byron. An excellent, critical study.

MUSIC

BLUME, FRIEDRICH *Classic and Romantic Music*, W. W. Norton & Company, Inc., New York, 1970. The last five chapters deal with nineteenth-century music. Blume's writing demands a good musical and cultural background, for he ranges from purely musical discussions of rhythm, melody, tonality, and so on to conceptual theories relating to history and aesthetics. Some of his ideas, imaginative and suggestive, may also be found to be controversial.

EINSTEIN, ALFRED *Music in the Romantic Era*, W. W. Norton & Company, Inc., New York, 1947. Excellent introduction by a distinguished historian. The book is divided into three parts: "Antecedents, Concepts, and Ideals," "The History," "The Philosophy." The second part, by far the lengthiest, covers the music literature of the period from Schubert to the late-nineteenth-century nationalisms. The first part is especially valuable for its treatment of the romantic spirit in music. Unfortunately, the book contains no bibliography, and the index cites merely page references to persons only (thus, the name of Franz Liszt is followed by 57 references, otherwise unspecified except by page). In spite of these drawbacks, the book is a survey regularly consulted by students.

LONGYEAR, REY M. *Nineteenth-century Romanticism in Music*, Prentice-Hall, Inc., Englewood Cliffs, N.J., 1969. In the Prentice-Hall History of Music Series, this volume, available in paperback, is both practical and useful. Starting with Beethoven, Professor Longyear traces the romantic movement through its early flowering in Mendelssohn, Schumann, Chopin, and Berlioz, to its later maturation in Wagner and Brahms, to the various nationalistic manifestations in Russia, Scandinavia, and other countries, and finally to its twilight at the very end of the century. One brief chapter is devoted to sociological aspects and to performance practices. Selective and up-to-date bibliographies.

STRUNK, OLIVER *Source Readings in Music History: The Romantic Era*, W. W. Norton & Company, Inc., New York, 1965. A collection of writings by the literary forerunners of musical romanticism (for example, Jean Paul, E. T. A. Hoffmann) and composer-critics of the nineteenth-century (for example, Schumann, Liszt, Wagner).

Chapter 13 ∘ *The twentieth century*

Ideas and arts in the twentieth century

A DETACHED OBSERVER, VIEWING THE PERIOD FROM 1700 TO 1900, WOULD have had cause for optimism about the future. The eighteenth century had brought some enlightenment to the fields of politics, economics, philosophy, and religion. It was possible to hope that through the use of reason, man would eventually solve most of his problems. Another dimension, added in the nineteenth century, acknowledged the emotional life of humanity. The idea of progress in all aspects of human activity dominated the minds of most thinkers. At the threshold of the twentieth century, things looked good.

But something happened as the dissonant voices of the nineteenth century gained strength. Kierkegaard, Fëdor Dostoevski and Nietzsche, each of whom had looked deeply into the human soul, came to be recognized as prophetic. They had anticipated some of the absurdities that were to confront mankind in the next century. In *Fear and Trembling* (1843), Kierkegaard retells the story of Abraham and Isaac. His powerfully drawn portrait of Abraham, who is forced to make a paradoxical, absurd "leap into faith," sums up a theme common to his other writings (*Either / Or, The Concept of Dread*). With *The Brothers Karamazov* (1880) and *Crime and Punishment* (1866), Dostoevski reveals the inadequacies of human reason in powerful novels that dramatize the anguish of sufferers from guilt and sin. And Nietzsche proclaims that God is dead.

The pain and anxiety those writers expressed has become a common theme, heavily orchestrated and *fortissimo,* in the twentieth century. Cultural historians like Oswald Spengler (*The Decline of the West,* 1918), Pitirim Sorokin (*Social and Cultural Dynamics,* 1937), and Arnold Toynbee (*Civilization on Trial,* 1948) have cast serious doubt on the nineteenth-century theories of progress hailed by optimists like Auguste Comte (1798–1857) and Herbert Spencer (1820–1903). For the proposal of a steady march upward, these twentieth-century thinkers have substituted a view based on cultural births and decays, wide swings in the mentality of a society, and failures of civilizations to meet challenges from within and without.

At the beginning of this century a profound thinker, Albert Einstein, published his theory of special relativity. This and his later unified field theory (1929, but discarded for a more ambitious one in 1949) shattered whatever smugness scientists and philosophers had felt about the

Figure 13.1 • *Marcel Duchamp:* Nude Descending a Staircase, No. 2 (*1912*). *A cubist figure represented in temporal succession by multiplication.* (**Philadelphia Museum of Art; The Louise and Walter Arensberg Collection.**)

secure, ordered world of Newtonian physics, which was now challenged by a relativistic flux in which traditional notions of time and space have no fixity apart from the relative positions from which we make our measurements. In their fascinating account of the history of relativity and quantum mechanics (*The Evolution of Physics,* Simon & Schuster, Inc., New York, 1938, p. 33), Einstein and Leopold Infeld clarify man's new relationship to the so-called real world around him:

> *Physical concepts are free creations of the human mind and are not, however it may seem, uniquely determined by the external world. In our endeavor to understand reality we are somewhat like a man trying to understand the mechanism of a closed watch; he sees the face and the moving hands, even hears its ticking, but he has no way of opening the case. . . .*

If the physical universe, once thought to be so ordered and open to measurement and observation, is dependent on place and time and our view of it clouded by imperfect and limited senses, how relative must all man's knowledge be?

Artists and art critics have felt, at least intuitively, the impact of relativity, for Einstein's theories have had far-reaching consequences. By showing simultaneous front and side views, Pablo Picasso in his *Girl before a Mirror* (1932; Plate 5) relativizes space. Marcel Duchamp does not attempt to freeze motion; rather, he tries to catch its ongoing relativity in his famous *Nude Descending a Staircase, No. 2* (1912; Figure 13.1). Novelists like Marcel Proust (*Remembrance of Things Past,* 1911–1922) and James Joyce (*Ulysses,* 1922, and *Finnegans Wake,* 1939) explored the new awareness of subjectivity early in the century. Stream-of-consciousness techniques break up the neat, logical order of time and space into the more disordered, subjective time found in the memory. After World War II, writers like Michel Butor (*Modification,* 1957), Nathalie Sarraute (*Portrait of a Man Unknown,* 1958), but more especially Alain Robbe-Grillet (*Jealousy,* 1959) continued to develop the sense of the relativeness of the real. For example, in *Jealousy*

Figure 13.2 • *Vincent van Gogh:* Starry Night. *Postimpressionism or early expressionism presented through the strong, dark, swirling colors of an uncontrolled sky.* (Collection, The Museum of Modern Art, New York. Acquired through the Lillie P. Bliss Bequest.)

Figure 13.3 • *Edvard Munch:* The Cry. *Early expressionism: a pictorial horror story as vivid as a nightmare.* (Courtesy of Munch-museet, Oslo.)

Figure 13.4 • Oskar Kokoschka: **The Bride of the Wind** *(1914). An expressionistic setting of a love scene, unreal yet suggestive of an inner psychological state.* (Public Art Collection, Basel.)

Robbe-Grillet plays with a series of scenes that crop up throughout the novel as musical motives do in a sonata. Each scene is clearly described but is viewed from different positions and from different times, almost as if observers from other planets were reporting it: Other eyes within the dining-room scene, as an instance, report from above, below, and at various other angles from the central table, each pair of eyes seeing an event from its own relative position.

Sigmund Freud (1856–1939) has added an important new dimension to our understanding of the human personality. Freud's organization of personality into the *id, ego,* and *superego,* his views on the dynamics of personality (psychic energy, instinct, anxiety, and the unconscious), and his formulations of personality development through such now common terms as *identification, sublimation, repression, regression, fixation, defense mechanism, Oedipus complex,* and *libido* have influenced not only his own fields of medicine, psychology, and psychiatry but other human activities as well. Many of his ideas have affected the thinking of theologians, philosophers, novelists, artists, social workers, politicians—indeed, of everyone who makes an attempt to understand what it is that motivates man as an individual and men in general.

In the arts a number of movements, notably expressionism and its many offshoots, drew inspiration from Freud. Vincent van Gogh (*Starry Night,* 1889; Figure 13.2) and Edvard Munch (*The Cry,* 1893; Figure 13.3), in the first wave of expressionists, echoed Freud's early explorations into the horrors of the unconscious. Haunting, disturbing pictures, either in technique or subject matter, brought these pictorial artists close to the psychologist. Picasso (in his blue and Negro periods), Georges Rouault, Henri Matisse, and Oskar Kokoschka (Figure 13.4) continued the expressionistic movement in the first two decades of this century. To express inner meanings through outward forms meant bringing to painting, drama, literature, and music a sense of insight into the strange world of dreams, fantasy, and raw, uninhibited emotions. Naturally, splinter movements developed, each with its own aesthetic creed: *Die Brücke* (The Bridge), *Die blaue Reiter,* (The Blue Rider), fauvism, dadaism, surrealism, and certain aspects of cubism and futurism. Movements like these emphasized new drawing techniques and use of color combined with erotic, irrational, and dreamlike elements reminiscent of Freud. During the first two decades of this century, expressionistic impulses appeared in operas such as Richard Strauss's *Salome* (1905)

In Pablo Picasso's Girl before a Mirror *(1932),
space, time, elements of fantasy, and classic
ideals are blended in the style of late cubism.*
(Collection, The Museum of Modern Art, New
York; gift of Mrs. Simon Guggenheim.)

Plate 5

(a)

(b)

Two versions of surrealism: (a) Joan Miró: Carnival of Harlequin.
*Painted in the middle 1920s, this canvas is a fantasy of a
colorful party with numerous possibilities for symbolic interpretation.*
(Albright-Knox Art Gallery, Buffalo, New York; Room of
Contemporary Art Fund.) *(b) Salvador Dali:* Inventions of the
Monsters. *A 1937 creation, with explicit sexual symbolisms.*
(Courtesy of The Art Institute of Chicago; Joseph Winterbotham
Collection.)

Plate 6

Although rather widely separated in time from impressionism, abstract expressionism can be thought of as its descendant: (*a*) Claude Monet's Impression: Sunrise *was created in 1872 and suggests forms and colors instead of proclaiming bold patterns.* (Musée Marmottan, Paris; photo Routhier.) (*b*) *Willem de Kooning:* Composition (1955). *The process of abstraction has proceeded so far as to produce a sense of disorder and chaos; yet the painting is unified by dynamic rhythmic energy.* (The Solomon R. Guggenheim Museum.)

(*a*)

(*b*)

Plate 7

Karel Appel: Angry Landscape. *Dating from 1967, this example of late expressionism combines brilliant coloration with violent, distorted figures in a primitive and barbaric synthesis.* (Collection: Jimmy J. Younger—Houston, Texas.)

Plate 8

and *Electra* (1909). But the best examples are found in works by Arnold Schoenberg: the monodramas *Erwartung* (1909) and *Die glückliche Hand* (1913) and what eventually became his most widely known work, the song cycle *Pierrot lunaire* (1912). The musical language of these compositions exploits dissonance, extreme ranges, sudden dynamic changes, and bizarre subject matter. Béla Bartók's opera *The Castle of Duke Bluebeard* (1911) and pantomime *The Miraculous Mandarin* (1919) set grotesque stories with weird symbolisms to highly dramatic music. Perhaps the greatest opera of the century is Alban Berg's *Wozzeck* (1926), a drama of violence that explores the inner torments of a primitive, unintelligent, emotionally unbalanced soldier living in a world without reason, a world of fantasies, nightmares, and chaotic imaginings, a world distorted with hopelessness, fear, and oppression. Even in architecture, elements of fantasy and unreality appear: Erich Mendelsohn's Einstein Tower near Berlin (1921), Hans Poelzig's Grosses Schauspielhaus in Berlin (1919), and Rudolf Steiner's Goetheanum II in Dornach, Switzerland (1928). Later Le Corbusier's Chapel of Notre Dame du Haut at Ronchamp, France (1955; Figure 13.5), with its

Figure 13.5 • Le Corbusier (Édouard Jeanneret): Notre Dame du Haut at Ronchamp, France. This example of organic architecture is fitted into the landscape with its free form and its massive roof supported by white concrete. (Lucien Hervé, Paris.)

Figure 13.6 • Yves Tanguy's Indefinite Divisibility *expresses the dreams of surrealism: fantastic shapes, shadows, infinite background, and a sense of desolation.* (Albright-Knox Art Gallery, Buffalo, New York; Room of Contemporary Art Fund.)

massive roof, curved walls, and windows of varying sizes and shapes, would create a strange, uncanny impression, especially on one standing within the structure. In Pampulha, Brazil, Oscar Niemeyer's Church of St. Francis merges masses of curved concrete, colorfully painted tiles, asymmetrical patterns, and baroquelike ornamentation. Experienced from the interior, Le Corbusier's chapel and Niemeyer's church surround the visitor with a kind of dreamlike, enchanted, almost holy unreality. Seen on a flat-surfaced color reproduction, these interiors could be mistaken, at least from a distance, for abstract-expressionist paintings.

During World War I, the dada movement was born. In proclaiming the supremacy of the irrational, dadaists produced strange paintings and collages (scraps of various materials pasted on a background), wrote incoherent poems, and assembled noises, musical sounds, and words from various languages; they were protesting against an ordered society, which they felt had failed. The movement was short lived, but its negative thrust, which carried the seeds of self-destruction, had opened further avenues of expression in the arts. By externalizing the spontaneous, uninhibited depths of the human mind, the dadaists anticipated a more affirmative movement, surrealism.

In his *First Manifesto of Surrealism* (1924), André Breton insisted that a superior reality, especially appropriate for the artist, transcends the reality of reason. The former is the reality of the unconscious mind and dreams, which is truer to the real self than the artificial reality of the outer world. Taking Breton's definition of surrealism as "thought dictated in the absence of all control exerted by reason, and outside all aesthetic or moral preoccupations," Hans Arp, Paul Klee, Joan Miró (Plate 6a), Yves Tanguy (Figure 13.6), René Magritte, Giorgio De Chirico, and Salvador Dali created weird paintings. Monsters, strange landscapes, phallic symbols, fanciful forms are colorfully combined to suggest dreams and fantasies. In Dali's *Inventions of the Monsters* (1937; Plate 6b) a wild scene is set before the viewer. Ghostlike heads, masked cupbearers, distorted nudes, a vast, receding horizon, a burning giraffe, and a strange dog frame the central altar on which a symbolic Venus figure is set. Consistent with the importance of the erotic in Freud, this painting reveals Dali's obsession with sexual symbolism.

During the 1930s and 1940s the roots of another movement began to take shape: abstract expressionism. Its origins can probably be traced as far back as the impressionism of the last third of the nineteenth

Figure 13.7 • Auguste Rodin: Nijinsky. *A postimpressionistic view of the dancer that expresses the bizarre aspects of his inner dynamism.* (Permission S.P.A.D.E.M. 1972 by French Reproduction Rights, Inc.)

century, in which French impressionists had gradually replaced the traditional techniques of representation (by means of cleanly drawn lines, colors, and contours) with a variety of novel techniques involving the subtle use of light and shade, shimmering colors, and hazy visual impressions. Subtle effects with color and changing intensities of light fascinated painters like Edouard Manet, Auguste Renoir, and Claude Monet; so Monet's *Impression: Sunrise* (1872; Plate 7*a*) catches a fleeting moment in vague outlines, as if seen through a haze or fog. The greatest sculptor of the time, Auguste Rodin (1840–1917), had tried to capture the spirit of Honoré de Balzac (1799–1850) by creating an impression of the novelist's sheer physical bulk. For his bronze *Balzac* (1897), Rodin made numerous preliminary studies, from heads and busts to full figures of Balzac nude and clothed. The suggestiveness of his final conception captures, as Rodin had hoped, the writer's "relentless labor" and "magnificent courage." Likewise, his statue of Waslow Nijinsky (1912; Figure 13.7), rough and unfinished, reveals expressionistic traits in its powerful twisted torso, the grotesque head and arms, and the suggestive inner explosiveness and potency of the famous Russian dancer. In Monet and Rodin photographic likeness changes to impressions of form, color, and line. Finally even the natural resemblances to objects and shapes disappear (compare Figures 13.8 and 13.9), and pure expression, with no external reference, becomes the aim (Figure 13.10).

One of the earliest efforts in abstract expressionism can be found in Vasili Kandinski. In works like *White Line, No. 232* (1920) the artist produces a feeling evoked by colors and patterns, with no recognizable objects. Willem de Kooning (Plate 7*b*), Franz Kline, Mark Rothko, and Jackson Pollock (*Lavender Mist*, 1950) spearheaded the idea of abstract expressionism since the end of World War II. The individualism of abstract expressionists has splintered the movement into many subdivisions, each of which settles on some set of principles (Figure 13.11). One such group has found a source of inspiration in the intuitive, natural expression of children's, folk, and primitive art, incorporating in their essentially abstract paintings not only the spontaneity but also the violence and distortions suggested by those sources. Karel Appel's *Angry Landscape* (1967; Plate 8) provides a good example.

If relativism and Freudian psychology have exerted strong influences on the arts, another force has been the philosophy of *existentialism.*

Figure 13.8 • Alberto Giacometti: Man Pointing *(1950). Although fantastic, this spindly, attenuated figure yet bears more or less of a realistic resemblance to a human being. (The Tate Gallery, London.)*

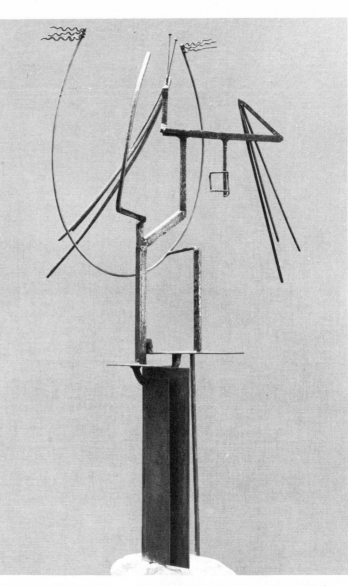

Figure 13.9 • In Julio González's Woman Combing Her Hair *(1931–1933) the human reference has nearly disappeared in abstraction; the linear construction molds mostly space to suggest the subject. (Nationalmuseum, Stockholm.)*

Figure 13.10 • Reuben Nakian: Rape of Lucrece (1953–1958). *An abstract treatment in steel of a classical theme.* (Courtesy the artist and Egan Gallery, New York; photograph by Rudolph Burckhardt.)

Twentieth-century existentialism has been traced to nineteenth-century writers like Kierkegaard, Dostoevski, and Nietzsche. In Kierkegaard, for example, we find that the basic term in human life is "anxiety"; being alive is an "experiment in anxiety." Human life is primarily controlled by three determinants: the inevitability of death, the uncertainty that pervades life, and the sense of guilt. In Kierkegaard's philosophy there is a God, even though the Dane sensed that man was on the way to a dehumanization in which he would eventually become no more than a useful commodity in a depersonalized world. The most important spokesman of existentialism in our time, Jean-Paul Sartre, does not permit man to find refuge even in the comfortable mythology of religion. Frankly atheistic, Sartre argues that human personalities make themselves since they have no prior essence. No one (God, he says, does not exist) can have an idea or plan ahead of time. We exist first and then, through our choices, define ourselves. "Existence is prior to essence," Sartre's famous dictum, is well explained in his own words:

Atheistic existentialism, of which I am a representative, declares with greater consistency that if God does not exist there is at least one being whose existence comes before its essence, a being which exists before it can be defined by any conception of it. That being is man, or as Heidegger has it, the human reality. What do we mean by saying that existence precedes essence? We mean that man first of all exists, encounters himself, surges up in the world—and defines himself afterwards. If man as the existentialist sees him is not definable, it is because to begin with he is nothing. He will not be anything until later, and then he will be what he makes of himself. Thus, there is no human nature, because there is no God to have a conception of it. Man simply is. . . . Man is nothing else but that which he makes of himself. That is the first principle of existentialism. . . .*

In Kierkegaard's view Abraham is forced to make an "absurd leap into faith"—to believe in God's goodness and in His commandment to sacrifice Isaac. In Sartre's philosophy man is forced to choose constantly, being absurdly aware that no real or true values attach to the

---

*Jean-Paul Sartre, *Existentialism and Humanism* [Philip Mairet (trans.)], Methuen & Co., Ltd., London, 1948, pp. 27–28.

Figure 13.11 • Mark Tobey: Above the Earth *(1953). An example of abstract expressionism in which forces, colors, and energies are suggested.* (Courtesy of The Art Institute of Chicago; gift of Mr. and Mrs. Sigmund Kunstadter.)

decisions he makes. One common denominator underlies most existential thought: the "absurdity of being."

Camus's *The Myth of Sisyphus* draws a painful picture of the meaninglessness of existence: "Is life worth living?" he asks; if not, does it not follow that man must commit suicide? For Camus, this is the only serious problem facing man. With his appetite for clarity, order, and knowledge, man must endure in a universe where knowledge, order, and clarity are impossible and where death makes all human endeavor futile. How does one survive with this bleakness? Neither God nor reason provides an answer: One must be able to live, according to Camus, without hope. This pessimism, transferred to literature in general, has given us many heroes of modern fiction who are in search of personal identity, who seek to have their humanity recognized, who desperately long for understanding, compassion, or even justice in a neutral but seemingly malevolent world. At times these heroes do not even rate the dignity of a name: In the novels of Kafka (*The Trial,* 1925, and *The Castle,* 1926), a mere initial is used (an early anticipation of the anonymity of credit-card and social-security numbers). The hero struggles to find answers, but there are none. Beyond the borders of an ordered, stable world, knowing neither himself nor his responsibilities, being aware that he stands terribly alone, he is free, totally free. But at what a cost, for he is also totally responsible! He cannot pin responsibility on some God-given essence or on heredity, environment, education, upbringing, or psychological complexes. He makes himself by choice and thus is totally, frighteningly responsible.

Other writers exploring the problems of meaninglessness are Friedrich Duerrenmatt (*Traps,* 1960), Colin Wilson (*Ritual in the Dark,* 1960), Max Frisch (*I'm Not Stiller,* 1958), Natalie Sarraute (*Portrait of a Man Unknown,* 1956), T. S. Eliot ("The Love Song of J. Alfred Prufrock," 1917, and "The Hollow Men," 1925), Samuel Beckett (*Waiting for Godot,* 1953), Joseph Heller (*Catch-22,* 1955)—to name among many just a few novelists, poets, and playwrights. Much of their literature portrays man as cut off from what is sane, safe, secure, and solid. These and other recent works call attention to the unpredictability of life, the illogical randomness of events. In Marc Saporta's *Composition No. 1* (1963), an imaginative literary effort, the reader is instructed to shuffle the unbound pages before reading the novel; throwing the pages on the floor and regathering them in haphazard fashion produces a random

Figure 13.12 • Eero Saarinen's Dulles Airport at Chantilly, Virginia. Dating from about 1962, the sweeping, curved roof supported by rhythmic ranges of pillars expresses the logic of the twentieth century. (Ezra Stoller © Esto.)

Figure 13.13 • Frank Lloyd Wright: Kaufmann house, Bear Run, Pennsylvania (ca. 1937). Another example of organic architecture in which the international style is fitted to the landscape with strong horizontal lines. (Bill Hedrich, Hedrich-Blessing.)

Figure 13.14 • *Antoine Pevsner:* Construction in Space *(1929). Abstract engineering raised to the level of art.* (Public Art Collection, Basel; Hoffman Foundation.)

ordering of their time and events. In his mural paintings James Rosenquist juxtaposes incongruous images—light bulbs, grass, spaghetti, a pair of ballerina's legs—within a single frame. By exploring new techniques, many contemporary artists have questioned traditional procedures by emphasizing spontaneity, chance, randomness, improvisation, and the unpredictability of "happenings." They attempt to circumvent culturally imposed inhibitions in order to produce a new kind of art.

Although one aspect of the arts and ideas of the twentieth century has delved into man's emotional nature, with its instinctive, intuitive feelings and its irrationalities and contradictions, another aspect is represented by the search for clarity and order (Figure 13.12). There are still those who listen to the claims of reason. Continued application of reason, the scientific method, and intelligent hypothesis represents for them the rational way—in art, music, communication, and life in general. They seek to control their artistic and social environments (Figures 13.13 and 13.14) by careful selection, definition, and clarification, leaving as little as possible to chance. They prefer the self-corrective methods of science to the assertions of authority and are suspicious of mystics—social, religious, and artistic—who receive some sort of private instruction from on high. Recognizing their human fallibility, they nevertheless labor to make ideas clear, operations efficient, and knowledge secure.

One way to make ideas clear is to study language. Semanticists in this century have written extensively about language by examining words, grammar, syntax, symbols, comparisons, relationships. They have generally tended to point out that our thinking rests in large measure on how we employ words and how we respond to them. Popularizers like Stuart Chase (*The Tyranny of Words,* 1938), I. A. Richards and C. K. Ogdon (*The Meaning of Meaning,* 1936), and S. I. Hayakawa (*Language in Thought and Action,* 1939) warn of the vagueness and imprecision surrounding the manner in which we communicate through language. One influential philosophical view, logical positivism, rejects traditional metaphysics and all its trappings of thought, arguing for a vigorous application of scientific method in all thinking. Leaders of this movement were Rudolph Carnap (*Philosophy and Logical Syntax,* 1935) and A. J. Ayer (*Language, Truth and Logic,* 1936).

While word scientists like Carnap and Alfred Korzybsky (*Science and Sanity,* 1933) worked to develop greater precision in verbal communication, technical scientists have introduced automation. Activities from

Figure 13.15 • Julio Le Parc: Continuel Lumière Formes en Contorsion *(ca. 1966). This nearly 7-foot-high motorized aluminum and wood construction, synthesizing light and motion, combines simplicity and complexity, order and change.* (Courtesy Galerie Denise René; André Morain photograph.)

simple clerical work to extremely complicated analyses are now often handled by machines. Norbert Wiener's *Cybernetics* (1948) and his later layman's version, *The Human Use of Human Beings* (1950), not only gave us a new word but made us aware of the range of problems arising from increasing automation. In two anthologies, *Dimensions of Mind* (1960), edited by Sidney Hook, and *Mind and Machines* (1964), edited by Alan Anderson, the relationships between the human brain and the machine are examined. With the fantastic sophistication of machines today, we may not be far from the horrors of Karel Capek's *R.U.R.* (1921), the drama that coined the word ''robot.'' Yet most of the contributors to the two anthologies sound no urgent alarm, although they are a bit fearful that the power of the machine may be somewhat like that of the angry jinni released by the poor Arab fisherman in the *One Thousand and One Nights*.

Norbert Wiener raised some of the problems fundamental to a machine-oriented society, and Marshall McLuhan has popularized one important aspect of such a society: the role of electronic communication. A new technology of our time, communication via electronic media, is rapidly transforming society. For centuries man had communicated verbally; messages were slow in arriving and often inaccurate and misleading. With the development of written languages and the later invention of printing, man's thinking came to be shaped by dependence upon the more precise written and printed word, that is, by the nature of the medium through which he communicated. We now live in a radically different world, according to McLuhan, which encourages active engagement. Electronic technology brings immediacy. We become involved because the older time lag has practically disappeared. Television, the movies, and rapid travel teach more than the family, the church, or the school. On a global scale this new technology is eliminating time and space differences. In *The Medium Is the Massage* (1967), McLuhan, the high priest of technology, brilliantly states his case that media exercise an enormous control over thought and feeling. But who controls the media?

Modern man, it would seem, must live between two extremes: order and total control, giving rigid security, and disorder and freedom, giving frightening insecurity. Like the Savage in Aldous Huxley's *Brave New World* (1932), man is offered a choice between a civilization that has chosen ''machinery and medicine and happiness'' and an existence that involves danger, inconvenience, suffering, and sin, including ''the right to grow old and ugly and impotent; the right to have syphilis and cancer; the right to have too little to eat; the right to live in constant apprehension of what may happen tomorrow.'' Generally speaking, the artist in the twentieth century has preferred freedom (the choice of the Savage) because it offers a challenge to the creative mind. With no holds barred, he can artistically portray the human condition in all its facets.

Happily for most of us, the possibilities at the moment are not limited to the either-or faced by Huxley's Savage. While some modern artists (Hans Hartung, Pierre Soulages, Georges Mathieu), musicians (John Cage, Earle Brown, La Monte Young), novelists (Franz Kafka, Alain Robbe-Grillet, John Barth), and philosopher-historians (Reinhold Niebuhr, Jacques Maritain, and Arnold Toynbee) may belittle the role of reason in human affairs, the fact is that none of them has completely renounced it. However critical their views of artistic order, of political and moral liberalism, of scientific method, of rational discourse, they have not completely forsaken that side of the human coin; the power of eighteenth- and nineteenth-century enlightenment, in spite of the disillusions of all the wars in *this* century, cannot be lightly ignored. However painful and slow, some progress has taken place. No doubt man cannot now be—and perhaps can never be—a god on earth. He remains a mixture of success and failure, of reason and irrationality, of the ugly and the beautiful. And all his facets find expression in art (Figure 13.15). As ever in the history of man, art in the modern world continues to explore and share the rich diversity of his subjective experience.

Musical style

Many ''isms'' have been identifiable in twentieth-century arts and ideas. Sometimes groups of artists have clearly defined their aims, whereas at other times some general spirit or technique has been shared by several otherwise independent artists and works. Histories of many of these movements have yet to be written. Shifting ideas within society and the changing convictions of the creative men themselves often blur the distinctions. The job of sorting out the isms is especially difficult because we stand so close to them in time and because we are faced with so much overlapping. A partial listing of isms and movements in addition to those mentioned or described in the preceding section quickly points up the problem: in the visual arts, abstract art, abstract imagists, action painting, *art nouveau*, assemblage, concrete art, constructivism, *De Stijl*, happenings, international style, junk art, magic realism, the metaphysical school, the Nabis, neoimpressionism, neoromanticism, neoplasticism, op art, pop art, post impressionism, precisionists, psychedelic art, realism, regionalism, social realism, synthetism; in the literary arts, dadaism, expressionism, humanism, impressionism, liberalism, naturalism, neoromanticism, realism, regionalism, surrealism, theater of the absurd; and the share contributed by twentieth-century music, aleatoric music, atonality, electronic music, folkloric music, futurism, *Gebrauchsmusik*, happenings, jazz, junk music, microtonal music, *musique concrète,* nationalism, neoclassicism, neomodality, neotonality, pandiatonicism, polytonality, postromanticism, serialism. This highly casual list throws together terms that name specific techniques common to a number of works and terms suggesting a general spirit—aesthetic, philosophical, or social. In music, for example, some compositions may be linked more closely by their similarity of musical techniques than by any adherence to a ''movement''; so in such cases it might be meaningful to treat procedures rather than isms. But it is also useful to describe and discuss an ism even though works contained within any single category may represent different musical techniques. We shall use the second method in the next few pages as we examine impressionism, neoromanticism, folkloric music, expressionism, neoclassicism, and recent departures from tradition.

IMPRESSIONISM

In the late nineteenth century, French artists, such as Manet, Cézanne, Monet, and Renoir, developed a style that attempted to paint visual impressions, not in our current photographic sense but in ways that suggested momentary, fleeting images, clouded visions, and blurred outlines. By avoiding clear-cut lines, using light and color to catch shifting moods, and choosing subject matter (water, sunrise) in which shade and nuance were important, they created impressions of the external world.

A parallel musical movement, centering mainly in France but influential elsewhere, also came to be known as ''impressionism.'' With some justification, Claude Debussy's name is the principal one linked with musical impressionism although Maurice Ravel, Frederick Delius, Charles Tomlinson Griffes, Edward MacDowell, Alban Berg, Béla Bartók, Igor Stravinsky, and many other composers have written music that at times sounds impressionistic even when the main body of their work might be described more appropriately in other terms.

Music of the classic and romantic periods had emphasized a homophonic texture in which melody was a major factor: thinking of Mozart, Schubert, and Tchaikovsky, for example, immediately brings to mind some of the melodies they wrote. Impressionists, however, only hint at melody, which with them is more often a by-product of harmony than a strong, generating force in and of itself. Short, fragmented motives are more common than lengthy, lyrical melodies. The listener is less likely to ''follow the melody'' than he is to ''feel an impression'' of a melody. Sometimes it is as hard to put one's finger on the melody as it is on a bold, clear dividing stroke in an impressionistic painting. Melodic phrase structure, accordingly, avoids the symmetry of 4 + 4 measures in favor of short phrases, which are often repeated immediately in another register. Major, minor, modal, whole-tone, and various altered scales are all used in impressionistic melodies.

Harmony is perhaps the most important feature of this music. Composers seemed to enjoy the sensuous qualities of seventh and ninth chords, chromatically altered as well as diatonic; traditionally, such chords required resolution as they were dissonances which were to be resolved to consonances. In impressionism, however, complex chords are often unresolved, the music gliding from one dissonant chord to another. Sometimes the composer will retain the same chord structure, moving it up and down a scale, but more often he merges one complex sound into another to create vagueness with regard to well-defined tonal goals.

Rhythms are as fluid and flexible as the melody and harmony are. Passages with a steady, regular pulse are not uncommon, but change and flexibility are heard more frequently. These changes emphasize a rhythmic freedom that allows for slight delays, hesitations, prolongations, increases, and decreases in motion—a *rubato* affecting the total musical texture. Frequently the tempo is slow, moving with a leisurely, unhurried, and wayward pace. Seldom does impressionistic music insistently pound like a Beethoven symphony. Compound triple meters ($\frac{6}{8}$, $\frac{9}{8}$) are much in favor.

Like their fellow artists in painting, impressionistic composers exploit color, seeking shadings and nuances in their handling of the orchestra. The flute, oboe, English horn, and clarinet are given exquisite solo passages, frequently set against a background of lush sonorities in the strings (bowed, *pizzicato,* or *tremolo* and often muted). French-horn solos also provide rich, mellow sounds. Brass instruments are used sparingly, usually to add mere touches of color; heaviness is avoided. Together with the woodwinds, the string section forms the nucleus of the orchestra. Because of the complex harmonies employed, composers often divide the strings so that a six-note chord, for example, is spread through several octaves. Effects like *col legno* (hitting the strings with the stick part of the bow), *sul ponticello* (playing close to the bridge), and harmonics add special flavor to the more traditional ways of playing. Of additional instruments, the harp is most important: From a single plucked note at the right moment to a series of sweeping *glissandi,* this instrument makes vital contributions to the tone colors of impressionistic pieces. As in impressionistic painting, sensitive, delicate, subtle blending is essential.

The general dynamic level of impressionistic music is soft. This is a language of suggestion, not blunt assertion. The slight difference between *ppp* and *pp* counts. Extremely delicate shading is crucial. Very loud passages are not often found. When they do occur, they tend to be short-lived, brilliant outbursts rather than sustained sections.

Texture is almost exclusively homophonic, or at least it is not polyphonic. The harmony, however, moves frequently in masses of sound, unlike music of the classic and romantic periods, where strong melodies stand out against chordal backgrounds. In impressionism, melodies usually blend with the background of sound as chords move to one another although melodies are occasionally heard against chordal backgrounds. A frequent combination is a solo woodwind and strings. Sometimes the texture is very thin, transparent to the point where each participating instrument can be distinguished; but often it is thick, mainly because of the kinds of chords used.

During the last half of the nineteenth century the larger forms of composition (symphony, sonata, concerto) continued to expand. Even smaller forms (like ternary form) broadened and became more complicated. Impressionists reacted against this "bigness" not only by introducing novel ideas in harmony and tone color and melody but also in matters of form. Generally they avoided "developmental" forms (for example, sonata-allegro) and favored free forms not easily defined. Partly owing to programmatic intentions, many of their pieces are short: they simply attempt to catch a mood, an atmosphere, an idea; then the moment is over. Thematic development is rarely present. Sounds, sonorities, bits of melody, and rhythmic touches are played with independently of those larger tonal considerations which Beethoven and Brahms struggled with in order to achieve unity. Here unity stems more from tone painting than from structural organization, and consistency of impression prevails over the coherent working out of a form. Piano pieces, songs, and modest orchestral compositions were well suited to the musical language of impressionism although one opera, Debussy's *Pelléas et Melisande* (1902), ranks among this century's greatest.

For an example of impressionism, listen to *The White Peacock* by Griffes, the first in the following section. Representative Pieces. In the section Other Important Music, the compositions listed under Debussy will provide additional examples.

NEOROMANTICISM

Nineteenth-century romanticism, you will recall, favored the grand gesture: stirring climaxes, big forms, startling contrasts, accomplished by furious string passages, loud brass fanfares, drawn-out *crescendo*s. Impressionism, on the other hand, was mostly a language of understatement; it hinted, it suggested, it whispered, mainly through the various musical devices described in the preceding paragraphs. Although impressionism influenced much musical thinking, especially between 1890 and 1915, and other movements and techniques also reacted against the romantic spirit, romanticism did not completely die out. The prefix "neo-" means a new or recent form; so neoromanticism (and later, neoclassicism) may be understood as a return to the ideals of a previous time, but with a significant difference: the musical (or artistic) language has changed.

Being a follower, even when the language is new, involves risks. Critics have often bitterly attacked composers like Edward Elgar, Gustav Mahler, Jean Sibelius, Sergey Rakhmaninov, Howard Hanson, Samuel Barber, Norman Dello Joio, Gian Carlo Menotti, Ernest Bloch, and others, in whose music they see traces of an outmoded romanticism. Although such criticism may or may not be justified, it persistently crops up whenever neo- attaches itself to a term. Yet many great compositions, paintings, novels, and dramas have been neo–something or other, works that have often extracted the best from the older style and added some new insights.

In melody the neoromantic composer continues to work with the long extended lines of his nineteenth-century models. But the melody now embraces a wider range, is characterized by larger leaps, and contains an abundance of nonharmonic notes, that is, notes dissonant to the underlying harmony. Phrase structure also becomes more irregular and less predictable.

Neoromantic composers were, of course, aware of current musical developments, and their harmonic vocabulary naturally reflected some of the changes taking place. Although they increased the level of harmonic dissonance, it was kept within the bounds of propriety. Many were influenced by the rich sonorities of such impressionists as Debussy, and others enjoyed the momentary dissonance caused by the merging of two streams of sound. But few went to the extremes of constantly dissonant harmony.

The rhythms strongly resemble those of composers like Schumann, Liszt, Chopin, and Wagner, except that they are perhaps more complex, more difficult, and less easily anticipated. Yet they retain most characteristics found in nineteenth-century music: strong pulse, careful use of *rubato*, use of rhythm to create tension, and rhythmic patterns as unifying devices.

About the turn of the century the orchestra had reached enormous proportions. A wide variety of tonal colors encouraged composers to experiment with new tonal combinations; the alto flute, English horn, and bass clarinet appear in more conspicuous roles; more percussion is used; and the individual sections of the orchestra are increased in size. Yet the music remains basically melody with harmony, significantly enriched in tone color.

Practically the same kinds of dynamic marking are found in romantic and neoromantic scores. Generally speaking, the latter contain more directions. Composers, attempting to convey their musical intentions accurately, marked their scores very fully, not only with familiar symbols but also with more elaborate verbal explanations. Loud and soft passages were extended at both ends, leaving only noise and silence as the logical next steps.

Textures are basically homophonic, that is, melody with chordal background. But the very richness of this music encouraged frequent countermelodies. For example, against a string melody a French horn countermelody is heard—all against some harmonic background. The play of two or more melodic ideas in counterpoint was not entirely discarded.

Unlike the impressionists, these composers continued to work with forms like the sonata, symphony, or concerto. They felt at home in those forms which called for a development of themes or a lengthy exploration of an eloquently stated idea.

For examples, listen to Barber's *Adagio* for Strings and Hanson's Symphony 2, which are discussed under Representative Pieces 2 and 3. Certain works by Sibelius and Rakhmaninov will provide additional examples.

FOLKLORIC MUSIC

"Music of the people," as it is sometimes called, covers a diversity of styles and forms, from the simple folktune of humble rural origin to sophisticated city music by highly trained composers. Underlying this range of expression, which we call "folkloric," is the notion that the music stems from some fundamental base, from some deep wellspring of human existence, from some primordial instincts that unite the human race.

At one level we can speak of the music sung in simple settings by indigenous rural workers: Italian, Spanish, French, German, English, Hungarian, and Russian folksongs; hillbilly songs of America; and songs peculiar to certain geographical areas all over the earth. These songs tell of joy and sorrow; they relate to ceremony, war, work, play, and other activities. They serve many purposes: inspirational, practical, therapeutic, magical, and recreational.

Modal scales, especially a five-note pentatonic scale, form the basis for many of these tunes. Melodic range is restricted, keeping well within an easy singing range. However, some melodies are highly ornamented. Harmony usually consists of three or four basic chords. Of all the musical factors, rhythm tends to be the most complex. Although much of the music may move with a regular beat (especially, of course, music associated with dance and accompanying work), some of it is free and rhapsodic, well suited to the drama often expressed. Percussion instruments, a chord-playing instrument like the guitar, and maybe a treble instrument to alternate with or assist a voice may provide additional tone color. The texture is either monophonic or homophonic, and the forms are often sufficiently regular to permit the use of the same music for continuing narration.

We have noted that during the nineteenth century certain composers, especially in those nations seeking to establish national identities, found sources of inspiration in the legends and folk heritages of their respective countries. Reacting against the dominance of the German tradition (Beethoven, Brahms, Wagner), they found at their own doorsteps a wealth of musical material—tunes, dances, stories, heroes—sufficiently original to allow them to compete successfully with German supremacy.

At one end of the musical spectrum we find the often unwritten and frequently improvised folksongs handed down from generation to generation; at the other end that kind of music transformed into lengthier and more complicated compositions written down and played by trained musicians. In our century Béla Bartók and Zoltán Kodály (Hungarian), Leoš Janáček (Czech), Jean Sibelius (Finnish), Ralph Vaughan Williams (English), Manuel de Falla (Spanish), Carlos Chávez (Mexican), Heitor Villa-Lobos (Brazilian), and Aaron Copland (American) have drawn upon folk elements for extended and sometimes complicated compositions in a variety of genres: opera, ballet, piano music, songs, symphonies. In the notes to accompany the *English Folksong* Suite by Vaughan Williams (page 337) we discuss how such composers have treated folkmusic in serious compositions.

EXPRESSIONISM

As with impressionism, expressionism in painting had a counterpart in music. In fact, the two movements in both arts have been among the strongest influences of the period following romanticism. The *Har-*

vard Dictionary of Music partially defines expressionism as "music written in a deeply subjective and introspective style." Thus far the definition could apply equally to nineteenth-century romanticism. But expressionism, whose roots are found in the earlier movement, carried that style to its last gasp: It was a kind of end-of-the-century agony, which dwelt on the tensions and conflicts of man's inner life, externalizing this subjective turmoil in highly dissonant music. During the early 1900s, Arnold Schoenberg (*Erwartung*, 1909; *Pierrot lunaire*, 1912; *Die glückliche Hand*, 1913), Alban Berg (*Wozzeck*, 1925; *Lulu*, 1937), and Anton von Webern (Five Pieces for Orchestra, 1913) revolutionized the world of music by composing pieces that seemed to parallel canvases by Edvard Munch, Emil Nolde, Vasily Kandinsky, Georges Rouault, and groups like *Die Brücke* and *Der blaue Reiter*. From highly chromatic music with tenuous roots in tonality (a sort of extreme Wagnerianism), Schoenberg finally began to write music that seemed to have no roots at all in tonality—an atonal music. This was music in which each note owed allegiance primarily to itself, secondarily perhaps to a few notes surrounding it, but not at all to some tonal system in which gravitational pulls are in evidence.

In this style wide, awkward, angular leaps produce melodies that sound jagged and distorted, Melodic intervals are frequently dissonant: sevenths and ninths, augmented and diminished. Smooth contours, long lines, and stepwise motion are consistently avoided, and melodic lines, therefore, are hard to follow, for they deliberately instill feelings of uncertainty, even frustration, in listeners accustomed to tonally oriented music, where anticipation is possible.

If harmony is taken to mean pleasant agreement, then this music has no harmony; but in another sense, of course, expressionistic harmony is simply all dissonant. Like atonal melody, this harmony contains no expected progressions; chords (usually very dissonant) are sounded one after another with no apparent harmonic goals. Triads and seventh and ninth chords have disappeared. With the absence of tonal centers, the idea of modulation becomes meaningless, as do the terms major and minor. Since much of this music calls for chamber ensembles, where each instrument participates as an equal member, you will frequently encounter polyphonic textures. But individual lines often outline the notes of chords, resulting in pseudoharmonic feeling. So with the development of the twelve-tone system, contrapuntal thinking predominates although the sounding together of tones based on the tone row makes chords possible.

Both melody and harmony move very irregularly; changes in tempo predominate, often very sudden. Short, detached, *staccato* notes sounded in a quick cluster of melodic or harmonic pitches, irregularly placed accents, and sections of brief silence tend to eliminate any feeling of steady beat.

Expressionistic composers also experimented with unusual combinations of instruments. This is especially noticeable in music written for smaller ensembles, where the composers call for instruments like the mandolin, guitar, bass clarinet, and saxophone to play on equal terms with traditional instruments like the flute, oboe, violin, and cello. The ensembles not only use odd assortments of instruments but also exploit the tonal resources of each instrument: Extreme registers, extreme dynamics, and a stunning array of effects (trombone *glissandi*, flutter-tonguing, and the like) contribute to the intensive expression of the music. Schoenberg (and later Berg and Webern) was also fond of the voice, using it sometimes in a normal fashion (but with the usual jagged melodic outline), sometimes more like an instrumental tone color, and in some exceptional cases (as in his *Pierrot lunaire*) in a kind of speech song called *Sprechstimme*. This last technique, as has been explained before, sounds like a gliding wail; for the voice does not sing pitches but approximates them, loosely following the dynamics, rhythm, and general contours suggested by the score. One other effect, highly developed by Webern, is the idea of *Klangfarbenmelodie*, a melody fabricated out of tone color. Music of this sort (for example, Webern's *Five Pieces for Orchestra*) avoids thematic and motivic development, depending mainly upon more or less isolated tone colors and thin textures to achieve effects. Tone color literally creates the form, other factors (to the extent they are present) being subordinate.

In the early stages of expressionism, nearly all the pieces were relatively short. Schoenberg himself attempts to explain:

Harmonic variation could be executed intelligently and logically only with due consideration of the fundamental meaning of the harmonies. Fulfillment of all these functions—comparable to the effect of punctuation in the construction of sentences, of subdivision into paragraphs, and of fusions into chapters—could scarcely be *assured with chords whose constructive values had not as yet been explored. Hence, it seemed at first impossible to compose pieces of complicated organization or great length.* *

With the passage of time, the formulation of a "system," and continued experimentation, composers more confidently worked with atonality and all its implications, including the use of tonal elements in expressionistic music. This section may well conclude with a brief summary of Berg's expressionistic opera *Wozzeck*, in which the composer has given us a convincing, shaped musical experience without most listeners' being consciously aware that the music takes the following forms:

Act I. Five character pieces
 Scene I. "The Captain" [a suite]
  Praeludium
  Sarabande
  Gigue
  Gavotte
  Double I
  Double II
  Aria
  Reprise of the praeludium
 Entr'acte and finale
 [Four other scenes follow, each organized in various ways: for example, a military march, a passacaglia.]
Act II. A symphony in five movements
 Scene I. Introduction [comparable to an introduction to a Haydn symphony] followed by first movement in sonata form
  Exposition
  Repeated exposition [common to many classic symphonies]
  Development
  Recapitulation
 Entr'acte [continuation of recapitulation] and coda
 [Four other movements follow: a fantasie and fugue, a *Largo*, an extended scherzo and trio, and a rondo finale.]
Act III. Six inventions

*Arnold Schoenberg, *Style and Idea*, Philosophical Library, Inc., New York, 1950, p. 105.

[Each scene, separated by entr'actes that serve primarily as transitions, "invents" on some idea: a theme, a tone, a rhythm, a six-note chord, a tonality, and equal movement (toccata style).]

For examples of expressionism, listen to Arnold Schoenberg's *Pierrot lunaire* and Anton von Webern's Five Pieces for Orchestra under Representative Pieces 5 and 6. The music of these two composers, along with that of Alban Berg, is often associated with that movement.

NEOCLASSICISM

In the lean years during and following World War I, budgets were cut; compositions for big symphony orchestras stood little chance of being performed. Economics must thus be counted as one motivation for the rise of twentieth-century neoclassicism, which perhaps reached its peak in the late 1920s and the 1930s. Another—and probably more important—cause is a strictly human one: some creative minds are naturally attracted to aesthetic principles involving clarity, balance, and restraint. (As we have seen, expressionists, impressionists, and neoromanticists had preferred to emphasize spontaneity, imbalance, and vagueness.) However, the neoclassic composers used modern techniques with classic forms, and so both aspects must be present in works regarded as neoclassic: a modern musical language and an outlook that is fundamentally classic. Composers attracted to neoclassicism include Igor Stravinsky (Concerto for Piano and Wind Instruments, 1924), Sergey Prokofiev ("Classical" Symphony, 1917) and Paul Hindemith (series of *Kammermusik,* 1922–1928). American composers like Walter Piston, Roy Harris, Roger Sessions, Aaron Copland, and Elliott Carter, especially in works written up to the beginning of World War II, found the style congenial to their talents. Between 1920 and 1940 a vast number of solo and chamber-music works in the form of solo sonatas, sonatas for one instrument and piano, small ensembles such as string quartets and woodwind quintets, symphonic writing for small and large orchestras, and concertos poured from the pens of most major composers.

Melodies are usually clearly heard. They are much more jagged in outline than are those in Mozart, for example, and share the shape of expressionistic music; but they differ in one important respect: Expressionistic melodies are often short outbursts—disjointed spurts of notes—whereas neoclassic melodies have more continuity of motion; the listener can usually follow the melodic line even though it leaps about. Neoclassic melody uses a fairly orthodox structure, with thematic ideas, phrases, cadences, and more or less defined larger sections.

Harmony is usually dissonant, the degree of harshness varying with the composer and composition. Triads and seventh chords are occasionally heard, but usually the chords are complex combinations of intervals formed in a variety of ways, such as tone clusters, widely spaced notes, or simply a middle-register sonority.

Drive, excitement, and energy characterize the rhythm, which avoids the extreme fluidity of impressionism and the extremely irregular patterns of expressionism. Yet neoclassic music is often in odd meters ($\frac{5}{16}$, $\frac{7}{8}$) and changing meters, a succession of measures of differing lengths. This music moves; there is little that is static in a rhythmic sense.

Because of the strong emphasis on classic phrase syntax in melody and the dissonant harmonies and energetic rhythms, neoclassic composers generally do not emphasize tone color by seeking bizarre and striking effects. Given the limitations of a medium (for example, a sonata for violin and piano), composers use their instruments to best advantage in regard to register, various articulations, or dynamic levels. Balance is the goal, not tone color for its own sake.

In texture this music tends toward clarity, sharpness of detail, and sparseness in the use of instruments. Some movements are mainly polyphonic and others mainly homophonic, but most take advantage of both.

By adopting classic forms, neoclassic composers immediately had some basis for the organization of their music. Although their musical vocabulary was new and experimental, they acknowledged the need—at least as far as they were concerned—of periodicity (form-building units) if they were to make their music understandable. Classic forms like the sonata-allegro, rondo, theme and variations, ternary design, and fugue were modified to suit the requirements of changing vocabularies. Treatments of sonata form by Hindemith, rondo by Bartók, and theme and variations by Stravinsky, for example, are fascinating studies of adaptations of classic forms to twentieth-century music.

For examples, consult the sections on Stravinsky and Bartók under Representative Pieces 7 and 8. Almost all the music of Hindemith and Piston (see Other Important Music) will also provide good examples.

RECENT DEPARTURES

All the music we have been discussing in this section has been experimental in one sense. In 1915 the music of Schoenberg was viewed as a radical departure from, or even a decisive break with, the past. In the 1970s we have a different perspective: We now can see its debt to that past, and we are more likely to maintain that the break was not so great as we once thought.

Since the end of World War II, composers, as usual, have been experimenting; it is to be expected that their musical language would change along with everything else in society. In the last twenty years or so, the most radical experimentation has been stimulated by the advent of electronic music. But avant-garde composers have embraced many other creeds: aleatoric music, stochastic music, total serialism (see the discussion of preformed and unformed music in Chapter 8), and others, some of which may be associated with electronic styles or with more traditional musical instruments. In the following paragraphs we shall deal primarily with electronic music.

The notion of a tune is seldom found in recent electronic music. Earlier in this century, men like Alois Hába, Julián Carillo, and Harry Partch experimented with microtonal music, in which there were more than twelve half steps to the octave. The absence of precise, definable pitches is now common. A band of pitches moves up and down in blocks, or we hear a sequence of pitches so close in frequency that the melody, if we were to apply that term, sounds more like a fire siren. Continuity is often replaced by short rapid bursts of microtonal pitches sounding more like a *gestalt,* a form, than like a perceptible flow of melody. To speak of major, minor, or other scales in this music is meaningless. The terms ''consonance'' and ''dissonance'' hardly apply. Where melody in the traditional sense of the term can be detected, it tends to move in jagged outlines, leaping from high to low and most often in short isolated spurts; but in fact in much of this music the term ''melody'' simply is not pertinent.

If harmony means a set of chords bearing logical relationships to each other and to the composition as a whole, then the term ''harmony'' is likewise inapplicable. One is more apt to hear tonal masses, bands, and clusters of sounds. More important than the concept of consonance and dissonance (most of the music being acoustically dissonant) are the relative densities employed. Masses of simultaneous sounds may be very wide in range or very narrow or give the impression of being thick, dense, and heavy or transparent, thin, and light. The phrase structures created by Beethoven, by Wagner, and even by modern composers like Bartók and Hindemith, through their manipulation of melody, harmony, and rhythm (with sequences, cadences, and all the rest), have generally been discarded in favor of states of more or less tension generated by clusters of sounds.

Rhythm, as we have explained, refers to the organization of movement. If this recent music *is* music—and we maintain that it is—it follows that it has rhythm because it always has movement. Many sections of experimental music seem to move by additions of sounds to a rather static mass of continuing sound. The entrances create the impression that something is happening, that the mass is moving; such entrances may persist and merge into the mass, or they may momentarily "drop in" and say quick goodbyes. What is important is that the spaced entrances seem to move the music, but in a radically different way from the steady pulse and beat found in traditional music. Under such conditions terms like "fast" and "slow" have little meaning although we can speak of little or much activity. Where pulse *can* be felt, it is generally irregular. Electronic instruments, capable of sustaining extremely long notes or articulating extremely short notes—in both cases far beyond possibilities ever available to earlier composers—can create gigantic and tiny patterns that exceed the limits of human perception. Rhythmic patterns are molded to the incredibly slow and fast speeds of the machine, super-rhythms, or macrorhythms, so large as to be beyond the organizing span of our attention as well as microrhythms either so complex or so rapid that we fail to perceive them.

Among other elements important to recent electronic music are accent and dynamics. The intensity and rapidity of decay of an accent can be controlled and dynamic levels varied in the most sophisticated and subtle ways. Usually these aspects are intimately tied up with tone color and texture.

Of all elements tone color has received perhaps the most attention in the last two decades. In the first half of the century composers like Schoenberg, Bartók, and Stravinsky had achieved remarkable effects by exploring the tone-color resources of traditional instruments. In the bag of tricks revealed by more recent composers we may encounter new devices, requiring performers to tap, strike, or rub their instruments, to groan, hiss, and whistle, to tamper with their instruments (John Cage's prepared pianos for example), and to obtain weird effects on woodwind and brass instruments never dreamed of a half century ago. Moreover, electronic instruments have made it possible to alter the sound of traditional instruments in radical ways. Machines can also work with and combine natural sounds (rain, thunder, wind), artificial noises (automobile horns, factory whistles), and traditional instruments to produce musical collages, which in turn can be speeded up, slowed down, played backward. By calling attention to such resources, composers have made us sensitive to the vast variety of tone color surrounding us, and we have become aware of the immense potential in the world of sounds. Careful listening tells us that tone color itself—sounded in high, middle, and low registers, as thick and thin, isolated and in combination, soft and loud—is among the most fascinating elements to be heard in recent music.

From the section Representative Pieces listen to music by Xenakis, Berio, Erb, Cage, and Penderecki. These examples (14 to 18) survey some of the most recent techniques. The five preceding pieces (9 to 13), by American popular ensembles (Jacquet, Jones and Lewis, The Modern Jazz Quartet, Coleman, and Blood, Sweat and Tears), exemplify recent trends with roots in jazz.

Representative pieces

1. CHARLES TOMLINSON GRIFFES (1884–1920)

Before World War I a great many American composers were creating music of all types. Some important figures were Edward MacDowell, George Chadwick, Arthur Foote, and the highly gifted Griffes. Griffes followed the usual path in his day: he went to Europe to study music, but primarily to be a concert pianist, not a composer. During his European years he yielded to an insistent creative urge, first writing songs influenced by his German teaching. Later he found himself attracted to the exotic "oriental" style of the Russians and to the French impressionistic music in vogue during the early years of the twentieth century. In 1920 death cut short a promising career at the moment when Griffes was about to enter a period of full maturation.

As might be expected of a man who proposed to be a concert pianist,

Griffes wrote well for that instrument. His *Roman Sketches*, op. 7, are four works for piano, of which ○● "The White Peacock" is one, its original piano version dating from 1915 and the orchestral version, our recorded example, coming four years later. Like others of his generation, Griffes was attracted by the poetry of William Sharp (whose works were published under the name of Fiona Macleod); and since this music seems to have been inspired by Sharp's verses "The White Peacock," the complete poem as it appears in the preface to the score is given below:

Here where the sunlight
Floodeth the garden,
Where the pomegranate
Reareth its glory
Of gorgeous blossom;
Where the oleanders
Dream through the noontides;

. . .

. . . Where the heat lies
Pale blue in the hollows,

. . .

Here where the dream-flowers,
The cream-white poppies,
Silently waver,

. . .

Here as the breath, as the soul of this beauty
Moveth in silence, and dreamlike, and slowly,
White as a snowdrift in mountain valleys
When softly upon it in the gold light lingers:

. . .

Moves the white peacock, as tho' through the noontide
A dream of the moonlight were real for a moment.
Dim on the beautiful fan that he spreadeth,

. . .

Dim on the cream-white are blue adumbrations,

Pale, pale as the breath of blue smoke in far woodlands,
Here, as the breath, as the soul of this beauty,
Moves the White Peacock.

For the orchestral version the composer chose a standard instrumentation (four each of the woodwinds, two horns, three trumpets, two trombones, percussion, and the usual strings) plus two harps and a celesta. The additions play important roles in the composer's attempts to portray the colorful shimmering of the peacock. The effect of the piece is entirely typical of impressionism in music. The opening motive (heard twice) in the solo oboe, the chromatic melody that slithers downward in the solo flute, and a rhythmic motive employing dotted-note patterns are the important musical building blocks. In some form or other these three ideas are frequently heard.

The dynamic range is from *ppp* to *ff*, with carefully marked shadings involving much *crescendo* and *descrescendo*.

Generally speaking, the texture tends to be thick, mainly because of the complex sonorities (for example, seventh and ninth chords). Griffes often uses lush harmonies, usually in a descending series and often played by the harps, celesta, and strings.

Largamente e molto rubato ("Broadly with much *rubato*") gives the clue to the flexible rhythmic motion characterizing the music. Later, *con passione* and *tempo intenso* markings are reflected by increasing motion and louder music. The strings start the piece with mutes, but during the more active middle portions they are instructed to play without mutes. A last, short section is again played with mutes, and the piece concludes *molto dim. e rit.* ("getting much softer and slower").

Of the woodwinds, first flute, first oboe, and first clarinet figure prominently as solo instruments, the second instruments generally entering when a reinforcement of tone color is needed. Bassoons usually support the bass. Horns, trumpets, and trombones function as harmony instruments. Almost without exception, they double notes found elsewhere in the orchestra. Thus their role is to reinforce and to provide an additional tone color to the total ensemble. The string section functions harmonically as well as melodically. It frequently provides the background harmony for a flute, oboe, or clarinet solo. At other times the principal melodic interest is found in the first violins. Harps and celesta play only arpeggiated figures or chords. The colorful quality of these instruments adds much to the effectiveness of the composer's impression of "The White Peacock."

2. SAMUEL BARBER (1910–   )

Born near Philadelphia, Samuel Barber came from a musical family. He developed rapidly as a musician and at age 10 attempted an opera. Various European trips broadened his musical horizons, and fame came quickly in the forms of a Guggenheim Fellowship and the much-coveted Prix de Rome. Barber's Symphony 2 was given its premiere performance by Serge Koussevitzky and the Boston Symphony Orchestra. That commissioned work was followed by numerous other commissions, a testimony to the high regard Barber has continued to enjoy.

Arturo Toscanini introduced Barber's *First Essay for Orchestra* and the
○● *Adagio* for Strings, op. 11, at a concert of the NBC Orchestra in 1938. Since that concert, the latter work has become one of the most popular pieces ever written by an American composer. In its original version the *Adagio* was the slow movement of Barber's Quartet for Strings in b, composed in 1936. The composer must have realized that this movement expanded for string orchestra would provide the power, the sonority, the contrast, and the expressiveness needed to fulfill its potentialities. It is the string-orchestra version that is most frequently heard today and appears on our records.

The score calls for first and second violins, viola, cello, and double bass. The initial tempo is marked *Molto adagio* ("Very slowly") along with the indication *espr. cantando* ("expressively singing"). The melody is unusually consistent in its stepwise motion; its line is smooth-flowing and long, rising and falling quietly. Another motive provides a contrast: a dramatic leap upward, followed by the immediate repetition of the upper note. Together, these two melodic ideas dominate the 7- to 8-minute piece.

The harmonies consist mainly in triads and seventh chords. Although most of the sounds, taken singly, can be found in the triads and seventh chords of nineteenth-century music, in Barber's *Adagio* they often follow each other in unexpected ways. The general impression is one of thick, rich sonorities and a mild amount of dissonance.

Because the composer frequently divides the individual parts of his orchestra, the texture varies from four-part (minus the double bass) to nine-part (all the upper strings divided into two groups each, plus double bass).

As the music proceeds, the listener's attention shifts as the main stepwise melody is picked up by one section of the orchestra after another, the double basses being the only section never given the melody. The dynamic level, generally *piano* or *pianissimo*, rises and falls with this developing melody to emphasize the motion. About halfway through the piece, as the cellos play the expressive melody, Barber marks the music "with increasing intensity." From this point a steady *crescendo* finally reaches *fortissimo* at the climax of the movement. Here the texture is nine-part, and all the instruments are playing in very high registers. After a pause, a brief retransition, played *pianissimo*, modulates back to the home key for one last statement of the melody.

The *Adagio* is a hauntingly moving piece. The simplicity of its melodic ideas, the unusual flavor of its harmonies, the range of textures, and the intensity of its climax have obviously contributed to its popularity.

3. HOWARD HANSON (1896–   )

For about four decades, Howard Hanson was one of the most influential figures on the American musical scene. As Director of the Eastman School of Music (1924–1965) and founder of the Festival of American Music (in 1925), Hanson profoundly affected the development of American music, not only through his creative efforts but also by attitudes expressed in his teaching, lectures, and writings. As an administrator, Hanson toiled unceasingly to promote American music by encouraging the performance of music by young composers. He crusaded for recognition of American talent, and he worked to realize that goal by capitalizing on the various positions of power he held on national committees and as Director of Eastman. As a composer, he preferred to cast his musical ideas in the larger orchestral and choral forms. Big sound, thick textures, striking French-horn melodies, and brass fanfares are characteristic of his methods. In addition to symphonies and symphonic poems, his other major work is an opera, *Merry Mount,* first produced by the Metropolitan Opera Company in 1934.

If we permit the composer to speak for himself, he says, "I do not believe that music is primarily a matter of the intellect, but rather of the emotions. I have, therefore, aimed in this symphony [o Symphony 2, op. 30 (*Romantic*)] to create a work that was young in spirit, lyrical and romantic in temperament, and simple and direct in expression." These words, stated at the time of the 1930 premiere (by the Boston Symphony Orchestra) of the *Romantic* Symphony, when Hanson was 34, were supplemented almost sixteen years later when he remarked, "I believe that there are essentially two types of music, warm-blooded music and cold-blooded music, and every admixture of the two. The 'Romantic' is definitely warm-blooded music." *

Symphony 2 reveals Hanson's commanding mastery of large orchestral forces. Almost every instrument has "its time at bat," a technique that, incidentally, wins friends among the players, who are all given something important to do. The textures can range from thin to very thick, from crisp, brittle chatterings in the woodwinds to widely spaced chords covering almost the entire pitch range from contrabassoon to piccolo.

Played by four horns, the principal theme of our recorded example, movement III, uses a striking dotted-note rhythm pattern. It extends over the range of an octave and is heavily dependent upon the "strong" interval of a fourth. Shortly after the basses take the theme, an animated *fortissimo* section is heard. Here the horns (plus English horn and bassoons) sound vigorous thematic material over sustained chords in the brasses and strings (playing *tremolo*). The texture quickly thickens, and the accompaniment figure and principal theme briefly return (in horns and trumpets) before the *Molto meno mosso* ("Much less fast") section begins.

In this section the texture is quite transparent. Solo woodwinds and solo French horn are used contrapuntally, usually against a sustained chord in the strings. Just before *Più mosso* ("More motion"), two flutes play an *ostinato* pattern while a solo oboe and two clarinets play thematic material, the rest of the orchestra being silent.

At *Più mosso* the timpani and lower strings (*pizzicato*) set a steady rhythmic beat. Certain beats are marked with accents, giving an effect of syncopation. With the entrance of the "horn call," that strong theme clashes with the rhythmic beat of the strings (and bassoons). When the trombones enter, the tension of these cross rhythms is continued. The trumpet fanfare sounds against sustained chords in the strings, again *tremolo*. From here the texture becomes increasingly thick, until finally

*Quoted by Louis Biancolli in his program notes for the Philharmonic-Symphony Society of New York concerts of January 17 and 18, 1946.

the entire orchestra is involved. The dynamic level in this section is *fortissimo*. After a somewhat unexpected moment of silence, the coda begins, softly, in the strings. At this point the composer asks only for solo first violin, solo second violin, one stand (two players) of violas, and one stand of cellos—six players in all. The coda becomes more animated. As more instruments join in, the dynamic level increases and the texture thickens. Brilliant contrasts of families of instruments, especially the woodwinds against the trumpets, bring the movement to a close.

4. RALPH VAUGHAN WILLIAMS (1872–1958)

One important phase of twentieth-century music can be traced back to the nationalistic revivals characteristic of the nineteenth century. As poets, dramatists, novelists, and painters became increasingly aware of the heritage of their fatherland, they praised that past in works of art. A strong interest in the artistic possibilities of musical folk material captured the imagination of many composers, including Stravinsky (*Les Noces*, 1914–1923), Bartók (*Improvisations*, op. 20, 1920), Kodály (*Háry János*, 1926), Janáček (*Glagolitic Mass*, 1926), and Vaughan Williams, from whose o *English Folksong* Suite our recorded example is taken. Neoclassic, expressionistic, and most recently electronic styles have perhaps dominated the musical scene since the 1920s. Yet the folksong influence has persisted in the works of some composers; and in the last decade or so the folksong with guitar accompaniment has risen to enormous favor in American popular music.

At least three aspects of the folksong in urban music, two of which are fairly easy to describe, will be briefly discussed: Given a folk melody, whether it be Hungarian, English, Czechoslovakian, Romanian, or Russian, a composer may choose to preserve its fundamental simplicity. He takes the tune, sets it to a tasteful harmonic background, and then "orchestrates" it for small or large ensemble. This procedure is adopted by Vaughan Williams in our example, "Seventeen Come Sunday"; the melody is made strikingly clear, and the harmonies he provides are consistent with what one would expect for folksong harmonizations. (The original setting was for military band, but later Gordon Jacob transcribed the *English Folksong* Suite for symphony orchestra.) A second technique may use the folk melody as basic material but splinters, fragments, or shortens the tune, distorting its original rhythmic flow, its formal balance, and its melodic purity. Bits of the tune are present, but these bits are interwoven into a complex musical fabric involving dissonant harmonies, irregular rhythms, and phrase patterns foreign to the simple peasant tune. In such a sophisticated environment the tune has been transformed. Raised to the level of serious art, it is a Cinderella dancing with a prince, bestowing a fascinating grace, charm, and strength. Bartók's *Improvisations* provide excellent examples of this second treatment of folk music. In the third sense, folk music permeates the total personality and being of a composer. Without consciously using folksongs, he instinctively reflects the spirit of his national folk background. In his own imaginative world there is a heritage that exerts subtle influences on the music he composes. Extremely hard to pinpoint and even harder to describe, its flavor seems to be there: the Finn in Sibelius, the Czech in Janáček, the Hungarian in Bartók, the Romanian in Georges Enesco, and the English in Vaughan Williams.

5. ARNOLD SCHOENBERG (1874–1951)

In 1912 the appearance of ○ ● *Pierrot lunaire,* op. 21, brought quick fame to its composer, Arnold Schoenberg. Some might argue that the proper word is "infamy"; yet time has firmly placed the controversial work, like Stravinsky's *Le Sacre du printemps* of 1913, among those masterpieces which were also historically important events. As is true of *Le Sacre,* legendary stories surround *Pierrot lunaire,* most of them dating from the early days when the music was considered wild and incomprehensible. In his book *Music in the 20th Century* (W. W. Norton & Company, Inc., New York, 1966, p. 195), William Austin relates the following amusing, but telling, anecdote: "The conductor Alois Melichar reported that the first clarinetist in the Berlin Opera orchestra had played twenty rehearsals of *Pierrot* before anyone noticed that he was supposed to shift from a B-flat to an A clarinet from time to time!" For the first performance, October 16, 1912, forty rehearsals were needed; for the first recording, according to Schoenberg himself, two hundred!

What kind of music was this, in which trained musicians did not detect wrong notes played by an instrumentalist, that required many costly rehearsals, that caused a commotion in the world of music?

Pierrot lunaire is a cycle of twenty-one miniature melodramas for voice and a small instrumental ensemble. The ''three times seven'' lyrics by Albert Giraud, a symbolist poet, were translated into unrhymed German by Erich Hartleben. Eight separate instruments are needed (but, through doubling—one musician's playing several instruments—only five instrumentalists can perform the work): piano, cello, violin and viola, flute and piccolo, and clarinet and bass clarinet. In addition a singer recites the texts, and in most performances a conductor keeps the ensemble together.

The general tone of the work strongly resembles the moodiness and suggestive Freudian id found in expressionistic painting and poetry of the time. In seemingly haphazard fashion the poems hover about the moon, Pierrot, and the figures Colombine and Cassander, historical pantomimers. There is no logical, rationally developed narrative. Like the mixed-up chronology of a Robbe-Grillet post–World War II novel (*The Erasers* or *Jealousy*), time in the Pierrot pieces avoids logical sequence: Pierrot recites a blasphemous Mass in the evening; he has a vision of his last mistress (the withered hussy with a long neck) about to strangle him; he bores a hole in Cassander's skull, stuffs ''authentic Turkish tobacco'' into it, and puffs contentedly; but later Cassander fiddles on Pierrot's bald head. The novelty, strangeness, and contrasts are enhanced by distorted musical treatments of the text. When ''Pierrot saws away on his viola with a grotesquely long bow,'' the setting is not for viola but for cello.

Another remarkable feature, immediately noticeable to untrained ears, is Schoenberg's demanding challenge to the vocalist, who neither sings, chants, nor speaks. The composer calls the part a *Sprechstimme* (''speaking voice''), but the vocalist does not merely speak; rather, she suggests pitch inflections by gliding up and down, sometimes whispering, according to detailed indications of rhythm and approximate levels of pitch. In a deliberate reversal of tradition, Schoenberg wishes to avoid precise melodic intervals and on-pitch singing. Thus in all live performances of *Pierrot* you will hear new vocal lines although the general contours in the rise and fall of the voice will be somewhat alike.

Schoenberg's *Sprechstimme* moves about in an instrumental texture that constantly shifts in size, quality, and density. Unlike most nineteenth-century composers, Schoenberg does not keep his small ensemble busy most of the time. Instead, each of the twenty-one pieces has its own characteristic instrumentation, its own fresh tone color.

Compared to the music of Debussy, Strauss, and other composers of the time, *Pierrot lunaire* shocked its listeners because of its radical musical language. This music denied tonality; it was atonal. Music based on seven diatonic notes (a major or minor scale) plus five auxiliary notes (color or chromatic notes) had, in *Pierrot*, become twelve equal notes used with complete disregard for traditional consonances, the gravitational pulls of tonic and dominant, and other common expectations. The twelve equal notes are flung about, pulled apart at the joints, with large leaps to unpredictable pitches. Sharp dissonances—melodic, contrapuntal, and chordal, emphasizing major sevenths and minor ninths—abound in the score. Sudden changes in vocal and instrumental registers, abrupt shifts in dynamic levels, fluctuating paces in the *Sprechstimme,* and techniques like *pizzicato, glissando,* and *tremolo* all contribute to the changing moods of the individual pieces, of which the first, "Mondestrunken" ("Moon-drunk") is the recorded example.

The wine we drink with our eyes
the moon pours down in floods at night,
and a spring tide overflows
the silent horizon.

Desires, shuddering and sweet,
ride the floods in countless number!
The wine we drink with our eyes,
the moon pours down in floods at night.

The poet, awe-inspired,
revels in the sacred draught.
Heavenward, entranced, he lifts
his head and, reeling, sips and gulps
the wine we drink with our eyes.

Den Wein, den man mit Augen trinkt,
Giesst Nachts der Mond in Wogen nieder,
Und eine Springflut überschwemmt
Den stillen Horizont.

Gelüste, schauerlich und süss,
Durchschwimmen ohne Zahl die Fluten!
Den Wein, den man mit Augen trinkt,
Giesst Nachts der Mond in Wogen nieder.

Der Dichter, den die Andacht treibt,
Berauscht sich an dem heilgen Tranke,
Gen Himmel wendet er verzückt
Das Haupt und traumelnd saugt und schlürft er
Den Wein, den man mit Augen trinkt.

6. ANTON VON WEBERN (1883–1945)

Arnold Schoenberg's most famous pupils were Alban Berg and Anton von Webern, both also his lifelong friends. This trio of composers strongly affected the course of twentieth-century music: Schoenberg through his formulation of the twelve-tone system, Berg through a handful of small chamber works and his powerfully dramatic opera

Wozzeck, and Webern through the development of a musical style similar to pointillistic techniques in painting. Their contributions and influences extended far beyond the above-mentioned works and procedures, for the techniques of all three have been studied seriously by most later composers.

It was Schoenberg who imposed order on what was threatening to become musical chaos. Peering into the abyss of complete freedom in their handling of tones, composers in the early part of this century had adopted various alternatives to the older major-minor system of tonality: bitonal and polytonal music (writing in two or more keys simultaneously), chords in intervals other than thirds (fourths and fifths), freely dissonant counterpoint, decisions that the music of the future lay in microtones (more than twelve notes to an octave), and among other experiments music that was atonal, lacking tonal direction toward a tonic with its surrounding satellite harmonies. But the complete freedom seemingly offered by atonality created enormous problems of form, texture, harmony, rhythm, counterpoint, melody, and tone color. How were those experimenting composers to organize music, to make it coherent, to work according to some guiding principle?

Berg, Webern, and many of their followers accepted Schoenberg's suggestions, and so-called twelve-tone composition became one of the most widely adopted (and controversial) techniques of creativity in this century. Basically, the composer works from a "row" of twelve different notes, no one of which is repeated until all twelve are sounded. The row is manipulated by sounding it in its original form, its inversion (the intervals remain the same, but the direction up and down is reversed), its retrograde (the original played backward), and its inverted retrograde. In any of these forms any single note can be sounded in any octave without destroying the integrity of the row. Furthermore, each form allows several transpositions. Each can be used horizontally (as melody) or vertically (as in chords), and each can be subdivided, as in two groups of six notes each or three groups of four notes each, to lend distinct motivic patterns. Upon each row or section of a row are superimposed other elements, such as rhythm, dynamics, phrasing, and tone color. Although the possibilities for any one row of twelve notes are many, the presence of the row acts as a unifying factor that has helped many composers to shape and organize new music.

Alban Berg freely drew from Schoenberg, employing serial techniques when it suited his purposes. But generally he avoided theory or doctrine, preferring to call upon intuitive gifts to help him solve musical problems. His opera *Wozzeck,* with its big, rich orchestral setting and gripping plot, ranks at the top of twentieth-century works for the stage.

Schoenberg's other pupil, Anton von Webern, moved in a completely opposite direction: he attempted to distill music to absolute essences, and his entire output of compositions takes less time to play than Berg's opera does. His longest single work extends to about 10 minutes; the shortest lasts a few seconds. The recorded example, ○ ● Five Pieces for Orchestra, op. 10, takes about 4 minutes. His instrumental and vocal resources are usually modest in number, and even then his players and singers "rest" more than they play and sing.

Melody, mostly in large intervals, passes from one instrument to another, often one note to each instrument. *Klangfarbenmelodie* (melody constructed from the different tone colors of various instruments) becomes a characteristic feature of Webern's style. Imagine "My Country 'Tis of Thee" played by ten different instruments, each playing only one or two notes of the melody at a time and at irregularly spaced intervals and resting the remainder of the time. Then listen to Webern, where the melodies involve wide skips, where dynamic nuance and balance shift delicately, where instrumental colors sound individually and in combination, where effects of flutter tonguing or harmonics or mutes dab the thin textures, and where musical space (in the sense of texture) and musical time (in the sense of rhythm) appear to be almost empty and motionless. Economy of musical means prevails to an unprecedented degree. In Webern, the grandiose gestures of a Wagner or a Liszt have been replaced by whispers, a 3-hour opera by a 4-minute, five-movement orchestral piece in which one movement, the fourth, consists of only 6 measures of music.

The instrumentation of Five Pieces . . . calls for seventeen players: flute (doubling on piccolo), oboe, E♭ clarinet, B♭ clarinet (doubling on bass clarinet), horn, trumpet, trombone, mandolin, guitar, celesta, harmonium, harp, one violin, viola, cello, and bass, and percussion instruments like xylophone, glockenspiel, and snare drum. At no point does the entire ensemble play together.

In this music every instant is essential and everything counts. It calls for the most attentive listening precisely because it is economical, reduced in size, and subtle in its fragile musical relationships.

7. IGOR STRAVINSKY (1882-1971)

Igor Stravinsky, as did his counterparts in other countries, found sources of inspiration in the indigenous folklore and folksongs of his native land, and Russian folk elements appeared in his earlier works, *Le Sacre du printemps, Renard,* and *Les Noces* (the last completed in 1923). Moreover, after requiring very large orchestral forces in his celebrated *Sacre* (1913), the composer began to write for more modest-sized ensembles during the war period 1914 to 1918: Conceived as a dramatic spectacle for what he called a *théâtre ambulant*—a touring group to perform on a circuit of Swiss villages—the recorded example, ○ ● *Histoire du Soldat* (*The Soldier's Tale*), calls for seven instrumentalists and, in its completely staged version, a narrator.

Stravinsky himself related: "I discovered my subject in one of Afanasiev's tales of the soldier and the Devil. In the story that attracted me, the soldier tricks the Devil into drinking too much vodka. He then gives the devil a handful of buckshot to eat, assuring him it is caviar, and the Devil greedily swallows it and dies."* After finding other episodes and folk tales in which the soldier and the Devil appeared, Stravinsky eventually collaborated with a friend, C. F. Ramuz, who provided the final libretto. The moral of the tale (Stravinsky was already showing signs of being a musical preacher) is contained in the narration of the Great Chorale, a paraphrase of "You can't have your cake and eat it too," or "You cannot be at once what you are and what you used to be."

The stringent economics of the war years restricted the size of the ensemble, but this limitation turned out to be a blessing in disguise, imposing a severe artistic discipline from which the composer ultimately benefited. In the six Charles Eliot Norton lectures delivered at Harvard University about two decades later, Stravinsky observed: "The more art is controlled, limited, worked over, the more it is free . . . in art as in everything else, one can build only upon a resisting foundation . . . my freedom thus consists in my moving about within the narrow frame that I have assigned myself for each one of my undertakings."† Even in more

---

*Igor Stravinsky and Robert Craft, *Expositions and Developments,* Faber & Faber, Ltd., London, 1959, pp. 89–90.
†Igor Stravinsky, *Poetics of Music* [Arthur Knodel and Ingolf Dahl (trans.)], Vintage Books, New York, 1956, pp. 66, 68.

affluent times Stravinsky deliberately limited his resources, surrounded himself with obstacles, and then accepted and attempted to solve the musical challenges he imposed upon himself. Another factor affecting the choice of instruments for *Histoire du Soldat* was his discovery of American jazz. He said: ''The 'Histoire' ensemble resembles the jazz band in that each instrumental category—strings, woodwinds, brass, percussion—is represented by both treble and bass components. The instruments themselves are jazz legitimates, too, except the bassoon, which is my substitution for the saxophone. . . . The percussion part must also be considered as a manifestation of my enthusiasm for jazz.''*

The work is important for still another reason: It serves as a model for Stravinsky's later neoclassic compositions like *Pulcinella* (1919), *Apollon Musagète* (1928), *Perséphone* (1934), *Orpheus* (1948), and numerous instrumental pieces of the 1920s and 1930s. *Histoire* is lean, athletic, clear, and economical, standing somewhere between the moodiness and expressionism of Schoenberg's *Pierrot lunaire* and the fragile, distilled musical world of Webern's Five Pieces for Orchestra. Stravinsky's music sounds vigorous, assertive, witty, and even at times raucous and vulgar. The rhythmic vitality displayed by the instruments (especially the busy percussion), the jaunty fiddling of the violin, the imaginative musical treatment of the melodic lines, the combinations of tone colors, and the variety of spirit and style in the nine short movements have made *Histoire du Soldat* an important composition.

Four movements out of the original nine are presented here: (I) The Soldier's March, (IV) Royal March, (VI) Tango (one of Three Dances), and (VIII) the Great Chorale.

In The Soldier's March two instruments often play contrapuntally in exactly the same rhythm, usually against an oompah bass, which at times persists in its regularity against other metrical changes above it and at other times stops completely. The violin makes sporadic entrances, playing chords both with the bow and *pizzicato* and occasional arpeggiated figures.

In the narrated version just before the Royal March the speaker strikes blows with his fist and declares, ''Where am I going? Going to see the King!'' The double bass, supported by the violin's playing double and triple stops, provides the rhythmic pulse. Typically, its notes match the

*Stravinsky and Craft, *op. cit.*, p. 91.

beat at times and go against the beat at others. And at times the background rhythm simply rests. Together, these rhythmic procedures give a sense of flippancy to this and to other movements. With disregard for usual placement, Stravinsky sometimes has his bassoon playing in a register above the clarinet and violin. In all movements the composer carefully specified how his percussionist is to strike his instruments, with what special kind of stick (hard felt, cane with fiber head), and where (at the rim, in the center).

The Tango features the violin and percussion, with here and there a brief entrance of the clarinet. The tango element is clearly suggested in the rhythms, melodies, and double stops of the violin and in the deft rhythmic touches in the cymbals and drums. Yet it is a tango that has been twisted and distorted; it retains some of its shape but fascinates because of its deformity.

The Great Chorale is a caricature of the dignified older form. Choralelike suggestions are heard: echoes of "A Mighty Fortress Is Our God," the typical holds at places where the ends of text lines would normally appear, the comparative independence of each of the instrumental parts (à la Bach), and the relative length, texture, and rhythmic movement. But each aspect has been grotesquely transformed. The chords at the *fermata*s are arrived at in unexpected ways; the part writing, conceived for independent contrapuntal lines, is sharply dissonant; and although the length, texture, and rhythm convey the feeling of a chorale, it is a chorale addressed to the Devil, who incidentally had just disappeared at the end of the preceding movement. The Luther of "A Mighty Fortress" would be scandalized.

8. BÉLA BARTÓK (1881–1945)

The period from around 1925 to 1940 was rich in productivity for Bartók. Starting with the beginnings of *Mikrokosmos* (1926–1937), a set of over one hundred fifty piano pieces of increasing difficulty, Bartók wrote his last four (of six) string quartets (1927–1939), his second piano concerto (1930–1931), the violin concerto (1937–1938), the Sonata for Two Pianos and Percussion (1937), and one of his most moving works, ○ ● *Music for String Instruments, Percussion, and Celesta* (1937), the second movement of which is our recorded example.

This last work calls for two string orchestras (physically divided in baroque antiphonal fashion) plus a third group consisting of piano, celesta, harp, xylophone, timpani, and other percussion. To be most appreciated, this composition needs to be heard in a live performance, where the groups can be seen separated from each other and a genuine excitement results from watching the players, especially the percussionists. Throughout the entire work Bartók exploits the tonal resources of individual instruments and groups. The strings play trills, *pizzicato* passages (but sometimes in special ways), and *tremoli,* with mutes, with *glissandi,* and with other effects. The piano, Bartók reminds us, possesses strong percussive values; it can trill and articulate rhythms as well as sing out a melody. His treatment of percussion calls for *glissandi* in the timpani, brisk rhythmic punctuations on the xylophone, and shimmering *arpeggio*s on the celesta, to name but a few of many special effects.

The first movement of *Music for String Instruments, Percussion, and Celesta* starts in fugal fashion on the note A. It proceeds in a double series of entrances, one series ascending, the other descending, at the distance of a fifth, until the climax of the movement is reached with an entrance on E♮ (a tritone—three whole steps—from A). At this point another series of entrances works its way back to A, and the movement concludes on that one single note.

The second movement opens with a two-note figure, short-long in rhythm and melodically rising a minor third. The idea of short-long (or unstressed-stressed) plays an important part in the movement. The two-note figure can be heard with expanded and compressed intervals, for example, minor seventh and major second. It can also be found descending. Even the timpani constantly pick up the two-note pattern. Numerous thematic entrances are heard in which one group of notes is followed immediately by an inverted (upside-down) version. Bartók varies his textures, occasionally using strong unison passages (the opening measures), dancelike homophonic sections, contrapuntal passages in *pizzicato* strings, and a fugal section (near the end of the middle section). An unmistakable return to the opening material at the same tonal level marks the beginning of the last section of a large ternary form.

The third and fourth movements are equally interesting. An example of Bartók's ''night music,'' the third movement evokes an eerie atmosphere. Bartók assigns unusually prominent roles to the xylophone, celesta, and timpani in this slow movement. As the first movement, the form is laid out in an arch, in this instance *ABCDCBA*. The last movement contains altered modal scales, syncopations, and what one might call transformed folkdance tunes. The form is a somewhat complicated rondo, with references to the opening measures constituting the returns.

Bartók's style in general can be described as highly original, the product of an immensely gifted and intuitive musical mind. A great contrapuntalist, an imaginative tone colorist, he is also impressive in his remarkable sensitivity to form, perhaps the most difficult of all problems facing contemporary composers. In this respect Bartók resembles Mozart or Beethoven, for most of his music creates the impression of being inevitable. Although even the casual listener may often be aware of the structure that underpins the music, it is perhaps the trained listener who most appreciates this composer's strong sense of form.

Unfortunately, it was only after Bartók's tragic death in 1945 that the musical world fully recognized his genius. For a decade or so he was enthusiastically studied and copied by young composers, and his compositions were widely performed throughout the world. Then interest lessened somewhat, partly because of changing tastes and new techniques, especially electronic ones. Yet today his music occupies a secure place in the orchestral, chamber-music, and solo repertories, and it seems likely to be heard for many years to come.

9. ILLINOIS JACQUET (1922–   )

The roots of American popular music can be traced back many decades. In the late nineteenth century the young nation began to show evidence of its important musical future. At the same time divisions in its music, due in part to ethnic and cultural differences, also appeared. America sought, naturally enough, to imitate what it considered to be the highest attainments of western Europe: symphony, concerto, opera, and ballet. But its energies and its pragmatic, practical, attitudes looked more to popular forms like dance music, folksong, band concerts, minstrel shows, vaudeville, and light opera. For an adventurous, expanding nation music was to be identified with entertainment as well as with edification; "In the Evening by the Moonlight" or a lively square dance possessed an immediate attractiveness that Wagner's *Die Götterdämmerung,* with all its intense profundity, could not match.

Not the least of these popular stylistic branches were the dances, work songs, and religious music of black Americans. These gave a strong initial impetus to the development in this country of a distinctly original music—jazz—which continued to splinter into numerous styles (ragtime, blues, cool jazz, swing, hot jazz, rock), some already faded into history's dateless night, others vibrantly alive today, and still others enjoying periodic revivals. With the advent of the ragtime band, blues singing, and other forms of jazz, the world slowly began to acknowledge a powerful new musical force: American popular music. This music was exciting, different, colorful—a strong antidote to European seriousness. From its origins in the South this music spread throughout the country and finally began to have an influence on even such serious European composers as Milhaud and Stravinsky. The small jazz combos of the 1920s gave rise to the big-band era, the swing music of the 1930s and 1940s. At the end of World War II Americans were ready for other styles, the most important being rock in its many forms.

Until recently, most American popular music (sentimental ballads, Westerns, ragtime, jazz) has contained certain basic ingredients: a more or less singable tune, a set of fairly predictable harmonies, a regular phrase structure, and a steady, regular, underlying rhythmic beat. Starting from these given elements, the typical American popular singer or instrumentalist adds his highly creative interpretation, usually with a degree of freedom seldom permitted in traditional classical music. When a popular singer or instrumentalist characteristically ornaments a given tune, he almost automatically sets up melodic, rhythmic, and harmonic tensions, the general impression being one of imposing irregularity, that is, freely improvised lines, over a fundamental regularity, that is, underlying rhythmic pulse, harmonic patterns, and phrase structure. No matter how far the performer strays, he never loses his "instinctive" feeling for where the music is at any given moment, and he can always find his way back quickly.

In our recorded version of o "How High the Moon," Illinois Jacquet and his small combo provide a typical jazz treatment (we might even say a classic jazz treatment) of a recognizable tune. The ensemble consists of trumpet, saxophone, piano, guitar, double bass, and percussion. The performance uses a regular beat throughout, the rhythms near the end, however, becoming more complicated. A traditional 32-bar structure regularly repeats, with successive choruses featuring different instruments, until the last section; here for most of the entire chorus 2-measure units prevail. The first 32 measures of the piece feature the trumpet, the next 32 the guitar, 32 the piano, and 32 the saxophone. Following this, a section occurs where trumpet, saxophone, and percussion fragment the piece by taking successively only 2 measures at a time. In the last 8 measures the saxophone sounds an unmistakable repetition of the basic tune.

The material played by the featured instrument is constantly surrounded by the music of the background instruments, which momentarily come to the fore and then drop back as the featured instrument reenters. Note how regular the formal structure is; Mozart in his most classic moments is no more square and regular: 2 measures taken twice become a unit of 4, which combined with another such unit makes 8, and the 8 plus 8 give us half the piece, the two 16 halves forming one complete chorus; the first four choruses each feature one instrument. The excitement of the performance certainly does not stem from irregularities in the basic, underlying, beat and phrase structure. The tune itself undergoes metamorphoses; it is always there but not always easily recognizable. At the end it reappears in a relatively pure form, providing a kind of psychological gift to those listeners who had lost their way en route.

10. THAD JONES (1923–   ), MEL LEWIS (1929–   )

The preceding piece represented the more or less traditional small jazz combo whose roots can be traced back to men like King Oliver and Louis "Satchmo" Armstrong, the classics of earlier decades in this century. The Thad Jones–Mel Lewis orchestra can be viewed as either a revival or a vestige of the Count Basie–Benny Goodman big-band era of the late 1930s and 1940s—updated, of course, to suit modern tastes. In each instance, the nucleus consists of a set of trumpets, trombones, saxophones, and rhythm instruments. In Goodman's band the clarinet was Goodman himself, in the Jones–Lewis band Jones is featured on the flügelhorn, a brass instrument similar in shape to the trumpet and cornet. The attentive listener may detect a slightly deeper, more mellow tone quality, due in part to the flügelhorn's wider bore and modified shape as compared with the more common brass instruments named.

A brief comparison may be in order:

Goodman (ca. 1940)	Basie (ca. 1940)	Jones–Lewis (1970)
3 trumpets	4 trumpets	4 trumpets
2 trombones	3 trombones	4 trombones
4 saxophones	4 saxophones	5 saxophones
4 rhythm: piano, guitar, bass, drums	4 rhythm: piano, guitar, bass, drums	4 rhythm: piano, guitar, bass, drums
1 clarinet		1 flügelhorn
14 players	15 players	18 players

Both Jones and Lewis have had extensive experience playing in large groups, Jones almost ten years with Basie and Lewis as a drummer with Gerry Mulligan, Goodman, and other big bands; they have also played in small groups. Formed in 1965, their big band combines the best of two worlds:the small freely improvising combo and the clean, precise, accurately arranged ensemble necessary in big-band performance.

The recorded sample, ○● "Don't Ever Leave Me," is an opportunity to hear how thematic material is flung back and forth among several soloists and instrumental groups, how backgrounds may vary from simple percussion touches to complicated ensemble writing, and how textures, dynamics, and other musical elements can change abruptly within short periods of time. The phrase structure in "Don't Ever Leave Me" follows 4-measure patterns, each of which contains more varied material than the comparable regular phrases in the Jacquet version of "How High the Moon." In both pieces regularity of rhythm and phrase underlies the music, giving a firm foundation to its rhythmic and formal structure. Attention tends to focus, therefore, on the improvisations, contrasts in dynamics, differences in tone color, and the stretching of melody-related rhythms as far as they can be without complete destruction of a sense of direction and order.

11. THE MODERN JAZZ QUARTET AND GUESTS

Jazz, like romanticism, is hard to define. Its many splintering offshoots have created numerous styles, sometimes difficult to distinguish and even harder to describe. Since The Modern Jazz Quartet uses the term, it *does* play jazz, but in a style that is smooth, sophisticated, and related in various ways to traditional or serious music. This relationship is due, in part, to the guiding hand of John Lewis (1920–   ), whose creative ideas have sparked the ensemble since its inception in the early 1950s. Lewis, a pianist, composer, and arranger, studied at the Manhattan School of Music and sang with the Scholum Cantorum choral group. In him classical training is combined with a natural flair for jazz. A merging of both elements is often noticeable in the music played by The Modern Jazz Quartet. With this group we sense that formal construction and free improvisation complement each other, that the relationship between freedom and constraint is mutually beneficial.

In "Da Capo" (*Third Stream Music,* Atlantic ATC 1345), The Quartet (piano, vibraharp, bass, and drums) is augmented by The Jimmy Giuffre Trio, which adds guitar, clarinet, and another bass. Two basic musical ideas predominate: a jaunty, dancelike figure and a somewhat more sombre pastoral melody. The first emphasizes a rhythm of long-short-short notes played rapidly and built mainly around a major triad plus its minor seventh. The second idea moves in note values that are longer and mostly equal; this tune is mainly diatonic and stepwise.

The piece begins with an introduction, in which the clarinet, vibraharp, and then piano are heard over a pedal point in the double bass. Near the end of the introduction the piano plays repeated notes as a *ritardando* occurs, followed by a hold in the music and a brief pause. The first motive is then heard in vibraharp alone, and this brief section closes with another *ritardando* and a pause. The pastoral tune appears in the clarinet with a double-bass *arpeggio,* and it likewise slows down at the end of the section. Repeated listening to these opening sections will prove rewarding because much of what takes place in the remainder of the composition can be directly traced from the two initial musical ideas.

Like the preceding two pieces, "Da Capo" is firmly based on a regular phrase syntax, but there are many more rhythmic interruptions, accomplished by *ritardandi,* holds on certain sounds, and brief pauses. At times the beat is strong and steady; at other moments the music is almost without beat. To listeners familiar with the two musical ideas, the piece offers challenges as clarinet, vibraharp, and guitar improvise upon the tunes. At one spot, piano and vibraharp enjoy the competition of a duet;

at another, clarinet and guitar collaborate. Other interesting aspects can be found in the variety of accompaniments, the textures, the nature of the cadences (strong and weak), and the dynamic levels. Most of the time the piece resembles an intelligent and animated conversation but with the special simultaneity and coherence characteristic of the art of music.

12. ORNETTE COLEMAN (1930-   )

Illinois Jacquet, Thad Jones, Mel Lewis, and their Jazz Orchestra, and John Lewis and The Modern Jazz Quartet have all sparked lively discussions among musicians and jazz critics. In Ornette Coleman we encounter a figure whose music and style of playing have been both praised (''an innovator of the first water'') and severely damned (''overtouted'' and ''more and more of a bore''). Coleman creates controversy—usually heated controversy—rather than polite discussion. In the early 1960s he came on the scene, after years of wandering around in various bands, with a spectacular new style. To what extent his own self-teaching from harmony and theory textbooks was enhanced by contacts with, and help by, John Lewis and Gunter Schuller (present Director of the New England Conservatory of Music) can be only a matter of speculation; nevertheless, he appeared with a style so divorced from traditional concepts that he enjoyed the usual hero worship and suffered the scorn that any innovator must receive. In effect, his music often sounded atonal, it lacked regularity of beat, balanced phrase structure was abandoned, the usual chord patterns disappeared, and what emerged was a kind of raw, ecstatic, intense playing—the Freudian id brought to the level of musical articulation: Primitive, eruptive, powerful emotional utterances suggesting anguished and uninhibited wails are sometimes brought into contrast with music that sounds quiet, subdued, and tender. This range of expression stems largely from the astonishing variety of sounds that Coleman is able to elicit from the alto saxophone.

In 1962 he played in New York's Town Hall. Among the pieces performed was our recorded example, o● ''Sadness,'' in which he was accompanied by a string ensemble and percussion.

From the opening seconds the listener knows that this music is different. The first measures, in the strings alone, not only are atonal but are also microtonal, the string players sounding tones smaller than a half step. With the entire ensemble playing microtones, the effect is that of a band of sound pulsing back and forth in very narrow and wide ranges. In this mass of pulsating strings, traditional landmarks like exact pitches, triads, rhythm patterns, and other recognizable sounds are completely missing. Such a technique resembles the bands of sounds frequently used by composers of electronic music and by certain composers like Xenakis and Penderecki (see 14 and 18).

Coleman's improvisation above this background (occasionally complemented by percussion instruments) centers on two series of notes plus a third two-note figure. The first series consists of three ascending large-leap notes, the first two of which are in a dotted rhythm and the last (and highest) a much longer note. The second series consists of four ascending notes, roughly equal in duration and moving stepwise, followed by a *glissando* to a fifth note, the longest in duration and also the highest. In the first two appearances each series concludes with a two-note figure, the second note of which is lower in pitch and longer in duration. From these elements Coleman constructs his gripping improvisation against the accompaniment of throbbing strings and occasional percussion.

13. BLOOD, SWEAT AND TEARS

Compared with the preceding Ornette Coleman piece, the recorded example, ○● "God Bless the Child" (from *Blood, Sweat and Tears*), may seem fairly traditional in sound. Yet the music warrants the term "sophisticated." Concentrated listening will make you aware of a wealth of well-handled musical elements: improvisations, interludes, choralelike harmony, *ostinato* patterns, changing textures, and dynamic fluctuations.

To the traditional rock quartet add a quartet of jazz players plus a singer, and a new, exciting musical style has been created. After one brief abortive effort, Blood, Sweat and Tears coalesced into something distinct and successful enough to keep the wedding of rock and jazz alive and thriving. Nine versatile musicians now constitute the ensemble:

Alto saxophone and piano
Trumpet and flügelhorn
Trumpet and flügelhorn

Trombone and recorder
Organ, piano, flute, trombone, and vocals
Guitar, harmonica, and vocals
Drums, percussion, and vocals
Double bass
Lead vocalist

Although the vocal solo is cleanly articulated, the complete text is given below, partly for the form and partly for the message:

Them that's got shall get,
Them that's not shall lose,
So the Bible says,
And it still is news.
Mama may have,
Papa may have,
God bless the child that's got his own,
That's got his own.

And the strong seem to get more
While the weak ones fade;
Empty pockets don't ever make the grade.
Mama may have,
Papa may have,
God bless the child that's got his own,
That's got his own.

And when you got money,
You got lots of friends
Crowding round your door;
When the money's gone
And all your spending ends,
They won't be round any more—no, no more.

And rich relations may give you
A crust of bread 'n' such:
You can help yourself,
But don't take too much.
Mama may have,

And papa may have,
God bless the child that's got his own,
That's got his own.

And when you got money,
You've got lots of friends
Crowding 'round your door (wait a minute, children);
And when the money's gone
And all your spending ends,
They won't be around any more (no).

And (the) rich relations may give you
A crust of bread 'n' such:
You can help yourself,
But don't take too much.
Mama may have,
And papa may have,
God bless the child who can stand up and say,
"I got my own,
Every child's got to have his own."

14. YANNIS XENAKIS (1922–   )

Shortly after the end of World War II, modern electronic music made its tentative beginnings although the Hammond organ and some lesser known instruments had been producing music electronically for a number of years. But the spectacular first steps in this infant technique came in the 1950s, when the tape recorder made superimposed dubbings possible. One man could now really become a "one-man band": he could play both solo parts of the Bach two-violin concerto; he could sing a quartet by himself; or he could sound like ten guitars. By chopping and splicing tapes, changing the speed of the tape, and controlling intensities, he could eliminate wrong notes or poorly played passages, make a flute sound like a bassoon, and change the squeak of a mouse to the roar of a lion. He could mix natural sounds (wind, rain, water) with man-made sounds like traffic noise, ringing telephones, and animated conversation. As more sophisticated and complex electronic processes were developed, the range of opportunity for the electronic composer expanded, and with it a new musical vocabulary came into existence. In place of the older and traditional terms, we now speak and read about electronic music in such terms as the following: sine-wave generator, ring modulator, low-pass filter, acoustic-input transducer, linear control, readout, and digital-to-analog interface—along with some familiar words like formant, reverberation, and decibel.

In the early stages of electronic music two men, Pierre Schaeffer and Herbert Eimert, provided direction and impetus, the first mainly through practical experimentation and the second mainly through theory. Although a few older composers like Messiaen and Varèse were immediately attracted to the new music, its most consistent enthusiasts have been composers born in the 1920s and later (Xenakis, Luigi Nono, Stockhausen, Berio), some notable exceptions being Luening, Ussachevsky, Cage, and Babbitt, all born in the first two decades of the century. Indeed, almost all serious composers under age 40 have either written some electronic music, have experimented with it, or are conversant with its techniques and methods. The electronic-music movement continues to grow; but we stand so close to its birth that judgment on the merit of individual electronic compositions and the movement in general should be tentative and cautiously encouraging. In the long run those composers who have something significant to say will say it, regardless of the musical medium they happen to adopt.

In 1947 a young Greek musician, Yannis Xenakis, left Athens for Paris, where he studied with Honegger, Milhaud, and Messiaen, and because he held an engineering degree from the Polytechnic School in Athens, he became associated with the famous architect Le Corbusier. This combination of scientific, technical training with solid education in music shows itself clearly in his approach to musical composition. According to Xenakis, composing is subject to a principle of scientific order found in all phases of life and activity; with the vision of a mystic, he advocates an aesthetic creed that leaves nothing to chance, not even chance itself. A superrationalist, he builds randomness and unpredictability—even capriciousness—into his music through mathematical formulas of probability, but his belief in complete determinacy (in which all musical elements are totally controlled) also attempts to take into account some of the waywardness of the human condition. Thus everything in music—pitch, rhythm, dynamic level, articulation, texture, tempo, tone color, intensity, attack and decay, and all their combinations—acts according to principles of probability although each of these elements has its own strictly controlled independence, their combination being determined by statistical patterns and probability curves. In this calculus of probabilities we may not see the individual tree, but we *do* see the forest; in music we may not hear the individual sound, but we experience the mass of sound as we might the mass behavior of electrons in physics. Although the physicist cannot predict the behavior of a single electron, he can deal successfully with large numbers of electrons on the basis of statistical probability.

Shortly after composing ○● *Pithoprakta* (1955–1956), the recorded example, Xenakis turned to electronic music although he continued to write, as in this work, for conventional musical instruments. *Pithoprakta* is included here to show how the principle of determinacy in Xenakis's setting (using traditional instruments) contrasts with the following electronic piece, *Omaggio a Joyce* by Luciano Berio, which mixes electronic and vocal sounds in what appears to be a less controlled way.

For his orchestra of fifty instruments Xenakis requires twelve first violins, twelve second violins, eight violas, eight cellos, and six double basses, a modest-sized but typically balanced string group; additional instruments include two tenor trombones, xylophone, and wood block. The Greek title means ''actions by probabilities,'' and the work was originally composed on graph paper (a not-unusual procedure) to be then transcribed into conventional notation. Xenakis treats his instruments in a most unorthodox fashion. In addition to playing *pizzicato, glissando,* and *col legno* (with the wood of the bow), the string players also tap their instruments, sometimes vigorously, to create a continuous sound against which other string players emit melodic fragments. The sound density varies from thick to thin. At times the sustained tone colors persist in the background while repeated pitches, often in irregular rhythms, punctuate the mass of sound. The wood block occasionally plays a rhythmic counterpoint against plucked strings. At other times a brief moment of silence will prevail. Some may find the music chaotic; yet it is anything but chaotically conceived. Xenakis's aesthetic theories have been recently formulated in his book *Musiques formelles* (1963), by which time he had written a number of electronic pieces (*Diamorphoses, Concret PH, Analogique A* + *B, Bohor*). His theories are as controversial as his music, and they can give rise to heated discussions concerning the nature of art.

15. LUCIANO BERIO (1925-   )

In 1922 James Joyce (1882–1941) published *Ulysses,* a long novel reconstructing the experiences of a single day, June 16, 1907, in Dublin. In 1958 Luciano Berio composed a musical tribute (homage) to Joyce, o *Omaggio a Joyce,* our recorded example. Berio had good reason to choose Joyce, for the novelist was himself extremely sensitive to nuances of sounds as they applied to language, not hesitating to make up words that conveyed, through their resonance and sonorous qualities, sensations common to touch, smell, feel, and sound in human existence; and it was probably Joyce's skill in capturing the complexities of a single instant (the tick of a clock, the texture of a wall, the color of a dress, the odor of bacon frying) in words that stretch a moment into page after page of description that made it possible for him to write a complete novel covering the events of only a single day. *Ulysses,* like *Finnegans Wake* and other works of Joyce, should be read aloud because the novel pleases the ear as much as it does the mind.

In *Omaggio a Joyce* Berio salutes the master novelist by taking a single fragment from *Ulysses.* The composer recorded a woman's voice reading the fragment in English, French, and Italian. These vocal sounds are mixed in different ways with electronic sounds, the sound, shape, and musicality of the text gradually being converted into musical (electronic) sounds. Berio's interest in the relationships between music and language parallels the interest of the novelist, the musician starting from music and the novelist from the word; questions of order, grammar, syntax, combination, simultaneity, context, form, and tone color are common to both creative artists as they seek to communicate in meaningful ways. Language consists of phonations (successions of noises, pauses, transitions), degrees of differentiation (letters, syllables, words, and combinations of words), plus rules of usage. Berio gives us phonations; there are pauses, transitions, and inflected pitch levels. We also hear the sibilant ess, the hum of em, syllables, words, and words in combination. And we occasionally hear passages with normal usage, for example, "so lonely." Joyce could only approximate or suggest the effect of simultaneity, but Berio can bring to us not one but three or more levels of simultaneous events, a technique made possible by the tape recorder and other electronic instruments.

16. DONALD ERB (1927–   )

○● *Reconnaissance* is for instruments and electronic sounds. A composition in five fairly short movements, of which our recorded example is the third, the work requires violin, double bass, piano, percussion, Moog Synthesizer, and a Moog polyphonic instrument. It is a sextet but a very unusual one. The electronic Moog Synthesizer produces and imitates sounds by controlling various elements, such as pitches, durations, and intensities. The Moog polyphonic instrument has a keyboard with a four-octave range; instead of twelve pitches to the octave, as in the piano, organ, and harpsichord, this instrument divides each octave into forty-three units, thereby producing pitch changes that are microtonal. In traditional keyboard fashion the performers can play chords as well as single notes.

In this strikingly different sextet the composer has created contemporary chamber music in which each instrument participates on an equal basis. By playing the music (rather than having it prerecorded on tapes), the performers can convey a sense of personal urgency and dramatic tension comparable with other live performances of music. Each electronic instrument requires its own musician as, of course, do the traditional instruments. The latter, however, are used in extremely imaginative ways. You will hear percussion taps, slithering *glissandi* on the stringed instruments, microtones, extreme ranges, sirenlike effects, suggestions of imitations in melodic patterns, *pizzicato*, spots of sound resembling the late-nineteenth-century pointillistic techniques in painting, and a climax.

That the music seems expressive may possibly be a result of Erb's own approach to the craft and art of composition. He has made the following statement:

*To me composing is basically an intuitive process. A composer should be able to use what he knows about music in an instinctive manner rather than relying on systems. Neither am I interested in abdicating my responsibility as a composer to factors over which I have little or no control.**

*Donald Erb, record-jacket notes for the album containing *Reconnaissance*, Nonesuch H-71223.

17. JOHN CAGE (1912–   )

Years before John Cage made his appearance on the musical scene, French protesters had organized a kind of insanity called "dada." During World War I the movement rose to prominence and then rapidly faded, lingering on only into the 1920s. Dada was more than an art movement; it was a way of looking at life and at art. Reacting against the senseless inhumanity of the war, young poets, artists, dancers, intellectuals, and plain madcaps opposed almost everything. Dada (meaning a hobbyhorse and hence nothing) was given its own manifesto by Tristan Tzara in Zurich, March 23, 1918:

Dada: abolition of logic . . . memory . . . archeology . . . prophets . . . the future: Dada; absolute and unquestionable faith in every god that is the immediate product of spontaneity. . . . Freedom: Dada Dada Dada, a roaring of tense colors, an interacting of opposites and of all contradictions, grotesques, inconsistencies: LIFE.

Its adherents provoked, demonstrated, tricked, lampooned, desecrated, and abused while engaging in all sorts of nonsense and absurdity. Dada became too successful, probably dying because of a self-defeating popularity foisted on it by a willing, gullible public.

Similarly, musicians, critics, and audiences have never quite known how to take John Cage. Born himself only four years before the official birth of dada in 1916, he has promulgated unorthodox practices and theories that have severely tested the patience of audiences. Yet unlike the dada movement, which had a very short life, Cage's controversial creations, so reminiscent of dada attitudes, have continued to increase his popularity and influence.

In Cage's early music, pianos were "prepared" by placing various objects (paper clips, rubber bands, tops) on the strings. By striking the soundboard and the frame with hands and drumsticks, by leaning inside and plucking, tapping, and strumming the strings, he and his companion, David Tudor, created novel effects. Later he combined prepared pianos with tapes, radios, extra microphones, toy pianos, and among other things Slinkies (coiled springs that can wind their way down stairs). Toy trumpets and whistles were also called into action. Playing on, upon, beside, in, and under a piano creates entertaining diversions for audiences privileged to witness his programs. (One repetitious piece lasted about 35 hours, during which members of the audience arrived and departed. At the end a wit is said to have shouted, "Bravo! Encore!")

Is Cage for real? Opinion today holds that he is. From his early experimental music has evolved his use of chance, the abandonment of rational control by the composer over his materials. The term "aleatoric" (from Latin, *alea*, "chance") is used to describe this music. According to Cage, music happens randomly, but to Cage the term "music" means the entire spectrum of sounds in the world. Organization, coherence, "message"—if they occur at all—just happen to happen. Why not place a perforated grid on a sheet of music paper, mark through the holes, remove the grid, and play the notes now found on the sheet? Why not scatter pages of music on the floor, pick them up, and then play them in the resulting random order? Why not let a performer play when, where, and how he chooses? Why not mix and combine sounds as they frequently are mixed and combined in real life? By asking questions like these, Cage has provoked serious thought concerning the creative process; in lectures and writing he has given expression to controversial, stimulating ideas. The most significant composers of our time have reflected upon what he has had to say.

On the recorded sample the opening narration to Cage's happening
o *Variations IV* provides a brief background for Cage's activities and then explains the circumstances surrounding the "performance."

18. KRZYSZTOF PENDERECKI (1933–   )

In the most advanced musical circles there exists a growing appreciation for much of the avant-garde music written by contemporary Polish composers like Witold Lutosławski, Wlodzimierz Kotonski, Wojciech Kilar, Boguslaw Schaeffer, Henryk Górecki, and Krzysztof Penderecki. The last had greatness thrust upon him when he anonymously entered three different compositions in a 1959 national competition in Poland and won the three first prizes.

Although he has been working with electronic music since about 1961 (*Psalmus,* for single-channel tape recorder), he is better known for works like *Anaklasis* (1960) for strings and percussion, *The Dimensions of Time and Silence* (1960) for chorus and orchestra, *Threnody for the Victims of Hiroshima* (1960), the Stabat Mater (1961), *De natura sonoris* (1966) for orchestra, the Capriccio for Violin and Orchestra (1967), and his *St. Luke Passion* (1963–1965)—all written for conventional instruments and voices, used unconventionally.

Penderecki skillfully manages to exploit tone-color combinations, sometimes in massive sonorities but at other times with the most delicate nuances; as a person, he must possess a phenomenally acute sensitivity to sound. In his vocal writing he creates blocks of sound that often consist of whistling, humming, weird *vibrati,* and *glissandi,* as well as normal singing. In his instrumental style his string players strike, pluck, and bow in a variety of ways. He also produces equally strange effects in the woodwinds, brasses, and percussion. Essentially, the style emphasizes superimposed layers of pitches, timbre, dynamics, and varying textures rather than cleanly separate polyphonic lines. He is eclectic to the extent that he absorbs techniques from present and past composers and fits them into his own expressive style.

Penderecki's music seems to have the same immediate impact that works like Carl Orff's *Carmina Burana* (1936) and Alban Berg's *Wozzeck* (1914–1923) have had on many listeners. The three composers represent widely diverse aspects of twentieth-century music; their styles and talents differ, but in these works there is a kind of direct emotional and dramatic appeal often believed to be the real purpose of music.

The recorded excerpt from the o *St. Luke Passion* deals mainly with the appearance of Christ before Pilate and the multitude, as recounted in the twenty-third chapter of the Luke gospel. The Evangelist is a speaking part; Christ is sung by a baritone, and Pilate by a bass.

And the whole crowd of them, rising up, led	*Et surgens omnis multitudo eorum, duxerunt*
Him to Pilate. And they began to accuse	*Illum ad Pilatum. Coeperunt autem accusare*
Him, saying:	*Illus, dicentes:*
"We have found this man perverting our nation	*"Hunc invenimus subvertentem gentem nostram,*
and forbidding the giving of tribute to Caesar	*et prohibentem tributa dare Caesari,*
and saying that he is Christ the King."	*et dicentem se Christum Regem esse."*
"Art thou the King of the Jews?"	*"Tu es Rex Judaeorum?"*
"Thou sayest it."	*"Tu dicis."*
"I find no fault in this man."	*"Nihil invenio causae in hoc homine."*
And he sent Him away to Herod.	*Et remisit Eum ad Herodem.*
Herod questioned Him in many	*Herodes autem interrogabat Illum multis*
words. But He answered him nothing. And Herod mocked	*sermonibus. At ipse nihil Illi respondebat, sprevit*

Him, putting on Him a white garment and sent Him
back to Pilate. And Pilate, calling together the chief
priests, said to them:
"Behold, nothing deserving of death has been committed by him.
I will chastise him and release him."
"Away with this man, and release unto us Barabbas."
And Pilate again spoke to them,
desiring to release Jesus. But they cried again,
saying:
"Crucify, crucify him!"
"Why, what evil hath this man done? no cause
of death do I find in him."
"Crucify, crucify him!"

*autem Illum Herodes indutum veste alba et remisit
ad Pilatum. Pilatus autem convocatis principibus
sacerdotum, dixit ad illos:
"Ecce nihil dignum morte actum est el.
Emendatum illum dimittam."
"Tolle hunc, et dimitte nobis Barabbam."
Iterum autem Pilatus locutus est ad illos,
volens dimittere Jesum. At illi succlamabant,
dicentes:
"Crucifige, crucifige illum."
"Quid enim mali fecit iste? nullam causam
mortis invenio in eo."
"Crucifige, crucifige illum."*

Other important music

For some additional music by composers of this period, see the Music Index.

Rather than attempting to categorize every composer or piece, we have provided a list of important composers arranged by birthdate and including some of their most representative compositions not discussed elsewhere in this text.

Twentieth-century composers have frequently created music that is difficult to classify in traditional ways. For experimental or hybrid types the term "other" has occasionally been used below to mean music that is microtonal, electronic, computer generated, or of some other kind. For further information about specific composers or compositions the interested student can consult the later suggested bibliography.

CLAUDE (ACHILLE) DEBUSSY (1862–1918)

SONGS
Ariettes oubliées (1888).
Chansons de Bilitis (1899).
ORCHESTRAL MUSIC
Nocturnes: "Nuages," "Fêtes," "Sirènes" (1893–1899).
CHAMBER MUSIC
Quartet for Strings in g, op. 10 (1893).
Sonata for Flute, Viola, and Harp (1915).

JEAN SIBELIUS (1865–1957)

CONCERTO
For Violin and Orchestra in d, op. 47 (1905).
SYMPHONIES
1 in e, op. 39 (1899).
2 in D, op. 43 (1902).
5 in E♭, op. 82 (1915).
7 in C, op. 105 (1925).

ERIC SATIE (1866–1925)

ORCHESTRAL MUSIC
Gymnopédies (1888). Orchestrated by Debussy.
PIANO MUSIC
Pièces en forme de poire (1903).

RALPH VAUGHAN WILLIAMS (1872–1958)

OPERA
Riders to the Sea (1937).
CHORAL MUSIC
Fantasia on Christmas Carols (1912).
Five Tudor Portraits (1936).
SYMPHONIES
4 in f (1935).
7 (*Sinfonia antartica;* 1951–1952).

SERGEY RAKHMANINOV (1873–1943)

CHORAL MUSIC
The Bells (1913). For solos, chorus, and orchestra.
SONGS
Over 70, of which opus 21 (twelve songs) and opus 26 (fifteen songs)
   are representative.
CONCERTO
Rhapsody on a Theme by Paganini for Piano and Orchestra (1934).

ORCHESTRAL MUSIC

Symphony 2 in e, op. 27 (1907).

Isle of the Dead, op. 29 (1907).

PIANO MUSIC

Numerous preludes, études, *moments musicaux,* and other pieces, of
  which the preludes are perhaps most representative.

CHARLES EDWARD IVES (1874-1964)

CHORAL MUSIC

"Harvest Home" Chorales (1898–1912).

SONGS

Over 100.

ORCHESTRAL MUSIC

Symphony 3 (1901–1904).

Holidays for Orchestra (1904–1913).

Central Park in the Dark (1898–1907).

CHAMBER MUSIC

Sonata 2 for Violin and Piano (1903–1910).

Quartet for Strings 2 (1912).

PIANO MUSIC

Sonata (*Concord;* 1909–1915).

ARNOLD SCHOENBERG (1874-1951)

SONGS

Das Buch der hängenden Gärten, op. 15 (1908).

CONCERTO

For Piano and Orchestra, op. 42 (1943).

PIANO MUSIC

Six Little Piano Pieces, op. 19 (1911).

Suite for Piano, op. 25 (1924).

MAURICE RAVEL (1875-1937)

SONGS

Shéhérazade (1904). Song cycle for voice and orchestra.

Trois Poèmes de Mallarmé (1913). For voice, piano, two flutes, two clarinets, and string quartet.

CONCERTO

For Piano and Orchestra in G (1932).

ORCHESTRAL MUSIC

Rhapsodie espagnole (1907).

Boléro (1928).

CHAMBER MUSIC

Introduction and *Allegro* for Harp, Flute, Clarinet, and String Quartet
  (1906).

PIANO MUSIC

Sonatine (1903–1905).

Le Tombeau de Couperin (1914–1917).

OTTORINO RESPIGHI (1879–1936)

ORCHESTRAL MUSIC

Le Fontane di Roma (1917).

I Pini di Roma (1924).

ERNEST BLOCH (1880–1959)

CONCERTO

Schelomo (1916). For cello and orchestra.

BÉLA BARTÓK (1881–1945)

OPERA

The Castle of Duke Bluebeard (1918). In one act.

CHORAL MUSIC

Cantata profana (1930). For tenor and baritone, double chorus, and
  orchestra.

CONCERTOS

For Violin and Orchestra (1937–1938).

For Piano and Orchestra 2 (1931).

ORCHESTRAL MUSIC

The Miraculous Mandarin Suite (1919).

CHAMBER MUSIC

Sonata 1 for Violin and Piano (1921).

Contrasts for Clarinet, Violin, and Piano (1938).
Sonata for Two Pianos and Percussion (1937).
Sonata for Violin Solo (1944).
Quartet for Strings 5 (1934).
PIANO MUSIC
Improvisations (1920).
Out of Doors Suite (1926).
Mikrokosmos (1926–1937). Six books of graded piano pieces.

IGOR STRAVINSKY (1882–1971)

BALLETS
The Firebird (1910).
Petrouchka (1911).
Agon (1957).
CHORAL MUSIC
Canticum sacrum (1956). For tenor, baritone, chorus, and orchestra.
CONCERTOS
For Sixteen Instruments in E♭ (*Dumbarton Oaks;* 1938).
Movements for Piano and Orchestra (1960).
SYMPHONY
In Three Movements (1945).

ZOLTÁN KODÁLY (1882–1967)

CHORAL MUSIC
Psalmus Hungaricus (1923).
Missa brevis (1945).
ORCHESTRAL MUSIC
Dances of Galanta (1933).

EDGARD VARÈSE (1883–1965)

ORCHESTRAL MUSIC
Arcana (1927).
CHAMBER-ORCHESTRA MUSIC
Octandre (1924).

OTHER

Density 21.5 (1935). For flute solo.
Deserts (1954). For tape and instrumental ensemble.

ANTON VON WEBERN (1883–1945)

SONG CYCLES

Opus 15 (1917). With instrumental accompaniment.
Opus 25 (1935). With piano accompaniment.

CHAMBER MUSIC

Concerto for Nine Instruments, op. 24 (1935).

CHARLES TOMLINSON GRIFFES (1884–1920)

ORCHESTRAL MUSIC

Pleasure Dome of Kubla Khan (1919).
Poem for Flute and Orchestra (1919).

PIANO MUSIC

Roman Sketches, op. 7.

ALBAN BERG (1885–1935)

SONGS

Seven Early Songs (1905–1908). With piano.

ORCHESTRAL MUSIC

Three Pieces for Orchestra, op. 6 (1914).

HEITOR VILLA-LOBOS (1887–1959)

CONCERTO

For Cello and Orchestra 5 (1955).

ORCHESTRAL MUSIC

Dawn in a Tropical Forest (1954).

CHAMBER MUSIC

Bachianas Brasileiras 1 (1930). For eight cellos.
Bachianas Brasileiras 3 (1934). For piano and orchestra.
Bachianas Brasileiras 5 (1938–1939). For soprano and eight cellos.
Bachianas Brasileiras 9 (1945). For strings.

FRANK MARTIN (1890–   )

ORATORIOS
Le Vin herbé (1942).
In terra pax (1945).
Golgotha (1949).
CONCERTOS
For Harpsichord and Small Orchestra (1955).
For seven wind instruments, strings, and percussion (1949).
ORCHESTRAL MUSIC
Petite symphonie concertante (1946). For harp, harpsichord, piano, and
    two string orchestras.

JACQUES IBERT (1890–1962)

CONCERTO
For Flute and Orchestra (1934).
ORCHESTRAL MUSIC
Escales (*Ports of Call*) (1922).

BOHUSLAV MARTINŮ (1890–1959)

CONCERTOS
For Piano and Orchestra 4 (*Incantation;* 1956).
For Two String Orchestras, Piano, and Kettledrums (1940).
For Violin and Orchestra (1943).
ORCHESTRAL MUSIC
Partita for String Orchestra (1931).
Symphony 6 (*Fantasies symphoniques;* 1955).
CHAMBER MUSIC
Quartet for Strings 4 (1936).
Quintet for Piano and Strings 2 (1944).
Trio for Flute, Cello, and Piano (1944).

SERGEY PROKOFIEV (1891–1953)

OPERA
The Love for Three Oranges (1919).

CONCERTOS
For Violin and Orchestra 2 in g, op. 63 (1935).
For Cello and Orchestra 2, op. 125 (1950–1952).
ORCHESTRAL MUSIC
Symphony in D, op. 25, (*Classical;* 1916–1917).
Lieutenant Kije Suite, op. 60 (1934).
Peter and the Wolf, op. 67 (1936).

ARTHUR HONEGGER (1892–1955)

STAGE ORATORIO
Jeanne d'Arc au bûcher (1938).
SYMPHONIES
3 (*Liturgique;* 1946).
5 (*Di tre re;* 1951).

DARIUS MILHAUD (1892–   )

OPERA
Les Choéphores (1915–1916). Second of a trilogy.
CONCERTOS
For Percussion and Small Orchestra (1930).
For Harpsichord and Strings (*L'Apothéose de Molière;* 1948).
SYMPHONIES
Five for small orchestra (1917–1922).
CHAMBER MUSIC, SOLO PIECES, AND SONGS
A staggering number.

WALTER PISTON (1894–   )

CONCERTOS
Concertino for Piano and Orchestra (1936).
Concerto for Viola and Orchestra (1958).
ORCHESTRAL MUSIC
The Incredible Flutist (1938). Ballet suite.
Symphony 5 (1956).
CHAMBER MUSIC
Divertimento for Nine Instruments (1946).

CARL ORFF (1895–   )

STAGE WORKS
Trionfi (1935–1953). A trilogy of three large choral works, performed
    separately, with optional staging.
Catulli Carmina (1943).

PAUL HINDEMITH (1895–1963)

OPERA
Mathis der Maler (1934–1935).
SONG CYCLE
Das Marienleben (1923, revised 1948). For voice and piano.
CONCERTOS
Der Schwanendreher for Viola and Small Orchestra (1935).
Music of Mourning (*Trauermusik*) for Viola and String Orchestra (1936).
Theme and Four Variations for Piano and String Orchestra (*The Four
    Temperaments;* 1940).
For Piano and Orchestra (1945).
For Woodwinds, Harp, and Orchestra (1949).
ORCHESTRAL MUSIC
Mathis der Maler (1934). Symphony from the opera.
Nobilissima Visione (1938). Ballet suite.
Symphonic Metamorphosis on Themes by Weber (1943).
CHAMBER MUSIC AND SOLO PIECES
An enormous amount for various combinations.
PIANO MUSIC
Ludus tonalis (1942).

ROGER SESSIONS (1896–   )

CONCERTO
For Piano and Orchestra (1956).
ORCHESTRAL MUSIC
The Black Maskers (1923).
Symphony 3 (1957).

CHAMBER MUSIC
Quartet for Strings 2 (1950).
PIANO MUSIC
Sonata 2 (1946).

HOWARD HANSON (1896–   )

OPERA
Merry Mount (1933).
CHORAL MUSIC
The Lament of Beowulf (1926).
ORCHESTRAL MUSIC
Merry Mount Suite (1937).
Serenade for Flute, Harp, and Strings (1946).
Sinfonia sacra (1955).

VIRGIL THOMSON (1896–   )

OPERAS
Four Saints in Three Acts (1928).
The Mother of Us All (1947).
CONCERTO
For Flute, Strings, and Percussion (1954).

HENRY COWELL (1897–1965)

ORCHESTRAL MUSIC
Hymn and Fuguing Tune 1–8 (1943–1947).
Symphony 16 (*Icelandic,* 1962).
CHAMBER MUSIC
Sonata for Violin and Piano 1 (1945).

ROY HARRIS (1898–   )

CONCERTO
For Two Pianos and Orchestra (1946).
SYMPHONIES
3 (1938).

7 (1951).
CHAMBER MUSIC
Quintet for Piano and Strings (1936).
Quartet for Strings 3 (1939).

FRANCIS POULENC (1899–1963)

CHORAL MUSIC
Mass (1937).
Gloria in G (1961).
SONG CYCLES
Poèmes de Ronsard (1925).
Calligrammes (1948).
CONCERTO
Concert champêtre for Harpsichord and Small Orchestra (1928).
For Piano and Orchestra (1950).

OTTO LUENING (1900–   )

OTHER
A Poem in Cycles and Bells (1954). For tape recorder and orchestra.
Theatre Piece No. II (1956). For tape, piano, narrator, percussion, and
    wind instruments.

ERNST KŘENEK (1900–   )

OPERAS
Jonny spielt auf (1927).
Karl V (1938).
ORCHESTRAL MUSIC
Symphonic Elegy for Strings (1946).

AARON COPLAND (1900–   )

ORCHESTRAL MUSIC
Quiet City for Trumpet, English Horn, and Orchestra (1940).
A Lincoln Portrait (1942). With narrator.
Appalachian Spring Suite (1944).

PIANO MUSIC
Variations (1930).
Fantasy (1957).

HARRY PARTCH (1901–   )

OTHER
Oedipus (1951).
Plectra and Percussion Dances (1952).
Castor and Pollux (1952).
The Bewitched (1955).

WILLIAM TURNER WALTON (1902–   )

CONCERTOS
For violin and orchestra (1939).
For viola and orchestra (1928).
ORCHESTRAL MUSIC
Façade (1923, rev. 1942). For narrator and instruments.
Partita for Orchestra (1958).

ARAM ILYICH KHACHATURIAN (1903–   )

CONCERTO
For Violin and Orchestra (1949).
ORCHESTRAL MUSIC
Gayne Suites 1 and 2 (1942). Ballet.

LUIGI DALLAPICCOLA (1904–   )

OPERA
Il Prigioniero (1948).
CHORAL MUSIC
Canti di liberazione (1955). For chorus and orchestra.
ORCHESTRAL MUSIC
Due pezzi (1947).

DMITRI KABALEVSKY (1904–   )

CONCERTO
For Piano and Orchestra 3 (1952).
ORCHESTRAL MUSIC
The Comedians, op. 26 (1940).

DIMITRY SHOSTAKOVICH (1906–   )

CONCERTO
For Violin and Orchestra 2, op. 127 (1967).
ORCHESTRAL MUSIC
Age of Gold. Suite, op. 22 (1929–1930). Ballet.
Symphony 13, op. 113 (1962).
PIANO MUSIC
Twenty-four Preludes and Fugues, op. 87 (1951).

ELLIOTT CARTER (1908–   )

CONCERTOS
For Harpsichord, Piano, and Two Chamber Orchestras (1961).
For Piano and Orchestra (1964–1965).
ORCHESTRAL MUSIC
Variations for Orchestra (1955).
CHAMBER MUSIC
Quintet for Woodwinds (1949).
Quartet for Strings 2 (1959).

OLIVIER MESSIAEN (1908–   )

CHORAL MUSIC
Trois petites liturgies de la Présence divine (1945). For women's chorus
   and orchestra.
CONCERTO
Oiseaux exotiques for Piano and Small Orchestra (1955–1956).
ORCHESTRAL MUSIC
L'Ascension (1934). From organ original.

Chronochromie (1960).
ORGAN MUSIC
Messe de la Pentecôte (1951).
La Nativité du Seigneur (1936).

SAMUEL BARBER (1910–   )

CHORAL MUSIC
Prayers of Kierkegaard, op. 30 (1954).
SONGS
Hermit Songs, op. 29 (1953). Ten songs for voice and piano.
CONCERTOS
For Violin and Orchestra, op. 14 (1941).
For Flute, Oboe, Trumpet, and Strings (*Capricorn;* 1944).
ORCHESTRAL MUSIC
Medea Suite, op. 23 (1947). Ballet.
CHAMBER MUSIC
''Dover Beach'' for Voice and String Quartet (1931).

WILLIAM SCHUMAN (1910–   )

COMIC OPERA
The Mighty Casey (1953).
ORCHESTRAL MUSIC
Symphony for Strings (Symphony 5; 1943).
Judith (Choreographic Poem; 1950).

GIAN CARLO MENOTTI (1911–   )

STAGE WORKS
The Telephone (1947).
The Consul (1950).
The Unicorn, the Gorgon, and the Manticore (1956).

JOHN CAGE (1912–   )

OTHER
Sonatas and Interludes for Prepared Piano (1946–1948).

Concerto for Prepared Piano and Chamber Orchestra (1951).
Imaginary Landscape 4 (1951). For twelve radios.
4'33'' (1954). Don't miss this one!

BENJAMIN BRITTEN (1913–   )

STAGE WORKS
Albert Herring (1947).
Billy Budd (1951).
SONGS
Serenade, op. 31 (1943). For tenor, horn, and strings.
The Holy Sonnets of John Donne (1945).
Songs and Proverbs of William Blake (1965).
CONCERTO
For Violin and Orchestra in d (1939).
ORCHESTRAL MUSIC
Variations on a Theme by Frank Bridge (1937). For string orchestra.

From this point on, no breakdown into categories is given since much of the music could fall under our heading Other.

MILTON BABBITT (1916–   )

Du (1957). Song cycle for soprano and piano.
Vision and Prayer (1961). Soprano and electronic sounds.

LEONARD BERNSTEIN (1918–   )

Symphony (*Jeremiah;* 1943).
Serenade for Violin, Strings, and Percussion (1954).
Candide Overture (1957).

LEON KIRCHNER (1919–   )

Concerto for Piano and Orchestra (1952–1953).
Toccata for Strings, Winds, and Percussion (1956).
Quartet for Strings and Electronic Tape 3 (1967).

LUKAS FOSS (1922–   )

Time Cycle (1960). For voice and small ensemble.
Echoi (1963). Small ensemble.
Baroque Variations for Orchestra (1968).

YANNIS XENAKIS (1922–   )

Metastasis (1953–1954). For orchestra.
Concret PH (1958). Tape.
Bohor (1962). Tape.
ST/4-2 (1962). For string quartet.
Eonta (1963). Piano and brass.
Strategy (1964). For two orchestras.

LUIGI NONO (1924–   )

Epitaffio per F. Garcia Lorca (1953). For soloists, choir, and orchestra.
Espressione (1953). For orchestra.
Cori di Didone (1958). Choir and percussion.
Intolleranza (1960). Opera using tape background.
Omaggio a Emilio Vedova (1960). Electronic.
Canciones a Guiomar (1962–1963). For soprano, female chorus, and
      small instrumental ensemble.

GUNTER SCHULLER (1925–   )

Conversations (1949). For jazz group.
Symphony for Brass and Percussion (1949–1950).
Symbiosis (1957). For dancer, violin, piano, and percussion.
Concertino for Jazz Quartet and Orchestra (1959).
Triplum (1967). For orchestra.

LUCIANO BERIO (1925–   )

Mutazioni (1956). Tape.
Serenade for Flute and Fourteen Instruments (1957).

Visages (1961). Vocal and electronic sounds.
Circles (1961). Voices and percussion.
Sequenza IV (1967). For piano.

PIERRE BOULEZ (1925–   )

Polyphonie X (1951). For eighteen solo instruments.
Sonata for Piano 3 (1957).

EARLE BROWN (1926–   )

Music for Violin, Cello, and Piano (1952).
December (1952). For anything you want.
Available Forms I (1961). For eighteen players.
Available Forms II (1962). For orchestra.

DONALD ERB (1927–   )

Sonata for Harpsichord and String Quartet (1962).
In No Strange Land (1968). For trombone, double bass, and electronic
  sounds.

KARLHEINZ STOCKHAUSEN (1928–   )

Momente (1963, rev. 1965). Electronic.

KRZYSZTOF PENDERECKI (1933–   )

Anaklasis (1960). For percussion and strings.
Quartet for Strings (1960).
The Dimensions of Time and Silence (1960). For chorus and orchestra.
Polymorphia (1961). For forty-eight string instruments.
Canon (1963). For fifty-two strings.

Further readings

GENERAL BACKGROUND

ARNASON, H. H.   *History of Modern Art,* Prentice-Hall, Inc., Englewood
Cliffs, N.J., and Harry N. Abrams, Inc., New York, 1969. An unsurpassed single volume, covering painting, sculpture, and architecture in

261 superb colorplates, over 1,100 black-and-white illustrations, extensive bibliography subdivided into five categories, and a detailed index listing works (colorplates specified) and artists. Over 600 pages of text give a clear and informative picture of modern art.

DAVIDSON, ROBERT F., ET AL. (EDS.)   *The Humanities in Contemporary Life,* Holt, Rinehart & Winston, Inc., New York, 1960. The volume presents eighty-two extracts from eminent thinkers, a large percentage being of the twentieth century. Each of four parts ("Man in Contemporary Society," "The Impact of Scientific Thought," "The World of Intuitive Thought," and "The Search for Values in Contemporary Life") examines its theme from the point of view of artist, musician, scientist, or philosopher. Imaginative works (Frost, Yeats, Kafka), artistic credos (Wright, Le Corbusier, Klee), religious beliefs (Whitehead, Schweitzer, Niebuhr), and various other writings by distinguished figures (Carnap, Sartre, Dewey, Russell) probe deeply into perplexing human problems.

WEBER, EUGENE (ED.)   *Paths to the Present,* Dodd, Mead & Co., Inc., New York, 1960. See the reference in Chapter 13. Although Weber starts with romanticism, the bulk of this anthology presents late-nineteenth- and twentieth-century writings. Included are extracts from novels, poetry, essays, manifestos, critiques, and apologias. Selections outlining the aims of symbolism, expressionism, cubism, dada, and other movements are useful.

OTHER GENERAL AND SPECIFIC STUDIES

BARNETT, LINCOLN   *The Universe and Dr. Einstein,* Harper and Brothers, New York, 1948. Philip Wylie has remarked, "Everyone who has a mind, or who imagines he is a thinker, should understand this much [referring to Barnett's book] of Relativity as a minimum." Einstein's startling theories, Barnett shows, not only changed the world of physics but have had far-reaching implications in philosophical thought. A book for the layman, well written and provocative.

BARRETT, WILLIAM   *Irrational Man,* Doubleday & Company, Inc., Garden City, N.Y., 1958. Subtitled "A Study in Existential Philosophy," this book examines the origins and development of those philosophic positions which have emphasized guilt, dread, anxiety, absurdity, and the antirational. Barrett centers on four philosophers: Kierkegaard, Nietzsche, Heidegger, and Sartre. In Chapter 3 the author reflects upon existentialism and modern art, mainly literature (Eliot, Joyce, Faulkner, Hemingway).

BOWLES, EDMUND A. (ED.)   *Computers in Humanistic Research,* Prentice-Hall, Inc., Englewood Cliffs, N.J., 1967. Twenty-four essays by pioneer scholars in this new field. Various writers explain their use of the computer and speculate on the untapped potentialities. An eye opener for students in the humanities.

HOFFER, ERIC   *The True Believer,* Harper and Brothers, New York, 1951. This century has seen its share of fanaticism, and Hoffer, the homespun American philosopher, exposes its roots and describes the "guilt-ridden hitchhiker who thumbs a ride on every cause," joining a mass movement as a compensation for his own personal sterility. Hoffer, a rugged individualist, slashes with broad strokes, but he provides a convincing picture of what it is that motivates men to attach themselves to a "holy" cause.

HOOK, SIDNEY (ED.)   *Dimensions of Mind,* New York University Press, New York, 1960. In an era of "thinking" and "learning" machines, Sidney Hook and a group of distinguished psychologists, philosophers, and natural scientists explore puzzling issues relating to concept formation and mind-body relationship as well as the terrifying possibilities of those complicated monster machines which seem to approximate what we call thinking. What can one call something that chooses, predicts, learns, interprets, analyzes, abstracts, indexes, decides, perceives, discovers, and maybe even feels, lies, understands, and creates?

KAUFMANN, WALTER (ED.)   *Existentialism from Dostoevsky to Sartre,* Meridian Books (World Publishing Company), New York, 1956. A noted authority on Nietzsche traces in an introductory chapter the story of existentialism and then lets Dostoevski, Kierkegaard, Nietzsche, Rilke, Kafka, Jaspers, Heidegger, Camus, and Sartre speak for themselves. The extracts chosen are always to the point, which is that the movement does not allow a simple definition.

MCLUHAN, MARSHALL   *The Medium Is the Massage,* Bantam Books, Inc., New York, 1967. A book packed with explosive ideas, explanations, and suggestions on the confrontation of humanity with technology, especially those processes which are both electronic and communicative. Media fashion thought, they force change, and they educate through ways other than the written or printed word. Stimulating presentations with sufficient humor to keep the book from being deadly. A recording made to accompany the book captures the spirit of McLuhan's message (or massage?).

MEYER, LEONARD B.   *Music, the Arts, and Ideas,* University of Chicago Press, Chicago, 1967. Subtitled "Patterns and Predictions in Twentieth-century Culture." Meyer sets out "to understand the present—to discover some pattern and rationale in the perplexing, fragmented world of twentieth-century culture." A musician-philosopher, the author writes knowingly about artists and their works in all fields. Part II, "As It Is, and Perhaps Will Be," reflects on the present artistic scene and speculates (which Meyer admits is hazardous) on the future. A profound and erudite book, with Parts I and III of special value to musicians and Part II to all students interested in contemporary art.

SOKEL, WALTER H. (ED.)   *An Anthology of German Expressionistic Drama,* Doubleday & Company, Inc., Garden City, N.Y., 1963. A lengthy introduction by the editor traces the background of German expressionism in the first three decades of this century. Four short essays discuss aesthetic theory relating to the movement. Nine complete plays (by Kokoschka, Kaiser, Brecht, and others) in translation explore this early literature of "revolt."

MUSIC

AUSTIN, WILLIAM W.   *Music in the 20th Century,* W. W. Norton & Company, Inc., New York, 1966. A comprehensive and informative survey, with an exhaustive small-print bibliography of almost one hundred pages. For a single hardcover book, the best of its kind. Especially full in its treatment of Schoenberg, Stravinsky, Bartók, Hindemith, Webern, and Prokofiev, it also does not neglect the role of jazz. The extremely detailed index is very useful.

HANSEN, PETER S.   *Twentieth Century Music,* Allyn & Bacon, Inc., Boston, 1961. An introduction to modern music from 1900 to 1960. The author prefers to limit his survey by selecting a few representative compositions that best represent a composer or style. The composition is set against other factors necessary to understanding: the composer's personality, his other works, and the general cultural and musical milieu in which the work came into existence. Numerous musical examples are cited.

HILLER, LEJAREN A., JR., AND LEONARD M. ISAACSON   *Experimental Music,* McGraw-Hill Book Company, Inc., New York, 1959. A professor of music and a mathematician explain how music can be composed with an electronic computer. The first three chapters, dealing with aesthetic issues and the background of experimental music, are accessible to the average layman. These are thought-provoking and stimulating chapters. The last four chapters are considerably more technical and involved. The "Appendix" prints the full score of the *Illiac Suite for String Quartet,* which was produced by the high-speed digital computer (ILLIAC) at the University of Illinois as programmed by Hiller.

LANG, PAUL HENRY, AND NATHAN BRODER (EDS.)   *Contemporary Music in Europe,* W. W. Norton & Company, Inc., New York, 1968. Twenty contributors write convincingly about contemporary music in eighteen countries, including Hungary, Greece, and Portugal as well as France, Germany, and Italy. One ''Entr'acte'' on formal or informal music at midpoint, a concluding essay, ''Musical Composition in Modern Israel,'' and an introductory essay by Lang complete this excellent survey. The writing is generally descriptive and nontechnical.

SALZMAN, ERIC   *Twentieth-century Music: An Introduction,* Prentice-Hall, Inc., Englewood Cliffs, N.J., 1967. Useful as a reference and as a beginning survey, this paperback is a good initial purchase. In fewer than two hundred pages, the author covers a wide spectrum (styles, composers, nations, genres) and manages to include some mention of just about everyone of importance. The difficult subject matter is very well organized. Brief but pertinent bibliographies conclude each chapter.

SCHULLER, GUNTHER   *Early Jazz,* Oxford University Press, Inc., New York, 1968. The first of two projected volumes on the history of jazz, this study ends with the big-band and Duke Ellington styles of the 1930s. Numerous musical examples and some technical analyses. Twelve-page glossary of jazz terms and a selected discography.

SCHWARTZ, ELLIOT, AND BARNEY CHILDS   *Contemporary Composers on Contemporary Music,* Holt, Rinehart & Winston, Inc., New York, 1967. The editors present a cross section of European and American composers' asserting, in most instances, their artistic credos. The essays, mainly nontechnical, can be read with understanding and delight by the layman as well as by the trained musician and are as diverse in mood and style as the music of the composers themselves. Good, enjoyable reading.

SOUTHERN, EILEEN   *The Music of Black Americans: A History,* W. W. Norton & Company, Inc., New York, 1971. Mainly narrative and descriptive, this book traces the role of the black musician in the United States from around 1619 to the present. Each of the four major subdivisions (each containing four chapters) is prefaced with a lengthy table of important events. The author provides a useful, extensive bibliography and discography.

STEARNS, MARSHALL   *Jazz Dance,* The Macmillan Co., New York, 1968. Written mainly by a college professor who has specialized in Chaucer, the book is an engaging compilation of history spiced with anecdotes. The subtitle, ''The Story of American Vernacular Dance,'' reveals the author's area of interest. Excellent bibliography includes a list of films in which jazz dances appear. Basic Afro-American dance movements are recorded in a special system of notation (Labanotation).

STUCKENSCHMIDT, H. H.   *Twentieth Century Music* [Richard Deveson (trans.)], McGraw-Hill Book Company, Inc., New York, 1969. A paperback (of some two hundred fifty pages), slightly longer than Salzman's book. Both, given their limitations of size, jointly provide a good introductory survey although the Stuckenschmidt is disadvantaged by its lack of index. On the other hand, it is more idea oriented, at times reflecting on matters of aesthetics and art. Like the Salzman, this book contains information about the latest experiments and trends in avant-garde music.

Part 4 ∘ *Ethnomusic*

A few decades ago it might have been difficult to convince American students that the music of peoples outside Western civilization was worthy of serious attention. At best those students would have admitted that the indigenous music of Asia, Africa, Oceania, and the Americas might indeed be called "music," that, being simple or "primitive," it might tell us something about the early development of Western music, and that perhaps the student of anthropology could round out his overall view of a culture by knowing something about its music and related social functions.

But since World War II, Americans have increasingly come into contact with nonwestern cultures and their musics.

Military occupation, the Peace Corps, and the urge to travel have all contributed to such contact. In addition there have been the burgeoning record industry throughout the world, the transformation of colonies into developing nations with a desire to retain and propagate their musical traditions, and the increased tendency to accept the ideas of cultural relativism and racial equality. So it is now probably unnecessary to convince anyone that nonwestern cultures have music, that in many cases it is extremely sophisticated, and that professional musicianship is an important factor in its existence. It has become increasingly clear that the music of other parts of the world can be enjoyed by the Western listener if he

will take the trouble to find out something about its structure (that is, its form) and its aesthetic principles.

The world of music consists of styles and repertories that are somewhat analogous to languages. Each must be learned in order to be understood. The casual listener may learn a bit of a musical language by hearing a couple of records, just as a casual tourist may pick up a few words of a spoken language in a day's travel through a foreign country. This sort of acquaintance is helpful although it is a long way from there to either musical or linguistic fluency. So the purpose of Chapter 14 is to provide a start on some of the things found in a few representative music cultures outside the West.

Chapter 14 ∘ Music of other cultures

THERE ARE ONLY A FEW ELEMENTS WHICH MOST NONWESTERN MUSICS HAVE in common and which contrast them with the art music of the West One such is the absence of musical notation; this is replaced by oral (spoken) or aural (heard) tradition. Although some of the Asian civilizations have notation systems, these are not normally read by a performer as he plays or sings; they are used instead as permanent records of materials even though they are not so precise as the Western system. Thus in most of the world's cultures music is learned by being heard. One result is the possibility of making changes in a standard form—which permits each performer to create his own version of a composition. Cultures vary greatly in the degree to which such freedom is actually accepted: In some African societies and among the North American Plains Indians the changing of a composed piece is encouraged; in Japanese and Chinese music, on the other hand, there is evidence that pieces are now performed very much as they were centuries ago. The existence of aural tradition makes it necessary for composers to create music that will be accepted readily by musicians and listeners; they must create what is capable of being memorized rather easily and what contains unifying factors sufficient to permit understanding without analysis of a written form. If their music fails these conditions, it will die.

In other respects nonwestern musics differ as much from one another as each of them does from Western music. The realm of nonwestern music includes the world's simplest musics as well as systems whose sophistication easily rivals that of the West: It contains tribal cultures in which almost everyone knows the entire musical repertory and in which there are no professional musicians except for those who are also the priests or medicine men, whose religious functions make it necessary for them to be the main singers; and it embraces complex musical societies with cultivated art music, enjoyed by intellectual and economic elites, performed by highly trained musicians, based on complex systems of music theory, aesthetics, and philosophy, and surrounded by popular and folk musics consumed by other segments of society.

Most cultures have professional musicians in some sense of the word. Among the Plains Indians of North America, for example, the owners of collections of ceremonial objects known as "medicine bundles" knew many songs because each object had one or several songs associated

This chapter is contributed by Bruno Nettl.

with it, songs that provided the object with its supernatural power. These medicine men had musical knowledge far beyond that of their fellow tribesmen. They were respected for their supernatural power as well as for their ability to sing although such matters as musicianship itself and voice quality apparently did not enter into consideration. Today the Plains Indians have men who are said to be "singers" or "drummers," who perform in public for social dances, and who receive some payment for this; they do not, however, make their living as full-time musicians. By contrast, in the high cultures of Asia musicians frequently come from musical families and study with their fathers or uncles. They spend many years in disciplined effort, learning the theoretical system as well as the techniques of performance and the repertory. But in both North America and Asia music is not something that comes into being without effort or is made up on the spur of the moment or in the heat of emotional experience. It almost always comes from a long and relatively complex tradition of thought. In this respect it is everywhere similar to the music of Western civilization.

The music of nonwestern cultures is often said to be more "functional" than Western music is—the latter existing largely for listening alone. Such statements may be taken to mean that the music of nonwestern cultures is frequently an integral part of important activities (such as work and dance and particularly religion) and that the music of a nonwestern culture expresses some of the most essential feelings and patterns of the culture. These assertions are largely correct; but they can equally be applied to Western musics, especially if we take into account more than just classic music but folk and popular music as well. The study of nonwestern musics may make us aware of the enormous importance of music as a major expressive component of *all* human culture, for no culture without some kind of music has ever been discovered.

All this makes it important to point out that one of the interesting aspects of music in all the world's cultures is the way it is used—its role and its function. To understand a little of the music of a nonwestern culture, we must approach it with sensitivity toward its special uses. It is necessary to know not only what activities music accompanies but, more significant and much more difficult to comprehend, what the culture's view of music is. For example, we must realize that in certain Islamic societies constraints are put on music, that secular music is not fully approved, and that musical activity is often relegated to members of lower classes or minority groups. In India, on the other hand, music forms an important part of the Hindu religion and is highly respected. Among the Indians of the North American Plains music seems to have provided a kind of stamp of approval for any important activity; for nothing was done properly without its appropriate song. In contemporary Amerindian (American Indian) societies and among other minorities music symbolizes group identity. This seems also to have been the case with music associated with specific clans and other groups in certain tribal societies. Just what is actually considered to be "music" also varies from culture to culture: Some include bird and animal calls or exclude certain kinds of chanting or include types of formalized speech. So an understanding of attitudes about music and musical thought in a nonwestern culture adds immeasurably to an understanding of its musical language.

A person who does not travel to a distant country to study its music will rarely accumulate sufficient material from anthropological and musicological literature to gain this kind of cultural information. Nevertheless, he can approach the other, strictly musical, side more readily through careful and analytical listening.

Rhythm

Compared with many nonwesterners, the typical European or American is very unsophisticated in his perception of rhythmic organization and subtlety. Rhythm has been developed much less in Western classic music than in many other musics, particularly those of India, Indonesia, and Africa. Only in some contemporary Western forms, such as jazz, has a similar level of rhythmic development been achieved. Perhaps the reason is one with general implications: Different cultures evidently develop different elements of music. In Western music harmony has been developed to a high degree of sophistication while rhythm has been neglected. In India, on the other hand, rhythm and melody have been developed but harmony has largely remained absent. In Indonesia sensitivity to tone color and to fine distinctions in pitch have been stressed. Amerindian music has seen substantial developments in the direction of melody but not of harmony. African music (though generally much more complex than Amerindian is) has continued to rely upon short fragments as the basis of melody but has had substantial development of harmony and rhythm.

Pitch organization

Those listening to nonwestern music for the first time might find that some of it sounds strange and even, in their frame of reference, "wrong." Each music has its own system, rules, and principles. For example, the listener may notice that the scales, tones, and intervals—the system underlying the use of musical pitch—differ from those used in most Western music. We may not be able to reproduce the intervals on the piano because some may be smaller than the smallest interval of our chromatic scale, the half step. More frequently, they will be larger than a half step and in between two of our accepted intervals. For example, the typical interval of *slendro,* one system of Javanese music, is about halfway between a whole step and a step and one-half. Elsewhere, the so-called neutral third, between three and four half steps, is particularly common. In Middle Eastern music a three-quarter tone, halfway between a half step and a whole step, is important. Getting accustomed to such intervals may require a good deal of careful listening.

The number of tones actually used in a piece may be far smaller than they would be in a typical piece of Western music. Pentatonic scales (five tones) are very popular throughout the world. Some tribal cultures make use of only three or four tones in all their songs.

The series of tones that we call a "scale" varies greatly from culture to culture. One idea is very widespread, however: that of "mode." A mode, in the broadest sense of the term, is a group of melodic characteristics that unite a large number of musical compositions or (if the music is improvised) performances. Typically, a mode has a scale. Certain tones (and the intervals between them) are used, and certain of these tones have greater importance than others. Most important, perhaps, is the fact that certain melodic formulas, or typical successions of tones, characterize a mode. Finally, a mode usually has some rather easily defined character that is often described in nonmusical terms such as love, aggression, peace, or devotion. In India the mode concept is called *raga.* If we state, for example, that an Indian composition is cast in a particular *raga,* we know that it has a certain arrangement and hierarchy of tones, that we can expect it to contain at least some of a group of melodic fragments, and that it is intended to convey a particular mood.

Harmony and counterpoint

Harmony, so important to us, is actually either absent or handled in a completely different way in most nonwestern music. The simultaneous sounding of several pitches is usually interpreted not as a conceptual unit, or chord, as in most Western music, but as a result of the simultaneous performance of related melodies.

The relationship of different voices or instruments performing together is usually very close and may originally have come about through coincidence. For example, two persons singing the same tune but beginning at different times will involuntarily produce a canon, or round. The type of polyphony called "parallelism" is produced by two singers trying to sing the same song but starting at different pitches. A type of polyphony called "heterophony," consisting in several variations of the same melody performed simultaneously, could have been first produced by two singers trying to sing together a song of which they knew differing versions. The importance of this heterophonic principle in the development of the music of East Asia is enormous. The accompaniment of a melody by a single, drawn-out note, or drone, is also important in world music and could have been invented by a singer accompanied by a friend who could not carry a tune.

All these hypotheses regarding the origin of harmony or polyphony are based on the assumption that an effect first created by error was eventually found attractive enough to become part of the system. No doubt there were cultures in which there was no counterpoint or harmony and whose performers occasionally commited such errors. Only in certain cultures did they become accepted, whereas in others they continue to be regarded as mistakes.

Tone color

One of the most important differences among the musics of the world is in their application of the singing voice and of tone color in general. Most Americans think of the Western trained singer as exhibiting the "natural" or "normal" way of using the voice, but of course this way is no more natural than is any other. Each culture has its own way of producing sound, and it is possible that each style of singing expresses some of the basic values and attitudes of the culture.

In most East Asian and Middle Eastern singing we find a strained, rather tense-sounding vocal color. African singing is usually more relaxed and has a wide variety of vocal effects. Much North American Indian singing is harsh and raucous. The singing of the Navaho and Apache Indians has a peculiar nasal tone, while that of the Pueblo Indians is often low and growling. According to Alan Lomax, who has studied singing styles throughout the world, there is some correlation between cultures in which there is repression of sexual activity, lack of good cooperation among people, a tendency toward oppression of the masses by an elite, and lack of equality of the sexes and high, nasal, ornamented, tense singing. There is also a correlation of cooperation, equality of the sexes, democratic tendencies, and sexual freedom with relaxed singing, good blending of voices in group singing, and the development of vocal harmony and polyphony. Although these correlations are based on small samples of music and conclusions cannot be drawn from them until both the musics and the cultures from which they come are studied in much more detail, this theory indicates that the character of a culture has a lot to do with the kind of music it produces.

There is little doubt that a particular singing style persists in a culture longer than other traits of the music do. Thus, throughout the many changes that African music has undergone in its transportation to various parts of the New World, the way of using the voice has remained very much the same. The new popular music of Middle Eastern cities retains the vocal style of older, traditional Middle Eastern music.

The typical instruments of a culture often produce tone colors similar to those found in singing. Indian and Middle Eastern playing of bowed string instruments differs from Western violin playing much as the singing styles of the cultures differ. The percussive and buzzing sounds of African music, found in drumming or xylophone playing, in the plucked string instruments, and in the manipulation of rattles and wind instruments, are reflected in the sharp and varied attacks and the humming and yodeling techniques of African singing. Furthermore, many cultures seem to have certain sound ideals that are exhibited in the typical instruments. Javanese and Balinese music stresses percussive melody instruments, such as gongs and xylophones. The Middle East and south Asia have instruments capable of sustaining long notes with ornaments (this is found even in the plucked string instruments of the area). Africa, as we have already said, stresses percussive and buzzing sounds and has thus developed mainly plucked strings, not bowed instruments.

Form

The structure of nonwestern compositions is usually rather tightly conceived. Contrary to the Western listener's first impression, this music is not customarily free from structural and aesthetic principles, and it is not aimlessly improvised. Because of the absence of written notation, organization must usually be rigorous; specific form types exist. In some cultures they have a theoretical basis, names, and known history. In others they cannot be explained verbally by performers but nevertheless have a deeply rooted tradition. Forms are seldom related to European types, such as sonata or rondo, but are often just as complex in their use of unity and variety as creative principles.

Music of other cultures in the modern world

For the Western listener one of the first attractions of music of other cultures was the notion that this music originates in man's primordial past. It was believed that the various nonwestern musics have not changed for thousands of years and represent earlier stages in man's musical development. This view has been demonstrated to be quite unrealistic. Although rates of evolution vary enormously from culture to culture, there is no doubt that each of those musics has a long history, that it has been influenced by other cultures, and that change has also come about through the creative activity of each culture's artists. Even the simplest cultures have music that must be very different from early man's musical expression.

It should not be surprising to find, therefore, that recent developments in global communication and in the mass media have also had an impact on nonwestern musics. This impact has frequently been denounced by persons who feel that it is causing the destruction of ''pure'' indigenous musics, whose authenticity is being ruined by the introduction of Western instruments, scales, notation, radio, and records. Actually no such destruction seems to have come about. No doubt things have changed under the influence of Western musical thought, but the changes are generally absorbed without causing complete abandonment of the traditional patterns. Typically, the result is a kind of blending, in which those elements of the music which are shared by both sides or which have been developed in somewhat similar fashion by both the nonwestern and the Western systems become prominent. And, also typically, those elements of the music which have reached the greatest sophistication in the nonwestern system have survived.

Thus, for example, the music of India survives, but those of its *raga*s which are easily intelligible to Westerners have become more prominent. The Western violin has been adopted but is played so as to produce a typically Indian tone color. Similarly, Western musical thought has caused the theoretical system of Persian music, once rather loose, to be tightened up to resemble Western music theory. But the sound of Persian music remains only slightly changed. In North American Indian culture the use of music primarily for religious experience has changed to one of entertainment. The original functions are being destroyed, but new ones, related to the functions of music in Western society, with the accompanying emphasis on professional musicianship, have replaced them.

It is difficult now to find nonwestern music that has in no way been affected by the West. But other aspects of these cultures have also been affected. Just as the world's peoples continue to retain much of their earlier values, customs, and philosophical systems, they retain the essential aspects of their music, taking advantage of certain elements of Western musical thought and technology as it fits their needs, without completely abandoning their traditions.

The following sections, devoted to the musics of a selected group of cultures, are intended to provide a sample of their wealth of musical styles and background. General characteristics of the music are illustrated by references to specific examples. The best way to approach this wide variety of world music is to begin with intensive listening to a small number of recordings. This may be followed by more extensive listening, with attempts to outline structures and to compare stylistic features according to the descriptions in this chapter and the general principles of musical structure explained in this book.

SIMPLE TRIBAL MUSICS

Throughout the world there are cultures that have lived for centuries in relative isolation. They have small populations and what appears to us to be rudimentary life styles. Their material culture and technological skills are poor; but they have sometimes developed the arts of music, design, sculpture, and oral literature to high degrees of sophistication.

Figure 14.1 • The Australian didgeridoo, as played at an aboriginal corroboree. The tapping-stick player on the right provides rhythmic interest. (Australian News & Information Bureau.)

LISTENING 14.1

In this chapter all examples are contained on the last record of the student set, *Listening for the Experience of Music.*

Here are two examples of primitive music making:

● Music of the Australian didgeridoo.
● Mboko song from Equatorial Africa, with musical-bow accompaniment.

To be sure, compared with our operas, symphony orchestras, and electronic-music studios, the music of these peoples appears to be relatively simple. But this simple music turns out, on close examination, to be more complex than our first impression would lead us to believe. The most important lesson it provides for the American listener is that very basic technical and musical devices can be exploited to provide an extremely high level of musical interest and sophistication.

Take, for example, the songs of the Yahi Indians of northern California, as sung by the world-famous Ishi (died in 1916), the last known North American Indian who grew up without at least some experience in Westernized culture. Ishi's repertory consisted of songs that last no longer than 10 seconds. (In performance, each is repeated many times.) Each has only two to four, at the most five, tones in the range of a fourth or fifth. But within this limited framework the composers of Yahi songs used a large variety of forms and musical devices—forms based on melodic sequences, on contrasting tone materials in the two or three sections of a stanza, on inversion of a theme, on variation. We must not assume that Yahi composers could not have broken out of the severe limitations of brevity and tonal simplicity had they wished to do so. Rather, for reasons we are ignorant of, they seem to have imposed these limitations on themselves and to have tried to exhaust the possibilities that could be realized within them.

Another example of primitive materials turned to good account is the aboriginal Australian didgeridoo (Figure 14.1; and hear the first item in LISTENING 14.1), a straight, hollowed-out branch or thin log about 4 feet long, which is played as a trumpet. It normally produces only one pitch. Although this instrument would appear to have few possibilities for providing musical interest, the players of the didgeridoo, by altering the shapes of their mouths, change the emphasis on different overtones to emit a variety of tone colors. They also perform a number of rhythms, wringing all possible versatility from this simple instrument.

A somewhat similar situation exists with the musical bow, a single-stringed instrument shaped like a hunting bow. Found primarily in Africa, South America, and parts of southeast Asia, its resonator can be a gourd, a pot, a basket, or the player's mouth or chest cavity. If the shape or opening of the resonator can be manipulated, that is frequently done to gain a number of tone colors that adds variety to the simple two- or three-note scale of the instrument (LISTENING 14.1).

As in most cultures of the world, music loomed large in the lives of the Amerindians before their continents were invaded by Europeans. Music accompanied many of their activities. Most important, it was one of the main ingredients of religion; in the thought of many cultures it was the medium through which supernatural power was transmitted to man. Thus many tribal groups believed that songs were the evidence of a medicine man's ability. Frequently it was thought that songs were created by supernatural forces and given to men through dreams and visions. Each of the hundreds of Indian tribes had its own large repertory of songs and pieces.

It is fairly easy to learn to recognize North and some South American Indian music: It is typically vocal, and there are few melody-producing instruments, especially in North America, although flutes are an important exception. There is a large variety of forms, but a great many of them fall into a dual pattern in which the song is presented and is then repeated in part or with a variation. The entire procedure is repeated several times, either with the same words or with new ones. The style of singing is characterized by rather harsh, tense-sounding voice production.

But there are also important differences among tribes and areas. Thus the Pueblo Indians of Arizona and New Mexico have very long, winding musical forms, usually using the pattern described above, especially in their ceremonial kachina songs (listen to the first example in LISTENING 14.2). These are sung in a low growling voice. The Navaho of the same area have forms in which two contrasting sections, one high and one low, are alternated time after time. The music is sung with a somewhat nasal sound, high in the singer's vocal range and sometimes with falsetto (LISTENING 14.2) Indians of the eastern United States had many songs that used the call-and-response patterns found in African and Afro-American music. The Indians of the Great Plains used the above-mentioned incomplete-repetition form almost constantly, adapting it to a sharply descending melodic line and performing songs in a particularly tense, pulsating style of singing (the last item in LISTENING 14.2).

It is interesting and important to note what happened to their music when the Indians were converted from members of independent tribes

LISTENING 14.2

Music of North American Indians:
- Zuñi Indian rain dance.
- Navaho Indian night chant.
- Blackfoot Indian war dance.

or nations to units in a downtrodden minority in the United States.

By the latter nineteenth century, Indians had tried to shed their tribal differences in order to face the white man together. Important among these attempts at unity was the Ghost Dance religion of the 1880s. This was a somewhat revolutionary movement that sought, through a special ceremony brought from northern California and the revival of some forgotten Indian practices, to make headway against the encroachments of the dominant culture. The musical style of the tribes of the desert area of Utah and Nevada was brought to other tribes and associated with this movement so that an intertribal Ghost Dance style of singing became established for a time.

Somewhat later a religious movement more friendly to whites and incorporating elements of Christianity became permanently established in many United States tribes. This was the peyote movement. Again, it carried with it a particular musical style, which came from the Apache and Navaho tribes, who had used the peyote cactus (its buttons are intoxicating when eaten) as early as the eighteenth century. This style is distinct from the main tribal style. Wherever Indians use peyote, the peyote-song style can be readily identified by its quick drumming, special meaningless syllables, and soft, liquid-sounding vocal style.

In the middle of the twentieth century a pan-Indian style, again attempting to do away with tribal distinctions, became prominent. It is based on the Plains style of singing. Although in many ways it shows the technical and musical influences of Western society, its sound seems to be still purely nonwestern and Indian. The recorded example of Blackfoot Indian music (LISTENING 14.2) illustrates this style in a song of the war dance, a strictly social dance now widespread among Plains Indians. These Indians have much more intertribal contact today than they did in earlier days, now intermarrying, moving, and visiting from reservation to reservation. The record was made at a dance that was part of a festival called North American Indian Days, during which most members of the Blackfoot tribe living on the reservation gather for dancing, singing, and entertainment. Many tourists are present, and a number of white Indian hobbyists will actually participate in the dancing. The Indian Days is a modern event that has essentially supplanted the sun dance, a religious ceremony of earlier times, during which all the bands of a tribe joined together for worship as well as social intercourse. The Indian Days singers are a group of professionals, known for their ability to sing rather than for a supernatural power that permits them to sing. The song was probably composed by one of the two or three dozen song makers on the reservation instead of coming to him in a dream. And the audience, rather than being impressed by the mana of the song as would have been the case centuries ago, listens to the excellence of the performance. Thus the song functions within a modern Indian social context; but its sound is still definitely Indian.

The form of the song is simple. A short motive is sung by the leader and repeated by a second soloist. Then the entire group of eight singers performs a descending phrase, which is followed by a final phrase approximately an octave lower than the beginning. This is a variation of the initial phrase. It thus adheres to a standardized form found in most of the modern Blackfoot social dances. In contrast to the greater variety of forms found in older songs, standardization makes it possible for people to learn a new song very quickly—which is desirable where singers from neighboring reservations wish to visit and participate. Although the form itself is simple, the performance is made interesting by increasing intensity throughout the five repetitions. The first two

(a)

Figure 14.2 • (a) A Blackfoot dancing group around a large drum. (This photograph was posed for early in the twentieth century.) (b) Rattles are the conspicuous musical instruments in this Hopi dance. (Courtesy of The American Museum of Natural History.)

(b)

"stanzas" are sung relatively softly. Drumming is on the rim of the big bass drum (Figure 14.2a) around which the singers sit. The third and fourth stanzas are louder, become gradually faster, and have regular drumming on the skin. The fifth stanza has irregular drumming, which at one point stops and then ends with a rousing *crescendo*. This variety in the performance shows the change from a ritualistic to a kind of concert function in much Indian music.

Indian music is generally changing in style, influenced by the changes from tribal orientation to pan-Indian orientation and from ritual to entertainment. At the same time, rather than dying out, it is increasing in popularity with Indians and with their white sympathizers. It has become for the Indians of the United States one of the main vehicles in the expression of their "Indianness" and their belief in the importance of their past and cultural traditions. This attitude is one that the Indians share with other minority groups in North America.

AFRICAN

African music is of great interest to Americans because it is the basis of the large variety of musical styles that emerged in the Afro-American communities of North and South America and the Caribbean. These had great influence on many types of Western music, particularly jazz.

The music of black Africa is surprisingly homogeneous, especially given the numerous different cultures, languages, and even racial groups that exist on the continent. Yet if we listen closely to the music, we find that the various regions have special traits. Some of the most widespread are described in the following paragraphs.

Forms are quite short. A song will usually consist of many repetitions—not precise but with variations—of a short bit of music, a bit frequently divisible into two parts; one sung by a leader, the other by a responding group; or one a tone higher than the other; or one monophonic, the second polyphonic. This principle of dualistic structure is important in African music and can be observed at various levels.

There is a good deal of polyphonic music. Voices may proceed in parallel motion, a third, fourth, or fifth apart. Occasionally we find a melody performed against a drone of a single long or repeated tone. Imitation, resulting in simple rounds, is sometimes used. Most frequently, however, an accompanying instrument or voice presents a

Figure 14.3 • In contemporary Africa drumming may serve to accompany recreational or concert activities. (Ghana Consulate-General, Information Section.)

short, simple, repeated pattern (an *ostinato*) while another voice produces a somewhat longer but also repeated melody that is independent of the *ostinato* but coincides with it at certain points.

Rhythmic complexity is perhaps the chief characteristic of African music, especially that of western Africa. The combination of performing and perceiving various rhythms is fascinating. For example, a widely used device is the hemiola, the simultaneous or successive use of duple and triple meters:

Sometimes hemiola is used in arrangements in which the meters do not begin at the same time:

Another characteristic is the extensive variety of instruments, most of which produce a percussive sound. Drums (Figure 14.3), of course, come first to mind. Rather than being subsidiary or accompanying instruments as they are in most Western music, they are usually the most important and prestigious, indispensable for significant religious and political ceremonies. In some tribal groups there are many different types of drum: those with two skins, some tubular ones, some that look more or less like tambourines, small kettledrums, skinless drums made of hollow logs to be struck—all in various sizes and producing various pitches and all with different sounds, uses, and social meaning. Then there are xylophones of many types, ranging from those which can be suspended from a cord around the player's neck to those made of large planks laid across two small logs. Related to the xylophones are zanzas, or mbiras (Figure 14.4), made of several metal or bamboo tongues which are intended to be plucked and which are tied to a bridge nailed across a small board (around 6 by 8 inches). These instruments are unique to Africa and a few Afro-American peoples. Many string instruments, most of them plucked, are utilized. Most typical are zithers, consisting of strings stretched along either a board, a long box, a thick bamboo tube, or a partially hollowed, troughlike piece of wood. Harps and lyres, which probably came down from Egypt millennia ago, are

Figure 14.4 • Three types of zanza.

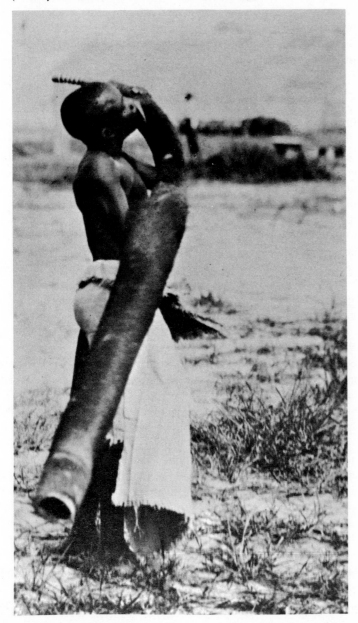

also found. Bowed string instruments are rare and were probably brought from the Middle East in more recent times. The simplest of all African string instruments is the musical bow that we have previously mentioned; its string is plucked or struck as accompaniment to singing. So it is easy to see why we say that many of these instruments have a percussive sound. For wind instruments it may not be so obvious, but even flutes and horns (Figure 14.5), made of wood, metal, natural horn, or ivory, are in a sense handled percussively. Such effects can result when a group of these instruments, each sounding only one tone, performs a melody during which each individual plays only at the moment his own note must be sounded.

African instruments are likely to be played solo, in homogeneous groups or families, and in ensembles in which radically different sounds are combined.

Generally percussive tone and a preference for a sort of buzzing undertone pervade African music. These contrast interestingly with the tense, ornamented, melodic sound of music that characterizes the Middle East but has been introduced to those African cultures which have become Moslem, such as the Hausa of Nigeria and many tribes of eastern Africa.

An important characteristic of African music is its close relationship to language. Here, more than in most other cultures, the character of language influences, and is in turn influenced by, music and its concepts. Most African languages are tone languages: That is, the meaning of a word is partly determined by its pronunciation pitch pattern. Obviously, when words are set to music, the composer must somehow take into account their pitch patterns; otherwise the words may be misunderstood. Although this question has hardly been studied, it seems that African composers do not follow these pitch patterns all the time but use them very often. The language tones are the basis for the signaling on ''talking'' drums, horns, whistles, and other instruments for which African cultures are famous, and in strictly musical situations as well sentences may be translated into melodies that become the foundations of instrumental pieces and improvisations.

Language and music are also closely associated in other ways. Story telling is very developed, and various myths, legends, entertaining tales, and ceremonial speeches form one of the most important aspects of life. Many of the stories contain songs that, presented in responsorial (echo) form, provide opportunities for audience participation. In some

LISTENING 14.3

African music:
- Badouma paddler's song from Equatorial Africa, for men's voices. .
- Yaswa *marimbas* from Equatorial Africa: three xylophones.
- Elephant song of the Mbuti pygmies, Republic of the Congo.

cultures instrumental pieces are said to have words that are known but not actually performed.

Finally—and perhaps most important—African music is characterized by improvisation on the basis of short melodic ideas, departures from the norm, and freedom to add individual creativity to tradition.

The recorded examples of African music illustrate many of these points. The first in LISTENING 14.3, from Equatorial Africa, is a choral song sung while paddling. The choral part moves primarily in parallel thirds. A short bit of music is repeated with variations. There is no percussion accompaniment, but there is rhythmic complexity, especially with syncopation.

The example in LISTENING 14.1 is a song accompanied on the musical bow, which is held in the player's mouth in order to provide changing emphasis on overtones. As a result, you will hear two melodies: that produced by the fundamental tones (of which there are only two, in regularly alternating groups of six notes) and that produced by the most audible overtones, which present variations on the basic theme.

The second example in LISTENING 14.3, also from Equatorial Africa, is performed by three xylophones. The lower two provide an *ostinato* accompaniment while the upper one presents variations on a short motive. The hemiola effect results from the lower two xylophones' playing a slow triple meter while the upper one plays a triple meter at twice the speed of the accompaniment.

The last example in LISTENING 14.3 is performed by a group of Mbuti pygmies from the Congo. Here a complex polyphonic structure is created by several voices' moving in various kinds of motion, with melodic bits thrown together and melodies broken up by alternation of several performers. Again, a short phrase is the basis of variations. Particularly to be noted is the open, relaxed manner of singing, in which the many voices blend so well as to be indistinguishable.

AFRICAN INFLUENCES ON WESTERN MUSIC   The student of nonwestern music is, of course, interested in the way in which the music of other cultures has influenced that of the West. Most frequently studied is the relationship of African music to the music of North and South America and the Caribbean.

When Africans first came to the New World, they brought with them their songs and instrumental pieces. As time went on, they learned the folk and popular music and the hymns of white Englishmen, Frenchmen, Spaniards, and Portuguese. They began composing new songs, using elements from their old as well as from their new musical environments. Today it is unlikely that pure African melodies survive in the Afro-American repertories except perhaps in those of Haitians and Afro-Brazilians, which have preserved their African cultures intact to the largest extent. But it is noteworthy that African style elements have been retained even where the basic melodic material has been entirely composed in the New World.

The most important elements of African music were carried to the New World by the slaves who were forced to come from Africa during the sixteenth to the nineteenth centuries. These elements are heard very clearly in the music of the tightly knit, relatively isolated black communities of certain Caribbean islands, such as Haiti, of the Guyanas, and of the northeastern Brazilian province of Bahía, where there have always been very few whites. Elsewhere, in the English-speaking West Indies (Jamaica, Trinidad, the Bahamas, and smaller islands) and in areas in which blacks had more contact with Spanish culture, such as Cuba and Puerto Rico, there developed musics with less African influence. But even in the culture of North American blacks, the African background accounts for the distinctiveness of the folk music and the difference between it and the folk music of the white Americans. African elements are also found in the popular music of Afro-Americans and in such universally accepted types of music as soul and jazz. However, the survival of African musical characteristics in the Americas often depended on the survival of other aspects of African culture. If general cultural patterns survived, they made possible the survival of Africanisms in the accompanying music. Thus in Haiti and Bahía the religions are a mixture of African and Roman Catholic elements, and African deities are often identified with Catholic saints. In these areas the drumming patterns associated with particular deities in western Africa are still found but now associated with the individual Afro-American cults and sometimes with the saints.

The elements of African musical style that have survived in the New World are naturally those which have been most thoroughly developed in Africa. Most significant is the emphasis on rhythm, from which comes the importance of the beat, syncopation, and other rhythmic complexities of jazz and the wide use of percussion instruments. The use of call-and-response patterns is as common in New World black music as it is in African. The ways in which Afro-Americans use the human voice, typically distinct from those of white Americans, are closely related to the African vocal styles, particularly to the relaxed, open, well-blended sounds such as are heard in the last example of LISTENING 14.3.

One of the most characteristic features of Afro-American music is the use of improvisation: The stanzas of many folk songs are really variations on a theme; the forms of jazz and urban blues are essentially improvised variations over a repeated series of chords. Ornamentation is also important in both African and Afro-American music, but here we cannot be sure that it has African roots since it is also important in the singing style of English-American folk music.

Certain other characteristics of African music seem not to have survived to a great extent in Afro-American music. The typical short forms of African music have been replaced by longer tunes similar to those of European folk- and popular songs. Polyphony, widespread in Africa (but not important in western Africa, the ancestral home of most American blacks), has not been greatly developed in Afro-American music.

One explanation for the dramatic survival of African music in the New World and the adoption of its elements into white music may be the essential similarity between African and European music. Both culture areas, for example, use diatonic scales. The two musics are certainly not identical, but compared with, say, Indonesian or American Indian music, they appear to be more closely related. As blacks have participated more fully in all aspects of American culture, their rich musical heritage has exerted more influence on every level of American music.

INDIAN

The music of India is relatively well known to Americans largely because Indian culture, religion, and philosophy have since the 1950s held a great attraction for Westerners. Also, the technical virtues of this music appeal to our music value structure, for Indians have developed a complex system of music theory that enables them to discuss music in a manner similar to ours. Yet we should remove certain misunderstandings.

For example, Indian music is thought to be essentially instrumental and the sitar regarded as its main mode of expression. In fact singing is the most basic kind of performance in Indian music. All musicians are expected to learn the musical system first through singing, and much

Figure 14.6 • A form of north Indian sitar, but lacking the customary sympathetic strings. (Government of India Tourist Office.)

Figure 14.7 • Carnatic vina player with his instrument. The decorated gourd may serve a resonating function.

that occurs in instrumental music is an imitation of vocal techniques.

Indian music is also thought to be largely improvised. Much of it is; but we must understand that the improvisations are created according to traditional patterns, rules, and forms that are rigorously maintained, just as there are many set, composed pieces that are learned with precision and handed down from generation to generation with great exactitude. There is a huge population of highly trained, professional musicians in India, particularly in the intellectual centers of Delhi, Benares, Bombay, Calcutta, and—perhaps most important—Madras. Those artists who have become famous in America are not necessarily the most highly respected in India.

Finally we should be aware that, although Indian music has changed greatly in the course of the last several hundred years and is now undergoing the influences of Western culture, it continues to maintain its integrity as a distinct system and a separate repertory.

Northern and southern Indian music are the two main branches of this art. They are similar in many ways, but it is not hard to tell them apart. North Indian, or Hindustani, music is the music of the Indo-European-speaking peoples and is somewhat related to the music of the Middle East. It makes use of the sitar (Figure 14.6) and the sarod (both large lutes with sympathetic strings that vibrate along with those that are plucked) as well as other instruments such as the oboelike surnay. To us it sounds much more emotional and less structured than does the music of south India, which is also called ''Carnatic.'' The latter music, of the Dravidian-speaking peoples, may represent a historically older type. It makes use of the vina, a very large lute with four melody strings and three drone strings (Figure 14.7). Many complex song forms and several improvisation types are easily distinguished.

Both north and south Indian music make important use of singing; both depend on a drone (an instrument that continuously sounds the tonic or basic tone and sometimes also the fifth above it) as a point of musical orientation throughout a performance; and both use the concepts of *raga* and *tala,* elaborate systems of melodic and rhythmic organization, as bases of composition and improvisation.

The concept of *raga* is extremely characteristic of Indian music. It is one of the many manifestations of the concept of mode discussed above and thus shows India to be related to the Middle East and the Mediterranean world. In India, however, this concept of mode is carried to much greater degrees of complexity than it is elsewhere. There are hundreds of *raga*s, subdivided into principal and derivative *raga*s in southern India and into *raga*s (male), *ragini*s (female), and *putra*s (children) in northern India.

The concept of *tala* is similar to that of *raga* except that it deals with rhythm rather than melody. *Tala* organizes music in a metric fashion, as do the meters of Western music, but it does so in a more complex way. In Carnatic music there are three kinds of units of which a *tala* cycle (or metric unit) may be composed: *laghu* (which may consist of 3, 4, 5, 7, or 9 beats), *dhrutam* (2 beats), and *anudhrutam* (1 beat). Among the most widely used *tala*s are the following:

Adi   *Laghu* (4 beats), *dhrutam, dhrutam,* or 4 + 2 + 2.
Triputa   *Laghu* (3 beats), *dhrutam, dhrutam,* or 3 + 2 + 2.
Rupaka   *Dhrutam, laghu* (4 beats), or 2 + 4.
Jhampa   *Laghu* (7 beats), *anudhrutam, dhrutam,* or 7 + 1 + 2.

Much of the improvised material in Indian music is not metric—not in *tala*. When *tala* is used, it is customarily indicated by the presence of a drum: in northern India normally the tabla drum (Figure 14.8), actually a set of two small drums of which one produces a variety of pitches, in the south customarily the mridanga, a large and heavy barrel-shaped drum with skin at both ends. Both types of drum are beaten with the hands and fingers, and various strokes, producing different sounds, are distinguished in a way similar to the distinction among tones of a scale.

Although Indian music can be performed by solo instruments or voice, a concert is usually performed by an ensemble. In southern Indian music the leader is a singer or vina player. He is supported throughout the performance by the tambura, a large lute that provides the unending drone. The drummer joins in those parts of the music which are cast in a particular *tala*. He may also play an extended solo near the end of a performance. There may also be a melody-instrument player, who supports the singer in unison in the composed pieces and who repeats each of his phrases after him in the slow improvisations. Most typically, this instrument is now the European violin played in a distinctive Indian style: held against the player's chest rather than under his chin. There may also be a second percussion instrument. In Carnatic music the

Figure 14.8 • In Afghanistan, the far north of the Indian subcontinent, the tabla drum becomes these versions: tunble (above), dubla (lower right), and naghares (lower left). (Government of India Tourist Office.)

ghatam—an earthenware pot—is used to provide a distinct contrast to the tone color of the mridanga, with which it may alternate in exciting duets of rhythmic competition. There are many variants of this ensemble arrangement, but the roles of the instruments are always maintained. The music is essentially soloistic and, except for the drone, monophonic.

A full-blown Indian performance of a *raga* may be very long, lasting up to an hour or two. So an Indian concert, consisting of one or two *raga*s and several shorter composed pieces, may go on for several hours, as determined by the mood of the musicians and the receptivity of the audience. The performance of a single *raga* in Carnatic music may have all or only some of the following sections and types of improvisation; those which appear normally do so in the order given below:

ALAPANA, OR RAGA IMPROVISATION   This section explores the *raga,* dwelling at length on its important tones and showing its typical melodic motives. In the most traditional performances its overall melodic contour is arc-shaped. It works up to a climax fairly near the ending and then drops off. It is usually slow, meditative, and nonmetric and thus does not have a *tala* and does not use the drum. The accompanying violin, if present, repeats each of the soloist's phrases. The first item in LISTENING 14.4, sung by one of south India's greatest female vocalists, illustrates a very traditional way of performing an *alapana*.

TANAM   Although this section also has no *tala* and thus no drum, the improvisation has more rhythmic interest and less emphasis on melodic development than the *alapana* has. It is particularly suited to the vina, but occasionally it appears also in vocal music. Repetitions of one note and extended improvisations over motives of two or three notes are common. An accompanying violin is not used.

KRITI   This is a type of composed song, usually consisting of three sections: *pallavi, anupallavi,* and *charanam.* Many *kriti*s were composed in the early nineteenth century, some hundreds of them by south India's most revered composer, Tyagaraja (1768–1846); but many also date from the twentieth century.

The three sections are typically related as follows: *Pallavi* consists of perhaps a dozen musical lines, the first presenting a short theme, the second repeating it, the third presenting a variation of it, the fourth repeating that, the fifth presenting yet another, perhaps more extended, variation, and so on; *anupallavi* presents a second theme, usually a bit higher, which is treated in the same repetitive and variational style, at

LISTENING 14.4

Indian music:
- Beginning of *alapana* in *raga Sankarabharanam,* sung by Shrimati M. S. Subbulakshmi, accompanied by P. M. S. Gopalakrishnan, violin.
- *Kriti Raghuvamsa* in *raga Kanadakutuhalam, tala Adi,* performed by Nageswara Rao, vina.

the end of which material from the *pallavi* section may be brought in; *charanam* presents yet a third theme, usually intermediate in pitch, which is treated similarly but is followed by a partial or even a complete repetition of the *anupallavi*. The great emphasis on repetition and variation indicates that the method of composing must be closely related to improvisation. Yet *kriti*s are composed and handed down in oral tradition with considerable accuracy. A *kriti* is cast in a specific *tala*, the drum may be used, and an accompanying violin may play in unison with the soloist. Being essentially a song, a *kriti* usually has words, most often of a devotional character, but it is also performed instrumentally.

The characteristic form of a *kriti* is illustrated by the following scheme of the piece in LISTENING 14.4. Each letter represents one line of music, corresponding to a line of the poetic text.

Pallavi $A_1A_1A_1A_1B_1A_1B_1A_1B_2A_1B_2A_2.$
Anupallavi $C_1C_2C_2C_3C_3C_4C_4C_2DDE_1E_1E_2A_1B_2A_2.$
Charanam $FFFGG$ plus all the *anupallavi*.

NIRAVAL   This is a type of improvisation usually based on the tune of one line of a *kriti*. Words are used if the performance is vocal, with *tala* (and drum). *Niraval* is usually quick and rather melodic in character and tends to consist of the basic line presented many times in alternation with short, improvised passages.

SVARA KALPANA   This is another type of improvisation that is sometimes (but not so frequently as *niraval*) based on the musical theme of a *kriti*. It too has *tala* and drum. When performed vocally, it contains, instead of words, the tone syllables of Indian music that correspond to our do, re, mi, fa, sol, la, ti, do: *sa, ri, ga, ma, pa, dha, ni, sa*. The chief musical characteristic of *svara kalpana* is its virtuosity. The performer delivers rapid ornamented passages, often in a *staccato* style, to produce a great variety of rhythmic patterns. This section may also include a part in which soloist and drummer alternate, the drummer imitating in detail the rhythmic pattern of each phrase given by the soloist. This sort of musical competition between soloist and drummer is expressed in other ways as well and lends to this section an enormous degree of excitement. Drum solos lasting up to 15 minutes are also included and may occasionally end the performance.

Northern Indian music has a somewhat different system of structuring a performance, but the principles are the same. The musicians move from a slow, meditative section to one with rhythmic interest but without *tala,* proceed to material with *tala* and including the tabla, and end in a section in which their technical virtuosity is fully exhibited.

MIDDLE EASTERN

The *raga* system of India, with its enormous emphasis on improvisation, has counterparts in Iran, Turkey, and the countries of the Arab world. In these Middle Eastern nations traditional music is built around somewhat less complex systems of modes, called *maqam* in Arabic and *gusheh* or *dastgah* in Persian. This music, like Indian classical music, is performed vocally or instrumentally. It makes some use of the drone (but much less than Indian music does). It may be accompanied by a drum and also by an instrument that repeats the soloist's melodic phrases. As in Indian music, the most significant improvisations are not metric. Again as in Indian practice, a Middle Eastern performance consists of the rendition of one mode, and the performer may select the types of improvisation, set compositions, and other materials. But in comparison with the large scale of Indian music, with its broad sweep of melody and form and its incredibly intricate rhythmic organizations, Middle Eastern music is simple. Its forms are shorter and the scale and meter are more European-sounding. To sum up, Middle Eastern music may be regarded as a miniaturized and extremely subtle art.

LISTENING 14.5 is Persian classical music. It illustrates a short performance of one mode, *chahargah,* which has a scale with four intervals that cannot be played in our tempered system: two three-quarter tones and two five-quarter tones. It is played on the tar (Figure 14.9), a large lute with frets, a long neck, six strings, and a belly of skin.

The performer first plays a short *chahar mezrab,* a metric virtuoso piece, in which he shows his versatile technique. Then he plays three sections, or characteristic melodies, of the mode, each a bit higher than the previous one and each ending like the first in order to provide unity. Although these sections are improvised, it is likely that each performer, once he has arrived over a period of years at a satisfactory way of playing a mode, continues to play it more or less the same way every time. So the music is not completely improvised. Each player has his own way of presenting it, in each performance making minor changes but

LISTENING 14.5

• *Dastgah* of *chahargah* from Iran, performed by H. Zarif, tar.

Figure 14.9 • *Iranian tar.* (Consulate General of Iran.)

also sticking to a certain order of musical events, themes, and mannerisms that make it possible to identify his playing.

The fate of Middle Eastern classical music during the twentieth century is an interesting commentary on the role of traditional musics in modern industrialized society. Iran provides a good example. After a period of flowering a few centuries ago, classic music declined in popularity to the point where it was almost unknown at the beginning of this century. At that time it was confined to a very small group of musicians and their wealthy patrons. After the onset of a more nationalistic spirit in the 1920s the traditional arts of Iran were revived, partly with government help, and today Persian classic music is taught at universities and conservatories and is heard on television and radio. At the same time Western elements of musical thought and practice have exerted influence. Persian classic music is no longer confined to small gatherings or garden parties but can be heard in concert halls. This has necessitated the introduction of orchestras into a once essentially soloistic style. Instead of taking place in the household of a master to which students are attached, instruction is carried on in the Western fashion, that is, through weekly lessons. Western instruments have been added to the traditional ones; the most widely used instrument in Iranian music is today the violin. Western musical notation has been adopted. As a result the nature of the learning process and of the concept of improvisation seems to have changed radically. The open acceptance of elements of westernization has lessened the conflict between the modern and the traditional. It has enabled the classic music to survive, even though in changed forms.

FAR EASTERN

The musics of Indonesia, Japan, and China illustrate the enormously rich and varied musical culture of the Far East. This huge area, home of more than one-third of the world's population, has some common cultural patterns but is also tremendously varied.

In contrast to India and the Middle East, where the musics are essentially soloistic, the Far East has a great deal of ensemble music, ranging from small chamber groups to the large gamelan orchestras of Java and Bali, the Japanese court orchestra, and the Chinese opera orchestras. The relationship among the instruments in these ensembles is largely

Figure 14.10 • A gamelan orchestra performing. Various gongs and xylophonelike instruments are visible. (Consulate General of the Republic of Indonesia.)

heterophonic—several variations of the same melody are performed simultaneously, perhaps along with additional percussion and other accompaniment. Another characteristic of this large area is the interest in a variety of contrasting percussion instruments: gongs, drums, bells.

The most spectacular use of percussion appears in the gamelan orchestras (Figure 14.10), which until recently were very numerous in Indonesia. The largest of these had forty to fifty players. Most of them performed on instruments related to the xylophone but principally made of bronze instead of wood. **LISTENING 14.6** includes a short lecture by

LISTENING 14.6

Indonesian music:

- Illustrated explanation of the gamelan by Jaap Kunst.
- *Kapi Radja*, performed by the gamelan of the Dancers of Bali.
- *Baris*, performed by the gamelan of the Dancers of Bali.

LISTENING 14.7

- Music of the Japanese court orchestra.
- Chinese *Sai Shang Ch'ü (Song at the Frontier)*, performed on the p'ip'a.

Jaap Kunst, the outstanding scholar in the field of Javanese music, who explains the instruments and the way in which they interact. The following paragraphs briefly summarize his views:

Three groups of instrument functions can be defined. One group of instruments plays the melody more or less unembellished, the lowest ones playing each note once and the higher ones quickly repeating each note twice or four times. Another large group paraphrases the melody, partially through improvisation. The same principle is followed: Low instruments play few notes; high ones are active. A third group, the gongs, organizes the rhythmic structure. The lowest gong marks the end of each long phrase. It is difficult to identify each group—let alone each instrument—in a recording because of the mass of similar yet slightly different tone colors. You may be able to perceive this structure to some extent, however, in the second example of LISTENING 14.6, which illustrates the largest of the gamelan types.

Changes in tempo and dynamics are highly significant elements of gamelan music. As Professor Kunst points out, the drummer functions as conductor, and he does this by manipulation of tempo. The last item in LISTENING 14.6 is an example of *baris,* a type of music based on an old folk tune. We first hear a very short phrase (eight notes) repeated twenty-three times. Minor changes in tempo and important changes in loudness provide variety and interest. The end of this section is marked by a substantial slowing down, initiated by the drummer-conductor, followed by a new section, with a new theme.

Gamelan orchestras are found throughout Java and Bali, in cities, villages, courts, streets, and theaters. They serve all levels of society, from princes who themselves conduct large orchestras of virtuosos to beggars in the streets who can hear four- or five-man ensembles playing for pennies thrown by passersby.

The Japanese court orchestra, on the other hand, was until recent times heard only by the small proportion of Japanese associated with the Emperor's court or with certain Shinto shrines. Therefore it is not suprising that the sound of the court orchestra's music, *gagaku,* is rather different from that of other kinds of Japanese music. The first example in LISTENING 14.7 illustrates one type of *gagaku.*

As do the gamelan, the Japanese orchestra consists of highly trained musicians. But unlike the gamelan, *gagaku* has a large variety of instruments and tone colors, providing broad contrasts compared to the blending sound scheme of the gamelan. The most important melody instruments are a short, oboelike instrument, hichiriki, and flutes. A mouth organ, sho, with seventeen pipes, provides a harmonic background. String instruments are used only in certain kinds of pieces; they are the koto, a long, thirteen-stringed zither (Figure 14.11), and the biwa, a pear-shaped lute. They do not play the melody but perform short phrases or *arpeggio*s that have a rhythmic rather than a melodic function. Two or three different drums and a gong round out the ensemble.

The court orchestra described here preserves an ancient form of music making, which flourished as far back as 1,400 years ago. At that time various kinds of music and dance were imported into Japan from many places. Different sources and style origins are still distinguished: pieces of Chinese and Indian origin are *togaku;* those of Manchurian, Korean, and Japanese origin, *komagaku. Gagaku* and old forms of Buddhist music provided the foundation for many later kinds of Japanese music, such as that for kabuki and other theatrical genres and chamber music.

Like some of the other Far Eastern cultures, Japan developed systems of musical notation mainly indicating finger placement on the instruments. Although such systems are not normally used by musicians for

Figure 14.11 • *In modern Japan, the koto performs the same musical and social functions as the piano did in Victorian households.* (Consulate General of Japan.)

Figure 14.12 • A member of a Shantung traditional-music group playing the p'ip'a. (Chinese Information Service.)

Recordings

actually learning pieces, they function as historical documentation of this highly complex and sophisticated musical culture.

Perhaps even more so than Japan, China has a large variety of music, including concert music, court music and religious, chamber, theatrical, popular, and folk traditions, and a music history full of changing trends and developments. It has undergone influences from various parts of the world—India, Indonesia, the Middle East, and most recently Europe—which accounts for some of this great variety. There are many instruments: bells, stone chimes, drums, plucked and bowed strings, flutes, oboes, and trumpets. Here it is impossible to do justice to this great cultural tradition; but a brief examination of a recorded example (the second in LISTENING 14.7) may provide the beginnings of insight.

The example is performed on the p'ip'a (Figure 14.12), a pear-shaped lute with frets and four strings usually tuned A–D–E–A. It appears in ensembles and as a solo instrument, its players using such virtuoso techniques as *tremolo*, rolls, slaps, glides, and harmonics.

The p'ip'a frequently performs pieces of program music, which represent battles, romantic scenes, and other events reminiscent of the subject matter of program music in nineteenth-century Europe. The example is the sorrowful song of a noblewoman who was compelled for political reasons to marry a barbarian prince. We have here a beautiful, lyrical piece, which proves once again that nonwestern music, in addition to providing valuable insights into the nature of the world's cultures and of music generally, can give much satisfying musical experience to the American listener.

Records are an important source for study in this field but are too numerous to list individually. Among the series that provide useful materials are *Ethnic Folkways Library* (Folkways records), and *Musical Anthology of the Orient,* and *Musical Anthology of Africa* (Unesco). A comprehensive set of 220 LP records of African music is *The Sound of Africa* (International Library of African Music). Brief excerpts providing a good sampling of world music are to be found in Alan Lomax (ed.): *Columbia World Library of Folk and Primitive Music* (Columbia).*Songs of the Redman* (Soundchief Enterprises) is a set of modern Amerindian recordings used by many Indians interested in maintaining their traditions. *An Anthology of the World's Music* (Anthology), like the others mentioned here, is a representative sampling of Asian and African music with comprehensive notes. Many other labels feature recordings of Indian, African, and east and southeast Asian music. An important criterion for selection should be that authoritative and detailed notes are supplied on the contents and the circumstances under which they were recorded.

Further readings

GENERAL STUDIES

MALM, WILLIAM P.   *Music Cultures of the Pacific, the Near East, and Asia,* Prentice-Hall, Inc., Englewood Cliffs, N.J., 1967.
MERRIAM, ALAN P.   *The Anthropology of Music,* Northwestern University Press, Evanston, Ill., 1965. Gives information on the role of music in nonwestern cultures and the ways to go about studying this field.
NETTL, BRUNO   *Folk and Traditional Music of the Western Continents,* Prentice-Hall, Inc., Englewood Cliffs, N.J., 1965.

SPECIFIC STUDIES

KAUFMANN, WALTER   *Musical Notations of the Orient,* Indiana University Press, Bloomington, Ind., 1967.
KAUFMANN, WALTER   *The Ragas of Northern India,* Indiana University Press, Bloomington, Ind., 1968.
MCPHEE, COLIN   *Music in Bali,* Yale University Press, New Haven, Conn., 1968.
MALM, WILLIAM P.   *Japanese Music and Musical Instruments,* Charles E. Tuttle, Co., Inc., Rutland, Vt., 1959.
MERRIAM, ALAN P.   *Ethnomusicology of the Flathead,* Aldine Publishing Co., Chicago, 1967.
NKETIA, J. H. KWABANA   *African Music in Ghana,* Northwestern University Press, Evanston, Ill., 1963.

Three books by Curt Sachs view nonwestern musics in their historical contexts: *The Rise of Music in the Ancient World,* W. W. Norton & Company, Inc., New York, 1943, *The History of Musical Instruments,* W. W. Norton & Company, Inc., New York, 1940, and *The Wellsprings of Music,* Nijhoff, The Hague, 1962.

Specialized articles on nonwestern music as well as bibliographies may be found in the journals *Ethnomusicology* and *Journal of the International Folk Music Council.*

Music index

Subject index